THE
AMERICAN
WOMAN
1996–97

Edited by Cynthia Costello and
Barbara Kivimae Krimgold
for the Women's Research and Education Institute
Betty Dooley, President

W. W. NORTON & COMPANY

NEW YORK / LONDON

THE
AMERICAN
WOMAN

1996–97

WOMEN AND WORK

For information about permission to reproduce selections from this book, write to Permissions, W. W. Norton & Company, Inc., 500 Fifth Avenue, New York, NY 10110.

The text of this book is composed in 11/13 Bembo, with the display set in Centaur. Compostion and manufacturing by The Haddon Craftsmen, Inc.

ISBN 0-393-03929-3
ISBN 0-393-31431-6 (pbk.)

W. W. Norton & Company, Inc., 500 Fifth Avenue, New York, N.Y. 10110
http://web.wwnorton.com
W. W. Norton & Company Ltd., 10 Coptic Street, London WC1A 1PU

1 2 3 4 5 6 7 8 9 0

CONTENTS

List of Tables and Figures   7
Acknowledgments   15
Preface *by* Jean Stapleton   19

WOMEN AND WORK

A Perspective on America's Working Women *by* Cynthia Costello,
Anne J. Stone, *and* Betty Dooley   23
Affirmative Action: Understanding the Past and Present *by*
Jocelyn C. Frye   33

1. Women in the Workforce: An Overview *by* Diane E. Herz
   and Barbara H. Wootton   44
2. Work and Family: The Experiences of Mothers and Fathers in
   the U.S. Labor Force *by* Ellen Galinsky *and* James T. Bond   79
3. Women and the Unemployment Insurance System *by* Laurie J.
   Bassi *and* Amy B. Chasanov   104
4. Struggling to Survive: Welfare, Work, and Lone Mothers *by*
   Katherine McFate   127
5. Women's Employment Patterns, Pension Coverage, and
   Retirement Planning *by* Martha Priddy Patterson   148
6. Women and Pensions: A Policy Agenda *by* Cindy Hounsell   166

IN REVIEW JULY 1993–MARCH 1995   **177**

AMERICAN WOMEN TODAY:
A STATISTICAL PORTRAIT

1.	Demographics	249
2.	Education	269
3.	Health	281
4.	Economic Security	306
5.	Women in the Military	324
6.	Elections and Officials	334

Women in the 104th Congress	341
Congressional Caucus for Women's Issues	367
References	369
Notes on the Contributors	381
About the Women's Research and Education Institute	385
Index	387
About the Editors	409

LIST OF TABLES
AND FIGURES

WOMEN AND WORK

CHAPTER 1   Women in the Workforce: An Overview

Figure I-1   Percentage of Population in the Labor Force by Sex, 1948–1994   47

Table I-1   Selected Population and Labor Force Characteristics of Women, 1994   49

Figure I-2   Labor Force Participation Rates by Sex and Age Group, Selected Years   50

Table I-2   Families by Type, Presence of Children, and Labor Force Status of Family Members   53

Figure I-3   Work Schedules of Women with Work Experience, 1970 and 1993   55

Table I-3   Employed Persons by Occupation and Sex, 1974 and 1994   58

Table I-4   Employed Women by Occupation, Race, and Hispanic Origin, 1994   59

Table I-5   Employed Persons by Industry and Sex, 1974 and 1994   60

Table I-6   Self-Employed Persons by Occupation and Sex, 1994   62

Table I-7   Median Weekly Earnings of Full-Time Wage-and-Salary Workers, by Sex, 1979–1994   63

Table I-8   Median Weekly Earnings of Full-Time Wage-and-Salary Workers, by Occupation and Sex, 1994   64

Table I-9   Median Weekly Earnings of Full–Time Wage-and-Salary Workers, by Sex, Race, Hispanic Origin, and Educational Attainment, 1994   68

Table I-10   Median Weekly Earnings of Full–Time Wage-and-Salary Workers, by Age and Sex, 1994   69

Table I-11   Median Weekly Earnings of Full–Time Wage-and-Salary Workers by Race, Hispanic Origin, Union Status, and Sex, 1994   70

Figure I-4   Unemployment Rates of Adult Men and Women, 1948–1994   72

Table I-12   Labor Force Status and Reason for Unemployment by Sex, Race, and Hispanic Origin, 1994   73

Table I-13   Poverty Status of Persons 16 Years and Over in the Labor Force 27 Weeks or More by Race, Sex, and Hispanic Origin, 1993   76

Table I-14   Poverty Status of Primary Families with Members in the Labor Force 27 Weeks or More by Selected Characteristics, 1993   77

CHAPTER 2   **Work and Family: The Experiences of Mothers and Fathers in the U.S. Labor Force**

Figure II-1   Employed Parents' Participation in the Contingent Workforce by Sex, 1992   83

Table II-1   Employed Parents' Family Finances by Sex, 1992   86

Table II-2   Employed Parents' Access to Traditional Fringe Benefits by Sex   88

Table II-3   Employed Parents' Access to Flexible Time and Leave Benefits Policies by Sex, 1992   90

Figure II-2   Employed Parents' Aspirations for Job Advancement by Sex, 1992   93

Table II-4   Employed Parents' Division of Family Work by Sex, 1992   94

Figure II-3   Employed Parents' Responsibilities for Sick Children by Sex, 1992   96

Table II-5   Employed Parents' Reports of Job Burnout by Sex, 1992   98

Table II-6   Employed Parents' Reports of Stress and Coping Ability by Sex, 1992   100

CHAPTER 3 **Women and the Unemployment Insurance System**

Table III-1 Average Weekly Benefit Amount, by State, 1993   109

Figure III-1 Unemployment Rates by Sex, 1945–1993   112

Figure III-2 Unemployment Rates by Gender and Race, 1955–1993   113

Table III-2 Reason for Unemployment by Sex and Race, December 1993   114

Figure III-3 Recipiency Rate for Regular State Unemployment Insurance Programs, 1947–1993   115

Table III-3 Unemployed Workers Who Received Unemployment Insurance by Selected Characteristics, Sex, and Race, 1989–1991   117

Table III-4 Unemployment Insurance Benefit Levels by Sex and Race, 1989–1992   118

Table III-5 Unemployed Workers Who Meet the Unemployment Insurance Monetary Eligibility Requirements in Their State by Selected Characteristics, Sex, and Race, 1989–1992   120

Table III-6 Unemployed Workers Who Receive Unemployment Insurance as a Percentage of Those Meeting the Unemployment Insurance Monetary Eligibility Requirements in Their State by Selected Characteristics, Sex, and Race, 1989–1992   123

Table III-7 Family Poverty Rate among Unemployment Insurance Recipients by Selected Characteristics, 1989–1992   124

CHAPTER 4 **Struggling to Survive: Welfare, Work, and Lone Mothers**

Table IV-1 Level of Support Given to a Poor Family of Three by State, 1994   130

CHAPTER 5 **Women's Employment Patterns, Pension Coverage, and Retirement Planning**

Table V-1 Annual Pension Payments for Retirees Earning Benefits as Former Employees by Industry Sector and Sex, 1978 and 1989   150

Table V-2 Full-Time Employed Men and Women with Pension Coverage by Years of Service with Employer, 1988 and 1993   152

Table V-3   Full-Time Employed Men and Women by Years of Service with Employer, 1988 and 1993   152

Table V-4   Retirement Benefit Coverage among Full-Time Private-Sector Workers by Annual Earnings and Sex, 1993   153

Table V-5   Retirement Savings of $1,000 Annually for 30 Years When Invested at Different Risks and Returns   155

AMERICAN WOMEN TODAY: A STATISTICAL PORTRAIT

SECTION 1   Demographics

Table 1-1   Population of the United States by Race and Sex, 1990   251

Figure 1-1   Population of the United States by Age and Sex, 1995   252

Figure 1-2   Population of the United States by Sex, Race, and Hispanic Origin, 1995   253

Figure 1-3   Projected Composition of the Population by Race and Hispanic Origin, 1995, 2000, 2020, and 2050   254

Figure 1-4   U.S. Fertility Rates by Race of Child, 1960–1990   255

Table 1-2   Marital Status by Sex, Race, and Hispanic Origin, March 1993   256

Figure 1-5   Currently Married and Never Married Adults by Sex, Race, and Hispanic Origin, March 1993   257

Figure 1-6   Median Age at First Marriage by Sex, 1970–1993   258

Table 1-3   Families by Family Type, Race, and Hispanic Origin, 1970, 1980, 1990, and 1993   259

Table 1-4   Households with Unrelated Partners by Sex of Partners and Presence of Children, 1993   261

Figure 1-7   The Divorce Rate, 1970, 1980, 1990, and 1994   262

Table 1-5   Divorce Ratios by Sex, Race, and Hispanic Origin, 1970, 1980, 1990, and 1993   263

Table 1-6   Children's Living Arrangements by Race and Hispanic Origin, 1970, 1980, and 1993   264

Figure 1-8   Number of Men Per 100 Women by Age, 1992   266

Table 1-7   Living Arrangements of Women Age 65 and over by Age, Race, and Hispanic Origin, 1993   267

Figure 1-9   Women and Men Age 65 and Older Living Alone, 1970, 1980, and 1993   268

SECTION 2   **Education**

Table 2-1   Educational Attainment by Sex, Race, and Hispanic Origin, 1993   271

Figure 2-1   White, Black, and Hispanic Women Age 25 and Over with 12 or More Years of Education, 1970, 1980, and 1993   272

Table 2-2   College Enrollment by Sex, Race, and Hispanic Origin, 1976, 1984, and 1992   273

Figure 2-2   Women Enrolled in Colleges and Universities by Age, 1970, 1980, 1991, and 1998   274

Figure 2-3   Students Enrolled in Colleges and Universities by Sex and Full- or Part-Time Status, 1970, 1980, 1991, and 1998   275

Table 2-3   Women Awarded Undergraduate Degrees in Selected Fields, 1961/62–1991/92   276

Figure 2-4   Recipients of Postsecondary Degrees by Sex, 1959/60–1991/92   277

Figure 2-5   First Professional Degrees Awarded in Selected Fields by Sex of Recipients, 1991/92   278

Table 2-4   Women Awarded First Professional Degrees in Selected Fields by Race and Hispanic Origin, 1976/77 and 1991/92   279

Figure 2-6   Faculty with Tenure by Sex and Type of Institution, 1980/81 and 1992/93   280

SECTION 3   **Health**

Table 3-1   Life Expectancy at Birth and at Age 65 by Race and Sex, 1900–2010   283

Table 3-2   Life Expectancy at Birth by Sex, Race, and Hispanic Origin, 1995   284

Figure 3-1   Female Life Expectancy at Birth in Selected Industrialized Countries, 1990   285

Table 3-3   Prenatal Care for Mothers with Live Births by Race and Hispanic Origin of Mothers, 1991   286

Table 3-4   Infant, Neonatal, and Postneonatal Mortality Rates by
Mother's Race and Hispanic Origin, for Birth Cohorts,
1985–1987   287

Figure 3-2   Low-Birthweight Live Births by Race, Ethnicity, and
Hispanic Origin of Mothers, 1991   288

Table 3-5   Contraceptive Users Age 15 to 44 by Method and Age, 1988   289

Table 3-6   Women Experiencing Contraceptive Failure during the First
12 Months of Use by Marital Status, Poverty Status, and
Age, 1988   290

Table 3-7   Abortions by Week of Gestation, 1991   291

Figure 3-3   Leading Causes of Death for Whites and Blacks by Sex, 1991   292

Figure 3-4   Mortality Rates among White and Black Women from
Lung and Breast Cancer, 1950–1991   293

Table 3-8   Incidence and Death Rates for Selected Cancers among
Women by Cancer Site and Race, 1989   294

Figure 3-5   Breast Cancer: Incidence and Mortality Rates for White and
Black Women, 1991   295

Table 3-9   Women Who Had Selected Preventive Services in the Past
Year by Selected Characteristics, 1990   296

Table 3-10   Women Who Have Received a Breast Examination and
Mammogram by Selected Characteristics, 1992   297

Figure 3-6   AIDS Cases in Females Age 13 and Over by Race and
Hispanic Origin, 1987–1994   298

Table 3-11   Distribution of Newly Reported AIDS Cases among
Women Age 13 and Over by Race and Hispanic Origin,
1994   299

Figure 3-7   Persons Age 18 to 64 with Private Health Insurance by Sex
and Source of Coverage, 1993   300

Figure 3-8   Health Insurance Coverage by Sex and Type of Insurance,
1993   301

Table 3-12   Persons with No Health Insurance Coverage by Family
Relationship, 1993   302

Figure 3-9   Persons with and without Health Insurance Coverage by Sex
and Age, 1993   303

Figure 3-10　Persons Age 18 to 64 with No Health Insurance Coverage by Sex and Age, 1993　304

Figure 3-11　Persons Age 16 to 64 with No Health Insurance Coverage by Sex and Work Experience, 1993　305

SECTION 4　**Economic Security**

Figure 4-1　Median Family Income by Family Type, 1973–1993　308

Table 4-1　Median Income of White, Black, and Hispanic Families by Family Type, 1983, 1988, and 1993　309

Figure 4-2　Median Family Income by Age of Householder, 1973–1993　310

Figure 4-3　Median Income of Families with Children by Family Type, 1978–1993　311

Table 4-2　Sources of Income for Women Age 15 to 64 by Race and Hispanic Origin, 1992　312

Table 4-3　Poverty Status of Women and Men by Age, Race, and Hispanic Origin, 1993　314

Table 4-4　Poverty Rates of Unrelated Individuals by Sex and Age, 1993　315

Figure 4-4　Poverty Rates of Families by Family Type and Presence of Children, 1993　316

Table 4-5　Poverty Rates of White, Black, and Hispanic Families by Family Type and Presence of Children, 1993　317

Table 4-6　Sources of Income for Persons Age 65 and over by Sex, 1993　318

Table 4-7　Sources of Income for White, Black, and Hispanic Women Age 65 and over, 1993　319

Figure 4-5　Homeownership by Age of Householder, 1983 and 1993　321

Figure 4-6　Homeownership by Family Type, Presence of Children, Race, and Hispanic Origin, March 1993　322

Figure 4-7　Female-Headed Households by Type and Presence of Children, March 1993　323

SECTION 5　**Women in the Military**

Table 5-1　U.S. Active Duty Servicewomen by Branch of Service, Rank, Race, and Hispanic Origin, Fiscal Year, 1994　326

Figure 5-1   Department of Defense Active Duty Women Personnel by
Officer/Enlisted Status, 1972–1994   327

Table 5-2   Educational Attainment of Active Duty Department of
Defense Personnel by Officer/Enlisted Status and Sex, Fiscal
Year 1994   328

Table 5-3   Active Duty Personnel by Pay Grade Grouping, Branch of
Service, and Sex, Fiscal Year 1994   329

Figure 5-2   Positions and Occupations Open to Active Duty Women by
Service, as of October 1, 1994   330

Figure 5-3   Occupational Profile of Active Duty Women in the Defense
Department, Fiscal Year 1994   331

Table 5-4   Unemployment of Veterans by Sex, Race, and Hispanic
Origin, Annual Average, 1994   332

Figure 5-4   Median Income of Veterans by Sex, Race, and Hispanic
Origin, 1990   333

SECTION 6   **Elections and Officials**

Table 6-1   Voter Participation in National Elections by Sex, Race, and
Hispanic Origin, 1976–1992   336

Table 6-2   Voter Participation in National Elections by Sex and Age,
1976–1992   337

Table 6-3   Women in Elective Office, Selected Years, 1975–1995   338

Table 6-4   Women on the Federal Bench, 1995   339

Table 6-5   Female Presidential Appointees to Senate-Confirmed
Positions, 1977–January 1995   339

ACKNOWLEDGMENTS

THE SIXTH EDITION OF *The American Woman,* like the first five, has enjoyed a broad base of support from foundations, corporations, and individuals who have made generous financial or in-kind contributions to WREI and its work.

The American Woman series was launched with a grant from the Ford Foundation and supported by contributions from other donors. We are extremely grateful to the Ford Foundation both for its past assistance and for providing a grant to help in the preparation of this edition of *The American Woman.* Marcia Smith, June Zeitlin, and Helen Neuborne, in particular, have earned our gratitude for their support and ongoing advice. Alison Bernstein of the Ford Foundation deserves special thanks for her encouragement of *The American Woman* series.

Special thanks are also due the AT&T Foundation and the Revson Foundation, both of which provided crucial support to this project.

The other funders without whose assistance we could not have prepared this book are the American Express Company and Juanita Kreps. To each we extend our thanks. We would also like to acknowledge the support of AETNA; AFL-CIO; Akin, Gump, Strauss, Hauer and Feld; AMBAC; American Income Life Insurance Company; American Postal Workers Union; Association of Flight Attendants; ARCO; Avon Products Inc.; Chase Manhattan Bank; Chrysler Corporation; Citibank; Communications Workers of America; DC Comics; Eastman Kodak; Fluor Corporation; Ford Motor Company; Guinness America, Inc.; Johnson & Johnson; Martin Marietta Corporation; Motorola; National Education Association; Pfizer Inc.; Ryder Systems; Sara Lee Corporation; SmithKline Beecham; Time

Warner; United Auto Workers; United Distillers North America; and Warner-Lambert Company.

Members of WREI's board of directors have offered extensive practical help as well as continuing encouragement throughout all of the editions of *The American Woman*. Board chair Jean Stapleton has tirelessly spoken about every edition of *The American Woman* in towns and cities across the country. JoAnn Heffernan Heisen, Martina L. Bradford, and Carolyn Forrest have promoted the book enthusiastically in the corporate and labor communities. Thanks to Alma Rangel's initiative, *The American Woman* has reached many African American women's organizations in New York. Matina Horner and Juanita Kreps were especially helpful with respect to funding for the book. Indeed, the WREI staff is grateful to the entire board for its belief in the book and for its moral support.

Our editor at Norton, Mary Cunnane, and her assistant, Nicole Wan, consistently provided constructive advice and guidance, for which we are extremely appreciative.

A stellar advisory committee has been generous with wisdom, expertise, and encouragement. That committee consists of Eileen Appelbaum, Ann Bookman, Ellen Bravo, Mariam Chamberlain, Harriet Harper, Cynthia Harrison, Kelly Jenkins, Deirdre Martinez, Jill Miller, Irene Natividad, Sara Rix, Ann Schmidt, Margaret Simms, Bobby Spalter-Roth, Ronnie Steinberg, Anne Stone, and Cindy Taeuber. Sara Rix, who edited the first three volumes of *The American Woman,* deserves special thanks; her recommendations for this edition were, as always, right on target.

We wish to thank the individuals at the Bureau of the Census and the Bureau of Labor Statistics who so generously shared their time and expertise. Lesley Primmer, the former executive director of the Congressional Caucus for Women's Issues, was always generous with information, time, and expertise. I would like to thank Jill Miller for her support of *The American Woman* series and especially Wendy Blum for her wonderful messenger service. The writing and editorial assistance of Azar Kattan and Kitty Stone has been invaluable.

No book of this kind could have been produced without the hard work of WREI's entire staff. The core editorial team, led by senior editor Cynthia Costello and coeditor Barbara Kivimae Krimgold, dedicated countless hours to the research, writing, and editing of *The American Woman*. I cannot adequately express my appreciation for their contributions to WREI and *The American Woman*. The book benefited from Anne Stone's continuing contributions to WREI and *The American Woman* series—this time in the form of writing "In Review" and coauthoring the introduction to this book.

Special thanks are due Monique DeJong for a first-rate job in preparing the statistical section of the book. Bridget Rice, one of WREI's research assistants, worked tirelessly to prepare sections of "In Review" and tables and figures for the statistical section. I also would like to express my appreciation to Shanda Boyett, who jumped in to assist in the exacting process of preparing and editing the tables, figures, and text. Seven WREI interns— Danielle Briggs, Tess Jordan, Jennifer LeFevre, Elizabeth Matthews, Yvonne McNeese, Sandra Okóed, and Amy Shortridge—were invaluable, and without their energy and enterprise there would be no "In Review" section. Shari Miles, WREI's director of education and training programs, offered suggestions on the chapters. Georgia Sadler, our expert on women in the military, assisted with statistics and information on military women. Leigh Carter, WREI's development associate, helped with the review of chapters and the fund-raising efforts that made *The American Woman* possible. And Kathleen Stevenson Pagano helped in many ways with the preparation of this volume, guiding us through the labyrinth of computer technology necessary to prepare *The American Woman*.

Finally, I want to underscore that our funders, advisers, reviewers, and independent editors are not responsible for any errors or misstatements that may appear in the book. The opinions expressed in the book do not necessarily reflect the opinions of anyone other than the authors and editors of *The American Woman*.

BETTY DOOLEY
President
Women's Research and Education Institute

PREFACE

Jean Stapleton

THIS VOLUME IS THE SIXTH in a series of comprehensive reports on the status of women in the United States prepared by the Women's Research and Education Institute (WREI). Published every other year, *The American Woman* assembles the latest available information about women's successes and setbacks in many aspects of their lives. The series has become a reliable almanac, summarizing where American women are and reflecting upon where they are going.

Nurturing the series from the first volume's appearance in 1987, the board and staff have made *The American Woman* a vehicle for assessing women's status in the policymaking process and politics, as well as in society. These books have reinforced the organization's persistent contributions to improving the status of American women, and they offer solid testimony to the effectiveness of the strong leadership centered at WREI.

A brief look backward. The first three editions of *The American Woman* covered a broad array of topics, highlighting, for example, the educational status of women of color, the legacy of the women's movement of the past three decades, and women's status in the military. The fourth edition, published in the spring of 1992, hit the mark by covering women's roles as political players—as candidates, officeholders, and voters—in what became a breakthrough year for women in American politics as a record 48 women were elected to the U.S. House of Representatives and five to the Senate.

The fifth edition of *The American Woman* focused the spotlight on women and health care. Through chapters on women's health status, reproductive health, the health problems of women of color, and long-term care, this volume explored the contradictions and omissions in our present health care system.

With the publication of this sixth edition, WREI turns to a topic of vital concern to all American women and their families: women and work. Of course, we all know that women have always worked—as mothers and as keepers of the hearth. And many women, especially the disadvantaged, have struggled for generations to combine household and paid work—usually with little help and limited resources. What is different today is that recent changes in the economy and the family have propelled the majority of women into the workplace.

What hasn't changed very much is that whether women work for pay or not, they retain primary responsibility for the household and child care. This will come as no surprise to the female readers of this volume whose efforts to "balance" the demands of paid work and family often leave them tired and frustrated. The women who head families by themselves feel these pressures most intensely.

Working women know that change is long overdue. For starters, work schedules need to be made more flexible so that working women—and men—can better tend to their paid work and family responsibilities. Flexibility by itself, however, is not enough. Faced with rising living costs and shrinking paychecks, working women need a living wage, good benefits, and equal opportunity to advance in the workplace. Is this too much to ask?

We live in a country that defines itself as a "land of opportunity." For far too long, women and people of color were shut out from the jobs available to others. Today we can take great pride as a country in the opening up of employment opportunities to women and people of color. It would be untenable, however, if the clock were to stop now.

As we cross over into the next millennium, it is my hope that we will look back on the last decade of the twentieth century as a time when women's equity in the workplace was affirmed, not eroded. Women cannot afford to be passive about their right to equal opportunity. I believe that the time has come for women as voters and as workers to be insistent—to be militant, if need be—that our hard-fought gains not be taken from us!

WOMEN AND WORK

A Perspective on America's
Working Women

Cynthia Costello, Anne J. Stone, and Betty Dooley

THIS BOOK—THE SIXTH VOLUME IN WREI's *American Woman* series—focuses on the status of the roughly 60 million women in America's workforce. The essay that follows this introduction addresses affirmative action—how it has helped working women and people of color and why the efforts to eliminate affirmative action are so unsettling. Chapter One gives the big picture—an overview of trends and current data on such subjects as the kinds of jobs women hold, their earnings, and the types of labor market problems they face. Chapter Two compares how well working women and men have been dealing with the conflict between the demands of work and the demands of family. Chapter Three is a groundbreaking analysis of the unemployment compensation system with women's employment patterns in mind. Chapter Four assesses the job and earnings prospects for women who are or who have been on welfare. Chapters Five and Six conclude with an analysis of pension coverage among today's working women and the policy changes that could increase women's income security in old age.

These chapters highlight the hazards of generalizing about female workers on the basis of their gender alone. To begin with the good news, a great many women are doing well in the workforce—well enough to raise the wages of that statistical construct the "typical" female worker, higher than they've ever been before. As Diane Herz and Barbara Wootton report in Chapter One, women's median earnings have been increasing both in real terms and relative to men's earnings, a development that is directly related to the fact that the typical female worker of today has more education than her counterpart in years past.

These encouraging trends are largely a reflection of what has been happening at the higher end of the employment scale in the still-growing service sector of the economy, where well-educated women have been able to take advantage of increasing opportunities for well-educated workers of both sexes. Not only are women as well as men in managerial and professional occupations earning more in real terms than their counterparts in the past, but the women in these occupations have actually been gaining on the men.

Women now make up respectable proportions—though still a minority— of the highly paid professionals who just a generation ago were almost all male, and to judge by enrollment in law and medical schools, those proportions will continue to increase. The proportion of managers among working women is approaching the comparable proportion of managers among working men.

It is still true that women of color are considerably less well represented in managerial and professional occupations than are white women. But it is also true that over the past dozen years the proportion of black working women who are managers and professionals increased by nearly one-third— the same rate as among white women. (Of course, a faster rate would be necessary in order for black women to catch up with white women.) Among college-educated women the earnings gap between whites and blacks has virtually disappeared. That is to say, college-educated black and white women now have comparable earnings.

To skim the daily newspaper or cruise the television channels leads one to conclude that women have made considerable headway in gaining highly visible, powerful positions. Admittedly the breakthroughs have been uneven: Although there is no longer any novelty in a female Cabinet member, or a female astronaut (unless she is a shuttle pilot), or a woman leading the prosecutorial team in a notorious murder trial, few women can be found among the "captains of industry." And the fact that women slightly predominate among the top officials at the Justice Department is still considered front-page news.

The prospects of managerial and professional women—and men—look favorable, even though most of those women would probably agree that sex discrimination has by no means disappeared from the workplace. The U.S. Department of Labor's Glass Ceiling Commission reported recently that this infamous barrier remains very much intact. Evidence also suggests that the conflict between job and family priorities may prevent, inhibit, or divert many talented and accomplished women from reaching the highest pinnacles of success, especially in the private sector.

While women's gains in professional and managerial occupations have increased the odds that a working woman has the same type of job her father had, this holds true only if he was a professional or other white-collar worker. Women have made virtually no headway in the skilled construction trades and other traditionally male blue-collar occupations. Because the majority of female workers work in service, sales, and clerical jobs—60 percent in 1994—today's female worker is likely to be employed in a job traditional to her gender.

What is different for today's typical white female worker is that unlike her mother, she will probably work steadily for pay from the time she leaves school until she reaches retirement, even when her children are small. This is a familiar pattern among black women, who have for generations combined paid jobs with family responsibilities, but it is rather new among white women.

For women who have children, the work-family balancing act is a major preoccupation and cause of stress. "Working Women Count!," a survey conducted by the Labor Department's Women's Bureau in 1993, drew an avalanche of comments from working mothers about the difficulty of finding good child care and employers' lack of flexibility in accommodating workers' family obligations. Although working mothers at every level grapple with the problem, Ellen Galinsky and James T. Bond demonstrate in Chapter Two that managing the conflicting demands of work and family is especially tough for women whose jobs give them little or no control over their own work schedules and whose resources and employment options are limited. It is surely toughest of all for single mothers. The child care dilemma is a difficult one for many women, no doubt made more painful by recent reports in which child development experts pronounced most child care—whether family care or institutional care—far from adequate, especially for infants.

The women surveyed in "Working Women Count!" put "too much stress" at the top of their list of workplace problems, even ahead of the pocketbook issues. Whether or not she is a member of what Secretary of Labor Robert Reich has called "the anxious class," the average working mother of today surely belongs to "the tired class." She is working more hours at her paid job than she—or her counterparts in earlier times—used to work, and she is more likely than they were to have a very small child or an elderly parent to care for. She, her family, and her productivity as a worker might well benefit from alternatives such as a flexible schedule and the chance to do some of her work at home via telecommuting, but employers rarely offer these options to nonsupervisory workers. Indeed, the majority of workers who enjoy flexible schedules are not only managers but men.

Flexible schedules are not, however, among working women's top priorities for changes in the workplace, according to the Women's Bureau. At the top of the list are health care insurance for all employees and improved pay scales. Both are high priorities for between 60 and 70 percent of women, whatever their occupation, whatever their race.

The failure to enact health care reform in the 103d Congress has left working women and men with greater insecurity about their ability to provide health care for themselves and their families. The last edition of *The American Woman* focused on women's health and insurance status in great detail. The statistical section of this edition shows that today 13 million women and 16.7 million men of working age lack private or public health insurance. It also shows that most people of working age who have no health insurance are actively employed. Working women are less likely than men to get health insurance from their employers, but more likely to get health insurance through a spouse's employer or a public program. In the absence of health care reform, the number of uninsured working Americans is continuing to grow. It is no wonder that the "Working Women Count!" survey found that working women feel insecure about their health insurance status and future.

The problem of inadequate pay and benefits is most acute for women in the low-wage workforce. For these workers, the news is bad. The same structural shift to a service economy that has benefited skilled and educated women—and men—has increased the economic disadvantages for less well-educated and low-skilled workers.

These workers suffer because of the disappearance of the high-wage, high-benefit manufacturing jobs that allowed even poorly educated heads of household (mostly men—and a few women) in previous generations to provide a secure base of support for a family on a single income. Now, in addition to the reality of low wages and few benefits, the job security of poorly educated men and women is diminished. Two incomes are usually needed to support a family, and many workers are experiencing downward rather than upward mobility.

It is becoming harder and harder for low-skilled workers of either sex to find full-time jobs or jobs that are permanent or provide health and pension benefits. American employers' use of part-time and contingent workers has burgeoned in recent years. Part-time and contingent workers—a category that includes temporary workers, independent contractors, and leased employees—may account for as many as 32 million American jobs, according to the Department of Labor. While employers like to stress that using contingent workers helps companies to stay competitive by allowing them to adjust quickly to the ebbs and flows of demand, a major advantage for employers is that they usually can avoid providing contingent workers with such benefits as health insurance and pension plan coverage. And of course, employers can terminate contingent workers immediately upon completion of a given work task since these workers have no guarantee of job security.

Women predominate in the contingent and part-time workforce partly because this kind of work meets the requirements of some women, at least for the short term. A part-time or temporary job can be workable for a woman who wants flexibility to meet her family responsibilities, whose household does not need to rely heavily on her earnings, *and* who does not need health insurance through her job. (At the same time years of employment in a part-time or temporary job can leave these women without adequate earning potential or benefits in the event of divorce or widowhood.) A part-time or temporary job can also be just the ticket for an older woman (or man) who wants to supplement her (or his) Social Security income, perhaps to help pay for a health insurance policy to cover what Medicare doesn't.

Part-time or temporary work may become less acceptable to women who are supplementary earners in their families, especially if job security and health insurance benefits for primary earners continue to diminish. Meanwhile, the pool of workers who will accept low wages and who are without health insurance helps employers resist pressures to provide better pay and minimum benefits to the workers who do need them. These are the women and men—and they are disproportionately people of color—whose households depend heavily on their earnings, who have no health insurance coverage from other sources, and who take part-time or contingent jobs only because they can't find other work. Nearly two million of the women who worked part time last year did so involuntarily—that is, they would have been working full time if they had been able to find the work. One in every four of the black and Hispanic women who work part time would take full-time work if she could get it; this is more than twice the comparable proportion among white women.

As Laurie Bassi and Amy Chasanov point out, part-time and contingent workers are unlikely to qualify for unemployment compensation if they lose their jobs. Nor, as Martha Priddy Patterson and Cindy Hounsell emphasize in their chapters, do most of them qualify for pension coverage from their employers, raising serious concerns about the long-term economic security of the American workforce. Low-skilled workers in part-time and contingent jobs are truly vulnerable. Because they know they can be readily replaced, they are in a weak position to demand better wages, benefits, and working conditions.

The research presented in these chapters shows that organizing through labor unions would probably improve the prospects of low-skilled contingent workers. The low-skilled workers with the best pay, benefits, and working conditions belong to labor unions. On average, both women and men who belong to unions earn more money and have better benefits than their counterparts who do not, and the differential between women's and men's earnings is smaller among union members than among nonmembers.

But existing labor laws, which were designed when the typical job was permanent, full time, and in a fixed workplace, make organizing the contingent workforce very difficult. Indeed, that is undoubtedly one of the reasons employers find contingent workers advantageous. After President Clinton was elected, advocates for low-wage workers began to press for reforms that would help contingent and contract workers organize. Their hopes were badly dampened, if not extinguished, by the congressional elections in 1994.

Indeed, the welfare overhaul under way in this Congress could worsen the situation of America's low-skilled workers, especially women. As Katherine McFate cautions in Chapter Four, research suggests that precipitating welfare mothers into the low-wage workforce will be at the expense of the women already in it. The fundamental problem for workers who are ill equipped by training and education for good jobs is that they often cannot lift themselves and their families out of poverty even if their work effort is strong. This is especially true in the case of women who maintain families. Among women-maintained families with at least one family member in the workforce for at least half the year, the poverty rate is nearly 20 percent. The rate is even higher—nearly 25 percent—if the families contain children.

No doubt because working is now the norm for middle-class women with children, there is now widespread sentiment that if poor people on public assistance are able to work, they ought to work, regardless of whether they have small children at home. However, not much consideration seems to be given to the costs versus the rewards of work for workers with few skills. The jobs they can get are not only the jobs least likely to pay enough to support a family but also the jobs least likely to provide health insurance. Yet a mother who leaves the Aid to Families with Dependent Children (AFDC) rolls to take a low-wage job—and as McFate shows, many women do just that—soon loses eligibility for Medicaid for herself and her children. She must find child care for her children, and quality child care that she can afford is very scarce.

The Earned Income Tax Credit (EITC) for low-income families with children may supplement a woman's low earnings, but it probably will not provide sufficient income for a woman to buy health insurance or to pay for child care. And for the long term it's important to remember that while the EITC does in effect increase her current earnings, it does not build a woman's earnings record for the Social Security benefits that she will depend on in her retirement.

The President and his Secretary of Labor, Robert Reich, place great emphasis on education and job training and retraining as American workers' best hope for success in a rapidly changing workplace. It is hard to quarrel with the goal of equipping workers with the skills required for jobs that pay living wages and provide adequate benefits, but this goal optimistically assumes that there will be enough good jobs available. Research shows that a substantial proportion—possibly the majority—of the jobs that have been created in the last few years are low-wage jobs that provide few benefits. Without changes in public- and private-sector policy, this trend is unlikely to change.

By itself job training is unlikely to bring the hoped-for results. Even in the days when politicians were willing to commit substantial sums of money to job training, few programs succeeded in moving people with serious educational and skills deficiencies into *good* jobs. One reason is that no good jobs for low-skilled workers have come along to take the place of the lost manufacturing jobs that paid good wages and provided good benefits in the past. A second reason is that comprehensive job training programs are costly. If the country were serious about preparing people for rewarding work, policymakers would begin with major improvements in the education of children.

Ensuring that women have choices is surely at the very heart of the push for women's economic equity. However, the importance of equipping low-skilled women to make a decent living for themselves and their families should not blind us to the implications for women of the increasingly desperate plight of low-skilled men. The earnings capacity of better-educated women gives them the power to choose to marry or not to marry or to leave a bad marriage. But it is largely the earnings capacity of better-educated men that allows their wives to choose *not* to work for pay or to work only part time. And it is usually the earnings capacity of men that determines whether there will be adequate child support if the parents break up. In short, when men lack earnings capacity, women have fewer choices.

So there is ample reason for women's advocates to be deeply concerned about the growing number and proportion of low-skilled men in their prime working years (age 22 to 58) who don't have steady jobs. Of those men with less than a high school education, scarcely more than half worked year round, full time steadily through the decade of the 1980s, down from 68 percent in the 1970s. One in 10 worked only sporadically, if at all, in the 1980s, compared with one in 20 in the 1970s. Half the men with less than a high school education earned less in the 1980s than in the 1970s. For black males as a whole the trend was depressingly similar to the trend for men who did not finish high school: The proportions without steady work were almost identical.

The reason, again, is largely that there are no longer enough good, steady jobs to go around for men with few skills, and the gap grows wider daily. With corporate downsizing, the number of jobs that pay a living wage is steadily decreasing.

What it means to men not to work and not to be able to support or contribute financially to a family is beyond the scope of this discussion. But here are some of the practical implications for women who have chronically unemployed or underemployed men in their lives. Men without work may make it difficult for their partners to keep working. It's reportedly quite common for men to try to sabotage the efforts of women trying to work their way off welfare. There's little incentive for women to marry since they can anticipate no economic benefit from marriage and could find themselves worse off. And there's little prospect of a reasonable level of child support should a marriage end in divorce.

These points certainly bear pondering, perhaps especially by those who blame the "welfare system" for poverty and dependence. A woman who works year round, full time at the current minimum wage will not make enough to keep herself—not to mention a family—above the poverty line. Requiring women with marginal skills to work at marginal jobs is no substitute for a serious nationwide commitment to upgrading the skills and "employability" of women *and* men with marginal skills—and to ensuring that there are decent jobs available and truly open to these workers.

As long as female workers face challenges and problems that stem either from their gender (such problems as sex bias and sexual harassment) or from their typically heavier responsibilities for child care, it will be necessary to examine the situation of female workers as a special case. Nevertheless, it would be a mistake to overlook the fact that the same labor market developments and general economic trends that affect male workers affect female workers too, although not always in the same way.

Take, for example, the narrowing of the wage gap—the differential between the median weekly earnings of women and men. Closing this gap has been a key objective of women's equity advocates for many years. As Diane Herz and Barbara Wootton report, between 1979 and 1994 the gap narrowed by about 13 percentage points—but only partly because women's real earnings increased. The larger factor was that men's real earnings declined. Analysts at the Economic Policy Institute say that the male earnings drop-off—which until lately was confined largely to men with no more than a high school education—has now become apparent among college-educated men as well.

As the purchasing power of men's earnings has dropped, married-couple families have kept up with inflation only because more wives are working and wives are working more hours. Beyond the obvious financial gain, there are other advantages in having two people share the responsibility of bread-winner. The family is better able to ride out a layoff or job loss. Two working parents are more likely to share child care; this generally turns out to be a plus for fathers and children as well. A working woman may feel entitled to more say in important family decisions. And of course, knowing that if necessary, she can earn her own living allows a woman to make decisions about her marriage for other than financial reasons. To judge by all we really have to go on—intuition, common sense, personal experience, and the experiences of friends—the growing importance of wives' earnings is altering family dynamics in fundamental ways.

There's little doubt that for many men, adjusting to what amounts to a shift in the family balance of power is not easy. And it is frightening for anyone to see his or her earning power decline. Whether for these or other reasons, many men appear to feel aggrieved and threatened. And for men no less than women, it turns out, the personal is political. The big news of the 1994 congressional elections was the white male vote, which was larger than usual. It was so large that it changed the political landscape altogether.

Some men seem inclined to think that women (and "minorities") are to blame for the decline in their earnings. The cry has gone out to do away with affirmative action to save the endangered white male, and at this writing, affirmative action appears to be hanging by a thin thread.

Jocelyn Frye describes the controversies surrounding affirmative action in her essay in this volume. Despite the intensity of the debate over affirmative action, experts agree that it has nothing to do with the decline in men's earnings. This decline stems from big, international trends over which individual workers (and American politicians) have little or no control, such as the loss of good blue-collar jobs in heavy manufacturing and the loss of middle-management jobs as a result of widespread corporate restructuring and downsizing. The increase in women's median earnings (still far below the median for white men) stems mostly from the improvement in women's educational levels. So doing away with affirmative action is unlikely to have any impact on white men's earnings, even though it is undeniable that affirmative action has been a positive force in women's lives, helping them get better jobs than they would have gotten otherwise.

While many white men may perceive that the playing field is now level—even that women and minorities have an edge—working women certainly don't see it that way. More than half the respondents to the Women's Bureau survey said that ensuring equal opportunity in the workplace was a priority for them. And of the concerns working women most wanted to tell the President about, "unequal or unfair pay" and "lack of equal treatment and equal opportunity" ranked second and third respectively—outweighed only by the work-family conflicts mentioned earlier.

To the question "What do America's working women want?" the survey provides clear answers. Pocketbook issues are very important. "Health care insurance for all employees" and "improving pay scales" were the two top priorities for the women who answered the survey. These were followed by on-the-job training, equal opportunity, more responsibility on the job, and paid family leave.

The chapters in *The American Woman* conclude that many of the needs voiced by working women can be met only through changes in public policy. An increase in women's pay, universal access to health care, and labor law reform that facilitates organizing among contingent workers are policy changes that would give working women—and men—a big boost. In addition, working women are counting on the President and Congress to uphold—rather than abandon—their commitment to affirmative action. It is our hope that the readers of this book will agree that working women deserve no less!

Affirmative Action: Understanding the Past and Present

Jocelyn C. Frye

IN A RECENT ARTICLE ABOUT AFFIRMATIVE ACTION, Roger Wilkins (1995) writes, "The past is hugely important, since we argue a lot about who we are on the basis of who we think we have been, and we derive much of our sense of the future from how we think we've done in the past. In a nation in which few people know much history, these are perilous arguments, because in such a vacuum, people tend to weave historical fables tailored to their political or psychic needs." Nowhere are the perils of talking in a vacuum more evident than in the case of affirmative action, where understanding the past and present experiences of women must play an integral part in shaping future affirmative action policies and protecting existing programs. Indeed, while debate about the merits of affirmative action has taken center stage in 1995, little attention is being given to history. For women, this history is particularly critical because many of the discriminatory barriers facing women today in employment, education, and business are rooted in long-standing views of "proper" gender roles and women's capabilities.

THE HISTORICAL FRAMEWORK

For years qualified women were shut out of employment, education, and business opportunities solely because of their sex and/or race. Women were excluded partially because of a traditional view of women's "proper" role, which confined women's responsibilities and ambitions to home and family. This traditional view did not conceptualize women (usually thought of exclusively as white women) outside the home, for example, as workers or business owners. Women who worked did so mostly in traditional female jobs and usually at lower wages than men, implicitly because their work was less valued and less respected. A disproportionate number of women of color worked when compared with white women, and they often were relegated to the lowest-paying, least-valued jobs (Needleman 1993).

Women's choices generally were limited from their earliest school years through high school; girls and later young women frequently were tracked into certain careers and cut off from other educational opportunities. Those who did pursue higher education often were discouraged from pursuing careers in such fields as engineering or medicine. As late as 1968 newspaper want ads often were segregated by gender—one section for the "male" (usually better-paying) jobs and a separate section for the "female" jobs. As a result, women were systematically excluded from many opportunities without regard to their qualifications.

Understanding this historical context is critical to grasping the important role that affirmative action plays for women. Affirmative action programs have been one of the tools used effectively in the contemporary struggle to open new doors for women, combat gender-discriminatory policies, break down traditional limits on women's choices, and expand the conception of appropriate roles for women. Reviewing history also provides insight into the attitudes that continue to engender sex discrimination. Unfortunately, many affirmative action opponents pay little attention to history or to the ongoing reality of discrimination.

WHAT IS AFFIRMATIVE ACTION?

Clouding the current debate about affirmative action is the lack of a clear understanding of what affirmative action is and what it is not. Affirmative action generally means positive steps taken by a company, organization, agency, or institution to end discrimination, to prevent its recurrence, and to create new opportunities that previously were denied to qualified women and people of color. In practice, for example, affirmative action programs range from special efforts to alert women and people of color about job openings to more assertive strategies, such as special training programs targeting people of color and women, minority scholarships at academic institutions, or goals and timetables to measure and encourage increased participation by women and people of color. Examples of lawful affirmative action programs are varied.

- In order to increase the number of women involved in the construction industry, a Chicago real estate developer established an outreach program called the Female Employment Initiative. The program creates opportunities for women in the building trades through special training programs, counseling and information services, and referral listings that identify available women workers for employers.
- A number of universities and employers have developed initiatives to provide specialized counseling and training to encourage women to enter engineering and other technical programs.
- Other employers have instituted targeted reviews by senior management staff to identify promising women candidates for consideration when senior job opportunities emerge. These programs may also include mentoring programs and ongoing leadership training for women to develop their understanding of the corporate culture and enhance their prospects for promotion.

All these programs are used to counteract ongoing sex and race discrimination that too often taints decisions about jobs, education, and business opportunities.

Equal in importance to the question of what affirmative action is, is an explanation of what affirmative action is not. To the extent that affirmative action is controversial, much of the controversy stems from misconceptions and myths about how affirmative action works. The Supreme Court has made clear that a lawful affirmative action program must apply only to qualified candidates, have a strong reason for being developed, and be narrowly crafted to minimize negative effects. This means that despite myths to the contrary, a program cannot promote unqualified individuals over qualified individuals. Nor can a program set rigid, inflexible numbers (or, in other words, quotas) that must be met regardless of the available pool of qualified candidates. Rather, programs may rely on flexible numerical goals to measure progress in expanding opportunities as long as the numerical goals take into account the relevant pool of qualified women and people of color. Even in its most recent decision toughening the standard used to evaluate race-based government affirmative action programs, the Supreme Court nonetheless made it clear that properly designed affirmative action programs are valid.

Affirmative action programs must respect the rights of men and whites; programs cannot require that male workers be discharged to make way for female workers, for example. The Supreme Court has ruled, in one instance, that a public employer cannot lay off more senior white workers to protect the jobs of less senior black workers. Nor can men and whites be excluded from opportunities. Indeed, affirmative action's core principle is that all candidates must have the chance to compete and to have their qualifications compared.

Affirmative action also must be temporary, designed to end when the program's goals are met. The Supreme Court approved a voluntary affirmative action plan to increase the number of black craftworkers at one company, for example, in part because it was a temporary measure designed to correct one specific problem—the serious underrepresentation of black craftworkers—and then end.

Despite the real facts about how affirmative action works, opponents frequently mischaracterize affirmative action programs to perpetuate negative myths about the individuals who benefit from such programs and to build fear and resentment in the general public. Recent polls indicate that Americans firmly support affirmative action to create opportunities for women and people of color, while they vigorously oppose quotas and preferences for unqualified candidates. Not surprisingly, then, the current strategy of affirmative action critics is to redefine affirmative action as a synonym for quotas and preferences and to judge affirmative action in a vacuum without acknowledging its role in battling ongoing discrimination.

WHY AFFIRMATIVE ACTION IS NEEDED

The best way to assess the need for affirmative action accurately is to look at affirmative action in context as a response to discrimination. While the days of segregated job ads are gone, sex discrimination still persists.

CURRENT DISCRIMINATION AND AFFIRMATIVE ACTION

The Equal Employment Opportunity Commission (EEOC) reports that more than 25,800 claims alleging sex discrimination were filed in fiscal year 1994 alone; complaints of sexual harassment increased by more than 13 percent (Equal Employment Opportunity Commission 1994). And persistent discrimination underlies the very real wage gap that continues to depress women's earning power. Discrimination keeps disproportionate numbers of women stuck in low-wage jobs with limited opportunity for advancement and success.

Several recent court cases involving grocery store chains present a very vivid picture of how discrimination against women persists. In these cases female employees were routinely segregated into low-wage, dead-end jobs with little hope for advancement, while men were hired for jobs that led to management opportunities. Women also were denied access to training programs and were pushed into part-time rather than full-time jobs against their wishes. Black women often were given the lowest-paying "female" jobs. In one case, when a black woman asked her manager about promotion opportunities, her manager said that men would not work for a woman, let alone a black woman (Swisher 1994). In short, promotions into management and other leadership opportunities were few and far between.

Affirmative action, however, has made a real difference for these women. Female employees challenged many of the discriminatory grocery store practices and won. Several stores, including Lucky Stores and Safeway, have implemented affirmative action programs designed to open up management opportunities for qualified women. Lucky Stores' newly created affirmative action programs have led to increased numbers of women in entry-level management jobs and have doubled the percentage of women store managers, assistant managers, third-rank managers, and fourth-rank managers. Safeway's program has expanded opportunities for women applying for middle- and upper-level management jobs.

Far from being an isolated occurrence, the discrimination experienced by women in the grocery store cases reflects an all-too-common reality for many women and people of color. Indeed, recent social science studies confirm that discrimination continues to exclude women and people of color from meaningful opportunities. Recent tests conducted by the Fair Employment Council of Greater Washington (FEC) illustrate how discrimination works. For example, two women—one African American and the other white, both with identical credentials and background—were sent to a suburban Washington employer who had advertised for a receptionist/typist. The African American woman submitted an application, was interviewed briefly, but heard nothing. A short while later the white woman submitted an application, was interviewed, and was offered a better, higher-paying position as a personal assistant to the manager. Even after the white woman turned her offer down, the employer was uninterested in hiring the African American woman for either position when she followed up with phone calls (Bendick 1995).

The two women in the FEC test were part of testing studies—studies that pair white and minority candidates, called testers, who have identical work experiences, backgrounds, demeanors, interviewing skills, and physical builds, and then send the members of the pair separately to apply for the same job—to investigate whether white and minority job applicants are treated differently. The FEC, using black/white testing pairs, found substantial evidence of discrimination. In a 1992 study almost half of the white testers received job offers, compared with only 11 percent of the black testers. In cases where black and white testers received the same job offer, almost 20 percent of white testers were promised a higher starting wage than black testers. All in all, FEC tests have found that nearly one employer in four discriminates by treating minority applicants significantly worse than nonminority applicants (Bendick 1995).

A not-so-surprising result of these discriminatory practices is that white men still dominate the upper-level managerial jobs in most fields. For example, the recent fact-finding report issued by the bipartisan Glass Ceiling commission (1995) revealed that less than five percent of senior managers (vice president and above) in Fortune 1,000 companies were women and people of color, even though women constitute 46 percent of the overall workforce and people of color constitute 21 percent of the overall workforce. Moreover, women continue to face significant barriers when seeking higher-paying, nontraditional jobs, particularly in the skilled and construction trades. Overall in 1993 women were only 0.6 percent of auto mechanics, 0.9 percent of carpenters, 0.7 percent of plumbers, 1.1 percent of electricians, and 3.5 percent of welders (Bureau of Labor Statistics 1994).

Qualifications and merit still too often take a backseat to the old boys' network and old-fashioned discrimination. Even when women get jobs, they earn less than men. Although women's wages have risen, men are still more likely to be high-wage earners and women are disproportionately low-wage earners. For example, 16.4 percent of white men were high-wage earners (earning $52,364 or more annually) in 1992, compared with only 3.8 percent of white women, 1.6 percent of black women, and 1.8 percent of Hispanic women. In contrast, only 11.6 percent of white men were low-wage earners (earning $13,091 or less a year), compared with 21.1 percent of white women, 26.9 percent of black women, and 36.6 percent of Hispanic women (Bureau of the Census 1994).

Not only do white-male earnings outpace the earnings of white women and people of color, but white men also get a better return on their education.

- College-educated Hispanic women earn almost $1,000 less annually than white male high school graduates and nearly $15,000 less than college-educated white men.
- College-educated black women earn only $1,000 more annually than white male high school graduates and $13,000 less than college-educated white men.
- College-educated white women earn only $2,000 more a year than white male high school graduates and $12,000 less than white men with college degrees (National Committee on Pay Equity 1993).

In the face of such pervasive discrimination, affirmative action clearly has been one of the tools used to create new opportunities for qualified women and people of color. Because of affirmative action and other antidiscrimination measures, women have made significant progress.

- Women earn more. In 1963 women earned 59 cents for every dollar earned by men; today women earn 71 cents for every dollar earned by men.
- More women are in the pipeline for top jobs. In 1980 white women were 27.1 percent of all managers (middle and upper level) and women of color were 3.2 percent; by 1990 white women were 35.3 percent of managers and women of color were 6.9 percent (Institute for Women's Policy Research 1995).
- Women have moved into professional jobs previously occupied by men. In 1993, 18.6 percent of architects were women, compared with only 4.3 percent in 1975; 47.6 percent of economists were women, compared with only 13.1 percent in 1975; and 22.8 percent of lawyers and judges were women, compared with only 7.1 percent in 1975 (Costello and Stone 1994; Bureau of Labor Statistics 1994).

THE BENEFITS OF AFFIRMATIVE ACTION

The broader economic benefits of affirmative action are often ignored in the emotionally charged debate about its impact on specific individuals. The changing demographics of the workplace are a reality that cannot be ignored. Indeed, 75 percent of new entrants to the workforce between 1990 and 2000 will be women and people of color. A growing number of businesses, in fact, now recognize that affirmative action policies boost productivity and increase profits by creating a diverse workforce drawn from a larger talent pool, generating new ideas, targeting new markets, and improving workplace morale. In short, taking advantage of the diverse talents in the labor market is good for business.

Several recent studies conclude that diversity boosts a company's performance. A 1993 University of North Texas study pitted ethnically diverse teams of business students against all white teams for 17 weeks. At the study's end the university concluded that the ethnically diverse team viewed business situations from a broader range of perspectives and produced more innovative solutions to problems (Watson, Kumar, and Michaelson 1993). Also, a recent study by Covenant Investment Management rated the performance of the Standard & Poor's 500 companies on factors relating to the hiring and advancement of women and minority men. The stock market performance of the companies with good records of hiring and advancing minority men and women was 2.4 times higher than the performance of companies with bad records. Indeed, the 100 companies with the best hiring records earned an 18.3 percent average return on investment, while the 100 lowest-ranked companies earned an average return of only 7.9 percent (Glass Ceiling Commission 1995).

SCAPEGOATING AFFIRMATIVE ACTION

The intensity of the current affirmative action debate raises questions about why affirmative action has become such a target, particularly in light of the many other serious economic, safety, education, and health care problems facing this country. Perhaps it is precisely because of the complexity and difficulty posed by these other problems that decisionmakers and commentators instead target policies like affirmative action that are easily distorted and misunderstood. Rather than confront the serious economic problems that have forced cutbacks in jobs and strained the economic security of families, some have chosen to make affirmative action the easy target; critics blame expanded opportunities for women and people of color for white male job loss.

Another complication is that affirmative action forces us to confront the persistent sex and race discrimination that continues to undermine the goal of equal opportunity. As Roger Wilkins (1995) notes, acknowledging ongoing discrimination and the need for affirmative action and other antidiscrimination remedies challenges us to reconcile our broader philosophical ideals about who we want to be with the reality of who we really are. By ignoring existing discrimination and branding affirmative action as the problem, we use the jettisoning of affirmative action programs as a proxy for ridding ourselves of the very discrimination that affirmative action seeks to remedy.

And finally, there are also some who dislike affirmative action's success and seek to end affirmative action programs precisely because they have opened new opportunities. There remain in our society individuals who oppose the basic principle of equal opportunity and would reduce, rather than expand, choices for women and people of color.

Instead of talking about these issues honestly, opponents of affirmative action frequently obscure the debate with misleading objections. Many critics, for example, mischaracterize affirmative action policies as unfair preferences for women and people of color that disregard merit and place white males at a disadvantage. Yet these same critics overlook the myriad long-standing and powerful preference systems employed by many companies, agencies, and institutions long before affirmative action began. Many of these preferences continue today, and many, if not most, of their beneficiaries are white males.

For example, in 1994, 40 percent of the children of Harvard alumni who applied to Harvard were admitted, as compared with the 14 percent admission rate of nonalumni children. According to a U.S. Department of Education report, the alumni children who were admitted scored an average of 35 points lower on their Scholastic Aptitude Tests than other Harvard students. Another recent research report on higher education revealed that far more whites have entered the gates of the 10 most elite institutions through "alumni preference" than the combined numbers of all the blacks and Chicanos entering through affirmative action (Institute for the Study of Social Change 1991).

A 1992 National Collegiate Athletic Association survey of Division I colleges revealed that even though women represented more than one-half of the total student population, male athletes received more than two-thirds of the athletic scholarship dollars. Moreover, many men have access to scholarships specifically reserved for men only; for example, Bucknell University offers a scholarship for mechanical engineering students who are members of Sigma Chi Fraternity, and Middlebury College offers scholarship aid to male students from New Jersey.

Northwestern University sociologist Mark Granovetter, author of a book on how connections lead to employment, concludes that personal contacts account for between 30 percent and 70 percent of all hires (Granovetter 1995). Given that most managers are white men (approximately 95 percent of all senior managers, according to the Glass Ceiling Commission's 1995 report), it is not surprising that most of their personal contacts are also white men and that their hires and promotions are disproportionately white men.

There is little evidence to back up the claim that affirmative action discriminates against white men. In its March 1995 preliminary draft report on reverse discrimination, the Department of Labor concluded that only a small percentage of discrimination cases involve reverse discrimination claims ("Draft Report on Reverse Discrimination" 1995). Similarly, the EEOC found that between 1987 and 1994 race-based discrimination claims filed with it by white men constituted only 4.1 percent of all race-based charges and 1.7 percent of the total number of discrimination filings.

Others complain that affirmative action means that unqualified people move ahead. There may be instances where, for example, employers are sloppy and may not take the time to make sure that an affirmative action program operates in a lawful manner. But the remedy is to enforce the law to ensure that affirmative action programs are lawful, flexible, narrowly tailored, and effective, rather than eliminate affirmative action altogether. Moreover, in some cases individuals who complain about losing an opportunity to an unqualified person simply may be unwilling to admit that someone—perhaps a women or person of color—could be equally or more qualified.

Critics also charge that affirmative action stigmatizes women and people of color. But the stigmatization experienced by women and people of color existed long before affirmative action, and it undoubtedly would continue if affirmative action programs were eliminated tomorrow. Prejudice and discrimination, not affirmative action, stigmatize women and people of color. The sad reality is that some individuals make assumptions about the capabilities of others based on their race or gender, and many of those individuals will assume that certain groups, because of their race or because of their gender, are less capable or less intelligent.

CONCLUSION

Many opponents of affirmative action argue that women no longer need affirmative action and that women will not lose anything if affirmative action is eliminated. They point to the growing number of women in the workplace, the rise of female managers in companies, and the steady growth of new opportunities for women in careers traditionally dominated by men.

But make no mistake, the elimination of affirmative action will mean an erosion of the gains made by women. What critics ignore is that women have made gains *because of* antidiscrimination measures like affirmative action. While certainly some committed employers and institutions would continue efforts to expand opportunities for women and people of color without the steady force of affirmative measures, many would not. Eliminating affirmative action programs removes the incentive to pay attention to the makeup of a workplace or an institution and be vigilant about ensuring equal opportunity for all.

Moreover, cutting back affirmative action programs shrinks women's choices. Affirmative action programs have opened doors to new opportunities previously closed to women, particularly in nontraditional fields. Without affirmative action, organizations can easily revert back to old patterns of stereotyping "appropriate" roles for women.

Affirmative action has proven to be successful in opening doors for qualified women. The need for affirmative action remains great because sex discrimination continues to color decisions about employment, education, and business opportunities. Rolling back affirmative action would signal a retreat from our long-standing national commitment to women's equality and a return to the politics of exclusion and division that keeps the gate locked tight against qualified women and people of color.

ONE

★

WOMEN IN THE WORKFORCE: AN OVERVIEW

Diane E. Herz and Barbara H. Wootton[1]

HIGHLIGHTS

TODAY WORK AMONG WOMEN is the rule rather than the exception. Out of every 10 women age 16 and over, nearly six participate in the workforce. Labor force participation is even more common among women age 25 to 54; three-quarters of such women were either working or looking for work in 1994.

- Women of all races, ages, and marital status groups participate in the workforce in large numbers. Even among mothers more than half of those with children under age one work either full or part time.
- Women have made substantial inroads into some occupations tradition-ally dominated by men, particularly managerial and professional fields, such as law. Overall, however, women remain concentrated in service, sales, and clerical jobs. These jobs, which often pay lower-than-average wages, accounted for nearly six in 10 working women in 1994.
- The earnings gap between women and men declined substantially between 1979 and 1994. Still, women who usually worked full time in 1994 earned only 76 percent as much as men.
- Over the 1979–94 period women's earnings increased after inflation, while men's declined in real terms. Increases in women's earnings reflected additional years of work experience and educational attainment as well as movement into higher-paying occupations.

[1]The authors would like to thank the staff of the Division of Labor Force Statistics—espe-cially Linda Blount, Randy Ilg, and Dan Watson—for their assistance on this chapter.

- Women and men are equally likely to experience unemployment. Among women, black women and women of Hispanic origin are twice as likely as white women to be jobless.
- Women are somewhat less likely than men to be displaced from their jobs because men are more heavily concentrated in industries hardest hit by downturns. However, women made up a larger share of displaced workers—41 percent in the 1991–93 period—than a decade earlier, as displacement became more common in service-producing industries.
- Women are much more likely than men to be living in poverty despite participating in the labor force. Nearly a quarter of women who maintain families with children have family incomes below the poverty level despite the labor force participation of at least one family member for half of the year or more.

INTRODUCTION

Today work among women is the rule rather than the exception. In 1940 nearly three in 10 women in the working-age population were in the labor force—that is, they either held jobs or were looking for work. Labor force participation by women increased after World War II and through the 1980s, after which it remained relatively stable. In 1994 the 60.2 million women in the labor force accounted for about six of every 10 women in the working-age population. In terms of their proportion of the labor force, women accounted for 46 percent of the total in 1994, up from 24 percent in 1940.

This chapter provides an overview of women in the U.S. workforce and sets the stage for the chapters that follow. We present a brief history of changes in labor market participation of women since World War II and describe the types of jobs women hold, their earnings, and the types of labor market problems they face. Where possible, we illustrate how women's work has changed over the past several decades, as well as how women's labor market experiences vary by age, race and ethnicity, marital status, family type, and other characteristics.

Most of the data in this chapter are derived from the Current Population Survey (CPS), a monthly sample survey of households conducted by the Bureau of the Census for the Bureau of Labor Statistics (BLS). Where the CPS does not provide complete information, we draw on other sources.

TRENDS IN LABOR FORCE PARTICIPATION

HISTORICAL TRENDS

Most examinations of the influx of women into the labor force in the United States begin with World War II because the war period is often viewed as a watershed in women's involvement in market work. Some women, however—particularly young, single, and nonwhite women—participated in the labor force in large proportions even before the war. For example, nearly half of single women and women age 20 to 24 participated in the labor force in 1940. It is true, though, that the rapid increase of women's participation in the workforce was stimulated by women's movement into the workforce during the war years.

In the early 1940s severe labor shortages resulting from the wartime mobilization of men and the production requirements of the war began to create a greater demand for women in the labor market. As a result, 5.2 million more women were in the labor force in 1944 than in 1940, and the proportion of women age 14 and over who participated increased from about 28 percent to 36 percent during that period. After the war the proportion of women in the labor force dropped to 31 percent in 1946 but still remained above its prewar level. Some women, particularly those beyond childbearing age, were much less likely to withdraw from the labor force after the war than were others. For example, although the participation rate of women age 45 to 64 declined immediately after the war, it surpassed wartime levels by 1949 and continued upward after that. Figure I-1 illustrates increases in women's participation from 1948 onward.

In the 1950s steady labor force gains among women continued. In the 1960s and 1970s the influx of women, particularly married women, into the labor force accelerated for a number of reasons. The feminist movement was growing in strength and influence, providing encouragement for women to seek a larger role in the workforce—whether for increased autonomy, personal satisfaction, or other reasons. The achievements of the civil rights movement led to more equal treatment for women as well as minority groups. Birthrates were declining during this period, both reflecting and contributing to women's growing attachment to the labor force. In addition, women were attaining higher levels of education, and education tends to increase workforce activity. Finally, the economy was expanding, providing jobs for most who sought them.

During the early 1980s, despite back-to-back recessions and structural changes in the economy, women's labor force activity continued to increase,

Figure I-1 · PERCENTAGE POPULATION IN THE LABOR FORCE BY SEX, 1948–1994 (annual averages)

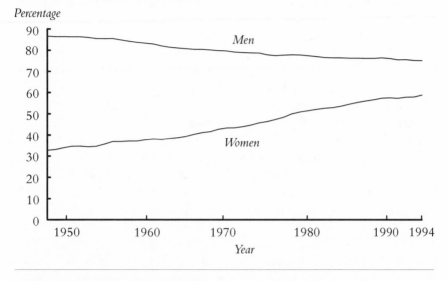

Source: Bureau of Labor Statistics 1994b.

although at a slower pace. As is typically the case, these recessions dispropor-tionately affected industries and occupations traditionally dominated by men.

During 1990–91 the rise in women's labor market participation essen-tially stopped. A recession during those years included an unusually large share of job losses in industries that employed many women, such as retail trade. It also led to increases in school enrollments by younger women (age 16 to 24) as many stayed in school because of relatively poor job prospects. After that, participation among women remained relatively flat. In 1994, 58.8 percent of women age 16 or older were either working or looking for work.

In contrast to the rise in labor force activity among women, the propor-tion of men in the U.S. labor force declined, though much more gradually, during the decades following World War II. In 1948, 87 percent of men age 16 and older either held a job or were looking for work; by 1994 that proportion had declined to 75 percent (see Figure I-1). The gradual reduc-tion in men's labor force participation primarily reflected the long-term trend toward early retirement, spurred by enhancements in the Social Security sys-tem and increases in the availability of private pension income. The expan-sion of the Social Security disability program also accelerated the decrease in participation among preretirement-age men (Ippolito 1989; and Have-man, DeJong, and Wolfe 1991).

CHANGES IN HOUSEHOLD AND FAMILY TYPES

Concurrent with the rise in labor force participation by women, a dramatic shift occurred in the structure of American households and families. Marriage rates in the United States peaked in 1946. After that, and particularly after 1970, men and women became more likely to defer marriage, and a growing share decided not to marry at all. At the same time the divorce rate escalated, peaking around 1980. Despite small declines in recent years, one in every two first marriages can be expected to end in divorce. Finally, particularly in the 1980s and 1990s, an increasing number of children were born to unwed mothers.

These factors led to substantial declines in the proportion of families that were married couples (with or without children) and increases in the proportion of families that were maintained by women. In 1994, 77 percent of all American families were married-couple families, down from 85 percent in 1975. And 19 percent were families maintained by women, up from 13 percent in 1975. In addition, "nonfamily" households increased as a proportion of all households over the period, primarily reflecting increases in the number of individuals living alone, including widows. The combination of these social trends has meant that women have increasingly relied on themselves for their own support and that of their families. Today even those women who do not currently maintain households or families are more likely to plan their work lives with that possibility in mind.

VARIATION IN LABOR FORCE PARTICIPATION

AGE

The entry of women age 25 to 54 into the labor force was the driving force in the rise of women's labor market activity after World War II. Three of every four women age 25 to 54 were in the labor force in 1994, twice the proportion for this age group shortly after the war. In 1994 women in their late thirties and early forties had the highest participation level of any age group; nearly eight in 10 were in the labor force (see Table I-1). In the early postwar period, by contrast, the highest rates were among women under age 25 (see Figure I-2). Increases in work by those age 25 and older eliminated the dip in participation among women age 25 to 34 that used to exist as many women left the labor force to have and care for their children. As a result, women's participation pattern by age now looks similar to that for men; participation increases steadily until the middle years, remains high,

Table I-1 · SELECTED POPULATION AND LABOR FORCE CHARACTERISTICS OF WOMEN, 1994 (numbers in thousands)

Characteristic	Population	Labor Force	
		Number	Percentage of Population
Total, 16 years and over	102,460	60,239	58.8
Age			
16 to 19 years	6,993	3,585	51.3
20 to 24 years	9,279	6,592	71.0
25 to 54 years	57,269	43,116	75.3
25 to 34 years	20,945	15,499	74.0
35 to 44 years	21,091	16,259	77.1
45 to 54 years	15,233	11,357	74.6
55 to 64 years	10,825	5,289	48.9
65 years and over	18,094	1,658	9.2
Race and Hispanic Origin[1]			
White	85,496	50,356	58.9
Black	12,621	7,413	58.7
Hispanic origin	9,014	4,765	52.9
Marital Status			
Never married	22,886	14,905	65.1
Married, spouse present	54,198	32,862	60.6
Widowed	11,073	1,945	17.6
Divorced	10,113	7,473	73.9
Married, spouse absent	3,911	2,461	62.9
Presence and age of children			
Without children under 18	66,810	35,455	53.1
With children under 18	35,373	24,191	68.4
6 to 17 years, none younger	18,248	13,863	76.0
Under 6 years	17,125	10,328	60.3
Under 3 years	10,026	5,724	57.1
Under 1 year	3,152	1,720	54.6
Men, total, 16 years and over	94,355	70,817	75.1

[1]Details for race and Hispanic origin groups will not add up because the data for the "other races" group are not presented and Hispanics are included in both the white and black population groups.

Source: Bureau of Labor Statistics (BLS) 1994b and BLS 1994c.

Figure I-2 · LABOR FORCE PARTICIPATION RATES BY SEX AND AGE GROUP, SELECTED YEARS

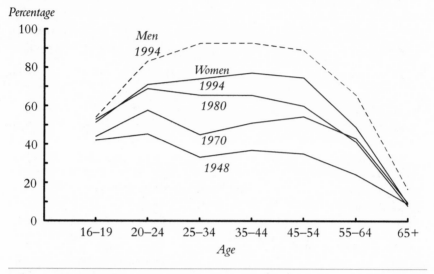

Source: Bureau of Labor Statistics 1994b.

and then begins to decline after age 50, as workers start to retire (Shank 1988).

Like women of other age groups, older women were much more likely to be in the labor force in 1994 than was the case for their counterparts in the past. Half of women age 55 to 64 were labor force participants in 1994, up from only a quarter in 1948. While adult women's labor force activity rose steadily for many decades, labor force activity of women age 16 to 19 fluctuated, as the employment situation for teens is more sensitive to business cycles than that for adults.

RACE AND ETHNICITY

Today women's labor force activity varies only slightly by race. In 1994 about 50.4 million white women and 7.4 million black women were in the labor force, representing about six of every 10 women in each race group (see Table I-1). Women of Hispanic origin were somewhat less likely to participate than were women in the other two groups; about 4.8 million, or 53 percent, were in the labor force in 1994.

In the past race differences in women's labor force participation were large. In 1948, 44 percent of nonwhite women either worked or looked for work, compared with 31 percent of white women. (Separate data for black women were not available from the CPS until 1972.) After that, and especially during the 1960s and 1970s, women's labor force activity increased among both white and black women. White women's participation rates increased more rapidly, however, and the gap between the two groups disappeared. The higher participation rates of black women in earlier years may have reflected greater economic necessity among black women. Black men's earnings have always been low compared with the earnings of white men, and their unemployment rates have been higher than those of white men. In addition, a relatively large share of black women have maintained families on their own. Such financial concerns have become increasingly important for women from all racial and ethnic backgrounds over the past several decades as family structures have changed and men's real earnings have stagnated or even declined.

While data from the CPS are not available for other racial and ethnic groups (the monthly sample is too small to produce reliable figures), decennial census data provide some insight into trends in their labor force participation (see Table I-1). Data from the 1980 and 1990 censuses of the population showed that over the decade, labor force participation also rose among female Asians and Pacific Islanders and among Native American, Eskimo, and Aleutian women. In 1990 there were only slight variations in participation rates among women of different racial and ethnic backgrounds. Asians and Pacific Islanders had the highest participation rate—60 percent—while Native American women had the lowest, 55 percent. (The census and CPS data are not strictly comparable.)

MARITAL STATUS AND THE PRESENCE OF CHILDREN

Marital status, especially when combined with the presence of children, still has a substantial effect on women's labor force activity. Historically, never married women and divorced women were those most likely to be employed or looking for work. This pattern has not changed completely, but the gaps in participation between groups of women have gotten much smaller as the result of rapid increases in participation among married women. In 1994, 74 percent of divorced women were working or looking for work—about the same as in 1975, when 72 percent of divorced women were in the labor force. Among married women, by contrast, the proportion in the labor force increased from 44 to 61 percent over the 1975–94 period. Fewer than two in 10 widows were in the labor force in 1994; their low participation rate reflected their considerably older ages, on average, than women in other marital status groups.

The presence of children continues to have an impact on women's work activity, but less so than in the past. In 1975 half of women age 25 to 44 with children under 18 were active in the labor force, compared with about three-quarters of women the same ages who did not have children. Both groups of women were more likely to participate in 1994, but increases over the 1975–94 period were greatest among women with children. As a result, the gap between the two groups shrank. In 1994, 70 percent of women with children under age 18 participated in the workforce, compared with 85 percent of those without children.

Women with school-age children are more likely to work than those with younger children; however, labor force participation has increased among all groups of women so that today most mothers—even those with the youngest children—are active in the labor market. Among mothers 76 percent of those with children age six to 17 (but none younger) were in the labor force in 1994, as were 60 percent of those with children under six. Those rates were up from 55 percent and 39 percent respectively in 1975 (the first year data for all mothers were available by the ages of their children). Returning to work shortly after childbirth is also common today. More than half of women with children under age one were in the labor force in 1994 (see Table I-1).

FAMILY TYPE

The rise in labor force participation among all women, including married mothers, has led to a substantial increase in the proportion of married-couple families in which both the husband and wife work. In 1994 such dual-earner married couples accounted for more than four in 10 families in the United States—up from fewer than one in 10 in 1940. The proportion of married-couple families in which the husband was in the labor force and the wife was not declined from two-thirds of all families in the 1940s and 1950s to only 17 percent in 1994 (Hayghe 1990). Even among married couples with children, dual-earner families have become the norm. Of 25 million married couples with children in 1994, both the husband and wife were in the labor force in two-thirds (16.6 million) of such families, up from 42 percent in 1975 (10.7 million out of 25.2 million) (see Table I-2).

More than eight million families with children under 18 were maintained by women in 1994. The number of families maintained by men was much smaller: 1.4 million. Families maintained by women now account for about a quarter of all families with children, up from 15 percent in 1975. About 68 percent of mothers in those families were in the labor force in 1994, up from 55 percent in 1975. These women usually need to work to ensure adequate support for their families, in part because many mothers who are

Table I-2 · FAMILIES BY TYPE, PRESENCE OF CHILDREN, AND LABOR
FORCE STATUS OF FAMILY MEMBERS (numbers in thousands)

	Number			Percentage		
Family Type & Presence of Children	*1975*	*1994*	*Change*	*1975*	*1994*	*Change*
Total families	55,698	69,211	13,513	100.0	100.0	—
Without children	25,638	34,523	8,885	46.0	49.9	3.9
With children	30,060	34,688	4,628	54.0	50.1	-3.9
Married–couple families	47,069	53,246	6,177	84.5	76.9	-7.6
With children	25,236	25,087	-149	84.0	72.3	-11.7
Father in labor force, mother out	12,822	7,055	-5,767	42.7	20.3	-22.4
Mother in labor force, father out	399	752	353	1.3	2.2	0.9
Both in labor force	10,678	16,642	5,964	35.5	48.0	12.5
Neither in labor force	613	637	24	2.0	1.8	-0.2
Families maintained by women	7,230	12,974	5,744	13.0	18.7	5.7
With children	4,400	8,211	3,811	14.6	23.7	9.1
Mother in labor force	2,635	5,610	2,975	8.8	16.2	7.4
Mother not in labor force	1,765	2,601	836	5.9	7.5	1.6
Families maintained by men	1,399	2,992	1,593	2.5	4.3	1.8
With children	424	1,390	966	1.4	4.0	2.6
Father in labor force	365	1,225	860	1.2	3.5	2.3
Father not in labor force	59	165	106	0.2	0.5	0.3

Source: Bureau of Labor Statistics (BLS) 1975 and BLS 1994c.

granted court-ordered child support have difficulty getting full (or any) payments from the fathers of their children. Many women who were not in the
labor force (and some who were) received assistance through Aid to Families with Dependent Children (AFDC).[2] Chapter Four in this volume focuses on the work experience of women receiving AFDC.

EDUCATION

Labor force participation among women increases dramatically with education. Women in the labor force in 1994 had completed more schooling, on
average, than those who participated in 1970. For example, the proportion
of women age 25 to 54 in the labor force who obtained a four-year college
degree increased from 11 to 27 percent over the period. In 1994 half of

[2]AFDC benefits were received by 4.8 million families with over nine million children in 1992.
Adult women constituted 3.9 million of the recipients.

women age 25 to 54 with less than a high school diploma were in the labor force. Three-quarters of high school graduates who did not go on to college and 85 percent of women who obtained a four-year college degree or more were in the workforce. Differences exist but are less pronounced among men, as men in this age group tend to work regardless of their educational level.

HOW MUCH DO WOMEN WORK?

WORK SCHEDULES

Not only are women more likely to work in the labor force today than in the past, but those in the workforce also spend more time at work than did women in earlier years. Women have increasingly opted to work both full time and year round, partly because of economic necessity but also because of movement into occupations that require full-time, year-round work.

Each March a supplement to the regular CPS includes questions on work activity during the prior calendar year, including usual weekly hours and the number of weeks worked during the year. Data from March 1994 showed that a majority of women who worked in 1993 not only did so full time (35 hours or more per week) but also did so for the entire year (50 weeks or more) (see Figure I-3). About 53 percent of women (33.5 million) who had any work experience during the year worked full time and year round, up from 41 percent in 1970. (About 68 percent of men worked year round and full time in 1993.)

While the number of women in the workforce increased dramatically between 1970 and 1993, the full-time/part-time split changed very little; in both periods about seven in 10 women who worked typically did so full time. The shift to full-time, year-round work, then, primarily reflected a movement of women into year-round work. In the past it was not uncommon for women to take time out of the workforce each year to care for their children, particularly during the summer months. Taking such time out became less common among both part-time and full-time working women over the period, particularly as women moved into occupations that required women to work all year (Rydzewski, Deming, and Rones 1993). In addition, women who were reentering the labor force often experienced a period of unemployment for part of the year. Such frictional unemployment became less common as women increasingly chose to work year round.

Mothers with children of school age are more likely than those with

Figure I-3 · WORK SCHEDULES OF WOMEN WITH WORK
EXPERIENCE, 1970 AND 1993

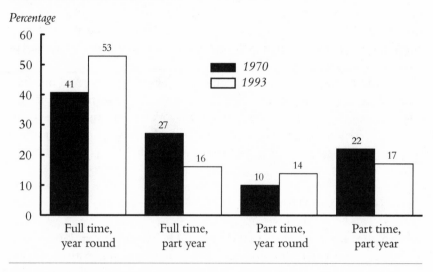

Source: Bureau of Labor Statistics (BLS) 1971 and BLS 1994c.

younger children to work both full time and year round outside the home.
In 1993, 56 percent of women with children between the ages of six and
17 worked such schedules, compared with 43 percent of women with children under age six.

MULTIPLE JOBHOLDING

Data on multiple jobholding dramatically illustrate women's increasing labor
force attachment. In 1994, 3.3 million women—or 5.9 percent of employed women—held two or more jobs, up from only 2.2 percent in 1970.
The proportion of multiple jobholders who were women rose from 16 to
46 percent. By contrast, the multiple jobholding rate among men actually
declined over the period, from 7.0 percent to 5.9 percent—now matching
the rate among women.

A larger proportion of women than men reported that they held multiple jobs out of economic necessity. In 1991, the most recent year with available information on reasons for holding more than one job, 44 percent of
women and 37 percent of men who worked at more than one job did so in
order to meet regular household expenses or to pay off debts. The likelihood of holding more than one job and the reason for doing so varied by
marital status. Women who were widowed, divorced, or separated were

about twice as likely (55 percent) as single women (28 percent) or married women (27 percent) to work at more than one job in order to meet regular household expenses. This is probably because on average, women who were widowed, divorced, or separated were more likely to have child support responsibilities than single women and to have fewer financial resources than those who were married.

One-half of the women who held multiple jobs in 1994 worked one full-time and one part-time job, compared with two-thirds of men. Multiple job-holding women were more likely than men to work two part-time jobs—about 33 percent of women versus 13 percent of men. And a very small proportion worked two full-time jobs: two percent of women and five percent of men.

THE JOBS WOMEN HOLD

Women are employed in every industry and hold nearly every kind of job. The types of work that women (and men) do reflect a combination of many factors, including:

- socialization, which can vary by gender and influences both the kind of work that men and women choose and how family responsibilities enter into work decisions;
- the amount and types of education completed by workers;
- the types of jobs that have expanded or declined; and
- discrimination, in some cases.

OCCUPATIONAL PATTERNS

Technological and organizational changes create new kinds of jobs all the time, making detailed comparisons over long periods difficult. Two major points can be drawn, however, from comparable data on broad occupational groups that are available for the past two decades. First, substantial shifts in the gender distribution of many occupations have occurred. Second, despite these shifts, women and men still tend to be concentrated in different occupations; women are highly overrepresented in clerical, sales, and services occupations, for example, while men are disproportionately employed in craft and laborer jobs.

Women have moved most rapidly into those occupational groups in which employment has been expanding. In the 1974–94 period, overall job growth was fastest among managers and professionals and slowest among operators, laborers, and farm workers. Women moved into managerial and professional specialty occupations in great numbers; in 1994 seven million women held managerial occupations, and the share of employed women who held such jobs more than doubled from 1974. The proportion of women working in professional occupations rose as well. By contrast, the share of women employed as operators, fabricators, and laborers fell over the period; in 1994 only eight percent of employed women held such jobs, down from 13 percent in 1974.

The occupational group in which women and men were most equally represented in 1994 was managers and professionals: About three in 10 employed women and men held such jobs. Gender differences were more dramatic among workers in other major occupational groups. For example, more than a quarter of employed women but only six percent of men worked in administrative support jobs. Women also were represented heavily in sales and services occupations. In fact, the administrative support, sales, and services categories together accounted for twice the share of employed women (57 percent) as employed men (28 percent). Men were much more likely than women to work in precision production, craft, and repair jobs—such as construction trades—or as operators, laborers, or farmers. Four of every 10 men held such jobs in 1994, compared with only one in 10 women (see Table I-3).

It is important to consider data for more detailed occupations because large occupational categories can mask underlying differences in employment by gender. Within professional specialties, for example, 85 percent of elementary school teachers employed in 1994 were women, compared with three in 10 computer systems analysts and scientists and fewer than one in 10 engineers. Differences were less pronounced among workers in managerial occupations, as women accounted for between 40 and 60 percent of employees in nearly every managerial job; at the extremes, however, only seven percent of construction inspectors but 80 percent of medicine and health managers were women.

The most pronounced differences in occupational employment by gender occurred in precision production, craft, and repair occupations; in 1994, for example, only one percent of carpenters and two percent of electricians were women. Differences by gender were also large among sales workers. While women accounted for one in every two sales employees overall, they constituted 80 percent of apparel sales personnel and only 30 percent of workers selling securities and financial services.

The occupational distributions of men and women in 1994, while still very different from one another, were much less so than only 20 years earlier. Table I-3 shows how women's share of employment in major occupational groups changed—or did not—during the 1974–94 period. Table I-3 highlights

Table I-3 · EMPLOYED PERSONS BY OCCUPATION AND SEX, 1974 AND 1994 (percent distribution)

Occupation	Men		Women	
	1974	1994	1974	1994
Total employed (in thousands)	53,024	66,450	33,769	56,610
Total percentage[1]	100.0	100.0	100.0	100.0
Managerial and professional specialty	22.0	26.5	17.6	28.7
Executive, administrative, and managerial	12.1	14.0	5.0	12.4
Professional specialty	9.9	12.5	12.6	16.3
Technical, sales, and administrative support	18.5	20.0	45.1	42.4
Technicians and related support	2.4	2.8	2.5	3.6
Sales occupations	10.1	11.4	11.0	12.8
Administrative support, including clerical	6.0	5.9	31.6	26.0
Service occupations	8.1	10.3	20.6	17.8
Private household	0.1	—[2]	3.6	1.4
Protective service	2.3	2.8	0.3	0.7
Service, except prvt. household & protective	5.8	7.4	16.8	15.7
Precision production, craft, and repair	19.7	18.4	1.8	2.2
Operators, fabricators, and laborers	25.4	20.4	13.3	7.7
Machine operators, assemblers, and inspectors	10.4	7.2	10.3	5.2
Transport. & material moving occupations	7.6	7.0	0.6	0.9
Handlers, equip. cleaners, helpers, & laborers	7.4	6.1	2.4	1.6
Farming, forestry, and fishing	6.2	4.4	1.6	1.2

[1]Percentages may not add to 100 because of rounding.
[2]Less than 0.05 percent.

Source: Bureau of Labor Statistics (BLS) 1974 and 1994b.

changes in some selected occupations during the same time. Women made substantial inroads into some areas, such as financial management and law but, even in 1994, rarely worked as carpenters or mechanics.

Patterns by Race and Ethnicity

Occupational employment among working women varies by race and ethnicity. A much larger share of white women (30 percent) than black (21 percent) or Hispanic (17 percent) women held managerial and professional specialty jobs in 1994 (see Table I-4). Both black and Hispanic women were more likely than white women to work in service occupations or as machine operators or laborers. About one-quarter of women in each racial/ethnic group worked in administrative support occupations. Occupational patterns partly reflected white women's higher average educational attainment than their black or Hispanic counterparts; 25 percent of white women (age 25 and older) in the labor force in 1994, for example, had completed a four-year college degree, compared with 17 percent and 13 percent of black and Hispanic women respectively.

Over the 1984–94 period (data for Hispanic women were not available in 1974) the proportion of women in each racial and ethnic group who held managerial or professional jobs increased substantially. At the same time the proportion of each group that worked as operators declined, largely because these occupations accounted for a declining share of employment overall. Private household work became less common among black women over the

Table I-4 · EMPLOYED WOMEN BY OCCUPATION, RACE, AND HISPANIC ORIGIN, 1994 (percent distribution)

Occupation	Total	White	Black	Hispanic Origin
Total employed women (in thousands)	56,610	47,738	6,595	4,258
Total percentage	100.0	100.0	100.0	100.0
Managerial and professional specialty	28.7	29.8	21.3	16.7
Executive, administrative, & managerial	12.4	12.9	8.7	8.3
Professional specialty	16.3	16.9	12.6	8.4
Technical, sales, & administrative support	42.4	43.1	38.4	39.1
Technicians and related support	3.6	3.6	3.4	2.5
Sales occupations	12.8	13.4	9.6	12.4
Administrative support, including clerical	26.0	26.2	25.4	24.2
Service occupations	17.8	16.6	25.7	25.6
Private household	1.4	1.3	2.0	5.1
Protective service	0.7	0.6	1.4	0.5
Service, except prvt. household & protective	15.7	14.8	22.3	20.1
Precision production, craft, and repair	2.2	2.1	2.6	3.4
Operators, fabricators, and laborers	7.7	7.0	11.6	13.3
Machine operators, assemblers, & inspectors	5.2	4.7	8.2	9.9
Transport. & material moving occupations	0.9	0.8	1.2	0.8
Handlers, equip. cleaners, helpers, & laborers	1.6	1.5	2.3	2.6
Farming, forestry, and fishing	1.2	1.4	0.3	1.9

[1]Percentages may not add to 100 because of rounding.

Source: Bureau of Labor Statistics 1994b.

period. In contrast, Hispanic women remained heavily represented among the 790,000 women doing private household work; they accounted for 28 percent of the group, four times their share of total employment.

Industries

Differences in industry employment patterns by gender to a large degree reflect differences in occupational employment patterns within industries. In 1994, three of every 10 men, but only one in every 10 women, were employed in manufacturing or construction industries (see Table I-5), where precision production, craft, and operator work is the norm (see Table I-3). By contrast, nearly twice the proportion of women (47 percent) as men (25 percent) were employed in service industries, including business, health, educational, and professional services.

As with occupations, differences among large groupings of industries can mask differences within industrial groups. For example, within the manufacturing industries more than seven in 10 apparel manufacturing workers in 1994 were women, compared with fewer than two in 10 workers in the manufacture of lumber and wood products. Similarly, in retail trade women

Table I-5 · EMPLOYED PERSONS BY INDUSTRY AND SEX, 1974 AND 1994 (percent distribution)

Industry	Men		Women	
	1974	1994	1974	1994
Total employed	53,024	66,450	33,769	56,610
Total percentage[1]	100.0	100.0	100.0	100.0
Agriculture	5.5	3.8	1.8	1.5
Mining	1.1	0.8	0.2	0.2
Construction	9.8	10.2	1.0	1.3
Manufacturing	28.2	20.6	18.0	11.4
Durable goods	18.4	13.1	8.4	5.5
Nondurable goods	9.7	7.5	9.6	5.9
Transportation & public utilities	8.6	9.4	3.6	4.4
Wholesale trade	4.9	5.0	2.3	2.4
Retail trade	13.7	15.4	20.1	19.0
Finance, insurance, & real estate	4.3	5.0	7.3	8.5
Services	17.6	24.7	41.7	46.9
Public administration	6.2	5.0	4.1	4.4

[1]Percentages may not add to 100 because of rounding.

Source: Bureau of Labor Statistics (BLS) 1974 and BLS 1994b.

constituted 82 percent of employees in gift and novelty shops and only 19 percent of those employed at motor vehicle dealerships.

One industry that has been the focus of much concern to researchers interested in women's employment has been the help supply service (temporary help) industry. Concern has been raised because jobs in this industry, which are disproportionately held by women, tend to pay lower-than-average wages and rarely provide health benefits. While the CPS does not provide specific information on employment in that industry, BLS's monthly survey of employers, the Current Employment Statistics survey, showed that in 1994 temporary help supply establishments employed two million workers, 55 percent of whom were women. Industry employment grew rapidly from 1982—when data were first collected—to 1994, expanding by more than 400 percent, compared with all-industry (private) employment growth of 28 percent over the same period. Temporary help supply accounted for about 2.1 percent of private nonfarm industry employment in 1994.

While many people think that temporary jobs are nearly all clerical positions, BLS's Occupational Employment Survey showed that only about four in 10 workers in the temporary help industry were actually performing clerical jobs in 1993. The industry also employed many health services, accounting, and production workers to fill temporary positions. Average hourly earnings for temporary workers, at $8.27 in 1993, were well below the all-industry earnings average of $10.83, reflecting in part the occupational composition of help supply services.

Self-Employment
Between 1974 and 1994 self-employment among women expanded from 1.6 million to 3.9 million. About three in 10 self-employed men and women worked as managers or professionals in 1994 (see Table I-6). Nearly as many women who "worked for themselves" worked in personal service occupations, including child care. Self-employed men were more concentrated in craft occupations, particularly carpentry. One researcher who examined earnings data from March CPS supplements found that men who were self-employed earned as much as or more than those who worked in wage-and-salary jobs, while self-employed women earned much less than their wage-and-salary counterparts (Devine 1994).

Home-Based Work
Among researchers interested in workers' attempts to balance work and family roles, there has been a growing interest in home-based work among both men and women. A May 1991 CPS supplement on work done at home identified 1.8 million women and 1.9 million men who worked at least eight

Table I-6 · SELF-EMPLOYED PERSONS BY OCCUPATION AND SEX, 1994
(numbers in thousands)

Occupation	Self-Employed		Percent Distribution	
	Men	Women	Men	Women
Total	6,757	3,891	100.0	100.0
Managerial and professional specialty	2,011	1,095	29.8	28.1
Executive, administrative, and managerial	1,105	495	16.4	12.7
Professional specialty	906	600	13.4	15.4
Technical, sales, and administrative support	1,203	1,178	17.8	30.3
Technicians and related support	66	26	1.0	0.7
Sales occupations	1,091	716	16.1	18.4
Supervisors and proprietors	539	308	8.0	7.9
Sales representatives, finance, & business	302	152	4.5	3.9
Sales workers, retail, and personal services	144	230	2.1	5.9
Administrative support, including clerical	45	435	0.7	11.2
Service occupations[2]	207	971	3.1	25.0
Protective service	10	1	0.1	—[3]
Service, except prvt. household & protective	196	968	2.9	24.9
Cleaning and building	66	117	1.0	3.0
Personal services	91	762	1.3	19.6
Precision production, craft, and repair	1,608	131	23.8	3.4
Operators, fabricators, and laborers	508	131	7.5	3.4
Farming, forestry, and fishing	1,220	386	18.1	9.9

[1]Percentages may not add to 100 because of rounding.
[2]Includes private households.
[3]Less than 0.05 percent.

Source: Bureau of Labor Statistics 1994b.

hours per week at home for pay. Since most home-based workers were self-employed, their occupational profile was similar to that of the self-employed. About 32 percent of women working at home for pay were managers or professionals, 28 percent were employed in personal service occupations, and 17 percent worked in sales. By contrast, more than half of men who worked at home were managers or professionals, and almost none held personal service occupations. In addition, there were significant numbers of men employed in skilled blue-collar jobs (13 percent), particularly in construction trades or as mechanics (Deming 1994).

Table I-7 · MEDIAN WEEKLY EARNINGS OF FULL-TIME WAGE-AND-SALARY WORKERS, BY SEX, 1979–94 (in current and constant [1994] dollars)

	Median Earnings		Ratio of Women's
Year	Men	Women	to Men's Earnings
Current dollars			
1979	291	182	62.5
1980	312	201	64.4
1981	339	219	64.6
1982	364	238	65.4
1983	378	252	66.7
1984	391	265	67.8
1985	406	277	68.2
1986	419	290	69.2
1987	433	303	70.0
1988	449	315	70.2
1989	468	328	70.1
1990	485	348	71.8
1991	497	368	74.0
1992	505	381	75.4
1993	514	395	76.8
1994	522	399	76.4
Constant (1994) dollars[1]			
1979	594	372	62.6
1994	522	399	76.4
Percent change	-12.1	7.3	—

[1]The Consumer Price Index for All Urban Consumers (CPI-U) was used to deflate the earnings series.

Source: Bureau of Labor Statistics 1994b.

Women were much more likely than men to work entirely at home, accounting for two-thirds of the 1.5 million workers who did so. Such women worked an average of 34.2 hours per week, compared with 39.1 hours for men.

WOMEN'S EARNINGS

Employed women earn less, on average, than employed men; however, the earnings gap has been declining for many years. In 1994 median earnings for women who usually worked full time were $399 per week, about 76 percent of the median for men ($522). As shown in Table I-7, the gap

Table I-8 · MEDIAN WEEKLY EARNINGS OF FULL-TIME WAGE-AND-SALARY WORKERS, BY OCCUPATION AND SEX, 1994 (numbers in thousands)

Occupation	Employed		Median Earnings			Ratio of Women's to Men's Earnings
	Number	Percentage Women	Total	Men	Women	
Total, 16 years and over	87,379	42.8	$467	$522	$399	76.4
Managerial and professional specialty	25,208	48.3	683	803	592	73.7
Executive, administrative, and managerial[1]	12,333	45.0	658	797	541	67.9
Financial managers	572	48.6	718	889	598	67.3
Managers, marketing, advertising, and public relations	524	34.0	851	1,027	631	61.4
Accountants and auditors	1,234	52.4	616	724	545	75.3
Administrators, education and related fields	563	56.7	768	930	634	68.2
Professional specialty[1]	12,875	51.6	705	809	623	77.0
Engineers	1,731	8.5	897	907	785	86.5
Physicians	358	23.2	996	1,063	815	76.7
Registered nurses	1,394	92.3	682	709	680	95.9
Teachers, college and university	547	36.4	839	890	771	86.6
Teachers, except college and university	3,388	73.8	621	693	603	87.0
Lawyers	448	31.0	1,116	1,237	917	74.1
Technical, sales, and administrative support	25,718	62.0	420	548	376	68.6
Technicians and related support[1]	3,174	48.4	534	622	466	74.9
Health technologists and technicians	1,181	78.2	461	556	440	79.1
Engineering technologists and technicians	830	18.6	565	591	457	77.3
Science technicians	227	35.2	517	576	452	78.5
Sales occupations[1]	8,470	42.9	450	575	324	56.3
Sales representatives, finance and business services	1,488	41.1	622	739	485	65.6
Sales workers, retail and personal services	2,934	56.1	283	366	242	66.1

Administrative support, including clerical[1]	14,074	76.6	392	482	374	77.6
Secretaries	2,604	98.8	383	—[2]	383	—[2]
Information clerks	1,149	88.6	322	372	318	85.5
Bookkeepers, accounting, and auditing clerks	1,080	89.0	374	410	371	90.5
Adjusters and investigators	1,257	73.7	418	502	403	80.3
Service occupations	9,486	49.6	294	350	257	73.4
Private household	324	96.0	179	—[2]	177	—[2]
Protective service[1]	1,951	14.2	517	538	430	79.9
Police and detectives	946	15.3	582	595	483	81.2
Service, except private household and protective[1]	7,211	57.1	271	293	256	87.4
Food preparation and service occupations	2,724	49.6	254	271	239	88.2
Health service occupations	1,482	85.6	281	310	276	89.0
Cleaning and building services	1,955	36.3	286	314	249	79.3
Precision production, craft, and repair[1]	10,795	9.0	504	515	370	71.8
Mechanics and repairers	3,753	4.3	519	519	520	100.2
Electrical and electronic equipment repairers	591	12.2	607	613	584	95.3
Construction trades	3,460	1.5	491	492	408	82.9
Carpenters	832	0.8	424	425	—[2]	—[2]
Precision production occupations	3,445	22.0	498	548	342	62.4
Operators, fabricators, and laborers[1]	14,745	23.1	373	406	293	72.2
Machine operators, assemblers, and inspectors	7,032	36.4	361	415	292	70.4
Transportation and material moving occupations	4,096	5.9	461	469	361	77.0
Truck drivers	2,286	2.8	467	471	330	70.1
Handlers, equipment cleaners, helpers, and laborers	3,617	16.8	311	319	279	87.5
Farming, forestry, and fishing	1,426	11.3	282	290	234	80.7

[1]Includes other occupations not shown separately.
[2]Data are not shown where base is less than 50,000.
Source: Bureau of Labor Statistics 1994b.

between men's and women's earnings declined substantially between 1979 and 1994. In 1979, when comparable data were first available, women who worked full time earned only 63 percent as much as their male counterparts. Over this period women's earnings increased faster than inflation, while men's earnings declined in real terms.

OCCUPATIONS

A major reason for women's lower median earnings is their general concentration in jobs that pay lower-than-average wages. (Job tenure, industry, and years of work experience also affect women's and men's earnings.) Median weekly earnings for full-time workers—both men and women combined—in all occupations were $467 in 1994; this compared to $392 for workers in administrative support, $283 for those in retail sales, and $294 for workers in service occupations—all occupational groups in which women are heavily represented (see Table I-8). However, movement by women into higher-paying occupations and increases in educational attainment and work experience contributed to the lessening of the earnings gap.

Even within occupations men typically earn more than women. Some of the pay differentials in the major occupational groups, such as in professional specialties and sales, reflect the fact that women and men work in different occupations within those categories. For example, in sales, women are often employed in lower-paying cashier or other retail sales positions, while men are more likely to work in higher-paying wholesale trade or financial services occupations. There is no clear pattern that determines which occupations have the smallest or largest earnings gaps—that is, women's and men's earnings are close to parity in some occupations dominated by women as well as in some occupations dominated by men.

Occupations in which the ratios of women's earnings to men's were lowest included financial managers (67 percent), retail sales workers (66 percent), and precision production workers (62 percent). Earnings were closer to parity among engineers (87 percent), bookkeepers (91 percent), and registered nurses (96 percent). Female mechanics and repairers, most of whom were employed as electrical and electronic equipment repairers, earned (on average) as much as their male counterparts. Even though women accounted for 92 percent of nurses but only four percent of mechanics and repairers, earnings ratios were quite similar.

EDUCATION

Women's earnings (and men's) are greatly affected by the amount of education they have completed, as education is often a prerequisite for entering higher-paying occupations. Among women in the labor force in 1994 those with less than a high school education who worked full time earned about 40 percent as much as those who had completed a four-year college degree ($248 versus $613).

Over the 1979–94 period more rapid increases in educational attainment by women than men contributed to the shrinking of earnings differentials as an increasing proportion of women earned the higher wages of college graduates. For example, the proportion of women age 25 to 64 in the labor force who had completed a four-year college degree increased from 18 percent in 1979 to 26 percent in 1994, while the proportion of men with such degrees grew more slowly: from 24 to 29 percent.

Still, earnings differences between men and women persisted at all educational levels. Women who completed high school, for example, earned, on average, 73 percent as much as comparably educated men, while those with at least a four-year college degree earned 77 percent as much as their male counterparts.

RACE AND ETHNICITY

Earnings also vary by race and ethnicity, with white workers earning more, on average, than either black or Hispanic workers regardless of gender. In 1994 white men who worked full time at wage-and-salary jobs earned the most of any group, followed by white women and black men. Black women and Hispanic men and women had the lowest earnings (see Table I-9).

Education dramatically increases earnings for workers in all racial/ethnic groups. Not only does education "pay off" in terms of earnings, but women with more education are also those most likely to work and least likely to experience unemployment. While earnings differences between men and women persist at each educational level, differences between racial groups of women within each educational level are small (while the gap between racial groups of men within each educa- tional level remains considerable). For example, black women with a college degree earned 93 percent as much as comparably educated white women in 1994. And black women with less than a high school diploma earned 95 percent as much as their white counterparts (see Table I-9).

Table I-9 · MEDIAN WEEKLY EARNINGS OF FULL-TIME WAGE-AND-SALARY WORKERS, BY SEX, RACE, HISPANIC ORIGIN, AND EDUCATIONAL ATTAINMENT, 1994 (in current dollars)

Race, Hispanic Origin, and Sex	Total	Educational Attainment		
		Less than a High School Diploma	High School Diploma, No College	Bachelor's Degree or Higher
Total	467	292	493	708
Men	522	315	572	798
Women	399	248	416	613
White	484	296	507	725
Men	547	318	590	821
Women	408	251	424	619
Black	371	278	389	599
Men	400	305	419	630
Women	346	239	362	574
Hispanic origin	324	260	400	613
Men	343	276	432	671
Women	305	225	357	561

Source: Bureau of Labor Statistics 1994b.

AGE

In 1994 the earnings gap between men and women was narrowest among the youngest workers. Earnings for women who worked full time peaked at around $450 per week among those age 35 to 44 and 45 to 54 years. Men's earnings peaked at $671 per week among those in their late forties and early fifties. Thus the gap between men's and women's earnings is higher for each successive age group of workers up to age 65 (see Table I-10).

Women age 20 to 24 earned 95 percent as much as men in the same age group. Such young workers have about the same amount of work experience and, regardless of gender, are concentrated in entry-level jobs. The earnings of younger workers may also be closer to parity because new entrants to the workforce are those most likely to benefit from hiring practices that are more equitable than in the past. Women age 35 to 44, by contrast, earned only 73 percent as much as men the same age, and those age 45 to 54 earned about two-thirds as much as their male counterparts.

The higher gap among the older age groups probably reflects a number of factors, including the fact that women in those age groups tend to have, on average, less overall work experience and less experience with their pre-

Table I-10 · MEDIAN WEEKLY EARNINGS OF FULL-TIME WAGE-AND-SALARY WORKERS, BY AGE AND SEX, 1994 (in current dollars)

| | Median Earnings | | Ratio of Women's to |
Age	Men	Women	Men's Earnings
Total, 20 years and over	531	403	75.9
20 to 24 years	307	290	94.5
25 to 34 years	479	397	82.9
35 to 44 years	617	448	72.6
45 to 54 years	671	450	67.1
55 to 64 years	603	398	66.0
65 years and over	441	336	76.2

Source: Bureau of Labor Statistics 1994b.

sent employer than men of the same ages. These differences most likely will lessen over time as successive cohorts of women are increasingly likely to work, particularly year round and full time. It also is possible that the cumulative effects of different experiences of men and women in the labor force have contributed to a larger earnings gap among older workers. For example, if men and women are generally treated differently by employers, that differential treatment would tend to have a cumulative effect with age, just as the choice of or dedication to one's career would. The effects of such influences are very difficult to estimate.

UNION MEMBERSHIP

As women have increased their presence in the labor force at large, they have also increased their presence in unions. In 1994, 6.6 million women were members of unions, up from 5.8 million in 1984. Over the decade the proportion of employed women who were union members remained relatively stable at about 13 percent, while the proportion of employed men who were union members fell from 23 to 18 percent. As a result of the increase in women's union membership, women's share of union employment increased gradually, from 34 to 40 percent over the period.

Women who are members of unions earn more than those who are not: median weekly earnings of $522 versus $377 in 1994. Union women's earnings even surpassed those of nonunion men (see Table I-11). The earnings benefits of union membership are strong for black and Hispanic women as well as for white women. Furthermore, the ratio of women's to men's earnings among union members (84 percent) was higher than that among nonunion men and women (76 percent).

Table I-11 · MEDIAN WEEKLY EARNINGS OF FULL-TIME WAGE-AND-SALARY WORKERS BY RACE, HISPANIC ORIGIN, UNION STATUS, AND SEX, 1994

Race and Hispanic Origin	Union		Non union		Ratio of Women's to Men's Earnings	
	Men	Women	Men	Women	Union	Non union
Total	621	522	495	377	84.1	76.2
White	640	546	513	386	85.3	75.2
Black	524	452	359	323	86.3	90.0
Hispanic origin	506	402	316	289	79.4	91.5

Source: Bureau of Labor Statistics 1994b.

PART-TIME WORKERS

Up to this point we have compared earnings of full-time workers. The earnings of part-time workers, however, are of particular importance to women because women are disproportionately employed in part-time jobs; about 28 percent of women and 11 percent of men worked part time in 1994. Since hours of part-time workers vary, comparisons must be made using hourly earnings figures. The CPS collects hourly earnings information for all workers who are paid hourly rates.

In 1994 median hourly earnings of men and women (combined) who worked part time and were paid by the hour were $5.65—about 63 percent of hourly earnings for those who worked full time ($8.98 per hour). Most of the differences in earnings between full- and part-time workers reflected the different occupational mixes of the two groups and the much younger average age of part-time versus full-time workers. A larger share of part-time workers than full-time workers, for example, is employed in retail sales or services occupations, where earnings are relatively low.

Women who worked part time in 1994 actually earned more per hour than men who did so: $5.83, compared with $5.24. This difference largely reflected the fact that women who work part time are often between the ages of 25 and 54 and perform a variety of jobs, while men who are employed part time are more often young people earning entry-level wages. Among women who worked part time, white women had higher median hourly earnings in 1994 ($5.91) than black women ($5.14) and women of Hispanic origin ($5.23).

MINIMUM-WAGE WORKERS

About six percent of U.S. workers who are paid hourly rates earned the federally set minimum wage of $4.25 or less in 1994. About 2.6 million women—eight percent of those paid hourly rates—and 1.6 million men (five percent) earned the minimum wage or less. In 1980–81 about 21 percent of employed women earned the minimum wage or less; that proportion declined steadily between 1981 and 1989, as the minimum wage remained unchanged at $3.35. Between 1990 and 1994 the minimum wage was raised twice; as a result, the proportion of women whose earnings fell at or below the minimum increased. (The hourly wage reported by workers does not include supplemental payments, such as tips.)

Although many minimum-wage workers are teenagers who work part time—often while they attend school—about seven in 10 minimum-wage workers were adults (age 20 and over) in 1994. Women accounted for two-thirds of the 2.9 million adults whose earnings were no more than the minimum wage.

While eight in 10 minimum-wage workers (age 16 and over) were white, black workers and those of Hispanic origin were still overrepresented among the group—that is, they accounted for larger shares of minimum-wage workers than of all employed persons. In 1993, 18 percent of workers who earned the minimum wage or less were wives in married-couple families, another 7 percent were husbands, and 8 percent were women who maintained families. Other minimum-wage workers included teenagers and grown children living in their parents' households, as well as persons living alone or with nonrelatives.

UNEMPLOYMENT AND OTHER LABOR MARKET PROBLEMS

While earlier sections of this chapter mentioned some labor market difficulties faced by women, such as concentration in low-wage occupations, this section focuses specifically on labor market problems including unemployment and poverty among workers. Women and men experience the same kinds of problems in the labor market; however, the reasons for those problems and their outcomes often differ by gender.

UNEMPLOYMENT

The most obvious problem that people in the labor force can face is the inability to find work when they look for it—that is, unemployment. Women now are about equally as likely as men to be unemployed, though that has not always been the case. (Chapter Three focuses on women and unemployment.)

In 1994 three million adult women, or 5.4 percent of the female labor force age 20 and over, were unemployed; the rate was exactly the same as that of adult men. Women were slightly more likely than men to be unemployed during the 1950s. The rapid entry of women into the labor force in the 1960s and 1970s meant that many more were seeking work at any point in time; as a result, unemployment rates for women increased relative to those for men (see Figure I-4).

By the 1980s many women had been absorbed into the labor force. Jobs continued to expand rapidly in many service-producing industries that tend to employ disproportionate numbers of women. And those women who worked were more likely to do so both year round and full time than in the past. As a result, the unemployment rate of adult women dropped a bit, narrowing the gap between women and men. At the same time unemployment among men increased, as men were disproportionately employed in industries that were hardest hit by economic downturns. During the two recessions in the early 1980s men's unemployment rates surpassed women's for the first time, after which the rates converged again (Howe 1990 and Goodman, Antczak, and Freeman 1993). Early in the 1990s men's unemployment levels again surpassed those of women during the downturn. In 1994 both rates stood at 5.4 percent (see Table I-12).

Figure I-4 · UNEMPLOYMENT RATES OF ADULT MEN AND WOMEN, 1948–1994 (annual averages)

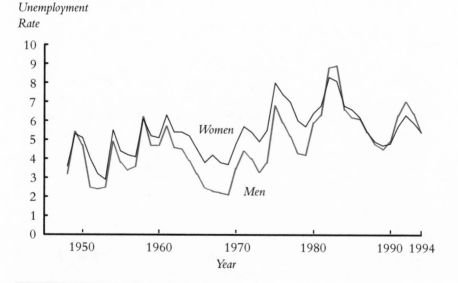

Unemployment Rate

Source: Bureau of Labor Statistics 1994b.

About 44 percent of unemployed women cited job loss or the completion of a temporary job as the reason they were seeking work in 1994, compared with 63 percent of unemployed men. By contrast, women were more likely than men to cite labor market reentry as the reason for their being without a job: 41 versus 25 percent. Women were also more likely to be entering the labor force for the first time. Men and women were about equally likely to be unemployed because they had left a job (10 and 11 percent respectively).

Black and Hispanic women were twice as likely as white women to be unemployed in 1994—a pattern that has persisted since data have been available. About five percent of adult white women in the labor force were seeking work, compared with 10 percent of black and Hispanic women.

DISPLACEMENT

As the economy has undergone structural changes in the last decades, there has been great concern about job loss resulting from those changes. For this reason every two years the BLS measures the extent of worker displacement. Displaced workers are persons age 20 and older who lost jobs because their

Table I-12 · LABOR FORCE STATUS AND REASON FOR UNEMPLOYMENT BY SEX, RACE, AND HISPANIC ORIGIN, 1994 (numbers in thousands)

Status	Total, 20 Years and over	Men	Women			
			Total	White	Black	Hispanic Origin
Civilian labor force	123,576	66,921	56,655	47,314	7,004	4,421
Employed	116,900	63,294	53,606	45,116	6,320	3,989
Unemployed	6,676	3,627	3,049	2,197	685	431
Unemployment rate	5.4	5.4	5.4	4.6	9.8	9.8
Total unemployed percentage	100.0	100.0	100.0	100.0	100.0	100.0
Job losers and persons who completed temporary jobs	54.4	63.3	43.8	46.5	36.4	41.1
Job leavers	10.6	10.1	11.1	12.3	7.6	8.4
Reentrants	32.2	24.8	41.1	38.1	50.2	41.5
New entrants	2.8	1.8	4.0	3.0	5.8	9.0

Source: Bureau of Labor Statistics 1994b.

plants or companies closed or moved, there was insufficient work for them to do, or their positions or shifts were abolished. Between 1991 and 1993, nine million workers were displaced from their jobs; about 3.7 million, or 41 percent, were women (Gardner 1995).

Women were less likely than men to be displaced because they often worked in industries with lower-than-average risks of displacement, such as the services industry. About 7.3 percent of employed women and 8.6 percent of employed men lost jobs from 1991 to 1993. The difference in these rates was smaller than in earlier years; between 1981 and 1983, for example, 7.7 percent of employed women but 9.9 percent of employed men were displaced. The narrowing reflected primarily a shift in the distribution of industries from which workers lost jobs. In the earlier survey 42 percent of displaced workers had lost jobs in manufacturing industries, compared with 27 percent of those displaced between 1991 and 1993. By contrast, the risks of displacement grew in finance, insurance, and real estate, as well as in trade (wholesale and retail combined), where a relatively large share of workers is composed of women.

Although their risk of displacement was greater, men were more likely than women to find other employment after displacement. Slightly more than six in 10 women displaced between 1991 and 1993 were reemployed in February 1994, compared with seven in 10 men. Displaced women were more than twice as likely as men to have left the labor force after losing their jobs: 19 percent versus eight percent.

Of those women who had lost full-time wage-and-salary jobs and had found new jobs, about three-quarters were again employed in full-time wage-and-salary work, while 18 percent were working part time and six percent were self-employed. In contrast, men were more likely to be reemployed in full-time wage-and-salary jobs (81 percent) and were less likely to be working part time (eight percent). Both men and women who lost and were reemployed in full-time wage-and-salary jobs earned about the same (on average, not adjusted for inflation) on their new jobs as on the jobs they had lost.

Involuntary Part-Time Work

Data from the monthly CPS allow analysts to divide part-time workers into those who work part time voluntarily and those who would have preferred full-time work—involuntary part-time workers. Comparable data are available only through 1993; 1994 data reflect revisions to questions on part-time work that were made as part of the 1994 CPS redesign (Cohany, Polivka, and Rothgeb 1994).

About 13.8 million women, or one in four of those who were employed in 1993, usually worked part time (less than 35 hours per week)—the same proportion as in 1970. Over the period, however, there was a gradual increase in the proportion of women working part time involuntarily; in 1993 about 18 percent of women who usually worked part time did so because of slack work or because of their inability to find full-time work, up from only eight percent in 1970.

In 1994 the count of part-time workers was higher—15.7 million—partly because the redesigned survey did a better job of identifying people who worked only a few hours per week. And the count of involuntary part-time workers was lower, as the revised questions required respondents classified as involuntary part-time workers to say both that they wanted full-time work and that they were available to take it. The number of women who worked part time involuntarily in 1994 was 1.9 million—or 12 percent of all women who usually worked part time. Both black and Hispanic women who worked part time were much more likely than white women to do so involuntarily; nearly a quarter of women in each of the two groups would have preferred to work full time, compared with 11 percent of white women.

"MARGINALLY ATTACHED" AND DISCOURAGED WORKERS

Women are overrepresented among those who are "marginally attached" to the labor force. These are persons who want a job, are currently available to work, have searched for work in the previous 12 months, but are not actively looking for work either because they think they cannot find any (discouraged workers) or for other reasons, such as child care problems, family responsibilities, or transportation problems. Women accounted for 54 percent of the 1.8 million persons in that group in 1994.

Women in the marginally attached group were less likely than men to cite discouragement over job prospects and more likely to cite other reasons for not actively searching for a job. About two in 10 women in the group, compared with nearly four in 10 men, reported discouragement as their primary reason. Among women, black women were slightly more likely than white or Hispanic women to report discouragement as their reason for not looking for work.

POVERTY AMONG WORKERS

Because women earn less than men and are more likely to maintain families on their own, their families are especially likely to be poor even when they work. Each year BLS reports on the number of individuals and families who are "working poor." Persons identified as working poor are those who, despite working or looking for work for at least half of the year (27 weeks or more), lived in families with incomes below the poverty level.

In 1993, the latest year for which data are available, about 4.1 million women (7.3 percent) and 4.1 million men (6.2 percent) who were in the labor force at least 27 weeks were living in poor families. Black women and women of Hispanic origin who were labor force participants were more than twice as likely as white women to be living in poor families (see Table I-13).

In terms of families, 4.2 million, or 7.5 percent of those with at least one member in the labor force for half of the year or more, had incomes below the poverty line. Poverty rates varied dramatically by family type, presence of children, and the number of labor force members (see Table I-14). Families maintained by women with children had by far the highest rates; fully 26 percent were poor despite the labor force activity of at least one member of the household. By contrast, the working poverty rate among married-couple families with children in which at least one member was working or looking for work was 7.2 percent. Regardless of family type, families that had two or more members in the labor force for at least half the year were much less likely to be living in poverty: 6.0 percent of families maintained by women versus 2.5 percent of married-couple families.

Table I-13 · POVERTY STATUS OF PERSONS 16 YEARS AND OVER IN THE LABOR FORCE 27 WEEKS OR MORE BY RACE, SEX, AND HISPANIC ORIGIN, 1993 (numbers in thousands)

Race, Sex, and Hispanic Origin	Total	Below Poverty Level	Poverty Rate[1]
Total	123,125	8,222	6.7
Men	67,126	4,146	6.2
White	57,949	3,235	5.6
Black	6,385	691	10.8
Hispanic origin	6,675	1,098	16.5
Women	55,999	4,075	7.3
White	46,881	2,760	5.9
Black	6,885	1,159	16.8
Hispanic origin	4,185	639	15.3

[1]Number below the poverty level as a percentage of the total in the labor force for 27 weeks or more.

Source: Bureau of Labor Statistics 1994c.

Table I-14 · POVERTY STATUS OF PRIMARY FAMILIES WITH MEMBERS IN THE LABOR FORCE 27 WEEKS OR MORE BY SELECTED CHARACTERISTICS, 1993 (numbers in thousands)

Characteristic	Total	Below Poverty Level	Poverty Rate[1]
Total primary families	55,769	4,155	7.5
Married-couple families	44,498	2,206	5.0
With children under 18	25,013	1,798	7.2
With one member in the labor force	14,535	1,444	9.9
With two or more members in the labor force	29,963	762	2.5
Families maintained by women	8,796	1,662	18.9
With children under 18	5,879	1,499	25.5
With one member in the labor force	6,131	1,503	24.5
With two or more members in the labor force	2,665	159	6.0
Families maintained by men	2,476	288	11.6
With children under 18	1,378	219	15.9
With one member in the labor force	1,615	247	15.3
With two or more members in the labor force	861	40	4.6

[1]Number below the poverty level as a percentage of the total labor force for 27 weeks or more.

Source: Bureau of Labor Statistics 1994c.

CONCLUSION

In summary, a substantial majority of women in the United States participate in the labor force. Women's labor force activity escalated after World War II, particularly in the 1960s and 1970s; today nearly six in 10 women either work or are looking for work. Changes in family structure have both influenced and been affected by women's participation in the labor force. Married-couple families in which the husband works but the wife does not have been replaced in large part by dual-earner couples and single parents. Clearly, women are more likely to engage in paid work to support themselves and their families than they were in the past.

Women are still concentrated in occupations, such as retail sales, services, and administrative support, in which they have always worked; however, women have made substantial inroads into some occupations, especially managerial and professional jobs, during the past several decades. As a result, women's earnings have grown and the gap between men's and women's earnings has diminished.

Finally, labor market problems—such as unemployment, displacement, and poverty among those who work—affect both women and men, but they affect them differently. Black and Hispanic women are much more likely than white women to suffer from such labor market difficulties.

All these issues will continue to be of interest for as long as women are active participants in the labor force. The chapters that follow focus on many of the topics raised here: work and family; women and the unemployment insurance system; women, poverty, and welfare; and women and pensions.

TWO

★

WORK AND FAMILY: THE EXPERIENCES OF MOTHERS AND FATHERS IN THE U.S. LABOR FORCE

Ellen Galinsky and James T. Bond[1]

HIGHLIGHTS

THROUGHOUT THE 1970s AND 1980s women with dependent children, particularly very young children, entered the paid labor force in unprecedented numbers. Although their participation rates have leveled off in the 1990s, employed mothers remain a significant force in the U.S. labor market.

This chapter sheds new light on the lives of employed mothers, drawing upon data from the *National Study of the Changing Workforce,* which surveyed a random sample of men and women in the U.S. labor force. The following findings underscore some of the key differences and similarities in life conditions and life outcomes between employed mothers and fathers.

- The personal demographics of mothers and fathers in the labor force—their age, ethnicity, and education—are fairly similar. However, their family demographics are quite different. While 23 percent of mothers in the workforce are single parents, only four percent of employed fathers are.
- Twenty-nine percent of employed mothers are in the contingent workforce—that is, they do not have permanent, full-time wage-and-salary jobs—compared with 13 percent of fathers. This difference is mainly due to more part-time employment among mothers. Among fathers, contingent workforce status is primarily due to seasonal work.
- Mothers earn significantly less per hour than fathers earn: $10.35 versus

[1]The authors would like to express their appreciation to the Carnegie Corporation of New York for the support to prepare this chapter.

$14.06. Their hourly earnings are 74 percent of fathers' hourly earnings. Mothers earn less than fathers annually: $19,962 versus $33,961. Their annual earnings are 59 percent of fathers' annual earnings. In addition, 27 percent of employed mothers, but only 17 percent of employed fathers, live in households with incomes under $22,500 per year—the poorest 20 percent of wage earner households with children in the United States.

- Despite the fact that employed mothers and fathers work in similar-size organizations (almost half work for employers with fewer than 50 employees), fewer mothers than fathers are eligible for coverage under the Family and Medical Leave Act because of mothers' higher rates of part-time employment.
- Mothers have less access to health insurance and paid vacations through their own jobs as the result of their contingent work status and the industries and occupations in which they work.
- Employed mothers and fathers have different criteria for taking jobs: Fathers are more likely to consider fringe benefits, management opportunities, and opportunities for advancement, while mothers give more emphasis to having control over their work schedules. Although mothers are less likely to want to move ahead than fathers, once they are in jobs, employed mothers are as committed and hardworking as men.
- Mothers assume more family responsibilities than do men. Among married wage-and-salary workers with children, women and men agree that the lion's share of the responsibility for maintaining the household belongs to women.
- Mothers are significantly more likely than fathers to miss work because of their children, and having a sick child is the major cause of family-related absenteeism for both mothers and fathers with children under 18.
- On five quality-of-life outcomes, employed mothers seem much worse off than employed fathers. By their own self-reports, employed mothers are more stressed, coping less effectively in their lives, more burned out by their jobs, less satisfied with their marital relations, and less satisfied with themselves as parents.
- Employed mothers exhibit more positive outcomes when they have:
  1. greater job autonomy, more control over their work schedules, more reasonable job demands, and greater job security;
  2. more equal opportunities for job advancement at their places of work;
  3. more access to flexible time/leave benefits and dependent care benefits at work;
  4. more supportive supervisors and a more family-friendly workplace culture; and
  5. husbands who take more responsibility for family work.

INTRODUCTION

As noted in Chapter One, 70 percent of women with children under age 18 participate in the paid labor force. This chapter discusses the challenges faced by employed mothers, challenges that often differ from those of women without children and from those of employed fathers.

Although much has been written about mothers in the workforce, most of the research illuminating what life is like for these women has relied on small-scale studies. Except for the nationally representative *Quality of Employment Survey,* conducted for the U.S. Department of Labor in 1977 (Quinn and Staines 1979), the most informative studies have been limited to specific communities, specific worksites, or specific topics, such as child care.[2] The *National Study of the Changing Workforce* (Galinsky, Bond, and Friedman 1993)—the first nationally representative, in-depth study of the U.S. workforce in 15 years—offers a contemporary perspective on the lives of employed mothers and the ways in which their lives differ from those of employed fathers.

The *National Study of the Changing Workforce* is an ongoing program of the Families and Work Institute in which cross-sectional surveys of the U.S. labor force are conducted every four years. The first round of data was collected in 1992 through hourlong telephone interviews with a random sample of households.[3] The findings discussed in this chapter pertain to 1,233 wage-and-salary workers—632 women and 601 men—who have children under 18 years of age living with them.

We speak of "differences" between employed mothers and fathers only when absolute differences reach statistical significance.[4] The reader will note that sample sizes sometimes vary substantially from item to item. This is be-

[2]See, for example, Baruch and Barnett 1987; Greenberger and Goldberg 1989; Greenberger and O'Neil 1993; Crouter 1984; Hughes and Galinsky 1988; Hughes, Galinsky, and Morris 1992; Piotrkowski 1979; Piotrkowski and Crits-Christoph 1982; Repetti 1989; Shinn et al. 1987; and Hofferth et al. 1991.

[3]The content of the survey was shaped both by prior research and by input from workers and managers at the organizations that sponsored the study: Allstate Insurance Company; American Express Company; AT&T; Commonwealth Fund; Du Pont Company; General Mills Foundation; IBM Corporation; Johnson & Johnson; Levi Strauss & Co.; Merck & Co.; Mobil Corporation; Motorola, Inc.; Rockefeller Foundation; Salt River Project; and Xerox Corporation.

[4]Generally we speak of "differences" between employed mothers and fathers when absolute differences reach statistical significance at $p < .01$—i.e., when there is less than one chance in 100 that the difference resulted from sampling error. We chose the significance threshold

cause of the conditional nature of some questions and because certain questions were asked only of randomly selected subsamples.

PERSONAL AND FAMILY CHARACTERISTICS

The study found few significant differences between employed mothers and
fathers in terms of personal characteristics. Employed mothers tend to be
slightly younger than employed fathers, to have slightly older children, and
to have somewhat different educational backgrounds. However, the study
revealed substantial differences between the marital status of employed
women and men: While 23 percent of employed mothers are single parents, only four percent of employed fathers are single and raising children
on their own.

JOB CHARACTERISTICS

There are substantial differences in the jobs held by employed mothers and
fathers and a concomitant disparity in their participation in the contingent
workforce, membership in labor unions, and number of hours worked per
week. In addition, mothers experience somewhat more interruptions in their
labor force participation than fathers. As discussed elsewhere in this book,
these factors significantly affect earnings, benefits, and retirement income.

Only eight percent of employed parents have more than one job, and
mothers are as likely as fathers to have secondary jobs. The findings presented
in this section pertain to the main job of those parents with more than one
job, unless otherwise indicated.

OCCUPATION

Fathers are more likely than mothers to be top- or mid-level managers, while
mothers are more likely to have professional jobs than are fathers. Not unexpectedly, many more mothers than fathers have administrative support
jobs, while many more fathers than mothers work as machine operators or

of $p < .01$, rather than the more customary $p < .05$, because of the relatively large samples
available for most analyses and the large number of tests performed. In our analyses the strat-
ified random sample is weighted to permit generalizations to the population of all employed
parents in wage-and-salary positions in the U.S. labor force. The design effect of weighting
is 1.22.

manual laborers. Employed mothers are significantly less likely than employed fathers to belong to labor unions.

CONTINGENT WORK

Overall, 79 percent of employed parents have permanent, full-time wage-and-salary jobs, while 21 percent are contingent workers of one sort or another; this includes part-time or seasonal employees, employees of temporary help agencies, and employees in temporary positions. Employed mothers are much more likely (29 percent) than employed fathers (13 percent) to be contingent workers (see Figure II-1). Employed mothers also have more access to part-time work than do fathers, in part because of employed fathers' concentration in industries where full-time positions are the norm. As a result, employed mothers are more than six times as likely as employed fathers to hold part-time jobs. Among mothers in the contingent workforce, the vast majority are employed part time, and four-fifths of mothers who work part time do so by choice. Employed fathers in the contingent workforce

Figure II-1 · EMPLOYED PARENTS' PARTICIPATION IN THE CONTINGENT WORKFORCE BY SEX, 1992

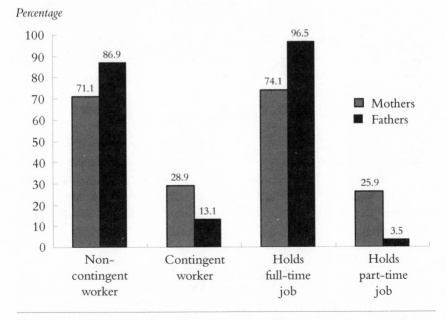

Source: Families and Work Institute 1992.

are more than twice as likely to hold seasonal—that is, part-year jobs—than part-time jobs.

HOURS WORKED

Because so many employed mothers work part time, it is not surprising that mothers work fewer hours on average than fathers. In their main jobs employed mothers are scheduled to work an average of 35.6 hours per week; fathers, 41.8 hours per week. When the actual hours worked per week are considered, the discrepancy widens somewhat. Women actually work 37.4 hours per week on average at their main jobs, compared with 46.7 hours per week for men. Considering time spent at all jobs, women work 38.3 hours per week on average, while men work 47.9 hours.

If we compare only parents with full-time jobs, the differences between employed mothers and fathers diminish; however, the difference in actual hours worked remains fairly substantial: Employed mothers actually work 41.6 hours at main jobs and 42.2 hours at all jobs, while fathers work 47.1 hours at main jobs and 48.2 at all jobs.

Employees in the *National Study of the Changing Workforce* were also asked the number of hours they would prefer to work each week. Employed mothers would prefer to work 32.5 hours—5.8 hours less than the number of hours they actually work. Fathers would prefer to work 41.2 hours per week, 6.7 hours less than the hours they actually work. Interestingly, although employed fathers work significantly longer hours, mothers and fathers do not differ very much in the number of hours they would like to cut back.

INTERRUPTION IN EMPLOYMENT

Employed mothers have experienced more interruptions in their labor force participation than have employed fathers. Excluding periods when employed parents were full-time students, employed mothers have dropped out of the paid labor force for more than a month 1.4 times on average. This compares with 1.1 times for employed fathers, a small but significant difference.

EMPLOYER CHARACTERISTICS

The size of an employer is particularly significant for employed parents because of the federal Family and Medical Leave Act of 1993 (FMLA), which exempts employers with fewer than 50 employees. Almost half of employed mothers and fathers work for employers with fewer than 50 employees and thus are not eligible for coverage by the FMLA. In addition, fewer employed mothers than fathers are eligible for coverage under the act because of mothers' higher rate of part-time work.

EMPLOYER SIZE

It is sometimes assumed that women are more likely to work for small employers than men are, but that is not the case among employed parents. There is no significant difference between fathers and mothers with respect to the size of their employers. Overall, just under half of employed parents work for employers with fewer than 50 employees at the local worksite, and 29 percent of parents work for employers with fewer than 50 employees in the United States. These are important figures in light of the exemption thresholds in the FMLA. The FMLA, which requires covered employers to offer eligible employees up to 12 weeks of unpaid medical and family leave annually, exempts employers with fewer than 50 employees within a 75-mile radius of the worksite.

Although employed mothers and fathers are equally likely to work for FMLA-covered employers, they are not equally likely to meet the requirements for employee eligibility—specifically, the requirement that employees must have worked at least 1,250 hours during the preceding year to be eligible for FMLA leave benefits. While 86 percent of employed fathers had worked 1,250 or more hours for their current employers during the preceding 12 months, only 73 percent of mothers had. This difference is due mainly to higher rates of part-time employment among mothers, not to shorter job tenure.

As a result, we estimate that 41 percent of employed mothers are covered by the FMLA, compared with 49 percent of employed fathers. It is ironic that women's choice to work part time—presumably for family reasons—places them at a disadvantage in terms of coverage by one of the major family-friendly laws in the United States.

THE EARNINGS DIFFERENTIAL

As shown in Table II-1, there is a large gender-related earnings differential. On average, employed mothers earn $19,962 annually, while employed fathers earn an average of $33,961. Mothers also earn significantly less per hour than employed fathers; however, the difference is less when we consider

Table II-1 · EMPLOYED PARENTS' FAMILY FINANCES BY SEX, 1992

	Mothers	*Fathers*	*Overall*
EARNINGS (in dollars)			
Mean annual earnings[1]	(n=491)	(n=482)	(n=973)
	$19,962	$33,961	$26,897
Mean hourly earnings[1]	(n=516)	(n=507)	(n=1,024)
	$10.35	$14.06	$12.19
Mean annual household income[2]	(n=534)	(n=520)	(n=1,054)
	$43,943	$46,071	$44,992
PERCENT DISTRIBUTION[3]			
Married parents:[1]	(n=485)	(n=576)	(n=1,061)
With nonemployed spouse	10.7	33.8	23.3
With employed spouse	89.3	66.2	76.7
Annual household income:[1]	(n=535)	(n=520)	(n=1,055)
Under $22,500	26.8	16.8	21.8
$22,500–$44,999	31.7	41.8	36.7
$45,000 or more	41.6	41.4	41.5

[1]Statistical significance = p<.001.
[2]Not statistically significant.
[3]Percentages may not add to 100 because of rounding.

Source: Families and Work Institute 1992.

hourly earnings. While mothers' annual earnings are only 59 percent of fathers' annual earnings, their hourly earnings are 74 percent of fathers' hourly earnings.

The mean annual household income for working parents in 1992 (before taxes) was $44,992 and did not differ significantly for employed mothers and fathers. Employed mothers are much more likely than employed fathers to be single parents without benefit of income from an employed spouse; this depresses the mean for women. However, employed fathers who are married are much more likely than employed mothers to have a nonemployed spouse; this similarly depresses the mean for men.

If we examine the distribution of income rather than the mean, however, we find that 27 percent of employed mothers—but only 17 percent of employed fathers—live in households with incomes under $22,500 per year, the poorest fifth of wage earner households with children in the United States. This overrepresentation of employed mothers in the lowest income group is largely due to the fact that more employed mothers are single parents with only one income. Single parents have significantly lower household incomes on average ($25,451) than married parents ($48,175), the majority of whom have employed spouses.

Employed mothers in two-earner families contribute about 40 percent of household income, while fathers in two-earner families contribute about 67 percent.[5] In light of employed mothers' generally smaller contributions to household income, it is not surprising that fewer than one in 10 rate their own jobs as more important than their husbands' jobs, compared with one-third of married fathers who rate their jobs as more important than their wives' jobs.

When employed parents with nonemployed spouses were asked about the main reason their spouses are not employed, 55 percent of men cited their wives' current dependent care responsibilities, while only nine percent said their wives had been recently fired, had been laid off, or could not find a job. In contrast, 42 percent of mothers with nonemployed spouses said their husbands had been recently fired, had been laid off, or could not find a job, and none mentioned current dependent care responsibilities as the reason for their husbands' nonemployment. In addition, a third of employed mothers with nonemployed spouses reported that their husbands were disabled versus only five percent of employed fathers who cited disability as the reason for their spouses' nonemployment.

Women are somewhat more likely than men to say that their families would not find it difficult if they did not have paid jobs. In contrast, men are much more likely than women to say it would be difficult if they did not have paid jobs.

In an effort to explain the large annual earnings differential between employed mothers and fathers, we sought to identify factors that differentiate employed mothers and fathers and are also correlated with annual earnings. For example, we have already noted that employed mothers are younger than employed fathers, and age is positively correlated with annual earnings. Likewise, we have reported that employed mothers are more likely to work part time, to work fewer hours, to have had more spells of more than a month out of the paid labor force, and to be contingent workers; all these factors are inversely correlated with earnings. Moreover, employed mothers tend to work in industries with lower pay scales. They are also less likely than employed fathers to belong to unions, and union members earn more.

[5]One would expect these percentages for random samples of employed mothers and fathers who are married to add to 100, and they come close to doing so in the current study.

ACCESS TO FRINGE BENEFITS

Data from the *National Study of the Changing Workforce* describe fringe benefits and personnel policies only in the most general terms. For example, we know whether a respondent's employer offers a group health insurance plan and whether family coverage is available, but we do not know anything about the quality of the plan or its cost to the employee. Similarly, we know whether the respondent's employer provides any leave for childbirth and parenting, but we do not know how much leave or who is eligible.

TRADITIONAL FRINGE BENEFITS

Traditional fringe benefits include health insurance coverage, pension plans, and paid vacation time. As shown in Table II-2, employed mothers have significantly less access than employed fathers to job-related health insurance; 16 percent of mothers have no access through their jobs, compared with 10 percent of fathers. Despite their more restricted access to job-related health insurance, employed mothers are no more likely to be uninsured than employed fathers (about nine percent of mothers and fathers are uninsured).

Table II-2 · EMPLOYED PARENTS' ACCESS TO TRADITIONAL FRINGE BENEFITS BY SEX (percent distribution)

Benefits	Mothers	Fathers	Overall[1]
Health insurance:[2]	(n=622)	(n=594)	(n=1,216)
None	16.4	10.4	13.5
Self only	6.3	4.8	5.6
Self and family	77.3	84.8	81.0
Pension plan:[3]	(n=611)	(n=587)	(n=1,198)
No	30.1	24.8	27.5
Yes	69.9	75.2	72.5
Paid vacation:[4]	(n=630)	(n=601)	(n=1,231)
No	25.4	13.8	19.8
Yes	74.6	86.2	80.2

[1]Percentages may not add to 100 because of rounding.
[2]Statistical significance = $p<.01$.
[3]Not statistically significant.
[4]Statistical significance = $p<.001$.

Source: Families and Work Institute 1992.

This is because they are much more likely (26 percent) than employed fathers (10 percent) to be covered by insurance from their spouses' jobs. Employed mothers are also less likely (75 percent) than employed fathers (86 percent) to receive paid vacation days.

Differential access to health insurance is fully accounted for by mothers' higher rate of contingent and part-time work. Differential access to paid vacation days appears to be a function of differences between mothers and fathers with respect to rates of contingent or part-time work, occupation, industry, and earnings. A full discussion of employer-provided pension plans is presented in Chapters Five and Six.

FLEXIBLE TIME AND LEAVE BENEFITS

As shown in Table II-3, employed mothers are significantly more likely than fathers to report that "employees" where they work can take time off for childbirth and parenting. (The survey was conducted before passage of the federal Family and Medical Leave Act.) In addition, mothers are much more likely than fathers to say that their "employer" allows employees to work less than full time. However, employed mothers are less likely than fathers to say that their employers allow extended lunch breaks for exercise, errands, and so forth if employees make up the time later.

Employed mothers and fathers do not differ with respect to having time off to care for a sick child or family member, having some flexibility in structuring work hours, or being allowed to do some work at home on a regular basis.

Flexible time and leave benefits appear to be of more interest and value to employed mothers than to employed fathers. A randomly selected one-third of respondents, whose employers did not offer flexible time and leave benefits, were asked about trade-offs they might make to obtain the benefit. Employed mothers are significantly more likely than fathers to say that they would or might (1) change jobs to be able to work part time and (2) trade job advancement to work part time, work at home regularly, and have control over the time they start and end the workday. These findings clearly reflect the greater emphasis that employed mothers give to their caregiving/homemaking roles when compared with employed fathers.

DEPENDENT CARE BENEFITS

The jobs of employed mothers and fathers do not differ with respect to offering any of the four dependent care benefits examined: flexible spending accounts for dependent care expenses (27 percent overall), child care resource

Table II-3 · EMPLOYED PARENTS' ACCESS TO FLEXIBLE TIME AND LEAVE BENEFITS POLICIES BY SEX, 1992 (percent distribution)

Benefits	Mothers	Fathers	Overall
Leave for childbirth or parenting:[1]	(n=597)	(n=561)	(n=1,158)
No	6.6	15.8	11.1
Yes	93.4	84.2	88.9
Time off to care for sick child or other family member:[2]	(n=613)	(n=572)	(n=1,185)
No	7.5	10.7	9.1
Yes	92.5	89.3	90.9
Part-time work or job sharing:[1]	(n=609)	(n=573)	(n=1,182)
No	34.2	55.5	44.5
Yes	65.8	44.5	55.5
Extended lunch break:[3]	(n=616)	(n=585)	(n=1,201)
No	58.2	49.5	54.0
Yes	41.8	50.5	46.0
Work less one day, make up later:[2]	(n=618)	(n=581)	(n=1,199)
No	55.3	57.4	56.3
Yes	44.7	42.6	43.7
Set own start and end times:[2]	(n=623)	(n=588)	(n=1,211)
No	73.9	71.9	72.9
Yes	26.1	28.1	27.1
Allowed to do some work at home on regular basis:[2]	(n=621)	(n=589)	(n=1,210)
No	75.9	74.9	75.4
Yes	24.1	25.1	24.6

[1]Statistical significance = p<.001.
[2]Not statistically significant.
[3]Statistical significance = p<.01.

Source: Families and Work Institute 1992.

and referral services (19 percent overall), on- or near-site child care (12 percent overall), and employer-paid child care subsidies (four percent overall).

REASONS FOR TAKING JOB WITH CURRENT EMPLOYER

Workers who had been with their current employers for fewer than five years were asked to rate the importance of twenty factors in their original decisions to take their jobs. It appears that men tend to put their provider role in the forefront when making decisions about where to work, while women give important consideration to their caregiving/homemaking role as well. Fringe benefits, management opportunities, and opportunities for advancement are more important to fathers than to mothers, while control over work schedule is more important to mothers. These findings parallel those related to the trade-offs that employed mothers and fathers are willing to make for benefits.

CONDITIONS ON THE JOB

Employed mothers and fathers have similar perceptions about the demands of their jobs, control over their work schedules, and job security. They also feel equally supported by their immediate supervisors at work. However, mothers do indicate that they have less autonomy on the job than fathers have.

WORKPLACE CULTURE

Employed mothers and fathers do not differ in their ratings of the "family friendliness" of their workplace cultures. Parents generally feel that their immediate supervisors are more supportive than their workplace cultures are. Overall, a third of parents surveyed agree that "at [their] place of employment employees have to choose between advancing in their jobs or devoting attention to their family or personal lives." Similarly, 34 percent agree that "there is an unwritten rule that you can't take care of family needs on company time," while an even larger percentage agree that "employees who put their personal or family needs ahead of their jobs are not looked on favorably."

DISCRIMINATION AND SEXUAL HARASSMENT

A small, randomly selected subsample of parents was asked about sexual harassment and discrimination. Employed mothers are more than twice as likely (17 percent) as fathers (seven percent) to have experienced "unwanted sexual attention" at work in the past five years. Likewise, three times more mothers (19 percent) than fathers (six percent) report that they have experienced discrimination on their current job.

FEELINGS ABOUT JOBS, EMPLOYERS, AND WORK

Both employed fathers and employed mothers are highly committed to doing their own jobs well. In addition, employed mothers and fathers are equally loyal to their employers. Almost two-thirds say that they are extremely or very loyal, and only six percent regard themselves as not loyal. Although mothers give much greater emphasis to family issues when deciding to take jobs, working mothers are just as committed to their employers as fathers are.

ATTITUDES TOWARD WORK

Employed mothers and fathers do not differ in the extent to which they feel they have made sacrifices in their careers for the sake of their families or sacrifices in their personal and family lives for the sake of their careers. Overall, almost a quarter of employed parents report that they have made a lot of sacrifices in their careers for the sake of their families, while 22 percent say that they have made a lot of sacrifices in the quality of their family lives for the sake of their careers. While mothers as a group may not "feel" that they have made more career sacrifices than fathers, previously presented findings suggest that employed mothers are more likely to have made family-related decisions that constrain career advancement and earnings, such as choosing part-time employment and taking more time out of the paid labor force.

Feelings of "sacrifice" may also vary in relation to aspirations. As shown in Figure II-2, employed mothers are more likely than employed fathers to want to stay at their current level of responsibility. For both mothers and fathers who want to remain at their present level, the main reason given is that they like their current jobs; 94 percent of fathers and 63 percent of mothers give this reason. For mothers, however, a second reason—mentioned by 29 percent of respondents—is dependent care responsibilities.

Interestingly, less than one in five mothers versus a quarter of fathers agrees with the statement "I prefer not to work too much." Likewise, mothers are less likely than fathers to agree that they would stop working if they had enough money. There is no difference, however, in how employed mothers and fathers rate their overall work ethic: Seventy percent rate it very strong.

FAMILY LIFE

Employed mothers take far more responsibility for family work than employed fathers. Among married wage-and-salary workers with children, women and men agree that the lion's share of the responsibility for main-

Figure II-2 · EMPLOYED PARENTS' ASPIRATIONS FOR JOB ADVANCE-
MENT BY SEX, 1992

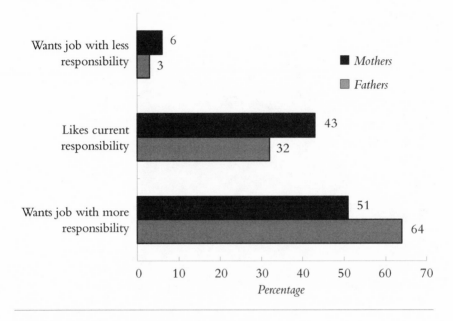

Source: Families and Work Institute 1992.

taining the household belongs to women (see Table II-4). For example, more
than four out of five employed mothers say they are primarily responsible
for cooking, cleaning, and shopping. Employed mothers are also more likely
to take charge of paying bills, although to a lesser degree than for other
household chores. The one difference in this pattern relates to making
household repairs. Women and men agree that this is a male domain. Fathers are more likely to view themselves as sharing household responsibilities equally with their spouses than mothers are to say that their spouses share
responsibilities on an equal basis.

There is more agreed-upon sharing when it comes to caring for children.
Among married parents with children under 16 years old, more than two-
thirds of mothers say that they take primary responsibility for the care of their
children, while only one in 20 fathers makes the same claim. However, 20
percent of mothers and 33 percent of fathers say that the care of their children is shared equally. Fathers with employed spouses are much more likely
(46 percent) to claim equal responsibility than are fathers with nonemployed spouses (10 percent).

Table II-4 · EMPLOYED PARENTS' DIVISION OF FAMILY WORK BY SEX, 1992 (percent distribution)[1]

Family Work Area	Mothers	Fathers	Overall
Cooking responsibility:[2]	(n=180)	(n=212)	(n=392)
Respondent	82.5	11.3	44.0
50–50 split	3.9	12.5	8.6
Spouse	13.5	76.2	47.4
Other	0.0	0.0	0.0
Cleaning responsibility:[2]	(n=180)	(n=212)	(n=392)
Respondent	81.4	5.8	40.5
50–50 split	10.0	24.4	17.8
Spouse	8.5	69.9	41.7
Other	0.0	0.0	0.0
Shopping responsibility:[2]	(n=180)	(n=212)	(n=392)
Respondent	89.2	11.3	47.1
50–50 split	7.5	27.1	18.1
Spouse	3.3	61.5	34.8
Other	0.0	0.1	0.0
Bill-paying responsibility:[2]	(n=180)	(n=212)	(n=392)
Respondent	66.6	32.5	48.1
50–50 split	14.6	17.1	15.9
Spouse	17.1	49.5	34.6
Other	1.7	1.0	1.3
Child care responsibility:[2]	(n=165)	(n=192)	(n=357)
Respondent	67.6	5.4	34.1
50–50 split	20.1	33.2	27.2
Spouse	12.3	61.4	38.7
Other	0.0	0.0	0.0

[1]Percentages may not add to 100 because of rounding.
[2]Statistical significance = $p < .001$.

Source: Families and Work Institute 1992.

CHILD CARE ARRANGEMENTS

Parents with children under 13 were asked a series of questions about their child care arrangements. The findings reveal that mothers and fathers have different experiences, largely because more employed fathers than employed mothers are married and more fathers have spouses at home to care for their children. For example, more than 76 percent of mothers rely on nonparental child care arrangements while they work, compared with 61 percent of fathers. When differences in marital status and employment status of spouse are taken into account, the child care experiences of employed mothers and fathers are similar for the most part. Overall, among parents with employed spouses and children under five years of age, 62 percent pay for child care services.

Among those who pay for child care, mothers and fathers report paying $3,172 annually on average for all children. This represents 8.5 percent of annual household income for the average employed parent. Very few employed parents receive any direct assistance from government or their employers in purchasing child care services. Overall, 96 percent of parents pay for child care entirely out of their own pockets. However, about three in 10 parents took advantage of the federal dependent care tax credit in the preceding year (1991), allowing them to pay for part of their child care expenses with pretax dollars.

Employed mothers and fathers both report the occurrence of about one breakdown in their usual child care arrangements in the three-month period preceding the interview. Among the 26 percent of mothers and fathers who seriously considered using a different arrangement for their youngest child, 59 percent found no satisfactory alternative, reflecting the lack of child care choices available to working parents in most communities across the country.

The one area in which differences between employed mothers and fathers appear to be clearly gender-related involves who stays home with a sick child (see Figure II-3). Although most parents say that "it depends" on the situation, twice as many mothers as fathers say that they regularly stay home with a sick child. By contrast, more fathers "typically" go to work when their children are sick than mothers do. Fathers with employed wives are much less likely than fathers with nonemployed wives to say that they typically go to work when their children are sick; nevertheless, even they are much more likely than employed mothers to leave sick-child care to their spouses.

WORK AND PERSONAL OUTCOMES

Although employed mothers and fathers feel equally successful at work and equally satisfied with their jobs, mothers experience higher levels of job burnout and report more home-to-job spillover. In addition, employed mothers are less satisfied with their marital relations, their parental roles, their children's status, and life in general. Finally, employed mothers report higher levels of stress than employed fathers.

WORK LIFE OUTCOMES

Mothers consider themselves just as successful in their work lives as fathers. Overall, more than 90 percent of employed parents feel that they are suc-

Figure II-3 · EMPLOYED PARENTS' RESPONSIBILITIES FOR SICK CHILDREN BY SEX, 1992

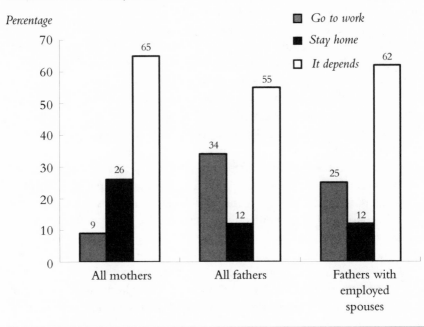

Source: Families and Work Institute 1992.

cessful in their work lives. Employed mothers and fathers with children under 18 report similarly high levels of satisfaction with their jobs. Overall, nearly nine in 10 say they are satisfied. In addition, 60 percent would take the same job again without hesitation.

However, employed mothers and fathers differ significantly in the degree to which they feel burned out by their jobs (see Table II-5). For example, 30 percent of mothers, in contrast with 23 percent of fathers, feel emotionally drained from their work often or very often; more mothers than fathers say that they often feel used up at the end of the workday or tired when they get up in the morning.

WORK-FAMILY OUTCOMES

Surprisingly, employed mothers and fathers do not differ in the extent to which they perceive conflict in balancing their work and personal/family responsibilities. Perhaps equally surprising is the fact that few mothers and fathers say that they experience a lot of conflict. However, four in 10 employed parents report some conflict in managing their dual responsibilities.

One of the main ways that work–family problems are expressed is through "spillover"—that is, the carrying over of the concerns, responsibilities, and demands of one part of life to another. Spillover can go in two directions: home-to-job spillover or job-to-home spillover. Employed mothers are no more likely than fathers to experience job-to-home spillover. During the three months preceding the interview, about one-third of mothers and fathers had experienced significant job-to-home spillover—not having enough time or energy for themselves or their families.

Not unexpectedly, given their greater responsibility for family work and caring for children, employed mothers are far more likely to experience home-to-job spillover than are employed fathers. Employed mothers are significantly more likely than employed fathers to say that they worked fewer hours, refused overtime, were distracted and less productive at work, and worried about their children on the job during the past year. However, employed mothers do not differ from employed fathers on other items, such as rearranging work schedules to meet family responsibilities, refusing business travel, refusing interesting work assignments, or having problems with either supervisors or coworkers because of family or personal responsibilities.

Another indicator of home-to-job spillover is absenteeism resulting from family responsibilities. Mothers are significantly more likely than fathers to miss work because of their children, and having a sick child is the major cause of family-related absenteeism for both mothers and fathers with children under 18. On average, mothers missed 0.64 days in the preceding three-month period while fathers missed 0.29 days, or about half as much time, to care for sick children.

SATISFACTION WITH PERSONAL AND FAMILY LIFE

Employed mothers are consistently less satisfied than employed fathers with various aspects of their lives away from the job. Mothers are less satisfied with their marital relationships than are employed fathers. Mothers are less satisfied with how they are doing as parents, and they are also less satisfied than fathers with how their children are doing. Finally, mothers are less satisfied than fathers with how things in their lives are going in general: Twenty-nine percent of employed mothers say that they are very satisfied, compared with 38 percent of fathers.

Table II-5 · EMPLOYED PARENTS' REPORTS OF JOB BURNOUT BY SEX, 1992 (percent distribution)[1]

In Past Three Months ...	Mothers	Fathers	Overall
Felt emotionally drained from work:[2]	(n=632)	(n=601)	(n=1,233)
Very often	15.9	10.1	13.1
Often	14.4	12.9	13.7
Sometimes	35.2	36.2	35.7
Rarely	23.8	25.4	24.5
Never	10.7	15.4	13.0
Felt used up at the end of the workday:[2]	(n=632)	(n=601)	(n=1,233)
Very often	24.9	16.7	20.9
Often	23.3	22.9	23.1
Sometimes	32.7	34.6	33.6
Rarely	13.4	18.8	16.0
Never	5.7	7.0	6.4
Felt tired when getting up in the morning to face another day on job:[3]	(n=629)	(n=601)	(n=1,230)
Very often	25.2	15.0	20.2
Often	22.6	19.9	21.2
Sometimes	28.6	34.1	31.3
Rarely	17.6	21.6	19.6
Never	6.0	9.4	7.7
Felt frustrated by job:[4]	(n=632)	(n=601)	(n=1,233)
Very often	14.1	11.1	12.7
Often	19.2	14.1	16.7
Sometimes	29.9	32.1	31.0
Rarely	24.1	28.4	26.2
Never	12.8	14.2	13.4
Felt burned out or stressed from work:[2]	(n=632)	(n=601)	(n=1,233)
Very often	16.4	10.2	13.4
Often	17.7	14.5	16.1
Sometimes	29.3	30.5	29.9
Rarely	25.9	29.5	27.6
Never	10.6	15.4	12.9

[1]Percentages may not add to 100 because of rounding.

[2]Statistical significance = p<.01.

[3]Statistical significance = p<.001.

[4]No statistical significance.

Source: Families and Work Institute 1992.

STRESS AND COPING

Employed mothers report higher levels of stress than employed fathers (see Table II-6). Mothers report being bothered by minor health problems (e.g., headaches, insomnia, stomach upsets) or feeling nervous and stressed more often than fathers.

Employed mothers also feel less confident than fathers about handling personal problems; 47 percent of fathers but only 36 percent of mothers feel very confident. In addition, twice as many mothers as fathers say that they are often unable to control the important things in their lives or are unable to cope with all the things they have to do. While 32 percent of fathers say that they *never* feel that difficulties are piling up so high they cannot overcome them, only 17 percent of mothers express such confidence.

CONDITIONS THAT FOSTER MORE FAVORABLE OUTCOMES

On five quality-of-life outcomes, employed mothers seem much worse off than employed fathers. By their own self-reports, employed mothers are more burned out by their jobs, less satisfied with their marital relations, less satisfied with themselves as parents, more stressed, and less able to handle their multiple roles effectively. These problems can be mitigated by the existence of certain conditions at home and at work. For example, mothers fare better when they are married, receive more help around the house, have employers that allow flexibility in scheduling. Employed mothers also fare better when they feel that they have autonomy on the job and that there is opportunity for advancement at work.

JOB BURNOUT

Interestingly, several aspects of employed mothers' family situations are significantly related to feelings of being burned out by their jobs. Single mothers, mothers with younger children, and those who have missed more work for child-related reasons report higher levels of job burnout than others. Women whose earnings account for a larger share of household income also report more job burnout.

As one might expect, women who work fewer hours or part time report significantly lower levels of job burnout than women who work longer hours, though the relationship between hours worked and burnout is not particularly strong. Having more flexible time and leave options on the job

Table II-6 · EMPLOYED PARENTS' REPORTS OF STRESS AND COPING
ABILITY BY SEX, 1992 (percent distribution)

In Past Three Months...	*Mothers*	*Fathers*	*Overall*
Bothered by minor health problems:[1]	(n=632)	(n=601)	(n=1,233)
Very often	9.5	3.2	6.4
Often	13.3	7.5	10.5
Sometimes	29.8	23.5	26.7
Rarely	37.0	45.9	41.4
Never	10.5	19.9	15.1
Felt nervous or stressed:[1]	(n=632)	(n=601)	(n=1,233)
Very often	14.0	6.4	10.3
Often	23.6	12.9	18.4
Sometimes	33.3	31.8	32.6
Rarely	24.4	36.3	30.2
Never	4.7	12.7	8.6
Felt confident to handle personal problems:[2]	(n=631)	(n=601)	(n=1,232)
Very often	35.6	47.3	41.3
Often	38.2	32.5	35.4
Sometimes	20.4	15.5	18.0
Rarely	4.7	3.8	4.3
Never	1.1	1.0	1.0
Felt unable to control important things in life:[1]	(n=632)	(n=599)	(n=1,231)
Very often	7.7	3.6	5.7
Often	14.5	7.6	11.2
Sometimes	28.7	25.4	27.1
Rarely	36.4	40.0	38.2
Never	12.7	23.3	17.9
Felt things were going your way:[3]	(n=632)	(n=601)	(n=1,233)
Very often	10.6	14.4	12.5
Often	33.5	36.2	34.8
Sometimes	39.1	35.4	37.3
Rarely	15.0	11.5	13.3
Never	1.8	2.6	2.2

(continued)

and having more dependent care benefits are associated with lower levels of
job burnout. Women with greater autonomy on the job and more control
over their work schedules report lower levels of job burnout, while those
who feel their jobs are more demanding and less secure report more burnout.
Perceiving more opportunities for persons of one's own race and gender to
advance at work, more support from one's supervisor, and a more supportive workplace culture are associated with less job burnout.

(Table II-6 continued)

In Past Three Months...	Mothers	Fathers	Overall
Felt you could not cope with all the things you had to do:[1]	(n=632)	(n=601)	(n=1,233)
Very often	5.6	2.0	3.9
Often	13.3	6.8	10.1
Sometimes	33.7	22.2	28.1
Rarely	35.0	46.2	40.5
Never	12.4	22.6	17.4
Felt difficulties were piling up so high you could not overcome them:[1]	(n=629)	(n=601)	(n=1,230)
Very often	5.6	1.0	3.4
Often	7.4	6.3	6.8
Sometimes	24.4	17.9	21.2
Rarely	45.4	43.1	44.2
Never	17.3	31.8	24.4

[1]Statistical significance = p<.001.
[2]Statistical significance = p<.01.
[3]No statistical significance.

Source: Families and Work Institute 1992.

SATISFACTION WITH MARRIAGE

Employed mothers who get more help around the house—mainly from husbands—feel better about their relationships. Women whose families depend more on their earnings—i.e., whose husbands contribute less to household income—are less satisfied with their marital relationships. Interestingly, several work-related variables are also predictive of marital satisfaction. Women who have more flexible time and leave options and more autonomy on the job feel more satisfied in their marital relationships. Furthermore, women who feel that their immediate supervisors at work are more supportive and who perceive greater advancement opportunities for employees of their race and gender are also more satisfied with their marital relationships.

SATISFACTION WITH SELF AS PARENT

Employed single mothers and mothers with more children are less satisfied than others with how they are doing as parents. Mothers whose earnings represent a higher share of household income—i.e., single mothers and women whose husbands contribute less—are also less satisfied with themselves as parents. Women who perceive greater opportunities at work for advancement by employees of their race and gender feel better about themselves as parents.

STRESS

Employed mothers are significantly less stressed when they miss less work for child-related reasons (mainly children's illnesses) and when their families are less dependent on their earnings. Having more options for flexible work schedules and leaves is also associated with lower levels of stress. Women who have greater autonomy on the job and more control over their work schedules report lower levels of stress, while women who feel that their jobs are more demanding and less secure report higher levels of stress. Women who have more supportive supervisors and more supportive workplace cultures report less stress, as do those who believe that there are better chances for advancement for employees of their race and gender at their current place of work.

ABILITY TO "COPE"

Employed mothers' feelings about their overall ability to handle problems—their ability to cope—are greatly affected by the issues discussed above. Again, certain life and work conditions contribute to women's sense of control over their lives.

Women feel more able to cope when they are married and when they have more help at home with chores and child care, mainly from their husbands. They are also more satisfied with their overall ability to handle problems when they have higher household incomes, which is largely a function of being married; however, women who contribute a higher proportion of family income—that is, single mothers and those whose husbands contribute less—feel that they are coping less effectively.

Job conditions that foster a greater sense of control include having more flexible time and leave options, greater autonomy, and greater control over work schedules. Perceiving more opportunities for persons of one's own race and gender to advance at work, more support from one's supervisor, and a more supportive workplace culture are also associated with more effective coping.

CONCLUSION

This chapter has examined a broad range of life conditions and life outcomes for employed mothers and fathers in wage-and-salary jobs. On average, employed mothers are more stressed, more burned out by their jobs, less satisfied with their marital relations, and less satisfied with themselves as parents than employed fathers. The most important analyses conducted for this chapter addressed the question "Under what conditions do employed mothers exhibit more favorable outcomes?" While some of the conditions affecting outcomes are clearly beyond the reach of private or public policy, a number are (theoretically at least) within the reach of both.

Findings reported in this chapter suggest that employed mothers might well benefit from changes in workplace policy and practice that:

- increase access to dependent care benefits and to flexible time and leave benefits;
- allow for greater job autonomy and control over work schedules, while placing more reasonable demands on workers and providing greater job security; and
- ensure all employees equal opportunities for job advancement, foster a more family-friendly workplace culture, and encourage managers and supervisors to be more supportive of their employees with respect to both job-related and personal or family matters.

This analysis also shows that working mothers need "help on the home front." If more husbands pulled their weight at home, the ability of working mothers to balance the demands of work and family would surely improve, and marital satisfaction might increase as well. These changes at work—and at home—could greatly enhance the lives of working mothers and their families.

THREE

★

WOMEN AND THE UNEMPLOYMENT INSURANCE SYSTEM

Laurie J. Bassi and Amy B. Chasanov

HIGHLIGHTS

THE UNEMPLOYMENT INSURANCE (UI) PROGRAM is an important first line of economic defense for the unemployed, sparing many the indignities of public relief. However, this important program, which was created as a part of the Social Security Act of 1935, has in many ways failed to evolve to meet the needs of today's labor force. This failure is particularly evident for unemployed women. The following points highlight how unemployed women fare in the UI system:

- Because of both monetary and nonmonetary eligibility requirements, unemployed women are substantially less likely to receive UI benefits than are unemployed men.
- Since women typically earn less than men, women are less likely than men to meet the minimum earnings requirements needed to qualify for UI.
- Among those who do meet the minimum earnings requirements, a variety of nonmonetary eligibility requirements appear to result in disqualifying a disproportionately higher percentage of unemployed women than unemployed men from receiving UI.
- Among unemployed individuals who do receive UI benefits, women tend to receive lower benefit amounts than do men. However, UI benefits typically replace a higher percentage of lost earnings for women than for men.
- Relaxing the monetary eligibility requirements for qualifying for UI would

increase the percentage of unemployed women who could qualify for benefits. The costs associated with expanded UI eligibility would be partially offset by a reduction in spending on means-tested programs.

- Minimum federal standards should ensure that workers with a substantial labor force attachment would meet state monetary eligibility requirements. These standards could correct the unfair treatment of low-wage workers—a disproportionate share of whom are women and minorities—within the UI system.

- Nonmonetary eligibility standards should seek to ensure that part-time workers and workers with caregiving responsibilities are treated equitably.

INTRODUCTION

This year marks the sixtieth anniversary of the passage of the Social Security Act. Together the three major programs created by the act were intended to provide both economic security and dignity for vulnerable members of the population. The Social Security Act created the Old Age and Survivor's Insurance program (OASI), a system for providing retirement income for the elderly; what is now called Aid to Families with Dependent Children (AFDC), to provide financial support for children without fathers; and, finally, the Unemployment Insurance (UI) system, which was intended by its founders to serve as the first line of economic defense for unemployed workers.

In 1935, when the Social Security Act became law, elderly and widowed women were particularly economically vulnerable. Consequently, OASI and AFDC were especially important programs for women. But since few women were members of the paid labor force, the UI program was much more relevant for men than for women.

Today women make up nearly half of the labor force and almost half of all unemployed workers. As a result, unemployment is at least as great a source of financial vulnerability for women as it is for men. The UI program, however, has not kept pace with these dramatic changes in women's status. As a result, unemployed women are much less likely to receive UI benefits than are unemployed men.

There are two basic obstacles that prevent many unemployed women from receiving UI benefits. The first is the UI system's monetary eligibility requirements—the amount that an individual must earn within a given period of time prior to unemployment. These requirements are expressed in terms of earnings, rather than in terms of hours of work. Because women typically have lower wages than do men, unemployed women are less likely to satisfy the UI program's earnings requirements than unemployed men are. In essence, the UI program discriminates against low-wage workers, the majority of whom are women. This problem is especially pronounced for black women.

The second major obstacle is a variety of nonmonetary eligibility requirements that unemployed workers must satisfy in order to establish and maintain eligibility for UI. These requirements, which can be both numerous and complicated, seek to ensure that a worker is involuntarily unemployed and available for and actively seeking work. Many of these requirements result in the disqualification of more women than of men.

The UI system is run through a complex federal-state partnership. The states set the rules that establish eligibility for UI. Much of the variation in these rules results in eligibility conditions that exclude low-wage workers, the majority of whom are women and minorities, from receiving UI. From the states' perspective, it may make sense to restrict eligibility to UI and let the low-wage workers receive welfare instead. States finance regular UI benefits, whereas the federal government pays for the majority of the costs for welfare programs. Federal standards for establishing both monetary and nonmonetary eligibility for UI benefits could eliminate many of these inequities.

HOW THE UNEMPLOYMENT INSURANCE SYSTEM WORKS

The goals of the Unemployment Insurance (UI) system are (1) to provide temporary, partial wage replacement for involuntarily unemployed workers who have a significant attachment to the labor market and (2) to serve as an automatic stabilizer for the economy by accumulating reserves during periods of prosperity that are then used during downturns. These program goals are attained through an "insurance" mechanism that pays benefits as a matter of right to those individuals who have worked and meet their state's monetary and nonmonetary eligibility requirements.

There are three separate types of programs that provide income support: (1) permanent, regular state UI programs, (2) federal-state Extended Benefits programs, and (3) temporary federal emergency compensation programs. This chapter focuses on the regular state UI programs.[1]

[1]For more detail on the Extended Benefits program and emergency compensation, see Advisory Council on Unemployment Compensation (1994).

FEDERAL-STATE RELATIONSHIP

While broad federal guidelines and laws ensure uniformity in areas considered essential, states maintain authority for designing the details of their UI programs' operations and benefits. The result is 53 varied state programs.[2] Although the U.S. Department of Labor maintains oversight responsibility, the states establish eligibility requirements, weekly benefit amounts, duration of benefits, and the tax schedules used to collect state UI taxes.

Federal requirements are imposed through the Federal Unemployment Tax Act (FUTA) and the Social Security Act. FUTA defines which employers must provide UI coverage to their workers and imposes federal payroll taxes on those employers. The Social Security Act provides the states with grants to fund the administration of their UI programs, establishes and allocates federal and state collections to various trust funds, and offers loan provisions to states that become insolvent.

COVERAGE

Individuals who are "covered" by the UI system work for employers who pay UI taxes on their wages. The percentage of the workforce covered by the UI system has increased over time. The most recent significant expansions in coverage were legislated in the 1970s, when state and local government employees, many household workers, employees of small businesses, and workers on large farms became eligible to receive UI for the first time. The current federal standards (FUTA) require that almost all employees who work for employers that pay wages of $1,500 or more in any calendar quarter be covered. As a result, in 1993 over 90 percent of all civilian employment in the United States was covered by UI. The two significant coverage exceptions are self-employed individuals and agricultural workers on small farms.[3]

ELIGIBILITY FOR UNEMPLOYMENT INSURANCE

Two broad categories of eligibility—monetary and nonmonetary—are used to determine whether an unemployed individual is eligible for benefits. Both

[2]The District of Columbia, Puerto Rico, and the Virgin Islands are considered states for the purposes of this discussion.
[3]Eight states provide more liberal coverage of agricultural workers than required by federal law. See Advisory Council on Unemployment Compensation (1995) for more information on coverage.

types of eligibility conditions are determined by the states, with only minimal requirements imposed by the federal government through FUTA. Monetary eligibility conditions ensure that those who receive UI benefits had a substantial attachment to the labor force prior to the onset of unemployment. Nonmonetary eligibility conditions are intended to ensure that UI recipients are able to work, available for work, and seeking work and that their jobs were terminated by their employers or they left their jobs for good cause. A more detailed discussion of these two types of eligibility conditions is presented later in this chapter.

BENEFIT LEVELS

With the exception of dependent allowances, which are offered in 13 states, UI benefits are not based on any factors related to individual circumstance. Rather, each state calculates the weekly benefit for which an unemployed individual is eligible on the basis of that individual's earnings and employment history. In 1979 UI benefits were partially taxed for the first time, and since 1986 all UI benefits have been subject to taxation. The result of this taxation is to reduce directly the net value of benefits.

States establish both minimum and maximum benefit amounts. In most states the lower the monetary eligibility requirement, the lower the minimum benefit amount. In 1994 the minimum weekly benefit amount varied from five dollars in Hawaii to $73 in Washington, and the maximum benefit amount varied from $133 in Puerto Rico to $347 in New Jersey.

The 1993 average weekly benefit amount for the United States was $180, ranging from $89 in Puerto Rico to $252 in Hawaii (see Table III-1). Although the average weekly benefit amount (in constant dollars) has declined slightly in the past two decades (from $192 in 1973 to $180 in 1993), it has not declined as sharply as average weekly wages (from $460 in 1973 to $363 in 1993).

An alternative measure of benefits is the replacement rate—the ratio of an individual's weekly UI benefits to his or her weekly wage prior to unemployment.

- On average, full-time, full-year workers who earn minimum wage have a weekly replacement rate of 55 percent, whereas workers earning $10 per hour have a weekly replacement rate of 50 percent and workers earning $15 per hour have a weekly replacement rate of 40 percent.
- At any given wage rate, average replacement rates are typically higher for part-time workers than for full-time workers.
- In the 13 states that provide higher benefits to individuals with depen-

Table III-1 · AVERAGE WEEKLY BENEFIT AMOUNT, BY STATE, 1993

State	Weekly Benefit Amount (dollars)	State	Weekly Benefit Amount (dollars)
Hawaii	252	West Virginia	167
Connecticut	234	Oklahoma	164
Massachusetts	234	Wyoming	164
New Jersey	224	Maine	163
District of Columbia	223	Vermont	163
Michigan	215	Idaho	162
Rhode Island	211	Arkansas	158
Minnesota	210	California	156
Pennsylvania	210	Kentucky	156
New York	200	Montana	151
Illinois	195	Georgia	150
Washington	192	North Dakota	150
Kansas	189	Arizona	149
Colorado	186	Missouri	149
Texas	184	South Carolina	147
Delaware	183	New Mexico	144
Ohio	183	Indiana	142
Wisconsin	183	Iowa	142
Utah	181	New Hampshire	142
Maryland	180	Nebraska	138
Oregon	180	South Dakota	131
Virgin Islands	177	Tennessee	131
Nevada	175	Alabama	129
Alaska	171	Mississippi	127
Virginia	169	Louisiana	119
North Carolina	168	Puerto Rico	89
Florida	167	U.S. AVERAGE	180

Source: U.S. Department of Labor 1994c.

dents, replacement rates are on average significantly higher for workers with families when compared to those for single workers at the same wage level.

Most full-year workers who are eligible for UI can receive benefits for up to 26 weeks (30 weeks in two states). In 1993 the actual average duration of benefits for all UI recipients in the United States was 15.9 weeks, ranging from 9.4 weeks in Alabama to 20.8 weeks in the District of Columbia.

FINANCING OF BENEFITS

The UI program is funded through a combination of federal and state UI payroll taxes imposed on employers, with state taxes financing most benefits in the regular UI program. These two taxes are based on separate taxable wage bases and tax rates.

Federal payroll taxes finance both the state and federal administrative costs of the UI system, the federal portion (50 percent) of the Extended Benefits program, and loans that are provided to states whose trust funds are insolvent.[4]

The federal payroll tax, established by FUTA, is currently a gross tax of 6.2 percent on the first $7,000 of an employee's salary. The federal government provides employers with a 5.4 percent credit on this 6.2 percent tax in states that have federally approved UI plans and do not have outstanding federal loans for their UI program. The resulting net tax rate of 0.8 percent (or $56 per worker earning $7,000 or more) provides a strong incentive for states to comply with the federal requirements; in the absence of the credit, the cost would be $434 per worker.

State payroll taxes are levied on employers to finance the state's regular UI benefits, as well as the state portion of the Extended Benefits program.[5] States must maintain a state taxable wage base that equals or exceeds the federal taxable wage base in order to receive the 5.4 maximum percent *federal* tax credit. As of January 1994, 41 states had a taxable wage base above $7,000, and the remaining 12 states had a taxable wage base of $7,000. The low taxable wage base tends to impose the burden of UI taxes disproportionately on employers of low-wage workers. To the extent that employers pass on a portion of the tax to their employees, low-wage workers, who are also the least likely to receive UI, are likely to be hurt by this regressive tax structure.

State taxes are required by federal laws to be "experience-rated." This means that the tax rate assessed on each employer is determined, to some degree, by the benefits that have been collected by that employer's former employees. Employers pay the assigned UI tax rate on the amount of their employees' taxable wages (i.e., those wages that fall below the state taxable wage base).

---

[4]Federal taxes also finance the Internal Revenue Service costs associated with the collection of these taxes, the U.S. Employment Service, and some data collection efforts.
[5]In four states—Alaska, New Jersey, Pennsylvania, and West Virginia—there are provisions to tax employees in addition to employers.

Within a state the entire schedule of tax rates is often adjusted either up or down on the basis of the state trust fund balance. During recessionary periods states with inadequate trust fund balances often shift the schedule of tax rates upward; conversely, during periods of low unemployment states tend to shift their tax schedules downward.

As a result of the range of both state taxable wage bases and tax rates, state taxes paid range from zero for some employers to more than $900 per worker for other employers. In 1993 the average *state* taxes collected per covered worker varied from $36 in South Dakota to $479 in Rhode Island.

RECEIPT OF UNEMPLOYMENT INSURANCE BENEFITS

Two facts characterize the receipt of Unemployment Insurance (UI) benefits in the United States. First, these benefits are received by a small and declining minority of the unemployed. Second, white men are significantly more likely to receive UI benefits than are white women, black women, or black men. The discussion that follows puts these facts into perspective.

TRENDS IN UNEMPLOYMENT

Historically women have experienced higher overall unemployment rates than men. During recessions, however, the gap between men's and women's unemployment rates has tended to narrow somewhat. A major reason for this is that women have been underrepresented in cyclically sensitive industries such as construction and manufacturing (see Figure III-1).

In the 1980s the gap between men's and women's unemployment rates began to close. In fact, since 1986 women's unemployment rates have remained slightly below men's. Although the recession of 1990–91 probably explains a part of this reversal, it does not appear to explain all of it.

These overall trends in unemployment mask major differences across racial and ethnic groups. Whites experience substantially less unemployment than do the two minority groups for which data are consistently available: blacks and Hispanics. Between these two groups, blacks experience higher unemployment rates than Hispanics. With some slight variations the pattern of women's and men's unemployment rates within racial groups mirrors that of the overall unemployment rates for women and men (see Figure III-2).

Figure III-1 · UNEMPLOYMENT RATES BY SEX, 1945–1993[1]

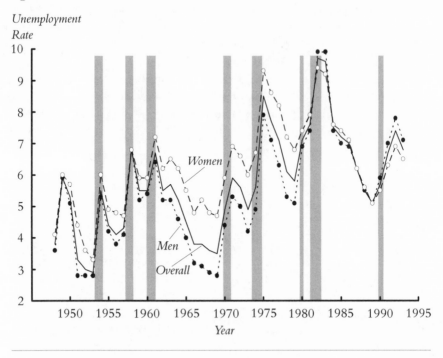

Unemployment Rate

Year

---

[1]Shaded regions represent recession from peak to trough.

Source: Council of Economic Advisors 1994 and U.S. Department of Labor 1994c.

REASONS FOR UNEMPLOYMENT

Unemployed persons are classified into four major categories: job losers, job leavers, reentrants, and new entrants. As is discussed in detail later, new entrants to the labor force are ineligible for UI; since they have no prior earnings, they cannot meet the program's monetary eligibility requirements. Similarly, reentrants to the labor force do not qualify for UI unless their absence from the labor force was brief. Depending on the exact circumstances under which they left their jobs, some job leavers may qualify for UI.

As Table III-2 shows, reasons for unemployment vary by gender and race. Men are more likely to be job losers than women are. Among those age 20 and older, in 1994, 63 percent of unemployed men were job losers, while only 44 percent of women were in this category. Unemployed women are much more likely to be new entrants or reentrants to the labor force than are unemployed men. Relative to unemployed whites, blacks are less likely to be job losers but are more likely to be new entrants or reentrants to the labor force.

Figure III-2 · UNEMPLOYMENT RATES BY GENDER AND RACE, 1955–1993[1]

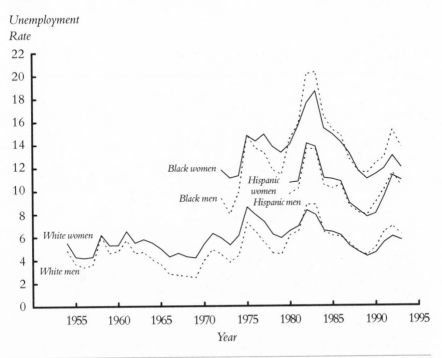

Unemployment Rate

Black women

Hispanic women

Black men

Hispanic men

White women

White men

Year

[1]Data for black men and women not available before 1972. Data for Hispanic men and women not available before 1980.

Source: Bureau of Labor Statistics 1989, 1992, 1993, and 1994a.

Since its inception the UI program has been designed to provide partial, temporary wage replacement for workers with a substantial labor force attachment who have lost their jobs through no fault of their own. Women (and minorities to a lesser extent) are more likely than men to be either new entrants or reentrants to the labor force. Consequently, the UI system is simply less relevant for unemployed women, a point that is discussed in detail below.

TRENDS IN RECEIPT OF UNEMPLOYMENT INSURANCE

In 1993 official Department of Labor statistics indicated that 31.5 percent of unemployed workers were among the "insured unemployed" (U.S. Department of Labor 1994c and Council of Economic Advisers 1994). Although this statistic is widely interpreted as the ratio of the unemployed who

Table III-2 · REASON FOR UNEMPLOYMENT BY SEX AND RACE, DECEMBER 1993[1] (percent distribution)

Reason for Unemployment	Total	Women			Men		
		All Races	White	Black	All Races	White	Black
Job losers	54	44	47	36	63	66	55
Job leavers	11	11	12	8	10	11	8
Reentrants	32	41	38	50	25	22	34
New entrants	3	4	3	6	2	1	3
Total percentage	100	100	100	100	100	100	100

[1]Data are for individuals 20 years of age and older. Percentages may not add to 100 because of rounding.

Source: Bureau of Labor Statistics December 1994c.

receive UI benefits to the total pool of unemployed persons, it actually overstates UI receipt. The weekly official announcement of "insured unemployment" is based on all UI *claimants,* rather than on UI *recipients.*

Some of these claimants have not received their first UI checks. Other claimants will ultimately be found ineligible for UI and will be denied benefits. Still others are temporarily ineligible; for example, when a claimant is determined to be unavailable for work (e.g., because of caregiving responsibilities), benefits are withheld until the claimant once again becomes available for work. If each of these three groups of nonrecipients is excluded from the official count, the percentage of the unemployed who actually received UI benefits in 1993 was only 28.7 percent.

The rate of receipt of UI among the unemployed has not always been this low. Figure III-3, which plots the time trend in the percentage of the unemployed who receive UI, indicates that UI has become less relevant to the unemployed with the passage of time.

The percentage of the unemployed who receive UI benefits tends to cycle up and down in inverse relation to the economy. During periods of relative prosperity a lower percentage of the unemployed have been laid off from their jobs and a higher percentage have quit their jobs. Since relatively few of the unemployed who have quit their jobs are eligible for UI receipt, a lower percentage of the unemployed are eligible for UI receipt during periods of low unemployment. During recessions a high percentage of the unemployed have been laid off from their jobs, increasing the likelihood that they will be eligible for UI. Despite these ups and downs, the overall trend in UI receipt among the unemployed is clearly downward.

Figure III-3 · RECIPIENCY RATE FOR REGULAR STATE UNEMPLOY-
MENT INSURANCE PROGRAMS, 1947–1993[1]

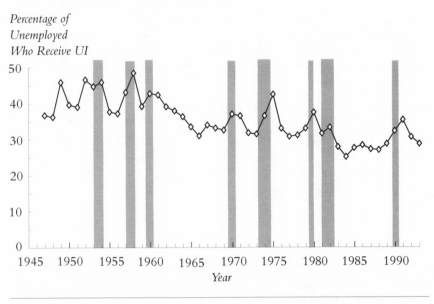

[1]Shaded regions represent recession from peak to trough. Calculation based on weeks
compensated, not weeks claimed.

Source: Council of Economic Advisers 1994 and U.S. Department of Labor 1994c.

The 1980s was an anomalous period in the UI program's history, even
given its overall downward trend. During a very sharp recession in 1981 the
ratio of the unemployed receiving UI plummeted—precisely when it would
have been expected to increase because of the high percentage of the unemployed who had been laid off from (rather than quit) their jobs.

While much of the decline in the utilization of the system in the early
1980s remains unexplained, some evidence suggests that changes in state laws
were an important source of the decline. Because many states entered the
recession of 1981 with unusually low levels of reserves in their UI trust funds,
some states chose to restrict eligibility for UI by raising the minimum earnings necessary to qualify for the program (in addition to or instead of raising state payroll taxes imposed on employers). States also tightened other
aspects of eligibility, increasingly disqualifying individuals for misconduct or
refusal of suitable work. While some of these restrictions represented voluntary choices on the part of the states, others were the result of financial
incentives that the federal government created (which still remain in effect)
for the states to crack down on their UI systems.

THE RACIAL AND GENDER COMPOSITION OF UNEMPLOYMENT INSURANCE RECIPIENTS

The percentage of the unemployed who receive UI benefits at some point during their unemployment spell is reported in Table III-3. These figures, which are based on an analysis of the Survey of Income and Program Participation (SIPP), cover unemployment spells that occurred between 1989 and 1992.

Although much of the UI system's long-term decline—that which occurred prior to the 1980s—remains unexplained, the results summarized in Table III-3 point to the broad outlines of the system's downward trend. Unemployed workers are more likely to receive UI benefits if they:

- earn relatively high wages;
- work in the manufacturing sector;
- work full time for the full year;
- are members of a union;
- live in the northeastern part of the country; and
- are job losers rather than job leavers.

Since the percentage of the workforce that is in possession of these attributes has declined, so, too, has the percentage of the unemployed workforce that receives UI benefits. And since each of these attributes is more likely to describe men than women, it follows that unemployed men are substantially more likely to receive UI benefits than are unemployed women. For similar reasons, whites are more likely to receive benefits than are blacks.

Table III-4 reports the average weekly UI benefit payment, as well as UI replacement rates (i.e., the percentage of an unemployed worker's lost earnings that are replaced by benefits) based on an analysis of the SIPP. The benefit formulas of many states explicitly calculate benefits as a fixed percentage of an unemployed worker's previous earnings, up to a maximum benefit amount. This cap has the effect of lowering the replacement rate for higher-wage individuals. As a result, men have higher average weekly benefit amounts but lower replacement rates than women (since men's average wages are higher than women's). Similarly, because whites have higher average earnings than blacks, whites' weekly benefit amounts are higher, but their replacement rates are lower, than blacks' weekly benefit amounts.

Table III-3 · UNEMPLOYED WORKERS WHO RECEIVED UNEMPLOY-
MENT INSURANCE BY SELECTED CHARACTERISTICS, SEX, AND
RACE, 1989–1991[1] (in percentages)

		Women		Men	
Characteristic	*Total[2]*	*White*	*Black*	*White*	*Black*
Overall	27	21	18	34	25
Hourly wage rate					
Less than $5.00	12	12	20	9	24
$5.00 to $7.49	31	31	40	28	38
$7.50 to $10.00	50	48	56	53	40
More than $10.00	63	39	—[3]	70	67
Poverty status prior to unemployment					
In poverty	16	12	12	22	17
Not in poverty	30	23	25	36	27
Occupation/industry					
Blue-collar, manufacturing	56	50	65	58	55
Blue-collar, nonmanufacturing	41	36	45	42	33
White-collar, manufacturing	56	50	30	62	—[3]
White-collar, nonmanufacturing	25	22	—[3]	32	38
Service	15	16	13	14	11
Hours of work					
Full-time, full-year	51	44	60	54	51
Part-time, full-year	27	24	37	30	27
Full-time, part-year	33	27	32	37	41
Part-time, part-year	10	11	8	10	4
Union status					
Member	61	42	48	68	57
Nonmember	29	25	25	33	30
Region of the country					
Northeast	38	30	28	45	44
South	21	18	19	26	18
Midwest	26	18	9	35	21
West	28	20	7	35	29
Reason for unemployment					
Job loser	44	40	41	49	35
Job leaver	8	6	11	10	19

[1]Because of missing data, less than half of the sample was used.

[2]"Total" includes only the four gender/race categories in the table.

[3]Estimate not available because of small sample size.

Source: Bureau of the Census 1990.

Table III-4 · UNEMPLOYMENT INSURANCE BENEFIT LEVELS BY SEX AND RACE, 1989–1992[1]

		Women		Men	
	Total[2]	White	Black	White	Black
Average weekly benefit amount	$169	$151	$134	$185	$149
Replacement rate	52%	57%	60%	49%	50%

[1]Simulated Unemployment Insurance weekly benefit amounts, not self-reported amounts.
[2]"Total" includes only the four gender/race categories in the table.

Source: Bureau of the Census 1990.

ELIGIBILITY FOR UNEMPLOYMENT INSURANCE BENEFITS

To be eligible for Unemployment Insurance (UI) benefits, an unemployed individual must meet certain monetary eligibility requirements and satisfy a variety of nonmonetary eligibility conditions. Both these categories of requirements, as well as the implications for women and minorities, are discussed below.

MONETARY ELIGIBILITY REQUIREMENTS

Monetary eligibility requirements are the mechanisms used by states to restrict UI eligibility to unemployed individuals with a substantial labor force attachment. These requirements, which vary from state to state, typically have three components.

First, earnings during the base period must exceed some minimum level.[6] Because earnings are equal to an individual's hourly wage rate multiplied by the number of hours worked, meeting the earnings requirement is most difficult for those who work at low-wage or part-time jobs. An individual working at the minimum wage ($4.25 per hour), for example, must work twice as many hours to qualify for UI as another individual who is employed at $8.50 per hour.

Second, most states also have a high-quarter earnings requirement, which specifies the minimum earnings level that an individual must have within at

[6]The base period is defined in most states to be the first four of the most recently completed five calendar quarters.

least one calendar quarter in the base period. Some individuals whose base period earnings are sufficient to qualify for UI do not have sufficient earnings in any single quarter to satisfy the high-quarter earnings requirement.

The high-quarter earnings requirement can be particularly problematic for part-time workers, especially for those who work at the minimum wage. For example, an individual working full time at the minimum wage for six months would qualify for UI benefits in all but one state. However, a person working half time at the minimum wage for 12 months would not qualify for benefits in nine states. In addition, although these two individuals have identical earnings in the base period, the first person satisfies the high-quarter earnings requirement in all states, but the second person does not satisfy the requirement in seven states. Arguably, the second individual's labor force attachment is at least as substantial as that of the first individual.

A third type of monetary eligibility requirement is that most states require that an individual have earnings in at least two of the four base period calendar quarters. This minimum quarters requirement has the effect of disqualifying recent entrants to the labor force who lose their jobs within the first three months of employment. The requirement can also result in the disqualification of a worker who has experienced one spell of unemployment, found a job, and then lost that job within three months. Although such workers may have a long history of labor force attachment, two spells of unemployment during one base year may make it impossible for them to qualify for UI.

Both together and separately these monetary eligibility requirements are designed to ensure that the UI program is available only to workers who have a substantial attachment to the labor force. However, because both the base period and high-quarter requirements are expressed in terms of earnings, rather than hours worked, their effect weighs most heavily on low-wage workers.[7] The high-quarter earnings requirement is most likely to disqualify low-wage, part-time workers, while the minimum quarters requirement is most likely to disqualify those who have recently entered or reentered the labor force.

Each of these requirements is likely to have a disproportionate disqualifying impact on women and minorities. Relative to men, women are more likely to be new entrants or reentrants to the labor force and/or to work in low-wage, part-time jobs. The same is true for blacks relative to whites. Therefore, women and minorities are less likely to qualify for UI benefits.

---

[7]Washington State is an exception; its base period earnings requirement is expressed in terms of hours worked.

Table III-5 · UNEMPLOYED WORKERS WHO MEET THE UNEMPLOY-
MENT INSURANCE MONETARY ELIGIBILITY REQUIREMENTS IN
THEIR STATE BY SELECTED CHARACTERISTICS, SEX, AND RACE,
1989–1992[1] (in percentages)

| Characteristic[1] | Total | Women | | Men | |
		White	Black	White	Black
Overall	56	54	35	64	47
Hourly wage rate					
Less than $5.00	56	58	54	54	57
$5.00 to $7.49	76	78	72	74	81
$7.50 to $10.00	92	91	95	93	90
More than $10.00	93	91	—[2]	94	95
Occupation/industry[3]					
Blue-collar, manufacturing	83	81	88	85	75
Blue-collar, nonmanufacturing	75	72	—[2]	75	76
White-collar, manufacturing	84	82	86	86	—[2]
White-collar, nonmanufacturing	70	70	—[2]	78	66
Service	55	57	47	58	45
Hours of work					
Full-time, full-year	93	95	96	92	92
Part-time, full year	88	91	89	86	84
Full-time, part-year	67	67	58	67	70
Part-time, part-year	42	45	37	42	32

[1]Because of missing data, less than half of the overall sample was used.
[2]Estimate not available because of small sample size.
[3]List of occupations/industries is not an exhaustive list.
Source: Bureau of the Census 1990.

The percentage of the unemployed who meet all of the UI program's monetary eligibility requirements is summarized in Table III-5.

NONMONETARY ELIGIBILITY REQUIREMENTS

A high percentage of unemployed workers who have worked for a full year
(either part time or full time) prior to their unemployment satisfy the monetary eligibility requirements for the Unemployment Insurance (UI) program.
Relatively few of the unemployed, however, actually receive UI benefits. A
part of the discrepancy between monetary eligibility and receipt of benefits
results from a variety of state nonmonetary eligibility requirements.
    One category of nonmonetary eligibility requirements pertains to the cir-

cumstances surrounding the unemployed individual's separation from his or her job; these requirements govern whether an unemployed individual will be determined to be eligible for UI. The second category relates to unemployed individuals' circumstances while they collect UI benefits; these requirements must be met on an ongoing basis for them to remain eligible for benefits.

Initial Nonmonetary Eligibility Conditions

Unemployed workers must meet three initial conditions to qualify for benefits. First, workers must not be unemployed as a result of a labor dispute. Second, workers who have quit must have done so for "good cause." Third, workers must not have been discharged because of misconduct.

The first of these conditions is likely to be more problematic for men than women since men are more likely to belong to unions. However, the second condition—voluntary separation without good cause—is likely to be more problematic for women than men.

A recent survey of the 53 state UI programs reveals wide variation in how voluntary separation for good cause is defined.[8] For example, when an individual leaves a job because the employer has imposed new employment circumstances (e.g., a change in work hours), that individual is eligible for UI in 15 states, potentially eligible in 25 states (depending on the exact circumstance), and ineligible in 13 states. Although changes in the hours that an individual is required to work could prove to be burdensome (especially for individuals with caregiving responsibilities), many states make no allowance for these burdens.

According to the state survey, most states make allowance for sexual or other discriminatory harassment to be good cause for quitting; however, only a few states include this allowance in their legislation or regulations. This omission is likely to be most problematic for minorities and women.

There are three additional aspects of the definition of good cause that are likely to be troublesome for women. The first is that a pregnant woman who leaves her job is likely to be found ineligible for UI unless she left as the result of a physician's advice. Second, although few states have explicit statutes denying benefits when an individual leaves a job because of marital obligations (including quitting a job in order to follow a spouse to a new location), most states do not consider these reasons to be good cause. Third, individuals who are employed by temporary agencies and do not accept subsequent assignments are often ineligible for UI (in at least 20 states);

---

[8]The Interstate Conference of Employment Security Agencies recently conducted a survey of the states, which provides more complete, current information than was previously available regarding nonmonetary eligibility conditions. For more detail on the survey results, see Chapter Eight in Advisory Council on Unemployment Compensation (1995).

women are more likely than men to be employed in these types of temporary jobs.

In the vast majority of states workers who quit their jobs without good cause are ineligible for UI for the entire duration of their unemployment. In five states, however, such individuals are allowed to receive benefits after a waiting period (typically five to 10 weeks).

Continuing Nonmonetary Eligibility Conditions

Once a determination has been made that an unemployed worker is eligible for Unemployment Insurance (UI), that individual must satisfy a variety of conditions on an ongoing basis to maintain eligibility. In particular, the person must: (1) be "able and available for work," (2) be actively seeking employment, and (3) not refuse "suitable work."

The first and third of these conditions tend to be more problematic for women than men. At least 30 states consider an individual unavailable for work if the person reports that he or she is seeking part-time (rather than full-time) work—even if the individual has a history of part-time work and meets all of the state's monetary eligibility requirements. A small number of states may, under some circumstances, define someone seeking part-time work as being available for work. But only one state (Pennsylvania) would consistently define such an individual as being available for work under most circumstances. This is clearly a problem for part-time workers; 28 percent of employed women were part-time workers in 1994 (Bureau of Labor Statistics 1994a).

Other aspects of determining an unemployed individual's availability for work can cause difficulties for low-wage workers (who are disproportionately likely to be women or minorities). For example, individuals might be found to be unavailable for work if they cannot work the night shift because public transportation is not available late in the evening or early in the morning. This determination is likely to weigh most heavily on low-wage individuals who do not have access to cars.

The problem has more serious consequences, however, if the person is found to have "refused suitable work" without good cause. These types of determinations are especially grave because the unemployed individual is often disqualified from receiving UI benefits for the remainder of his or her spell of unemployment (ineligible in 40 states). In most states individuals are found to have refused suitable work if they decline a full-time job offer because of family circumstances (ineligible in 28 states) or if the offer was for full-time work and they were seeking part-time work (ineligible in 37 states). Once again, these conditions are likely to be more problematic for women than for men.

It is not possible to determine the precise extent to which this array of nonmonetary eligibility requirements affects receipt of UI benefits because some individuals may choose not to receive UI even though they are eligible. Table III-6, however, does provide some insights.

Among the unemployed who meet their states' monetary eligibility requirements, white women are less likely to receive UI benefits than are either black men or women or white men. Among both men and women, those who have quit their jobs are far less likely to receive UI benefits than those who have lost their jobs. And eligible part-time workers are less likely to receive benefits than full-time workers.

The analysis reported here does not make clear distinctions between those

Table III-6 · UNEMPLOYED WORKERS WHO RECEIVE UNEMPLOY-MENT INSURANCE AS A PERCENTAGE OF THOSE MEETING THE UNEMPLOYMENT INSURANCE MONETARY ELIGIBILITY REQUIRE-MENTS IN THEIR STATE BY SELECTED CHARACTERISTICS, SEX, AND RACE, 1989–1992[1]

		Women		Men	
Characteristic	*Total*[2]	*White*	*Black*	*White*	*Black*
Overall	45	37	48	51	49
Poverty status prior to unemployment					
In poverty	40	30	45	44	57
Not in poverty	46	38	49	52	48
Hours of work					
Full-time, full-year	54	45	62	57	55
Part-time, full-year	30	27	—[3]	34	—[3]
Full-time, part-year	47	38	49	51	55
Part-time, part-year	22	23	20	23	11
Region of the country					
Northeast	62	55	59	66	69
South	39	32	50	40	37
Midwest	44	34	31	51	53
West	42	30	—[3]	50	55
Reason for unemployment					
Job loser	58	54	63	61	49
Job leaver	14	9	24	15	31

[1]Because of missing data, less than half of the overall sample was used.

[2]"Total" includes only the four gender/race categories in the table.

[3]Estimate not available because of small sample size.

Source: Bureau of the Census 1990.

who are eligible for UI benefits and choose not to receive them and those who are ineligible for benefits as the result of nonmonetary eligibility criteria. The results presented in Table III-6 are, however, consistent with the interpretation that much nonreceipt of benefits is involuntary. UI receipt among unemployed workers who met the eligibility requirements and were poor prior to becoming unemployed is substantially lower than among those who were not poor prior to unemployment for all groups except black men. It seems reasonable to assume that unemployed workers who are poor would choose to receive UI benefits if they were actually deemed eligible by the state. It is also reasonable to assume, therefore, that at least some (perhaps much) nonreceipt of UI benefits is the result of nonmonetary eligibility restrictions rather than choice.

Overall, approximately 18 percent of the unemployed are in poverty during the period in which they are unemployed. This is true for both the unemployed who receive UI and those who do not. Without UI benefits, however, one-third of UI recipients would be poor (see Table III-7). Con-

Table III-7 · FAMILY POVERTY RATE AMONG UNEMPLOYMENT INSURANCE RECIPIENTS BY SELECTED CHARACTERISTICS, 1989–1992[1] (in percentages)

Family Characteristic	Rates in Absence of UI Benefits	Rates Including UI Benefits	Reduction in Poverty Rates Attributable to UI Receipt
Overall	33	18	15
Race and sex			
White women	26	13	13
Black women	38	25	13
White men	36	19	17
Black men	33	25	8
Number of earners			
Working spouse	18	9	9
Nonworking spouse	46	29	17
No spouse	41	21	20
Number of children			
None	31	14	17
1 or 2	32	19	13
3 or more	47	37	10

[1]Simulated weekly benefit amounts, not self-reported amounts.

Source: Bureau of the Census 1990.

sequently, UI reduces poverty rates of those who receive it by approximately 15 percentage points.

CONCLUSION

A small and declining fraction of the unemployed receive Unemployment Insurance (UI) benefits. White men are significantly more likely to be eligible for and to receive benefits than are white women, black women, or black men. While some of the unemployed may choose not to receive UI benefits, many are involuntary nonrecipients.

Two major categories of obstacles prevent the unemployed from receiving UI benefits. First, some states set their monetary eligibility requirements sufficiently high that many part-time workers are unable to qualify for the program. This problem is especially pronounced for low-wage workers, a disproportionate percentage of whom are women and minorities.

A variety of nonmonetary eligibility requirements constitute the second category of obstacles. These requirements relate to both the circumstances by which an individual becomes unemployed and the individual's ongoing circumstances during unemployment. Individuals who quit their jobs must have done so for "good cause" or they will typically be ineligible for UI. Once eligibility has been established, the unemployed individual must be available for work, must be actively seeking work, and must not refuse a suitable job offer.

Some states' nonmonetary eligibility rules pose special problems for women and minorities. For example, some states do not have statutes that explicitly recognize harassment as a "good cause" for quitting a job. Other states disqualify individuals who are seeking part-time work from receiving UI. Many states disqualify an individual who has refused a job offer for night shift work (perhaps because of the unavailability of public transportation or child care). These, and a wide range of other nonmonetary determinations, are likely to disqualify a disproportionately high percentage of women and minorities from receiving UI benefits.

The current UI system is patently unfair to low-wage workers; with the exception of one state (Washington), states' monetary eligibility requirements dictate that low-wage workers must work more hours than high-wage workers to qualify for UI benefits.[9] Similarly, some states' nonmonetary el-

---

[9]Using hours of work rather than earnings in the base period as the basis for determining eligibility may create some administrative difficulties. The State of Washington, however, has demonstrated that it is possible to overcome them.

igibility requirements have the effect of disqualifying disproportionately high percentages of unemployed individuals who work at low-wage or part-time jobs. Both separately and together, the monetary and nonmonetary eligibility requirements disqualify large numbers of women and minorities from receiving UI benefits. The inevitable result is an expansion of welfare programs since many of the workers who are ineligible to receive UI end up on the welfare rolls.

From the states' perspective, this outcome may make sense since the states pay for the vast majority of the expenses associated with UI, but the federal government picks up much of the tab for means-tested programs, such as Aid to Families with Dependent Children. Although the outcome may be rational, it nonetheless discriminates against individuals who have the misfortune of earning low wages.

The establishment of minimum federal standards for making determinations of both monetary and nonmonetary eligibility determinations for UI benefits could correct these inequities within the UI system. These standards should specify that workers with a substantial labor force attachment be able to satisfy all aspects of a state's monetary eligibility requirements (e.g., both the base period and high-quarter requirements). And nonmonetary eligibility standards should seek to ensure that part-time workers and workers with caregiving responsibilities are treated equitably.

FOUR

STRUGGLING TO SURVIVE: WELFARE, WORK, AND LONE MOTHERS

Katherine McFate

HIGHLIGHTS

AID TO FAMILIES WITH DEPENDENT CHILDREN (AFDC) is the nation's primary source of cash assistance for needy children. Established in 1935 as part of the Social Security Act, it was originally designed to allow widowed mothers to stay at home and care for their children. However, as the program expanded its size and coverage in the 1960s and 1970s, it came to include a larger number of poor minority women, and work requirements were imposed on recipients. These requirements have become the major focus of reforms since the 1980s.

- In the 1980s states experimented with a variety of welfare-to-work programs designed to help the heads of AFDC households move into the private labor market. These programs were only modestly successful in improving the employment and earnings of recipients and helped very few become entirely "self-sufficient."
- Current reform proposals argue that setting strict limits on the amount of time a family can receive AFDC and imposing work requirements on heads of households is the only way to end welfare dependency. However, these proposals ignore the facts that many welfare recipients already mix government cash assistance and paid work and that the vast majority of AFDC users cycle on and off the program.
- The labor market prospects of AFDC recipients are poor. Recent research shows that average hourly wages for current and former AFDC recipients

are barely better than minimum wage ($4.25 per hour), that most jobs last less than a year, and that the majority of these jobs are clustered at the bottom of the occupational ladder. Moreover, they offer little opportunity for wage increases; wages improve only slightly with age or years of experience.

- For the majority of low-skilled lone mothers supporting children, continuous self-sufficiency is impossible as the result of the precarious and low-paid character of the employment available to them and the limited support services (e.g., child support payments, child care, health care, education and training programs) to which they have access.

- Work programs not only fail to address these problems but actively worsen the economic prospects of poor single-parent families by further depressing wages of low-skilled workers, reducing the resources available to poor families, and preventing families from developing the human capital to improve their earnings potential.

- The problem of long-term dependency cannot be solved within the welfare system. To promote long-term self-sufficiency among families headed by lone mothers, the government must ensure that child care, health care, and child support are available to these families as they move off welfare and as long as they remain in low-paying jobs. Improving the long-term employment and earnings prospects of low-income mothers will require major changes in our educational system, a more equitable wage distribution, residential desegregation coupled with vastly improved metropolitan-wide public transportation systems, and greater public investment in real job creation.

AN OVERVIEW OF INCOME SUPPORT FOR THE POOR

The United States has a meager system of income support compared with other industrialized nations (Esping-Anderson 1990; McFate, Lawson, and Wilson 1995). In countries with a strong union movement or powerful labor party, income support for jobless individuals is viewed as an entitlement of citizenship; in the United States cash assistance is a right earned by work or by one's status in a group society feels should be exempt from work expectations.

Consequently, no *federal* system of income support exists for nonelderly, able-bodied adults without children. Because of the strict eligibility requirements that govern Unemployment Insurance, fewer than four in 10 unemployed persons in the United States today actually receive unemployment benefits (*see* Chapter Three). Moreover, this assistance is time-limited: except in unusual circumstances, unemployment benefits are limited to six months.

Aid to Families with Dependent Children (AFDC), the program most Americans refer to as "welfare," is available only to indigent families with children. Less than half of all poor Americans receive assistance from AFDC (U.S. Congress 1994). Established by the Social Security Act in 1935, AFDC was designed to provide cash income assistance to needy children without fathers so their mothers could care for them at home instead of putting them in orphanages. AFDC was designed to allow lone mothers, most of whom were widowed or deserted, to stay at home instead of working.

For the first 25 years of the program two-parent families were excluded from receiving support unless the father was incapacitated. In 1961 federal rules were changed to allow states to give AFDC to children in two-parent households if the family head was unemployed. However, only half the states extended income support to this group (until a 1988 federal reform mandated that they do so).[1] AFDC for Unemployed Parents (AFDC-UP) represents only a small portion of the overall participant population (about seven percent of all AFDC families in 1993). Thus AFDC continues to be overwhelmingly comprised of poor families headed by lone mothers, the group it was designed to serve.

Although AFDC contains a number of federal rules and requirements, a great deal of state flexibility is built into its design. Each state sets its own benefit level according to its own evaluation of local living costs. This results in a wide variation in benefit levels: Mississippi provides only $120 a month for a family of three, for example, while Alaska provides $923 a month to such a family. In general, southern states, which have higher poverty rates, have lower benefits than states in other areas of the country. The median AFDC benefit is a mere $366 a month, about half the official poverty level for a family of three. Even when combined with Food Stamps, AFDC benefits typically provide only about 70 percent of the official poverty rate (see Table IV-1).

---

[1]The Family Support Act of 1988 mandated that all states establish AFDC for Unemployed Parents (AFDC-UP). However, states that did not previously have such a program can limit benefits to six months out of the year. And under current law the family is eligible only if the primary wage earner has a stable work history (i.e., was able to qualify for unemployment compensation the year before applying for AFDC) or worked six or more quarters in the previous three and one-half years before applying for AFDC. Also, if the primary wage earner works more than 100 hours a month, the family is disqualified. Thus, even with the 1988 reforms, AFDC contains provisions that discourage stable marriages to men with unstable employment records.

Table IV-1 · LEVEL OF SUPPORT GIVEN TO A POOR FAMILY OF THREE BY STATE, 1994.

State	Maximum AFDC Benefits (in dollars)	Maximum Food Stamp Benefits (in dollars)	Maximum Combined Food Stamps & AFDC Benefits (in dollars)	Maximum Combined Benefits as a Percentage of Federal Poverty Level	Benefits as a Percentage of Full-Time Federal Minimum-Wage Earnings
Alabama	164	295	459	.48	.67
Alaska	923	285	1,208	1.01	1.78
Arizona	347	292	639	.67	.94
Arkansas	204	295	499	.52	.73
California	607	214	821	.86	1.21
Colorado	356	289	645	.67	.95
Connecticut	680	192	872	.91	1.28
Delaware	338	295	633	.66	.93
District of Columbia	420	270	690	.72	1.01
Florida	303	295	598	.62	.88
Georgia	280	295	575	.60	.84
Hawaii	712	422	1,134	1.03	1.67
Idaho	317	295	612	.64	.90
Illinois	367	291	658	.69	.97
Indiana	288	295	583	.61	.86
Iowa	426	268	694	.72	1.02
Kansas	429	284	713	.74	1.05
Kentucky	228	295	523	.55	.77
Louisiana	190	295	485	.51	.71
Maine	418	271	689	.72	1.01
Maryland	366	295	661	.69	.97
Massachusetts	579	222	801	.83	1.18
Michigan	459	258	717	.75	1.05
Minnesota	532	236	768	.80	1.13
Mississippi	120	295	415	.43	.61
Missouri	292	295	587	.61	.86
Montana	401	276	677	.71	.99

(continued)

Table IV-1 (continued)

State	Maximum AFDC Benefits (in dollars)	Maximum Food Stamp Benefits (in dollars)	Maximum Combined Food Stamps & AFDC Benefits (in dollars)	Maximum Combined Benefits as a Percentage of Federal Poverty Level	Benefits as a Percentage of Full-Time Federal Minimum-Wage Earnings
Nebraska	364	287	651	.68	.96
Nevada	348	292	640	.67	.94
New Hampshire	550	231	781	.81	1.15
New Jersey	424	276	700	.73	1.03
New Mexico	357	289	646	.67	.95
New York	577	239	816	.85	1.20
North Carolina	272	295	567	.59	.83
North Dakota	409	273	682	.71	1.00
Ohio	341	295	636	.66	.93
Oklahoma	324	295	619	.65	.91
Oregon	460	293	753	.78	1.11
Pennsylvania	421	270	691	.72	1.02
Rhode Island	554	268	822	.86	1.21
South Carolina	200	295	495	.52	.73
South Dakota	417	271	688	.72	1.01
Tennessee	185	295	480	.50	.70
Texas	184	295	479	.50	.70
Utah	414	272	686	.72	1.01
Vermont	638	205	843	.88	1.24
Virginia	354	290	644	.67	.95
Washington	546	258	804	.84	1.18
West Virginia	249	295	544	.57	.80
Wisconsin	517	241	758	.79	1.11
Wyoming	360	288	648	.68	.95
Median	366	295	661	.69	.97

Source: U.S. Congress 1994.

Although the federal government does not set benefit levels, the funding formula for AFDC helps redistribute income across states. The federal government provides between 50 and 80 percent of the costs of benefits; the matching rate is inversely related to state per capita income. Thus the poor in poor states are dependent on federal funds for a larger proportion of their income than are the poor in wealthier states.

Unlike other federal entitlements, AFDC benefits are *not* automatically adjusted for inflation, and most states have allowed the value of AFDC grants to decline over time; the real value of the median grant has declined by over 47 percent since 1970 (U.S. Congress 1994). However, this decline has been partially offset by the rising value of Food Stamp benefits. More than 87 percent of AFDC families receive Food Stamps, a program that was federalized in 1972. Food Stamp benefits are fully paid by the federal government and *do* increase with inflation.[2] Still, the combined median value of AFDC and Food Stamp benefits has fallen by about 25 percent since 1979.

AFDC participation makes a family automatically eligible for Medicaid and some housing programs. As health care costs have skyrocketed, access to medical care has become an important concern for many poor families. There are widespread reports that the fear of losing Medicaid benefits keeps many mothers from leaving AFDC and brings others back to the system when they require medical assistance.

Although AFDC participation does qualify an individual for some low-income housing programs, two-thirds of AFDC recipients do *not* receive housing subsidies and have to use their AFDC checks to pay rent. Only nine percent of AFDC families live in public housing; another quarter receive housing subsidies (U.S. Congress 1994).

CHANGES IN THE AFDC POPULATION

The size and characteristics of the AFDC caseload have changed dramatically since 1960. Between 1960 and 1970 the AFDC caseload tripled (for reasons discussed in the next section). Caseloads then remained fairly stable until the late 1980s, when they increased again. Today almost five million families containing 9.4 million children receive income support from AFDC. This represents about 14 percent of all American children and five percent of the entire U.S. population (U.S. Congress 1994).

[2]Unfortunately the interaction between AFDC and Food Stamps creates a disincentive for states to raise benefit levels. The Food Stamp program reduces Food Stamp benefits by $0.30 for each $1.00 of AFDC a family receives.

Nevertheless, the size of the typical AFDC family has fallen since 1969: from four to 2.9 persons. In 1969 about half of all AFDC families contained three or more children. Today only about a quarter of AFDC families have three or more children; 42.5 percent have only one child; another 30.2 percent have two children. The welfare population mirrors the general trend toward smaller families.

The percentage of black families receiving AFDC rose rapidly in the 1960s, peaked in the early 1970s, when African Americans constituted almost 46 percent of AFDC families, and has since declined. Today about 39 percent of AFDC families are white, 37 percent are black, 18 percent are Hispanic, three percent are Asian, and three percent are Native American or other races. Contrary to public stereotypes, blacks have never constituted a majority of AFDC recipients.

The educational attainment of AFDC mothers has improved significantly over the past 20 years. In 1969 three-quarters of AFDC mothers had less than a high school education; less than three percent had attended some college. Today only 43 percent of AFDC mothers have not completed high school and 13 percent have attended some college, but only one percent have graduated from college (U.S. Congress 1994). However, their educational qualifications still lag far behind those of the general population. More than 85 percent of 24- to 35-year-old women today have a high school diploma, and almost one in four has a college degree (Burtless 1995).

Between 1969 and 1992 the average age of AFDC recipients—both household heads and children—declined. In 1969 a quarter of AFDC mothers were over 40 years old and about 40 percent were under 30 years old. Today only 12 percent of AFDC mothers are over 40 years old and 55 percent are under 30 years old. (However, the percentage of teenage mothers has not increased much. Teenage mothers represent only 7.6 percent of all AFDC family heads, up from 6.6 percent in 1969.) The shift in age is primarily the result of a reduction in the number of older mothers and an increase in the number of lone mothers in their twenties. Not surprisingly, as the proportion of young mothers has increased, so has the percentage of young children. About 45 percent of AFDC children are under five years old today, compared with 31 percent in 1969.

Despite these changes in the characteristics of AFDC families, public policy debates on welfare have focused on two developments: the increase in never-married lone mothers and the decrease in the number of welfare mothers who work. In 1969 about half of all AFDC families were headed by a widow or divorced or separated mother; about 28 percent were headed by an unmarried mother. By 1992 these proportions had been reversed: Over half (53 percent) of all AFDC household heads had never married, and less than a third were widowed or divorced. At the same time the percentage of AFDC mothers who were employed full or part time fell by more than half, from 14.5 percent in 1969 to 6.4 percent in 1992 (Administration for Children and Families 1994). These changes, coupled with the changing racial composition of the AFDC population and the fact that a majority of married mothers of young children in the U.S. population overall are now employed, have contributed to the erosion of the public's view of lone mothers as "deserving" of support.

CONDITIONAL ASSISTANCE: MORALITY, RACE, AND WORK

Since their inception, income support programs have been tied to questions of race and morality in the United States. Policymakers have been fearful that providing income support to able-bodied individuals will encourage sloth instead of enterprise, that the promise of income assistance will seduce individuals with weak work ethics into indolence. Fears of the corrupting influence of public aid have kept assistance levels low and Unemployment Insurance time-limited. Such fears also have led political elites to exclude certain categories of low-skilled workers—such as agricultural and domestic workers—from income support programs.

AFDC was initially designed to provide support to the widows or abandoned wives of blue-collar industrial workers. Recipients of assistance were individuals who found themselves without support *through no fault of their own*. Not all husbandless mothers were deemed worthy of such support.

When established, AFDC rules mandated intensive case management of all families enrolled in the program. Children had to be in a certified "suitable home" before they could receive support. Social workers were to investigate and monitor the family's needs and resources and the mother's "moral fitness." These regulations were used to exclude black mothers from receiving AFDC, particularly in the South, before the 1950s and 1960s (Amott 1990; Nelson 1990). As the records from congressional debates on welfare reform in the 1960s show, southern elites were very concerned that if AFDC were available to black mothers, the supply of live-in domestic help might dry up.

As the civil rights movement pushed for the end to all racial discrimination, welfare departments in both South and North were forced to end de facto practices that kept poor black families from receiving assistance. Yet even after African Americans were allowed to receive AFDC, they were often subject to "man in the house" rules and midnight raids to monitor their sexual activity.

Largely in response to such activity the National Welfare Rights Organization (NWRO) was established in the 1960s. As a result of NWRO's organized protests and legal action, AFDC was made more universally available to all poor female-headed families. The number of welfare recipients more than tripled between 1960 and 1970, and the number and proportion of African Americans using the program climbed until the early 1970s.

Black women, particularly poor black women, were at this time much more likely to be in the paid labor force than white women were. The irony was that poor black mothers won the "right" to receive AFDC and become full-time homemakers just as cultural changes (e.g., the women's movement) and economic stagnation conspired to make homemaking less attractive to (white) working- and middle-class mothers. Since the 1960s there has been a steady growth in the proportion of white wives and mothers entering the labor force (*see* Chapter 1).

As the number of black families on the welfare rolls increased, conservatives expressed concern that poor black women might "permanently" choose welfare over work. (Presumably this concern expressed a recognition of the limited and menial quality of the jobs available to black women.) Although AFDC was established to enable poor, white, working-class mothers to stay at home with their children, as the pigment of the welfare population darkened and more middle-class mothers entered the workforce, legislators began to reconsider this objective. In 1967 policymakers began to tamper with "work requirements" for AFDC recipients, and in 1971 new legislation required all able-bodied AFDC recipients to register for the Work Incentive (WIN) program.

The WIN program began with an emphasis on improving the "employability" of AFDC mothers with school-age children. However, only a minority of welfare recipients—less than 20 percent of the eligible population between 1975 and 1980 (Rein 1982)—were served by the program. Sanctions were rarely applied for nonparticipation. Administrative responsibility for the program was divided between the Department of Health, Education, and Welfare and the Labor Department, resulting in turf battles and low accountability. Nonetheless, the WIN program represented the beginning of a growing consensus that school-age children did not need full-time, stay-at-home mothers and that AFDC should encourage some mothers to work, at least part time.

In the early 1980s conservative critics, emboldened by the Reagan Administration, launched a concerted attack on the AFDC program. They reversed the causal relationship that "poverty causes welfare dependence" and instead argued that the availability of AFDC had created a "culture of dependency." All a poor woman needed to do to escape poverty was to marry a man who worked full time and work part time herself, they claimed. Conservatives charged that the availability of AFDC gave poor women the option not to marry and/or not to work.

Paradoxically, new research by liberal researchers that appeared around this time fueled the conservatives' arguments. Harvard researchers Bane and Ellwood (1983) developed a new way to analyze "spells" of welfare use based on longitudinal data that suggested welfare users were divided into two groups. One group used AFDC for short periods and then left the rolls; families in the other group used AFDC continuously for long periods. While the research showed that the great majority of families that ever relied on AFDC fell into the former group, the majority of families using AFDC at any given time were long-term users, according to this analysis.[3] Moreover, the long-term users fitted the public stereotype of welfare mothers: They were less educated, less likely to have married, more likely to have had a child as a teenager, and more likely to be African American than were short-term users. Length of time on welfare, or "dependency," became the new way of delineating the "undeserving" within the AFDC population.

The same data set (the Panel Study on Income Dynamics) was also used to examine intergenerational welfare use. Duncan, Hiel, and Hoffman (1988) showed that the great majority of young women (80 percent of blacks and 75 percent of whites) who grow up in households dependent on AFDC do *not* rely on AFDC as adults, but their results also showed that children from AFDC households were more than twice as likely to receive AFDC as adults than were children who grew up in households with no AFDC receipt. Conservatives interpreted the latter finding as support for their "culture of dependency" thesis and ignored the fact that the great majority of children who grow up receiving AFDC appear immune to its "corrupting" influence.

By the end of the 1980s the mantra of welfare reform had become "reduce long-term welfare dependency." At the federal level President Reagan pushed for universal "workfare," but the Democratic Congress instead passed legislation that allowed states to experiment with various approaches to moving AFDC recipients off the rolls and into the paid labor force. Few

[3]If this seems counterintuitive, the following analogy may make the results clearer. Consider a hospital ward in which three out of four of the beds are filled by patients with chronic illnesses. Over the course of the year the fourth bed is used by patients who stay an average of only one week. At the end of the year 52 patients were short-term users (of the one bed) while three patients were long-term users. However, at any given point in time three-quarters of the patients were long-term users.

observers defended the right of poor mothers to stay at home and raise children, even preschool children. If middle-class mothers had to work, poor mothers should work too.

States that chose to run WIN demonstration programs in the 1980s were allowed to establish Community Work Experience Programs (CWEP) or "workfare," job search, education and training, and/or work supplementation programs. By 1985, 47 states had adopted at least one option, but most relied heavily on job search, and only a few offered the full gamut of job search, education, vocational training, and support services (Nightingale and Burbridge 1987). Eight states contracted with the Manpower Demonstration Research Corporation (MDRC) to conduct rigorous random-assignment evaluations of their welfare-to-work programs, providing policymakers with detailed information about the effects of various interventions.

Most of the programs evaluated by MDRC invested relatively little in education and training for the client participants ($500 to $1,000 per person). Training typically involved job search techniques (how to fill out a résumé, prepare for an interview, hunt for a job), and sanctions were applied for nonparticipation. MDRC's evaluations showed that even these modest investments could increase the employment and earnings of participants and could do so in a way that was cost-effective for administrators—i.e., the earnings offset the program costs (Gueron and Pauly 1991).

However, the demonstration programs did little to reduce AFDC enrollments or the cost of AFDC because the participants did not earn enough to lift themselves and their families out of poverty. In fact, participants typically increased their earnings by only about $500 a year (Gueron and Pauly 1991). The programs did increase the work effort of a large number of AFDC recipients, and the participants contributed marginally more to their own support, but the goal of helping welfare recipients become self-sufficient remained elusive.

Nonetheless, when Congress passed the Family Support Act in 1988, it legislated that all states establish some kind of welfare-to-work program. The law required states to offer a range of employment, education, and training services under the Job Opportunities and Basic Skills (JOBS) program. However, the states were not required to operate the JOBS program uniformly, and each state could determine the groups targeted for services or required to participate in various program components.

The federal government paid 90 percent of expenditures on JOBS and required a participation rate of 20 percent in 1995 for nonexempt AFDC recipients. Despite the federal monies made available for JOBS and the favorable match rate, most states did not utilize the funds available. State governments did not want to invest their own funds in the child care and administrative costs that welfare-to-work programs required. In 1992 fewer than 500,000 individuals were participating in JOBS. Almost 40 percent were participating in educational programs, and another 16 percent were participating in some form of training; less than four percent were participating in work programs (CWEP) (U.S. Congress 1994).

Dissatisfaction with the AFDC system remained a potent political issue with voters in the 1992 and 1994 elections. Candidate Bill Clinton made welfare reform a prominent theme of his presidential campaign, promising voters to put a time limit on welfare use and to demand that "everyone who can work should work." The reform eventually proposed by President Clinton would have allowed two years of income support (with education or training services), followed by a work-for-minimum-wages program.

When the Republicans took control of Congress in 1995, they upped the ante. As of the writing of this chapter, they have called for a lifetime five-year limit on welfare receipt, the imposition of large-scale workfare programs, and the reduction of federal funds and standards for the AFDC program. Unfortunately the focus on time limits and work programs ignores more recent research about the way lone mothers actually mix income support with work and moves us farther away from the kinds of policies that lone mothers need to increase their economic independence.

LONE MOTHERS AND AFDC

Early research on welfare "spells" was based on annual income data that over-estimated continuous welfare use. More recent and sophisticated analyses using data sets containing monthly income reports instead of annual income records paint a more complex picture of the ways lone mothers use income support and earnings to support their families. AFDC mothers use income support in at least four ways.

EMERGENCY ASSISTANCE

About 70 percent of all individuals who enter AFDC leave within two years (Greenberg 1993; Pavetti 1992; Spalter-Roth, Hartmann, and Andrews 1993). Probably a quarter of these women do not come back. They initially turn to AFDC after some crisis—desertion, an unplanned pregnancy, loss of a job, etc.—and are able to marry or work their way off welfare and remain independent. The mothers in this group tend to have higher skills and more work experience than the other three groups. These women probably have families that can provide them with resources as well. This group of one-shot users probably represent no more than 15 percent of all AFDC users.

UNEMPLOYMENT ASSISTANCE

Of the 70 percent of AFDC users who leave AFDC within two years, a majority come back onto the system at some point in time. About 45 percent return within a year of leaving AFDC, two-thirds by the end of three years, and three-quarters within seven years. (In 1992 about 42 percent of new applicants had been on AFDC sometime before.) These "cyclers" typically "work their way off" AFDC in relatively low-wage jobs, often with extra income support from friends or relatives. They come back to the system when they lose their jobs, when a child is sick and needs access to health care through Medicaid, or when child care arrangements fall through.

These women cycle on and off of AFDC, using it as a kind of unemployment insurance system because they don't qualify for regular Unemployment Insurance. Research by the Institute for Women's Policy Research (Spalter-Roth, Hartmann, and Andrews 1993) indicates that about 45 percent of the mothers who ever use AFDC fall into this category.

EARNINGS SUPPLEMENTATION

According to official reports from the Department of Health and Human Services (Administration for Children and Families 1994), about 11 percent of AFDC households reported receiving some earned income in 1992, although only 6.2 percent of household heads reported that they were employed at least half time. The average earnings received ($462 a month) represented about 27 hours of work per week at the minimum wage. Some families continue to rely on AFDC even though they are working because their wages are so low.

Reforms in 1981 reduced the rewards for working part time by lowering the threshold point at which earnings would begin to be counted as income in determining grant levels. As a consequence of these changes, part-time work among AFDC household heads declined. However, ethnographic work (Jencks and Edin 1990) and research from the Survey on Income and Program Participation (Spalter-Roth, Hartmann, and Andrews 1993) suggest that a number of mothers work "underground"—i.e., they don't report earnings from the work they do. Probably 20 percent of AFDC mothers work and use AFDC to supplement their low earnings (although only half this number reports their earnings). These mothers would be considered long-term dependent.

INCOME SUPPORT IN LIEU OF WORK

About a quarter of all AFDC users stay on AFDC continuously for long periods of time and do not work, but 40 percent of these (about 10 percent of all AFDC users) are disabled. A good number of these women periodically look for work but fail to find employment. Others are caring for infants. A woman in this group typically has her first child as a teenager, does not have a high school diploma or work experience, and has very low basic skills. These women are disproportionately minority. About 15 percent of white and 30 percent of black applicants have a spell of welfare use that last longer than five years (Pavetti 1992).

The welfare reforms currently under discussion assume that all AFDC recipients fall into the first or last group. There is little recognition that cycling on and off welfare is a problem for more welfare mothers than is continuous "dependency." Nor is there much acknowledgment of the fact that the women who remain on AFDC continuously have characteristics that make them unlikely to be competitive in the private labor market. To recognize these facts leads to questions about the nature of the low-wage labor market and the kinds of opportunities that may or may not be available to poor mothers who rely on AFDC.

THE LABOR MARKET PROSPECTS OF LOW-SKILLED WOMEN

As Chapter One notes, the employment prospects of female workers have improved over the past 30 years. The U.S. economy has created more new jobs in the past two decades than any other advanced industrial nation (Freeman 1994). In addition, job growth has occurred most rapidly in those areas of the economy (the service sector, retail trade, administrative support) that employ more women. Job losses, on the other hand, have been concentrated in traditionally male blue-collar manufacturing industries. Thus low-skilled women have not fared as badly as low-skilled men in the industrial restructuring that has occurred since the early 1970s (Blank 1995).

Nonetheless, women with less than a high school degree have unemployment rates twice as high as those of women with some college education. Only about a third of women without a high school diploma are actually working in the paid labor force, compared with about two-thirds of those with a high school diploma. But even the high school graduates who end up relying on AFDC appear to have serious deficiencies in their basic skills.

Using data from the National Longitudinal Survey of Youth (NLSY), Burtless (1995) found that about three-quarters of the 25-year-old women in his sample who received AFDC continuously for one year scored in the bottom quartile on the Armed Forces Qualification Test, a culturally unbiased test designed to measure an individual's basic problem-solving ability. He notes that "the low educational attainment and poor test scores of welfare-dependent mothers severely restrict the kinds of jobs most can obtain."

New research by Spalter-Roth et al. (1995) confirms that former and current AFDC recipients tend to be employed in the lowest-paid female occupations: Almost two in five are maids, cashiers, nursing aides, child care workers, or waitresses (compared with one in 10 female workers overall in these occupations). These are low-wage occupations with high rates of part-time and contingent forms of employment. Food service jobs—the most common employment among welfare recipients—had an average duration of only 30 weeks and the lowest wages ($3.73 per hour in 1990 dollars). Cleaning service jobs paid slightly better ($4.08) and had the longest duration—44 weeks. But the women who cycle on and off welfare or who combine work and welfare had an average of 1.7 jobs in just two years and worked only an average of 13 months total over a two-year period. At this end of the labor market, jobs don't last long and people don't stay put.

The real value of wages has fallen for 80 percent of American workers since 1979, but the decline has been particularly acute among those at the bottom of the wage scale. Between 1979 and 1995 inflation eroded the real value of the minimum wage by 27 percent. In 1990 over a third of full-time, full-year workers without a high school diploma earned less than the poverty rate for a family of four. A full-time minimum-wage job (paying $4.25 an hour) pays only about $8,500 a year in wages.[4] The average hourly wage earned by current or former AFDC recipients in the late 1980s was only $4.29 per hour, barely above today's minimum wage (Spalter-Roth et al. 1995). Employers provided health care to former AFDC recipients only about a third of the time that they were working (Spalter-Roth et al. 1995). In general, the availability of health benefits for low-skilled workers seems to have fallen in the 1980s (Blank 1995).

Moreover, as low-wage jobs have become more short term and contingent, there appears to be less premium put on work experience and less wage growth for workers. Burtless (1995) shows that the women who rely on wel-

---

[4] A worker with children could receive another $3,500 a year from the Earned Income Tax Credit. Unfortunately many workers do not understand that this credit is available to them, and few employers automatically process the paper work to ensure that it is given on a monthly or quarterly basis instead of at the end of the year.

fare see very little increase in their earnings as they age or gain more work experience. Between 1979 and 1990 the average wage of AFDC-dependent women in his sample rose by less than one percent per year; other young women in the survey experienced earnings gains of almost five percent per year. Thus low-skilled women are consigned to jobs that pay them little more than minimum wage with few prospects for improvement over time, rarely offer health care benefits, and relegate them to the lowest tiers of the occupational structure.

MANDATING WORK

For a low-skilled lone mother, the private labor market represents a more risky economic future than the economic security offered by AFDC, Food Stamps, and Medicaid. If a mother worked full-time at a minimum-wage job and received the Earned Income Tax Credit, Food Stamps, and child care assistance, she would see her family only marginally better off financially from her efforts and would still not earn enough to lift a family of three out of poverty. If child care subsidies stopped or a family member required medical assistance, the economic advantages to work would quickly evaporate.

Since income from welfare mothers' private-sector employment has become so meager and uncertain, conservatives argue that the only way to ensure that poor women work is to make work a condition of income support or simply to put a time limit on the receipt of income support, thereby forcing mothers into the workforce. Reform proposals from Democrats as well as Republicans now contain work requirements.

Unfortunately these proposals fail to recognize the practical difficulties that large-scale work programs create. As discussed, welfare recipients' lack of education and basic skills does not make them attractive to private employers.

Even if aggregate demand at the national level is enough to absorb two to three million unskilled workers, many local economies would not be able to absorb the tens of thousands of household heads pushed into the local labor market. Poor people in the United States are not evenly distributed; they are concentrated in urban and rural areas where the demand for labor is weak. Mandating work does not create jobs.

Moreover, many labor economists agree that the immediate and lasting effect of rapidly increasing the low-skilled labor supply would be to depress already low wages even further (Burtless 1995; Blank 1995). In other words, the work for which AFDC household heads are qualified would become even less financially remunerative. Mandating work will exacerbate negative wage trends in the low-skilled labor market.

If work is mandated, the government and nonprofit organizations are likely to be asked to act as employers/supervisors of last resort for those rejected by the private labor market. The amount of time and effort involved in placing, supervising, and monitoring workers with little work experience, few skills, and little financial incentive to work is likely to be extensive, and administrative costs will increase. Moreover, if a mother with a young child is working, someone will have to pay for child care. (Remember that almost half of all children on AFDC are under five years old.) The Congressional Budget Office estimates that work programs will cost about $5,000 *more* per participant than the current system as the result of administrative and child care costs. Since research (Brock, Butler, and Long 1993) has shown that workfare assignments do *not* improve one's chances of finding private-sector employment at a later date, it is extremely unlikely that these costs would decline over time. Mandating work for AFDC recipients dramatically increases the cost of welfare.

When local governments take on the task of placing and supervising large numbers of welfare clients, there is a temptation to use them to replace low-skilled, unionized government employees since such "displacement" can create savings for financially distressed jurisdictions. (Indeed, the American Federation of State, County, and Municipal Employees charges that the City of New York has been consistently replacing union workers with General Assistance recipients as the former leave or retire.) Displacement practices reduce the supply of jobs with above-poverty-level wages that are available to the least-skilled workers, creating the potential for a cruel game of "musical jobs": When the music stops, more individuals may be left jobless, poor, and in need of assistance. Joblessness and local government fiscal problems reinforce each other.

Many policymakers suggest that nonprofit organizations should be the major source of work assignments for welfare recipients who cannot be absorbed in the private market. But preliminary results from a survey of nonprofit directors in 13 major cities conducted by the Joint Center for Political and Economic Studies suggest that nonprofits are wary of the time required to train and supervise inexperienced and poorly educated welfare recipients. A majority of the more than 1,300 nonprofit directors surveyed expressed a willingness to provide community service work assignments for welfare recipients. However, the most common number they report they could use was two (the median number was four), and the characteristics they believe they require (a high school education, work experience) are precisely the characteristics that many welfare recipients lack. The nonprofit sector will not be able to absorb the majority of AFDC recipients needing work under mandatory work requirements.

A mandatory work program would mean that adult heads of households with little education or work skills would be consigned to working at 70 percent of the poverty rate instead of engaging in activities (e.g., education and training) that could potentially improve their chances of obtaining unsubsidized employment at better-than-minimum wages. "Working-off-the-grant" creates a subtier of workers without the basic protections enjoyed by the general labor force.

Large-scale mandatory work programs could also have a detrimental impact on poor children and the neighborhoods in which they live. Many AFDC children live in neighborhoods of concentrated poverty and female-headed households, where the ratio of adults to children is already skewed toward children and where adolescent peer groups openly challenge the authority of parents. If residential patterns remain the same and significant numbers of the adults in AFDC households are forced into the labor force (with a lengthy commute to the job site), poor urban neighborhoods are likely to become more chaotic, more violent, and more dangerous places for children. This brings us back full circle to the original purpose of AFDC: to provide fatherless children with stable, if meager, income support so that their custodial mothers could be home to care for them. If society now feels that poor children would be better served by more formal child care arrangements during the day while their mothers work, then protecting children should involve upgrading and ensuring access to quality daycare and after-school care. Unfortunately this is not a central part of the welfare reforms now being proposed in Washington.

REAL WELFARE REFORM: MOVING TOWARD LONG-TERM SELF-SUPPORT

The current welfare reform debate treats "dependency" and "self-sufficiency" as if they were mutually exclusive and distinct states. In reality, of course, they are two ends of a continuum. Every citizen supports himself or herself on a mixture of earnings, interest, and public or private transfer payments.

The goal of welfare reform should be to move individuals on the "dependency" side of the support spectrum toward the "self-sufficiency" side, as family circumstances allow. Working 10 hours a week in paid employment will not make the mother of a young child "self-sufficient," but it will reduce her *level* of dependence on government and increase the income gained from her own effort. As her child ages, her goal might be to increase her working hours up to 20 hours a week or more. If all AFDC adults engaged in activity geared toward increasing their earnings from unsubsidized work, the *number* of individuals receiving some kind of government assistance might not decrease, but the nature of the relationship between the government and recipients would change in ways that most Americans would applaud.

"Dependency" is a value-laden word that has connotations of individual weakness and inadequacy. But the "dependency" of poor mothers on AFDC is primarily the result of weaknesses in the low-wage labor market. "Welfare dependency" among low-skilled mothers results from: (1) the recurring need for episodic income support as the result of tumultuous nature of the low-wage job market; (2) the need for long-term income supplementation because of the low wages available to low-skilled workers; and (3) the need for better preparation and placement in the labor market. These needs have grown over the past 30 years as the economy has changed. But government programs have failed to adjust to meet these needs.

Currently fewer than four in 10 unemployed Americans actually receive unemployment benefits. The proportion of the unemployed who receive benefits has declined over time as the stability of jobs, the number of full-time jobs, and wage rates have fallen. Until the Unemployment Insurance system is changed (*see* Chapter Three), part-time and contingent workers— a group comprised predominantly of women—will continue to require some kind of temporary income support for themselves and their families during spells of joblessness.

If the real wages of low-skilled workers remain low, then the government will have to supplement earnings to ensure that poor families have adequate support. The first and most important action the government could take to improve the circumstances of poor families would be to raise the minimum wage. The Department of Labor estimates that two-thirds of the individuals currently receiving the minimum wage are supporting families. If the minimum wage were raised to five dollars an hour and a family head received the maximum Earned Income Tax Credit ($3,500), her earned income would rise to just over the poverty level for a family of three.

For low-skilled parents, ensuring access to affordable health care and child care are important in both reducing episodic job losses and making low-wage work more remunerative. In 1991 the average weekly cost of child care for a preschool child was $63 a week, 37 percent of weekly earnings at minimum wage (U.S. Congress 1993). Poor mothers were twice as likely as non-poor mothers to rely on a relative for child care and so tended to pay less per week, but they still paid as much as 25 percent of their earnings for child care. This represents a severe "tax" on the earnings of a lone parent. Ensuring access to quality child care, and adjusting costs according to income, would help working mothers remain in the workforce more continuously and would provide another supplement to their wages.

Another way to supplement the wages of lone mothers and to encourage work would be to establish guaranteed child support payments. Although the rhetoric of welfare reform calls for stricter child support enforcement, current proposals rarely improve the living standards of poor mothers with regard to child support and may in fact worsen them.

If a family is receiving AFDC, only $50 a month of whatever child support is collected from the father is "passed through" to the family. The rest of the money goes to the state to offset the costs of AFDC. Thus a mother receiving AFDC would do better if the father made informal payments of $100 or $120 a month directly to her instead of paying the state. Stricter child support enforcement by the state could mean that although the father pays more money, the family sees less of it.

A child support assurance system that guaranteed a certain level of child support paid by the government each month ($250 for the first child, $50 for each additional child), regardless of the father's ability to pay, would do more to help poor families than the current system. The government would be responsible for collecting whatever a father could pay; the mother's payment would not be income-tested. Any money she earned she would keep in its entirety. This would provide a huge incentive to work. A child support assurance, with guarantees of affordable child care and health care, could dramatically decrease the number of poor families in need of other kinds of assistance.

Unfortunately a significant portion of the AFDC population is entirely dependent on government support for long periods because the education system failed it. As noted previously, almost half of AFDC household heads have not finished high school and a majority have very low basic skills. If these mothers are ever going to escape poverty through their earnings, they will have to improve their educational and skill levels. Targeted outreach to identify and intervene when poor youngsters begin to fail in school might prevent the need for support later in life. But public school reform has proved to be lumbering and incremental.

"Second chance" education and training programs for welfare recipients and other disadvantaged adults have a mixed record. They work better for women than men. They can increase the number of hours worked, but they rarely increase hourly wages. Training for welfare recipients is part of a very decentralized, fluid, federally financed system with poorly defined standards, little quality control, and volatile funding. The effectiveness of training programs for AFDC recipients is unlikely to improve until the United States invests in a modernized, national system of employment services (which includes training, retraining, and job placement services) like those of other advanced industrial countries (McFate, Lawson, and Wilson 1995).

Unfortunately it is unclear whether even major government reforms of the kind proposed here can affect the central problem facing low-skilled heads of households: the mismatch between the supply of low-skilled workers and the demand for their labor. The uneven distribution of work in the United States—across skill levels, households, and geographic regions—will challenge policymakers for the foreseeable future.

Until these labor market issues are dealt with, reforms of the AFDC system will do little to reduce the number of families that find themselves in need of income support. Without changes in the labor market and in other supports available to working parents, the reforms being discussed in Washington in the first half of 1995—time limits on AFDC receipt, mandatory work requirements, increasing decentralization in program rules and requirements—are likely to *increase* rather than reduce the poverty and hardship of single-parent families.

FIVE

★

WOMEN'S EMPLOYMENT PATTERNS, PENSION COVERAGE, AND RETIREMENT PLANNING

Martha Priddy Patterson

HIGHLIGHTS

WOMEN CHANGE JOBS MORE FREQUENTLY THAN MEN, have shorter tenure with an employer, earn less money, and take more time out of the workforce. These career patterns result in dramatically lower employer-provided retirement benefits (and Social Security benefits) for women than men. This makes women's individual savings for retirement especially important.

- Women who work year round and full time—53 percent of the approximately 60 million women who work in the paid labor force—are less likely than men to have employer-provided retirement plans. Moreover, more women than men work part time (and therefore do not qualify for employee retirement plans) or for employers who do not provide employee retirement plans.
- Since women change jobs more frequently than men—women stay with an employer for an average of 4.8 years, compared with 6.6 years for men—many women leave jobs before they reach the required years of service to qualify for employer retirement plans, usually five to seven years.
- In 1992 only one-third of recent retirees over age 55 received pension annuities based on their employment record. Among those retirees only 20 percent of women received pensions, compared with 47 percent of men.
- Women continue to earn less than men. Although the wage gap between men and women declined between 1979 and 1994, women working full time in 1994 earned only 76 percent of what their male counterparts earned.

- Because of differences in career patterns, earnings, and access to employer-provided retirement plans, women have smaller pensions than men. In 1989 women with benefits as retired employees received an average annual benefit of $4,330, less than half of the $9,460 men received.
- For employees with employer-provided retirement plans, the average plan replaces less than 10 percent of final earnings. If she has a 35-year working life, the average working woman receives about 20 to 40 percent of her preretirement wage from Social Security. Other retirement income for individuals comes primarily from preretirement savings or employment following retirement age.
- Lower wages result in lower public and private pension benefits for women than for men; in addition, they make it more difficult for women to save adequately for their longer period of retirement.
- Enforcement of the Equal Pay Act and other actions to increase women's wages and access to retirement plans may move women toward parity with men's rates of coverage in employer-provided retirement plans. At the same time, more income may enable women to achieve higher levels of saving to meet their retirement needs.

INTRODUCTION

In 1989 the average annual pension benefit earned by women receiving benefits as former employees was about 46 percent of the average annual benefit received by men ($4,330 versus $9,460). This was *down* from 1978, when female retirees received a benefit of approximately 51 percent of men's retirement benefits (see Table V-1). Clearly the trend in retirement benefits does not suggest parity for women (Beller and McCarthy 1992).

Only about one-third of recent retirees over age 55 received pension annuities based on their employment record, according to Beller and McCarthy (1992). Among those retirees, only 20 percent of women received pensions, while 47 percent of men received pensions. The Department of Labor reported that among all recent retirees in 1989, "The median retirement age of 62 is the same for men and women. Similarities end there. Comparing medians, men have 50 percent more service, 67 percent higher earnings, 200 percent higher benefits and 53 percent higher [final preretirement wage] replacement rates (Beller and McCarthy 1992)."

Employer-provided retirement plans are divided into two basic types:

- **Defined benefit plans** typically promise to pay an annual pension for as long as the retired employee lives, based on a percentage of the em-

Table V-1 · ANNUAL PENSION PAYMENTS FOR RETIREES EARNING BENEFITS AS FORMER EMPLOYEES BY INDUSTRY SECTOR AND SEX, 1978 AND 1989 (in dollars)

	1978		1989	
Industry Sector	*Men*	*Women*	*Men*	*Women*
All industries				
Mean	4,450	2,290	9,460	4,330
Median	3,480	1,630	7,020	2,570
Manufacturing				
Mean	4,730	2,880	8,190	4,600
Median	3,860	2,320	6,070	1,870
Nonmanufacturing				
Mean	3,970	1,780	10,550	4,200
Median	2,640	1,260	7,500	2,680

Source: Beller and McCarthy 1992.

ployee's salary multiplied by her years of service. An **integrated defined benefit plan** pays an annual benefit that is linked to Social Security. Companies with integrated defined benefit plans can deduct part of their employees' Social Security benefits from their pensions, sometimes reducing their pensions by as much as 50 percent. The Tax Reform Act of 1986 requires that a worker must still be left with half her pension after integration is applied, for the years after 1988.

• In **defined contribution plans,** the employer typically contributes a certain amount each year to the employee's account while she is working; that account will usually be paid in a lump sum to the employee at her retirement.

Neither defined benefit plans nor defined contribution plans are inherently "better" for women. Which type of plan is better depends on the individual woman and her circumstances. For example, defined benefit plans rarely require the employee to contribute her own money to the plan in order to participate. The employee does not need to take any action to participate in the defined benefit plan other than to meet plan requirements for minimum time with the employer, usually one year, and minimum number of hours worked during a year, usually at least 1,000. These same minimums typically apply to defined contribution plans as well. An employee with low earnings may benefit from a defined benefit plan, which, unlike most defined contribution plans, does not require her to contribute her own money in order to participate in the plan.

Usually, defined contribution plans tend to favor younger employees with fewer years with the employer because the contributions are linked not to age or length of service but simply to income. Additionally, younger workers have more years for those contributions to earn interest and grow before the money in the plan is needed for retirement.

Defined benefit plans tend to favor older workers with longer service because the amount needed to satisfy the employer's retirement obligation for the older worker will probably be higher than any contribution the employer might give under a defined contribution plan.

CURRENT PENSION STATUS

More than 60 million women in the United States today are employed in the paid labor force. In 1993, 53 percent of women who had some work experience during the year—or 33.5 million women—worked year round and full time. Approximately 68 percent of men worked year round and full time in 1993 (*see* Chapter One).

Women's participation in employer-provided retirement plans is increasing. In 1988 only 43 percent of women employed full time by private employers were participating in an employer-provided retirement plan. By 1993, 48 percent of women employed full time by private employers were participating in an employer-provided retirement plan. In part this is a reflection of the growing similarities in men's and women's years of service with an employer (see Tables V-2 and V-3).

Level of earnings and the likelihood of retirement benefit coverage are also strongly linked. Among full-time workers earning under $10,000, coverage is eight percent; among those earning $50,000 and over, coverage is 81 percent. Ironically, lower-paid women (under $35,000) are slightly more likely to have pension coverage than lower-paid men are (see Table V-4).

RETIREMENT PLANNING FOR WOMEN

Retirement planning for women in the workforce today is different from planning for men for several distinct reasons.

WOMEN LIVE LONGER

A woman who is 40 today is expected to live another 41 years. A man that age is expected to live another 36 years (U.S. Department of Commerce

Table V-2 · FULL-TIME EMPLOYED MEN AND WOMEN WITH PENSION COVERAGE BY YEARS OF SERVICE WITH EMPLOYER, 1988 AND 1993 (in percentages)

Years with Employer	1988		1993	
	Women	*Men*	*Women*	*Men*
Less than 1 year	13	18	11	14
1 to 4 years	37	39	39	39
5 to 9 years	63	62	63	61
10 to 14 years	70	73	71	70
15 to 19 years	72	77	77	78
20 to 24 years	75[1]	82[1]	85	80
25 or more years	—[2]	—[2]	84	84
All years of service	43	50	48	51

[1]Represents percentage with 20 or more years of service.
[2]Not available.

Source: U.S. Department of Labor et al. 1994.

Table V-3 · FULL-TIME EMPLOYED MEN AND WOMEN BY YEARS OF SERVICE WITH EMPLOYER, 1988 AND 1993 (in percentages)

Years with Employer	1988		1993	
	Women	*Men*	*Women*	*Men*
Less than 1	19	17	17	17
1 to 4 years	37	33	36	31
5 to 9 years	18	17	21	21
10 to 14 years	10	11	12	11
15 to 19 years	6	7	6	7
20 to 24 years	5	11	7	11

Source: Department of Labor et al. 1994.

1993). Not only do women live longer than men, but they also encounter greater long-term care expenses as the result of the chronic health problems associated with old age. The bottom line is that the longer a woman lives in retirement, the more money she needs. On average, then, today's 40-year-old woman will need income for at least five years more than her male counterpart.

Table V-4 · RETIREMENT BENEFIT COVERAGE AMONG FULL-TIME PRIVATE-SECTOR WORKERS BY ANNUAL EARNINGS AND SEX, 1993 (in percentages)

Annual Earnings	All Workers	Men	Women
Total	50	51	48
Under $10,000	8	7	9
$10,000–14,999	27	21	31
$15,000–19,999	42	35	49
$20,000–24,999	57	51	65
$25,000–29,999	62	61	64
$30,000–34,999	67	66	71
$35,000–39,999	73	74	72
$40,000–49,999	78	79	77
$50,000–74,999	81	81	80
$75,000 and over	81	82	78

Source: U.S. Department of Labor et al. 1994.

WOMEN EARN LESS MONEY

Women continue to earn less money than men. As Diane Herz and Barbara Wootton show in Chapter One, the earnings gap between men and women declined over the 1979–94 period. Still, in 1994 women who usually worked full time earned only 76 percent as much as men did. Earning less money has a geometric impact on retirement in three ways.

First, earning less money makes it more difficult to save for anything, including retirement. A woman who misses saving just $500 a year for retirement over 30 years will have her retirement account lump sum at retirement reduced by $39,500, assuming six percent interest. That lump sum could have given her annual benefits during her retirement of $3,100.

Second, both Social Security payments and most employer-provided retirement benefits are based on earnings while working. Social Security replaces about 20 to 40 percent of the average worker's final preretirement wage if we assume that a worker had at least a 35-year working life. The lower an individual's earnings, the higher the percentage of preretirement income Social Security replaces. However, low wages while working translate into low levels of Social Security and pension benefits.

Finally, as illustrated in Table V-4, the lower the worker's earnings, the less likely she is to have retirement benefit coverage while working although admittedly this link between income and coverage differs little between women and men.

WOMEN TAKE MORE TIME OUT OF THE WORKFORCE

Whether to care for children or for elderly parents, women tend to be out of the workforce more frequently than men. The direct effect of taking time out of the workforce is that women are not earning the right to retirement benefits during those years, nor are they earning money to save for retirement. The indirect effect is that women lose seniority, which is important for increased wages and promotions leading to wage increases. Women's employment in part-time jobs has a similar effect. Because by law pension plans do not have to cover most part-time employees, women often lose out on retirement benefits during their years of part-time employment. Fewer than 17 percent of part-time working women are covered by any type of retirement plan (U.S. Department of Labor et al. 1994).

WOMEN TEND TO HAVE LOWER JOB TENURE

Women over age 25 stay with an employer an average of 4.8 years, compared with an average of 6.6 years for men. Most employer-provided defined benefit retirement plans require an employee to work for the firm for at least five years before the employee "vests" or is legally entitled to any pension benefit she has earned. A woman who works for an employer for only 4.8 years may never vest in that employer's retirement plan. Additionally, many employers require that the employee work a full year before she is eligible for benefits under the employer's retirement plan. As a result, an employee who works continuously from age 18 to 65, but who has five different jobs, could lose five years of benefit buildup over her career in addition to the benefits lost as a result of jobs held for fewer than five years.

WOMEN ARE RISK-AVERSE IN THEIR INVESTMENTS

In many defined contribution pension plans, employees must choose among different investment options. Risk and return on investments go hand in hand. Certificates of deposit (CDs) are very low-risk investments, and they provide very low returns on investment. Bonds are riskier but provide higher returns than CDs in most cases. Stocks carry the highest risk but usually provide higher returns.

Studies and anecdotal evidence suggest that women tend to be less willing than men to make higher-risk investments with potentially higher returns. While this may protect women against potential losses, it also means that women need to save more money to have the same amount of income at retirement as an investor who is willing to risk more for a higher return.

To view this another way: Unless women invest with reasonable risk, for example, in stock mutual funds rather than in fixed-interest contracts (GIC), they will have a lower standard of living in retirement than they might otherwise have with the same level of savings. Table V-5 shows the outcomes of different investment strategies for an annual investment of $1,000 over 30 years in a tax-deferred retirement plan, such as an Individual Retirement Account (IRA) or a 401(k) plan. Depending on the investment strategy, the same $30,000 investment could pay about $5,000 a year during a 25-year retirement or $15,000 a year, about three times as much.

Unfortunately vendors appear to encourage this risk-averse tendency of women. Studies show that stockbrokers and banks selling mutual funds or other investments give female customers less time and attention and suggest more conservative, lower-paying investments for women (Wang 1994).

WOMEN ARE LESS LIKELY TO PREPARE FOR RETIREMENT

A recent telephone poll of 800 people age 25 to 64 found that only 30 percent of women, compared with 47 percent of men, were saving for retirement. Of those who were saving, only 46 percent of women reported that they started preparing for retirement before age 40. Thirty-five percent of women said that they felt uninformed about retirement, and 40 percent did not feel knowledgeable enough to make decisions about retirement plan-

Table V-5 · RETIREMENT SAVINGS OF $1,000 ANNUALLY FOR 30 YEARS WHEN INVESTED AT DIFFERENT RISKS AND RETURNS (in dollars)

Invested in:	Lump Sum at Retirement	Annual Income for 25 Years[1]
100% in stock mutual fund, 10% return	164,494	15,400
100% in government fund, 7% return	94,461	8,850
100% in fixed interest contract (GIC), 4% return	56,085	5,250

[1]Assumes a six percent rate of return during retirement.

Source: Patterson 1993.

ning on their own. The female respondents' total personal savings on average were $25,700, compared with $52,500 for men (Merrill Lynch 1993).

REDUCTIONS IN BENEFITS

As discussed above, women's career patterns tend to reduce benefits from retirement plans. Changing jobs and taking time out of the workforce have a dramatic and highly disproportionate effect on employer-provided retirement benefits. Missing as few as seven years out of the workforce and changing jobs as few as five times over a 40-year career can result in retirement benefits that are less than half of what could be expected from a one-job career. And that scenario assumes that the individual always works for an employer that provides a retirement plan; as noted earlier, more than half of American women working full time—as well as almost all of those working in part-time or temporary jobs—do not work for employers providing retirement benefits.

Typically an employee must wait one year before she becomes eligible for an employer's retirement plan and she must work at least 1,000 hours a year to accrue a benefit in a year. She must work for the employer for at least five years before she vests—that is, before she has a nonforfeitable right to take the benefit with her when she leaves. Before 1989 employer retirement plans could require employees to work for at least 10 years before their benefits vested.

By taking time away from work or by changing jobs, employees lose benefits. For example, if an employee leaves a job after only four years, she may lose the benefits that she has accrued over those years. If the employee goes on part-time status for a year and does not work at least 1,000 hours in that year, she may not earn a benefit for that year. Each time an employee takes a new job, she may not receive a benefit for her first year of service with the employer because she is not yet eligible to join the retirement plan.

Employees also lose benefits through preretirement inflation. For example, assume an employee earns the right to receive an annual benefit of $3,000 when she retires at age 65. The value of her $3,000-per-year pension will be decreased over the next 25 years by inflation. If inflation runs at two percent for those years, the buying power of her $3,000 annual payment will be reduced to 61 percent of its value, or $1,830, by the time she is 90. Once benefits begin at retirement, fewer than five percent of participants receiving retirement payments from defined benefit plans have those benefits adjusted for inflation through periodic cost-of-living adjustments or COLAs (Department of Labor 1991).

PRERETIREMENT CONSUMPTION OF RETIREMENT BENEFITS

Women may also lose retirement benefits if they receive a lump-sum benefit from their retirement plan when they leave an employer. Under the law, if retirement plan lump sums are not transferred to an IRA or to another employer's retirement plan, the employee must pay taxes on the money immediately and, in most cases, also a 10 percent penalty on the money. If the employee does not direct the plan sponsor to transfer the money directly to an IRA or to another tax-deferred employer plan, the plan sponsor must normally withhold 20 percent of the value of the lump sum for federal taxes before the sum is paid to the employee.

Cashing out these lump sums, even when they represent seemingly small amounts, can have a devastating effect on retirement income. For example, at age 57 cashing out one lump sum worth only about $11,000 can result in an employee's losing an annual retirement benefit of almost $2,000 per year for her *entire* retirement.

EXAMPLES OF WOMEN'S TYPICAL CAREER PATTERNS

The following examples provide illustrations of how women can lose employer-provided retirement benefits, even when they work almost continuously over the course of a long career. The examples compare pension income from a career with several employers to pension income from a single-job career. This is a useful device for demonstrating the loss of pension income that may result from job changes, while recognizing that a single-job career is becoming increasingly uncommon in today's changing economy. The scenarios cover Alice, a nurse now age 60, and Susan, a mid-level manager who is 50.

THE PLANS AND ASSUMPTIONS

The examples below assume that pension benefits earned after 1988 vest in five years and that benefits earned before 1989 vest in 10 years, the typical vesting schedule used by most employers as permitted by law. The assumed inflation rate is five percent per year; the assumed wage increase is six percent per year. The amounts contributed to the defined contribution plan are assumed to earn 7.5 percent annually, and any benefits that are rolled over to an IRA or other account are also assumed to earn 7.5 percent annually. All dollar amounts are stated in 1992 constant dollars. All salaries are based on 1992 average salaries for the position based on Bureau of Labor Statistics data.

Scenario 1: Alice, Age 60

Alice, now 60, began her nursing career at age 21. She has worked full time for six different employers over her 39-year career, and she now earns $36,750. She worked for eight years at her first job, with a large hospital, and then took one year off to care for her first child. She went back to work in the emergency room at a smaller hospital, worked full time for four years, and then took another year off to care for her second child. Next, Alice worked for seven years in a hospital nearer her home. She was offered a supervisory position at a different hospital and accepted that job, which she held for eight years. Alice then took a year off to care for her mother, who was terminally ill, and to help settle her mother's estate. She then joined a clinic specializing in children's care for six years. Two years ago Alice moved to her current job as supervisor of a neighborhood clinic. She plans to stay in this job until she retires.

If Alice retires at age 65, she will receive an annual pension of less than $4,650. Compare that with a pension of $12,700—the amount she would have received if she had been able to stay with one employer over her career or had received credit for all her years of service! Her pension is only about one-third of what it would have been had she stayed with one employer and still taken three years off over her 39-year career.

Basically Alice's dramatically lower pension results from lack of vesting. Over the years Alice left behind valuable retirement benefits at various jobs because she was unable to stay with her employer long enough to vest in the benefits. During much of her career the law allowed employers to require 10 years or more of service before an employee vested in retirement benefits— and Alice never stayed with any of her employers for 10 years or more.

Alice usually worked at her jobs for several years. If the five-year vesting required by today's law had been in effect during her entire career, she would have been entitled to all those lump sums except for the $977 from her second position, where she worked for only four years. Five-year vesting did protect Alice in her fifth job. She earned the right to an annual pension of $1,670, worth a lump-sum value of $10,700 when she left the job.

Throughout her career Alice might have partially protected herself through her own personal savings. Diverting just five percent of her income to a tax-free investment would have given her a lump sum of $2,660 when she left her first job. By retirement at age 65, this amount would have grown to approximately $14,700, assuming a five percent rate of return. If Alice had saved five percent of her earnings and invested the savings in a tax-deferred account over her entire career, her retirement account would have grown to $112,000 by age 65. This amount would pay her an annual retirement benefit of over $8,760 for 25 years.

Although Alice was unable to save throughout her career, there are several actions she can take today:

Investigate exact amount of Social Security benefits. First, Alice should contact the Social Security Administration to be sure that the agency has an accurate wage history for her. The Social Security Administration will also tell her what her expected benefit would be if she retired at 62, at 65, or at 70.

Examine current employer's pension plan. Second, Alice should look at her current employer's plan and determine at what age she can retire and what the reductions for early retirement before age 65 might be. If she retires now, she would receive an annual income from this job's pension of only $1,077, which, with her income from the prior job's pension, would give her an annual income of only $2,747. If she stays another five years, her annual pension from this job will be $2,960, more than twice its current value.

Consider a lump-sum payment form. To protect against inflation, Alice could consider taking one or both of her pensions in a lump sum at retirement and reinvesting the amounts.

Redouble savings efforts. Alice should redouble her efforts at saving now. She should look for investments that will protect against inflation. If she has her own home, she might consider trading down to a smaller, less expensive residence. If Alice chooses this option, she has time over the next five years to observe the housing market and sell at her convenience. Money remaining after the purchase of a smaller place should be invested for retirement income. Alternatively, she might consider renting part or all of her home if that could be made profitable.

Look for forgotten benefits. Alice should contact all her former employers and inquire about any potential retirement benefits.

Work after "retirement." Finally, Alice could consider a part-time job after retirement. After age 65 Alice can earn up to $11,280 annually (in 1995 dollars) without having her Social Security benefits reduced. At age 70 she may earn as much as she wishes without any Social Security reduction. Any pension benefits she may receive are not included in this limit. At any age she may have to pay tax on half of her Social Security benefits if she has income of more than $25,000 per year, which does include pension payments. (Couples pay tax on part of their Social Security benefits if they have income of more than $32,000.) She may need to pay tax on 80 percent of her Social Security if as an individual she has income over $34,000 per year.

Scenario 2: Susan, Age 50

Susan began working when she was 20 and has worked continuously since then. Over her 30-year career she has held five jobs. She currently earns $25,200 and plans to retire at age 65.

Susan worked as a secretary at her first job for four years for an employer without a retirement plan. She then worked for five years for an employer with a defined benefit plan, but she did not vest in it. Next, Susan took a job with a company for 10 years and vested in its defined benefit plan. After five years with a company which downsized, she went to work with her current employer, which offers a defined contribution plan.

When Susan retires at 65, she can expect an annual income from all of her employers' retirement plans of only about $4,700. This amount will represent about 16 percent of her final earnings. Compare this with the $8,300 she would have received annually from a single-job career under a defined benefit plan or the $10,600 annually she would have received under a defined contribution plan in a single-job career. Under these plans she could have received 29 percent or 37 percent, respectively, of her final earnings.

Although Susan had no retirement benefits from her first two jobs, she stayed for 10 years at her third job, which had a defined benefit plan integrated with Social Security. Because she stayed 10 years and because the Employee Retirement Income Security Act (ERISA) required vesting after 10 years, she had the right to retirement benefits when she left. Susan had earned a benefit with a lump-sum value today of $2,900, which will pay her at retirement $570 annually.

Her next job also offered a defined benefit plan, but she did not vest in the benefit she accrued. She was there for only five years, and the law did not require five-year vesting at that time. Susan's current employer's plan will provide her with annual earnings of $4,130 at retirement.

Susan's retirement account can grow significantly in the 15 years between now and her retirement. In addition, Susan can practice her own savings program for the next 15 years. Because her employer has a defined contribution plan, the company is also likely to have a 401(k) program to which she can contribute. That money is taken out of her pay on a pretax basis, and tax is not due on the earnings until she begins to withdraw it at retirement.

Susan can also fully fund an IRA each year. A $2,000 annual contribution to an IRA over the next 15 years will provide her with an account at retirement of $46,550 if it earns six percent annually or $54,300 if it earns eight percent.

RECENT POLICY CHANGES

A number of significant improvements in the laws governing employer-provided retirement benefits have been made since 1974. However, those improvements will not show their effects on retirement benefits until women whose careers are covered by those improvements retire. These improvements began in 1974 with the enactment of the Employee Retirement Income Security Act (ERISA), which required employers to hold the money for promised benefits in trust beyond the control of the employers or their creditors, ensuring that the money for promised benefits will be there at retirement. ERISA also required that employees vest in the promised benefits within 10 to 15 years and added a number of other protections for employees who are promised retirement benefits.

The Retirement Equity Act of 1984 required employers to count an employee's service as soon as she or he reached age 21, rather than at age 25, as permitted under earlier law. This was particularly helpful for women, who frequently work before they reach age 25 and then take time out of the workforce for family responsibilities after that time. That act also liberalized the so-called break in service rules by permitting a one-year maternity or paternity leave without counting such leave as a break in service.

The Tax Reform Act of 1986 further improved women's chances of actually owning a nonforfeitable right to retirement benefits they had earned. The act reduced the years of service required for vesting from 10 years of service for 100 percent vesting or 15 years for gradual vesting, to five years of service for 100 percent vesting and seven years for gradual vesting.

This 1986 law also increased women's chances for retirement security by making it more expensive to spend retirement benefits before retirement. The law imposed a 10 percent penalty on distributions received from retirement plans before reaching retirement, except in the case of the individual's death or disability or heavy medical expenses. The 10 percent penalty has, in fact, discouraged preretirement spending of employer-provided savings meant for retirement.

In 1992 the law was further amended to make it even more expensive to cash out these benefits before retirement. Under the 1992 change, retirement benefits paid in lump sums that are not rolled over to Individual Retirement Accounts or another employer's retirement plan are subject to a 20 percent withholding tax before the employer may distribute the money to the employee. This change too is designed to make the employee aware of the importance of saving retirement benefits for retirement.

Another important policy shift is the increase in the number of employer-provided retirement plans that permit the employee to receive and manage their retirement benefits when they leave an employer. While not legally mandated, this option provides employees with portability of benefits that many feel is critical to retirement income security. As employees leave a company, this option allows the employer to reduce the number of participants in its plan, saving the employer money. At the same time it gives the employees a chance to invest and protect the lump-sum amount from preretirement inflation.

These recent policy changes can benefit women entering the workforce or in the early stages of their careers, permitting them to earn and protect more retirement benefits.

STRATEGIES TO IMPROVE WOMEN'S RETIREMENT SECURITY

INCREASED WAGES

One policy goal the federal government can pursue successfully to increase women's pension coverage is stronger enforcement of the Equal Pay Act. This act does not regulate employee benefits directly and could not be used to directly increase pension coverage, but the secondary effects could be dramatic. Studies consistently show a strong correlation between pension coverage and average annual wages (see Table V-4). Higher-paying jobs are more likely to offer retirement benefits. Hence the most effective way to increase women's employer-provided pension coverage may be through the indirect, but important, policy goal of increasing women's wages and reducing the wage gap between men and women that has persisted in spite of the enactment of the Equal Pay Act more than 30 years ago.

INCREASED EMPLOYEE EDUCATION

A great deal can be done—and is being done—through educating women on how to plan for retirement. And employers are increasingly providing this education. In a study last year more than 55 percent of employers with more than 200 employees reported providing guidance on retirement planning in newsletters, and more than 32 percent reported giving such advice through seminars (KPMG 1994). Recent data also indicate that women are becoming more adept at using the retirement planning sources available to them. For example, women contribute to 401(k) plans at a rate about the same as or greater than their male colleagues.

Basic facts such as the importance of working for employers who offer pension plans, the consequences of leaving a job with a pension plan, and the importance of starting early to save for retirement and investing for the long term can literally make a tenfold difference in women's retirement income. This "financial" education involves basic concepts such as the time value of money and the relationship between investment return and investment risk.

The Securities and Exchange Commission (SEC), which enforces the Investment Adviser Act, could encourage employers to educate their employees about effective retirement planning by promulgating rules clarifying that such employer efforts will not make those employers "investment advisers" subject to SEC regulation under the act. Such rules would ease employer concerns about holding seminars and providing brochures and work sheets for retirement planning.

PROTECTING RETIREMENT FINANCIAL SECURITY

Individual women, helped by women's groups dedicated to improving the economic status of women, can take immediate and critical steps toward improving their retirement security. The need for women to build their own savings for retirement is immediate. They simply cannot wait for policy changes.

Women need to be educated about retirement savings in the earliest days of their careers. And they need to educate their colleagues. Every woman can and should take the following steps to improve her retirement financial security.

• Begin an automatic savings program today.
• Confirm her wage history with the Social Security Administration and find out how much she may potentially receive from Social Security.
• Learn about her employer's retirement plans, as well as plans from previous employers which may be overlooked or forgotten.

- Start contributing to any employer plan for which she is eligible.
- Open an IRA early in the year.
- Take a course in personal financial planning.
- Review her retirement savings investments.

Women should not have to act alone. Groups and organizations that promote women's equity should provide help to individual women on the important economic issue of retirement. There are several actions that these groups can take regardless of their basic missions or their budgets.

- Support the Pensions Not Posies program organized by the Pension Rights Center in Washington, D.C., and endorsed by such groups as the Women's Research and Education Institute, 9 to 5, and the Older Women's League. This campaign seeks media attention regarding women's pensions and is often focused on Secretaries Day. The program urges employers to reward their female employees with significant retirement benefits rather than with flowers one day a year. The campaign also has produced flyers that outline in clear, nontechnical language basic retirement plan features and important steps working women can take to begin retirement planning.
- Organize or cosponsor seminars on retirement planning for their members, focusing especially on the younger members who might otherwise feel that they do not need to start planning for retirement at an early age. This can be as simple as a luncheon speaker on the issue or as in-depth as a series of classes or workshops held after work.
- At the least, provide a list of available retirement planning opportunities or a bibliography of materials on retirement planning to their members.

THE FUTURE

Retirement security for women will remain a challenge as long as women continue to earn less money than men and experience more interruptions in their career patterns. Lower wages result in lower public and private pension benefits for women than for men. They also make it more difficult for women to save adequately for their longer period of retirement. Enforcement of the Equal Pay Act and other actions to increase women's wages and access to retirement plans may move women toward parity with men's rates of coverage in employer-provided retirement plans. At the same time more income may enable women to achieve higher levels of saving to meet their retirement needs.

But in the area of financial security an early start makes all the difference. Saving small amounts of money in one's twenties and thirties can make a big difference in retirement because the money saved has so many years to grow. Women who start later can also build a safer retirement with their own steady savings. Despite improvements in employer retirement plans or Social Security, women must be encouraged to start planning early and continuously for retirement.

SIX

★

WOMEN AND PENSIONS: A POLICY AGENDA

Cindy Hounsell

HIGHLIGHTS

IN CHAPTER FIVE, MARTHA PRIDDY PATTERSON DISCUSSES the effect of women's work patterns and earnings on their future pension income. As noted, women as a group are more affected by present pension policies than are men and are more likely to end their lives in poverty.

- Despite the dramatic increase in women's workforce participation, their access to and participation in pension plans have not increased at the same rate. The major reason is that women are concentrated in low-wage, service, part-time, nonunion, and small-firm jobs where pension coverage is less common.
- Although the pension laws are gender-neutral, inequities in the workplace and in family caregiving roles mean that women are less likely to be covered by pension plans. This eventually translates into financial problems and inadequate retirement income for older women.
- As long as women account for the majority of the elderly population and inequities in women's employment and caregiving responsibilities persist, the retirement profile for future generations of women will remain bleak unless important policy changes are made.
- Recommended policy changes include lowering the vesting requirements from five to three years for most plans, eliminating pension integration and backloading formulas, and instituting cost-of-living adjustments and portability provisions.

THREE-LEGGED STOOL

Policy experts illustrate the mechanism for providing adequate retirement income as a three-legged stool consisting of a Social Security retired-worker benefit, an employer-sponsored pension, and individual savings. Although none of these sources of income is assured, each is an essential element for replacing preretirement income.

Analysts estimate that employees must plan to replace at least 70 to 90 percent of preretirement income in order to maintain their standard of living after retirement. And since women live longer than men, they will need even more retirement income than men do. Because only a small percentage of older women receive pension income and most do not have significant personal savings, many women must rely on Social Security as their primary source of income.

The problem is that Social Security was meant to provide only a bare minimum or a "floor of protection." In 1994 the average Social Security benefit for retired female workers was $6,456 per year—$650 below the official poverty level for older adults and almost $2,400 less than an annual minimum-wage income. The fact that so many elderly women rely on Social Security as their only source of income is one of the major reasons that so many elderly women are poor.

The second leg of the retirement stool—private pensions—can provide an important source of income to women. However, only 13 percent of women age 65 and over are currently receiving a private pension, and the median annual pension income in 1992 was only $2,511 (Grad 1994).

The third leg of the stool—voluntary savings—is increasingly being emphasized as a major source of retirement income. However, statistics indicate that voluntary savings are not adequate to supplement Social Security. The median income from assets is only $1,059 a year for women age 65 and over.

POVERTY

Although the overall poverty rate for the elderly has declined over the past several decades, there are still pockets of severe poverty among certain groups. Older women are nearly twice as likely as older men to be living near or below the federal poverty level. The incidence of female poverty increases with age; while almost 21 percent of women age 65 to 74 lived below the poverty level in 1992, the poverty rate for all women age 75 and older was 24 percent. The poverty rate for women of color is even greater than for white women at each age: For black women the poverty rate for women age 75 and older was 43 percent, and for women of Hispanic origin, it was 35 percent.

MARITAL STATUS

The amount of pension benefits and the income that an older woman receives are directly related to her marital status. Unfortunately, however, being married is no guarantee that a woman will have sufficient income in retirement. Married women often count on their husbands' retirement benefits to support them in old age, but since women tend to outlive their husbands (and their husbands' retirement income), the poverty rate for widows age 65 and older is 21 percent.

The reforms of the Retirement Equity Act of 1984 (REA) have greatly improved the chances that a widow will continue receiving pension payments. The REA requires private pension plans to pay survivor benefits unless a spouse waives this protection in writing. One government study found that survivor benefit coverage has increased by 15 percent since the law took effect (General Accounting Office 1992).

However, problems still arise because the spousal consent forms that are used to waive the benefit are confusing. Many couples choose the larger benefit instead of the survivor benefit without understanding that as a result, a wife will not receive any benefit after her husband's death. Still others do not understand that even when they elect the survivor benefit, the widow will probably receive only half of the amount received while her spouse was alive.

A positive reform for women would be to provide either surviving spouse with a benefit equal to two-thirds of the benefit received while both were alive. However, this reform would reduce the benefit that the couple could receive while both were still living.

The REA also made an important start in helping divorced women get a share of their former spouses' pension plans by making it possible for pension plans to pay benefits directly to divorced spouses. However, it is still up to the discretion of state court judges to determine how much of her spouse's pension a divorced woman will receive.

Pension accrual may represent a couple's largest asset. However, many women continue to lose out on this important benefit because they do not have the legal and financial expertise needed to gain a share of the pension at the time of divorce, to ask for a survivor benefit, and to obtain a court order requiring that the pension plan pay benefits directly to the woman.

A positive reform for women would be to require a default option in which pension benefits are divisible unless the couple agrees in its separation agreement or under a court order that the benefits are not to be divided. Another positive step would be to require the Department of Labor to provide model language for court orders that could be distributed to attorneys and judges around the country.

PENSION COVERAGE FOR WOMEN

Low rates of pension coverage increase the likelihood that many women will retire without private pension benefits. The good news for women is that the gender gap in pension coverage for full-time workers has narrowed considerably: to three percent. In 1993, 48 percent of full-time female workers had pension coverage, compared with 51 percent for men. However, it is important to realize that the closing of this gender gap—a trend that began in 1972—is due in large part to declining pension coverage for men.

The bad news for women is that their coverage rate has improved mostly for employees who have some college education and who work full time, while there has been a decline in coverage for women with less than a high school education (Reno 1992). If all private-sector workers are included— part-time as well as full-time workers—the coverage rate for women remains at 39 percent, compared with 46 percent for men.

The large number of women who work for small firms are at a disadvantage because these companies are less likely to establish pension plans. In 1993 only 13 percent of full-time workers at firms with fewer than 10 employees reported pension coverage: 12 percent for men and 14 percent for women.

One way to expand coverage, particularly among small firms, is to educate employers about Simplified Employee Pensions (SEPs). With a SEP the employer contributes a percentage of the employee's salary to a defined contribution plan. Because the employer does not have to pay administrative expenses or file forms with the government, SEPs provide a realistic alternative to conventional and more complex pension plans.

Many women find themselves without pension coverage because they work for employers that sponsor pension plans but exclude some groups of workers—such as part-time workers or workers in certain job classifications—from those plans. There are no legal requirements that an employer must include all employees in a pension plan; employers are still able to exclude up to 30 percent of their workers from pension plans.

One reform that would help women (and men) would be to require plans to include all employees within an employer's single line of business who have worked for more than a year and are over age 21.

PENSION RECEIPT

Although the gap between men and women in pension coverage has been greatly reduced, the continuing disparity between men's and women's benefit accumulation still results in considerably smaller pension income for women.

Women are often unaware that their work patterns will result in lower benefit levels because of the complicated formulas used to calculate benefits. These formulas, which often favor longer-service, higher-paid, and older employees, can have a devastating effect on the dollar amount of workers' benefits. The two formulas that affect women's benefits the most are pension integration and backloading formulas. In addition, women's pension benefits are often dramatically affected by laws governing vesting and portability of benefits.

INTEGRATION

Pension integration has always hit female workers the hardest because women tend to dominate the lower-paid positions in the workforce. Many plans use pension integration to subtract part of a worker's Social Security benefit from her pension, thereby producing substantial savings for the employer.

The rationale for pension integration is that since Social Security replaces a larger percentage of the income for the lower-paid worker than it does for the higher-paid, an employer should be able to use the pension plan to offset the discrimination against the higher-paid employee.

A 1986 law instituted a requirement that a worker must still be left with half her pension after the integration formula is applied, but this provision is effective only for new benefits earned after 1988. Reform legislation that would benefit women and men calls for the elimination of pension integration altogether, effective for plan years beginning on or after the year 2002.

BACKLOADING

Women are also penalized by backloading formulas that give much greater worth to years worked closer to retirement age than to earlier years. Under a "fractional rule" backloading formula, the years worked between the ages of 55 and 65 can be worth four times as much as years worked between the ages of 25 and 35. A whiplash problem occurring now with company down-sizing is that when a mid-career worker leaves a company, the amount of the pension benefit remains at the same level until she reaches retirement age. A pension benefit terminated in mid-career may become virtually worthless by the time the worker retires.

VESTING

The typical worker changes jobs many times during her career. If she works for an employer for fewer than five years, a worker does not earn a right to a pension or vest under most plans. The most recent study by the Department of Labor shows that average job tenure for women is 3.8 years (Bureau of Labor Statistics 1992).★

Until 1989 most pension plans required 10 years of service with an employer in order to earn a benefit. Starting in 1989, most plans were required to reduce their vesting rules to five years, with the exception of multiemployer plans (union-negotiated plans under which more than one company pays into the plan). The change to five-year vesting has meant that 75 percent of women in pension plans are expected to earn a pension, compared with about 50 percent who would have earned a pension under the previous 10-year rule. While this represents a major reform, it still leaves a large gap. A study conducted by the Urban Institute estimates that if a three-year vesting provision were adopted for all plans, a million more women would be collecting benefits by the year 2002 (Zedlewski 1988).

Reforms to address this problem would require three-year vesting for single-employer plans or graded one- to five-year vesting. (Graded vesting currently is three to seven years—20 percent vesting after three years with an additional 20 percent each year until full vesting is reached after seven years.) For multiemployer plans, vesting should be reduced from 10 to five years. The Labor Department has estimated that the change in vesting from 10 to five years would result in benefits for an additional 1.1 million workers (Beller 1990).

★This job tenure statistic is based on women age 16 and over. It differs from the job tenure statistic of 4.8 years for women in Chapter Five, which is based on women age 25 and over.

PORTABILITY

Portability refers to the ability of employees to take vested pension benefits with them when they change jobs. Even if a woman vests, she may lose a substantial part of her earned benefit if she changes jobs before retirement. This is because the pension will be based on her wages as of the date she leaves the plan. If her benefit is from a traditional type of pension plan, such as a defined benefit plan, inflation will decimate the value of her fixed benefit long before she reaches retirement age. Portability reform would resolve this problem by allowing workers who change jobs to transfer their vested benefits to their new plans or to Individual Retirement Accounts.

INFLATION AND COST OF LIVING INCREASES

Since very few pension plans are indexed for inflation, the value of benefits continues to erode after retirement. And since women live longer than men, the impact of inflation is greater for them. One projection estimated that eight percent of the elderly living in poverty by the year 2020 will have become poor as the result of the erosion by inflation of their retirement income (Lewin/ICF 1987).

NEW TRENDS

Most recently the decline in employer-paid pensions suggests a decrease in the number of American workers who will receive adequate pension incomes in the future. The trend away from employer-paid pensions and toward do-it-yourself tax-deferred savings plans in which the employee contributes to her own retirement will further threaten the income security of older women. Because of lower earnings, women are less likely to accumulate significant benefits through tax-deferred savings plans. This development requires women to bear not only the burden of contribution but also the risk of investment.

The trend toward part-time and temporary employment, with the concomitant erosion of worker benefits, represents a fundamental change in the American workplace. The current law allows employers with pension plans to exclude people who work less than 1,000 hours a year. Even if the part-time or temporary worker manages to work the minimum required hours, she is not likely to remain on one job for the five years required under most plans to earn a benefit.

Reform legislation would protect part-time and temporary workers by providing pension credits to all employees working 500 hours or more a year.

Denying coverage to part-time workers who work fewer than 1,000 hours keeps a great many women out of their companies' pension plans. By giving them credit toward earning a pension, this reform would provide significant help for women, who make up almost two-thirds of the contingent workforce.

CONCLUSION

In order for pensions to provide a significant source of income for older women, several policy changes are needed. The private pension coverage rate of 39 percent for women workers needs to be expanded, the number of years required for vesting should be further reduced to accommodate the needs of a mobile workforce, pension integration and backloading formulas should be eliminated, and cost-of-living adjustments and portability provisions are needed in order to preserve earned benefits. These policy changes would greatly enhance the income security of elderly women and men.

In Review
July 1993–
March 1995

IN REVIEW:
JULY 1993–MARCH 1995[1]

"In Review" aims to cover key issues and developments of importance to American women over a recent period of time. An entire book would be required to include every significant occurrence, every state court decision and legislative initiative, and every newsworthy research development with implications for women. Nevertheless, the editors hope that what has been included here will help the reader recapture the flavor of a period when there were real gains for women in some areas and a stubborn resistance to women's equality in others.

1993

July 1 / The Association of American Medical Colleges reports that women accounted for the majority of students at nine of America's medical schools in 1992–93, and for the majority of new entrants at twice that many schools. Overall, 39.4 percent of medical students enrolled in 1992–93 were women—a record.

July 4 / The National Organization for Women (NOW) winds up its 27th annual convention, having reelected Patricia Ireland as its president. Embodying the convention theme—"Everyday Women, Extraordinary Acts"—Marilyn Jancsy and Sally Bartolo were featured speakers. They are

[1]The editors would like to thank Anne J. Stone for preparing "In Review" for this edition of *The American Woman*. Much of the credit for "In Review" in this edition belongs to Bridget Rice, who tackled a monumental task with spirit, intelligence, and determination. Special thanks are also due Shanda Boyett, Elizabeth Matthews, Yvonne McNeese, Jennifer LeFevre, Sandra Okoed, and Georgia Sadler.

former school cafeteria workers who recently won a pay equity suit against Everett, Massachusetts.

July 5 / More than a third of American households have no discretionary income, according to a publication released today by New Strategist of Ithaca, New York. The "Official Guide to American Incomes" reports that in 1992 only 64 percent of U.S. households had money left after paying for the necessities of life (food, taxes, clothing, and housing). Men living alone were most likely to have discretionary income; they were followed by married couples without children at home and women living alone. The emptiest pockets belonged to married couples with three or more children and female-headed households with no spouse present.

July 13 / A coalition spearheaded by the National Black Women's Health Project announces a campaign to repeal the Hyde Amendment, which prohibits Medicaid funding for abortions except in cases of rape or incest or when the woman's life is in danger. The amendment passed the House earlier this year, but the group hopes to persuade the Senate to repeal it.

July 14 / The Census Bureau releases a new report showing that single motherhood became considerably more common over the decade 1982–92: As of mid-1992 nearly one-fourth (24 percent) of never married women age 18 to 44 had borne a child, compared with 15 percent 10 years earlier. Out-of-wedlock childbearing increased among women of all racial and ethnic groups and all levels of education. Still, the percentage of single mothers was largest among black women (67 percent in 1992, up from 49 percent in 1982).

July 15 / The Senate Veterans' Affairs Committee approves a bill to expand VA health care services for female veterans. The legislation includes provisions to expand the sexual trauma counseling program, improve research relating to female veterans, and establish standards of quality for mammography screening.

July 27 / The House and Senate Armed Services committees approve their versions of the Department of Defense authorization bill. Both would repeal the last statutory barrier to women's equal participation in the military, the law that currently bans women from serving on combat ships. (By policy, however, women will continue to be barred from serving in the infantry, armor, and artillery.) Both bills also incorporate provisions of the Defense Women's Health Improvement Act of 1993, introduced last week by Representatives Patricia Schroeder (D-CO) and Marilyn Lloyd (D-TN). These provisions require military hospitals and health clinics to make available such services as Pap smears, mammograms, obstetric and gynecological care, menopausal care, sexual abuse treatment, and treatment of sexually transmitted diseases and to establish a Defense Women's Health Research Center to conduct research and develop treatments relating to servicewomen's health.

July 27 / The New Jersey Supreme Court rules unanimously that plaintiffs in sexual harassment cases must file suit within two years of the alleged harassment or lose the right to sue. The time limit is necessary, says the court, because the proof in these cases "generally depends on testimonial evidence. Depending on the memory and availability of witnesses, that testimony can dissipate or even disappear over time." However, the court says the two-year limit applies only to sexual harassment cases that arise after today. The court sends back to a lower court for trial the case that gave rise to today's decision, a suit filed by Jessica Montells two years and 10 days after she resigned her job, allegedly because of sexual harassment.

July 30 / In a memorandum released today, Congresswoman Nancy Pelosi (D-CA) expresses the view that the Clinton Administration's plan for expediting the exclusion of asylum seekers discriminates against refugee women who, for reasons relating to their gender, seek asylum in this country. According to Representative Pelosi, "internationally . . . it has been documented that refugee interpretations have ignored the persecution of women violating social norms, including violating marriage conventions, prohibitions on public expression, and contravention of religious-based lifestyle roles. Even more urgent today, the law has largely failed to recognize the political nature of seemingly private acts of harm to women, [such as] the practice of rape as a component of 'ethnic cleansing' in Bosnia. . . ."

July 31 / The Wesleyan Chapel Block of the Women's Rights National Historical Park opens in Seneca Falls, New York. The focal point of the block is the Wesleyan Methodist Chapel, where the First Women's Rights Convention was held in July 1848.

August 1 / Katherine A. Hagen takes office as deputy director general of the International Labor Organization. Ms. Hagen, a lawyer by profession, is the first American woman to hold this position.

August 1 / Cheryl Campbell Steadman and Marie Reynolds Garcia are sworn in as Texas Rangers, becoming the first women ever to serve in that fabled corps. Like all personnel admitted to the Rangers, both women are already experienced law enforcement officers.

August 2 / The House of Representatives approves legislation reauthorizing the Department of Education's Office of Educational Research and Improvement (OERI) through fiscal year 1997. The measure would require all data collected by OERI to be cross-tabulated, analyzed, and reported by sex, within race or ethnicity and socioeconomic status if possible. It would require OERI to fill directorships of the research institutes with qualified minorities and women. And it would give OERI the authority to seek ways to promote gender equity in all aspects of schools (policy, teacher training, and management).

August 3 / By a vote of 51 to 48 the Senate agrees to a measure ensuring that coverage for abortions will be available in federal employees' health insurance plans, effective October 1. The vote, on a procedural matter, was engineered by five Democratic women senators and took anti–abortion senators by surprise. Currently federal employees' health insurance plans can provide abortion coverage only in cases where the woman's life would be endangered by carrying the fetus to term.

August 5 / The Family and Medical Leave Act goes into effect, eight years after it was first introduced in Congress (*see* previous editions of *The American Woman*). The law allows workers at companies with 50 or more employees up to 12 weeks of unpaid leave in order to care for a new baby, an ill family member, or their own illness—without losing their health insurance coverage and with the assurance that they can return to the same or an equivalent job.

August 6 / The Senate confirms Sheila E. Widnall as Secretary of the Air Force. This is a historic first; no woman has ever before been secretary of any U.S. military service.

August 10 / For the third year in a row the policymaking delegates of the American Bar Association endorse a pro–choice position on abortion rights.

August 10 / Ruth Bader Ginsburg is sworn in as the 107th Supreme Court Justice. This brings to two the number of women on the nine-member Supreme Court.

August 11 / A nine-country study published today in the August issue of the *Journal of Population Economics* found that low-income American families are less likely to escape poverty than their counterparts in Canada and seven Western European nations that have more generous welfare benefits than the United States has. Greg J. Duncan of the Institute for Social Research at the University of Michigan was principal author of the study.

September 1 / The September issue of the *Quarterly Review of Biology* is devoted largely to Margaret Profet's new hypothesis about menstruation. Ms. Profet, a biologist at the University of California at Berkeley, theorizes that menstruation is a mechanism for regularly flushing the uterus and fallopian tubes of harmful microbes carried by incoming sperm.

September 10 / The Health Insurance Association of America (HIAA) airs the first of 14 "Harry and Louise" television advertisements opposing President Clinton's soon-to-be-introduced health care reform bill. This highly successful ad campaign runs from September 1993 through September 1994, at a cost to HIAA of $13.4 million.

September 20 / The Joint Committee on the Organization of Congress releases the results of a survey showing that most congressional staffers are poorly informed about the House or Senate Office of Fair Employment

Practices (OFEP) and would be reluctant to turn to an OFEP for help if they felt they had been discriminated against or harassed on the job. About 70 percent of the Hill aides who responded to the survey would have some reservations about contacting OFEP with an inquiry or to initiate a complaint. Their reasons include fear that their employer would retaliate and the belief that they would jeopardize their prospects of finding another congressional job. The survey was conducted for the Joint Committee by the Congressional Management Foundation.

September 21 / Clare Dalton, who six years ago sued Harvard University for sex discrimination after she was denied tenure on the Harvard faculty, accepts a $260,000 settlement from Harvard to end the suit. The money will be used to fund a new domestic violence institute that will be jointly sponsored by Harvard and Northeastern University, where Ms. Dalton is now a professor. Ms. Dalton is the wife of Robert Reich, the U.S. Secretary of Labor.

September 21 / The percentage of preschool-age children who were cared for by their fathers while their mothers worked increased sharply between 1990 and 1991, according to a report released today by the Population Reference Bureau. In 1991 fathers cared for the youngsters while mothers were at work in 20 percent of families where there were preschoolers with working mothers; the comparable percentage just one year earlier was 16.5. The report was based on Census Bureau surveys of working mothers about their child care arrangements.

September 23 / Vicki Van Meter, age 11, becomes the youngest female to pilot a plane coast to coast when she lands her single-engine Cessna in San Diego. She began the flight in Augusta, Maine. Because the law says she is too young to fly solo, Ms. Van Meter was accompanied by her instructor, who says he never touched the controls.

September 25 / The trustees of all-male Virginia Military Institute (VMI) vote to underwrite a military program for women at Mary Baldwin College, a women's college in Staunton, Virginia, some 30 miles from Lexington, the site of VMI. VMI, a state-supported institution, hopes thereby to avoid having to admit women to its own programs. A federal court has ruled that by establishing an equivalent program for women at another college, VMI may be able to satisfy the requirements of Title IX, which prohibits discrimination on account of sex in publicly funded educational institutions.

September 27 / According to today's *Washington Post,* two female employees of the Senate restaurant who were subjected to sexual harassment by a supervisor have been awarded monetary damages, along with guarantees of job protection and a written apology. *Post* reporter Helen Dewar writes that this is the first case to be resolved under the system created by the Senate last year to handle sexual harassment and job discrimination complaints.

September 28 / The Women's Research and Education Institute (WREI) presents its 1993 American Woman Award to Marian Wright Edelman, founder and president of the Children's Defense Fund, a national organization that advocates on behalf of children.

September 28 / The substantial grants awarded by the Howard Hughes Medical Institute to enhance education in the biological sciences are the subject of Judy Mann's column in today's *Washington Post*. According to Ms. Mann, the institute is "putting special emphasis on [university] programs that are trying to increase the participation of women and underrepresented minorities." She writes that the institute has already provided research support for 11,500 students, 56 percent of them women and 27 percent of them minorities.

October 2 / Ellen M. Lazarus is sworn in as president of the Federal Bar Association, the first woman in half a century to hold that office. Janet Reno, the first woman ever to serve as U.S. Attorney General, administers the oath.

October 7 / The Nobel Committee announces that the 1993 Nobel Prize for Literature will be awarded to novelist Toni Morrison. She is the first black woman (and the eighth woman) ever to receive the prize.

October 7 / The National Association of Women Judges gathers for its 15th annual conference. Of particular concern to the group are the conditions faced by the rapidly increasing number of women in prison and by their children. Eighty percent of incarcerated women are reportedly mothers, of whom 70 percent are single parents.

October 11 / Suzanne J. Doucette, an agent of the Federal Bureau of Investigation (FBI) who testified before the Senate in May regarding sexual harassment in the bureau, tells the press that she has been placed on unpaid leave, in "retaliation," she says, for her testimony. Ms. Doucette says she considers herself "constructively discharged" from the FBI and plans to turn in her badge.

October 11 / Ground is broken at Riverside Park in New York City for the Eleanor Roosevelt Monument, reportedly the first public statue of a president's wife in the country.

October 14 / At a forum sponsored by the Women's Bureau of the U.S. Department of Labor, experts on women's employment and working conditions call for changes in U.S. labor law to meet female workers' needs. Scholars and other participants in the conference, entitled "Labor Law Reform: Viewpoints from Working Women," explain that existing labor law was based on a dated model that applies to fewer and fewer American workers, especially women.

October 15 / John H. Dalton, Secretary of the Navy, announces that the Navy has censured three admirals and taken less serious administrative action against 30 other high-ranking officers in connection with the notorious 1991 Tailhook Association convention. Secretary Dalton calls the Tailhook affair "a failure of leadership" *(see The American Woman 1994–95).*

October 18 / By a vote of 80 to 15 the U.S. Senate approves an appropriations bill that includes provisions barring Medicaid-funded abortions except in cases of rape and incest or when the woman's life would be endangered by her carrying the fetus to term. The bill is slightly less restrictive than current law, which allows Medicaid-funded abortions only when the mother's life is in danger.

October 18 / President Clinton signs a proclamation declaring today National Mammography Day. Leaders of the National Breast Cancer Coalition present the President and Hillary Rodham Clinton with a petition asking for an increase in federal funds for breast cancer research. The petition contains 2.6 million signatures, a number said to represent the estimated number of American women who have breast cancer, whether they know it or not.

October 22 / President Clinton announces that he will appoint Geraldine Ferraro U.S. representative to the United Nations Human Rights Commission, a position with ambassadorial rank.

October 25 / The U.S. Senate confirms the promotion of Irene Trowell-Harris to the rank of brigadier general in the Air National Guard. She is the first black woman (and the third woman) ever to attain the rank of general in the National Guard.

October 27 / Accompanied by Hillary Rodham Clinton, President Clinton delivers the Administration's health care reform proposal, the Health Security Act, to Congress. This complex bill, which is intended to ensure universal health care coverage while controlling costs, is the result of nine months of work by the Administration's Health Care Task Force. It provides each American and legal resident with a health security card guaranteeing "health care that can never be taken away."

All American citizens and legal residents would be guaranteed a core package of benefits defined by the federal government. Most people and companies would buy insurance through large health care purchasing alliances—with employers contributing 80 percent toward the cost of insurance premiums and employees contributing 20 percent. Federal subsidies would be available for the poor, small businesses, and the self-employed and unemployed. Medicare would be maintained and enhanced with a drug plan and long-term home care. Major savings would be achieved by managed competition and limiting expected growth in Medicare and Medicaid.

October 28 / A federal district court jury in New York finds that Goldman, Sachs & Co., a leading New York investment bank, discriminated against Joanne T. Flynn because of her sex. Ms. Flynn, a former Goldman, Sachs vice president who thought she was on the firm's fast track, brought a sex discrimination suit against the firm after she failed to receive a promotion she was expecting and was fired shortly afterward. Whether Ms. Flynn may be entitled to monetary damages will depend on how Judge Kimba Wood rules on a Goldman, Sachs motion to overturn the verdict.

November 1 / A committee of the Institute of Medicine finds fault with the Women's Health Initiative, a multimillion-dollar project planned by the National Institutes of Health (NIH). According to the committee (composed of seven women and four men), the information the NIH study is expected to yield could be gathered in smaller studies at less cost. The Institute of Medicine is an independent group of experts that advises the federal government.

November 2 / Christine Whitman is elected governor of New Jersey. A pro-choice Republican, Ms. Whitman will be the state's first female governor.

November 9 / In a unanimous decision the U.S. Supreme Court rules in *Harris* v. *Forklift Systems* that victims of sexual harassment under Title VII of the Civil Rights Act may be entitled to compensation without having to prove that the harassment caused them psychological damage. According to the Court, "while psychological harm, like any other relevant factor, may be taken into account, no single factor is required." In its opinion, which was written by Justice Sandra Day O'Connor, the Court clarifies its definition of harassment, describing it as creating "an environment that would reasonably be perceived, and is perceived, as hostile or abusive."

November 9 / Catalyst, a nonprofit organization in New York, releases its latest study of women on the boards of the 1,000 Fortune 500 and Fortune Service 500 companies. The data are not encouraging: Overall, only 6.2 percent of the board seats are held by women, and nearly half of the companies have no women on their boards.

November 10 / A spokesman for the company that markets Norplant in the United States explains to a congressional panel why the contraceptive implant costs $365 in this country, nearly 16 times as much as it costs in Sweden and some other countries. An officer of Wyeth-Ayerst Laboratories says the price has been kept high so that Norplant will not be perceived by middle-class women as a poor woman's drug. He tells the House Small Business Subcommittee on Regulations, Business Opportunities, and Technology that in two years his company will make the implant available to federally funded family clinics at a reduced price.

November 14 / Interest in a business career has plummeted among U.S. college undergraduates, according to an article by Claudia Deutsch in today's

New York Times. The trend is particularly noticeable among women: Between 1987 and 1992 the proportion of freshman women who wanted to major in business dropped from 20 percent to 12 percent.

November 15 / The U.S. Supreme Court allows to stand a Mississippi state law requiring a woman under age 18 to obtain permission from both parents before having an abortion.

November 15 / The U.S. Justice Department files a brief arguing that a Virginia Military Institute–sponsored leadership program at Mary Baldwin College is not an acceptable substitute for admitting women to VMI (*see* September 25, 1993). The plan "allows sex discrimination to continue," according to Acting Assistant Attorney General James P. Turner.

November 16 / The U.S. Labor Department reports that the government has underestimated unemployment, particularly among women, for at least a decade. The undercount arose from a bias in the survey questionnaire used to collect the data; the bias caused many women who were looking for jobs to be counted as homemakers, rather than as members of the labor force. A redesigned questionnaire, which is being tested in parallel with the old one this year, will become the official survey questionnaire beginning in January.

November 17 / In a study released today the National Center for Fair and Open Testing reports that boys win three-fourths of the federally funded college scholarships intended to encourage students to go into math, science, or engineering. The reason: The scholarships—given by the National Academy for Science, Space, and Technology—are awarded solely on the basis of students' scores on a standardized test and do not take into account such other academic measures as grades. Girls tend to do less well than boys on this standardized test.

November 17 / The U.S. Court of Appeals for the Fourth Circuit upholds a federal district court's ruling that Shannon Faulkner may attend classes with cadets at the Citadel while the lower court hears her lawsuit challenging the Citadel's all-male admissions policy.

November 17 / The White House announces that President Clinton has nominated Ricki Tigert, an attorney who specializes in international banking law, to head the Federal Deposit Insurance Corporation (FDIC). If she is confirmed by the Senate, Ms. Tigert will become the first woman ever to head a federal banking agency.

November 21 / The Administration's Health Security Act is officially introduced in Congress, sponsored by 31 senators and 100 members of the House.

November 22 / The Agency for International Development (AID) makes the first grant in a five-year $75 million commitment to the International Planned Parenthood Federation. This is the first time AID funds have gone to the federation since 1984, when the Reagan Administration banned U.S. funding for international population programs that include information or counseling on abortion. The view of the Clinton Administration, according to J. Brian Atwood, administrator of AID, is that "free and uncontested access to information about family planning and to a range of methods and services is a fundamental human right."

November 24 / In an op-ed piece published in today's *Washington Post* Diane Ravitch takes issue with the conclusions in "How Schools Shortchange Girls," a report released in February 1992 by the American Association of University Women (AAUW) *(see The American Woman 1994–95)*. Ms. Ravitch, who was an Assistant Secretary of Education in the Bush Administration, asserts that "a review of the facts will show that our schools are not guilty of gender bias and girls are not victims of discrimination." Among the facts she cites to support her position: Fifty-four percent of all bachelor's degrees and 53 percent of all master's degrees are awarded to women.

November 24 / An analysis released today by the Council of Better Business Bureaus suggests that the glass ceiling is less of a problem in the nonprofit sector than in the for-profit sector. The group reports that women head 18 percent of the 222 best-known nonprofit organizations, but only 0.5 percent of the top 1,000 for-profit companies. The council also found, however, that women who head nonprofits earn on average 18 percent less than men who head nonprofits.

November 30 / The U.S. Supreme Court declines to hear the State of Colorado's appeal in *Roberts* v. *Colorado State University,* thereby allowing to stand lower court decisions that the university violated Title IX of the 1972 Education Act when it abolished women's softball as a varsity sport. The case is the first involving a Title IX college athletics complaint to come before the High Court.

November 30 / President Clinton signs the Department of Defense authorization bill for fiscal year 1994 *(see July 27, 1993)*. The bill repeals the law barring Navy and Marine Corps women from permanent assignment on combat ships and requires that all proposed changes in women's combat assignments be approved by the House and Senate Armed Services committees. The legislation also calls for the establishment of gender-neutral performance standards. Among the measure's other provisions of special interest to women: It authorizes women's primary and preventive health care services at military hospitals and clinics and allows the establishment of a Defense Women's Health Research Center. It also requires the Army to continue the breast cancer research program.

December 2 / The 104th Congress, which includes a record number of women, approved more legislative measures concerning women and families this year than any Congress in any year for at least a decade, according to an analysis released today by the bipartisan Congressional Caucus for Women's Issues. The caucus lists 30 measures, many of which were first introduced by caucus members as stand-alone bills and were subsequently attached to other legislation. According to Representative Patricia Schroeder (D-CO), cochair of the caucus, "almost every major bill that has gone through [the Congress] has had a strong women's component."

December 3 / The National Cancer Institute (NCI) announces that its guidelines will no longer recommend regular mammograms for women age 40 to 49 who have no symptoms of breast cancer. According to the NCI, research has shown that routine screening does not reduce the breast cancer death rate for women in their forties. The NCI's decision is controversial: Anticipating today's announcement, the American Cancer Society, the American Medical Association, and a number of other outside groups went on record last month opposing any change in the mammography guidelines. Still other groups, including the American College of Physicians and the National Women's Health Network, have recommended that routine mammography treatment start at age 50. A NCI spokesman says that for women 50 and over, "a regular program of mammography and clinical breast examination every one to two years will reduce the mortality [from breast cancer] by approximately one-third."

December 4 / The startlingly high incidence of injuries among young female cross-country runners is the subject of an article by Marc Bloom in today's *New York Times*. Mr. Bloom reports that their injury rate (61.4 injuries per 100 runners) exceeds the rate among athletes in any other high school sport, including boys' football. The data were collected by Stephen Rice, the author of an ongoing study of injuries to high school athletes. A combination of factors is probably responsible, reports Mr. Bloom. Among them is the fact that preadolescent girls and thin adolescent girls who train heavily are likely to have low estrogen levels, a condition associated with fragile bones (stress fractures of the leg are among the four most common injuries among female runners).

December 5 / The 32 winners of Rhodes Scholarships are announced today, and 17 of them are females, the largest number of women since 1976, when the scholarships were first opened to women. The selection criteria for Rhodes Scholarships include academic excellence, integrity, leadership ability, and athletic prowess. Winners attend Oxford University in England.

December 6 / Judith Rodin is named president of the University of

Pennsylvania, her undergraduate alma mater. She is the first woman ever appointed to head an Ivy League university. Penn is continuing a pioneering tradition: It was the first Ivy League institution to admit women. Dr. Rodin is currently provost of Yale University.

December 14 / The Illinois Court of Appeals rules that the State of Illinois cannot compel a woman to undergo a caesarean section against her will, even if her fetus's life will be endangered by a vaginal delivery.

December 17 / Senator Nancy Kassebaum (R–KS) issues a statement calling on Senator Bob Packwood (R–OR) to resign. She is the first Republican senator to do so. Referring to Senator Packwood's "war" with the Senate Ethics Committee, which is investigating charges against him involving sexual and official misconduct, Senator Kassebaum says, "I believe it will be increasingly difficult, if not impossible, for Senator Packwood to effectively perform the duties of his office. I believe he should resign."

December 20 / An article in today's *New York Times* features five girls from Brooklyn who, as fifth graders, built a six-foot-long suspension bridge out of Erector sets. Their construction took first prize in the school division of the 1993 Erector Set Contest. The girls, now in middle school, constituted the entire membership of the Civil Engineering Club at their elementary school (P.S. 147, in Bedford-Stuyvesant). The bridge was a club project.

December 20 / Releasing a 600-page study concluding that there is "no statistical link between marital status and readiness," the Defense Department scuttles the Marine Corps's ban on recruiting married personnel.

December 21 / The U.S. Conference of Mayors releases the most recent edition of its annual report, "Hunger and Homelessness in American Cities." The survey of 26 major cities found that families with children now account for 43 percent of the homeless population, up from 33 percent last year.

December 22 / Data released today by the American Association of Colleges of Nursing (AACN) suggest that one of the most female-dominated of all professions (97 percent female) could in time become significantly less so. The AACN reports that men account for nearly 12 percent of all undergraduate (baccalaureate) nursing students at colleges and universities and for roughly 15 percent of the students in postgraduate nursing programs for college graduates of non-nursing programs.

December 28 / President Clinton issues a directive requiring states to provide Medicaid coverage for abortions in cases of rape or incest. The Medicaid program is funded partly by the federal government and partly by states, some of which have laws that bar spending public funds on abortions unless the mother's life is in danger.

1994

January 1 / Women are twice as likely as men to suffer posttraumatic stress disorder sometime during their lives, according to findings published in this month's issue of the *Archives of General Psychiatry*. Researchers who studied a representative sample of American women and men between the ages of 15 and 54 found that 12 percent of the women, compared with six percent of the men, had posttraumatic stress disorder at some point. Half the female cases of this psychiatric disorder, which results from a traumatic experience, arose from the women's having been raped or sexually molested.

January 5 / A federal circuit court ruling appears to clear the way for Shannon Faulkner to begin classes at the Citadel next week. The U.S. Court of Appeals for the Fourth Circuit, which previously ordered the Citadel to admit Faulkner (*see* November 17, 1993), denies the Citadel's request for a rehearing of the matter.

January 6 / Child support enforcement agencies collected $7.9 billion in child support in 1992, 16 percent more than in the year before, according to a Department of Health and Human Services report made public today. Still, the report says, the funds collected represented only one-fourth of what was owed.

January 6 / Robert Vladeck, head of the federal Health Care Financing Administration, says that despite some states' objections, the Clinton Administration will not change its mind about requiring Medicaid coverage for abortions in cases of rape and incest (*see* December 28, 1993).

January 7 / The National Abortion Rights Action League announces that it is changing its name to the National Abortion and Reproductive Rights Action League, although it will continue to use the acronym NARAL. Kate Michelman, the organization's executive director, says that "our nation's focus should not be on abortion but on giving people the information and tools they need to make informed choices about their lives and their families."

January 9 / Two businesswomen call on women to "give the phrase 'the glass ceiling' a decent burial." In an op-ed piece in today's *New York Times* Dawn-Marie Driscoll and Carol R. Goldberg assert that women are making it into the top ranks; the trouble is, "women executives are still not very visible in the news media." The authors call on the media to use women as sources more often; they also urge female executives to offer their services as media sources.

January 11 / Survey results released today show that women in the first year of college have higher educational aims than their male peers. More than two-thirds of first-year women plan to earn advanced degrees, a proportion that not only is the highest in the survey's history but exceeds that (63 percent) of first-year men. The proportion of female freshmen planning to pursue medical, law, or doctoral degrees also exceeds that of their male counterparts (27 percent versus 26 percent). The survey of nearly one-quarter of a million first-year students at 427 colleges and universities is conducted annually by the Higher Education Research Institute (HERI) at the University of California at Los Angeles.

January 12 / Shannon Faulkner registers for classes at the Citadel (*see* November 17, 1993) but finds she won't be allowed to attend them this week. Chief Justice William Rehnquist has issued an order barring her from classes until at least Monday.

January 12 / Job sharing in upper-level jobs is the subject of Diane Kunde's column in today's *Dallas Morning News*. Ms. Kunde discusses a number of job-sharing women, including two who successfully divide the president's job at a bank in Highland Park, Illinois.

January 13 / Secretary of Defense Les Aspin announces a policy that is expected to open more specialties and assignments to women in the armed forces. In a memorandum to the services Secretary Aspin rescinds the risk rule that has banned women from serving in noncombat units and positions that exposed them to a risk of combat equal to or greater than the risk faced by the associated combat units. The risk rule is being replaced by a less restrictive rule that will take effect on October 1 of this year. The Secretary's memorandum directs the services to provide him with a list of units and positions that would remain closed to women under the new policy.

January 13 / Women who breast-feed have a lower risk of developing early (premenopausal) breast cancer than other women, according to a study published in today's *New England Journal of Medicine*. Breast-feeding does not, however, appear to affect the risk of developing breast cancer after menopause, which is when more than three-quarters of breast cancers occur.

January 14 / The U.S. Court of Appeals for the Third Circuit rules that a Pennsylvania law restricting abortion rights must go into effect before it can be challenged in court as causing an undue burden for women. (In 1992 the U.S. Supreme Court ruled that states could constitutionally restrict abortion as long as the restrictions did not place an "undue burden" on women.) Today's ruling means that Pennsylvania's law could take effect in about three weeks.

January 14 / Governor William Weld (R) of Massachusetts introduces legislation that would drastically alter the welfare system in that state. The bill would require most able-bodied adults already on the AFDC rolls to take a job within a year (new applicants would have only 90 days) and would reduce their cash grants considerably once they were working. The state would use the money saved to provide child care, health care, and child support to these workers. (Recipients unable to find other employment would be required to enroll in a transitional community service employment program.) Since teenage mothers, disabled mothers, the legal guardians of welfare-eligible children, and persons caring for disabled children would be exempt from the work requirement, Massachusetts officials estimate that about half of the state's 100,000 AFDC recipients would be affected by the plan, which must be approved by the federal government.

January 14 / A committee of the National Research Council releases its analysis of why there are still so few women among the scientists and engineers employed in private industry. One reason is that female scientists are heavily concentrated in the life sciences, behavioral sciences, and social sciences—fields in which private industry offers few career opportunities. However, the committee found that female scientists in industry contend with discrimination and sex stereotyping by male scientists. Moreover, since scientists lose out professionally if they don't keep their skills up-to-date, having children can hurt a woman's career. The committee urges corporate policies, such as on-site child care, that would allow women to return quickly to work after childbirth.

January 15 / Applications to women's colleges across the country have increased 14 percent in the last two years, and enrollment is at a 14-year high, reports Maria Newman in today's *New York Times*. According to Ms. Newman, academic experts attribute the trend to such factors as concern about sexual harassment and a belief by young women and their parents that girls are treated differently from boys in coeducational schools.

January 16 / The earnings gap is narrower in New York City than in the rest of the country, according to a new study released today by scholars at the Institute for Urban and Minority Education at Columbia University's Teachers College. The researchers report that the female-to-male earnings ratio for workers who worked full time in New York City in 1989 was 77.5, compared with 66.0 for workers in the country as a whole. The analysis was based on data collected by the Bureau of the Census.

January 16 / Ruth Marcus writes in today's *Washington Post* that while President Clinton has been slow in filling vacancies in the federal judiciary, his record of appointing women and minorities outstrips that of his predecessors. Ms. Marcus notes that white males accounted for less than half (18 of 38) of President Clinton's nominees for federal judgeships in his first year. The comparable proportions of white males among his predecessors' first-year nominees were respectively: Carter 88 percent (30 of 34), Reagan 91 percent (41 of 45), and Bush 74 percent (17 of 23).

January 18 / Governor Robert Casey (D) of Pennsylvania says his state will disregard the federal directive requiring Medicaid to cover abortions in the case of rape or incest (*see* December 28, 1993). Governor Casey, who is an outspoken opponent of abortion, says the federal government exceeded its authority to override states' laws. Pennsylvania law allows Medicaid to pay for abortions in cases of rape or incest only when the crime has been reported to local law enforcement or health officials.

January 20 / Shannon Faulkner attends her first class at the Citadel (*see* January 5, 1994). Pending the outcome in appellate court of Ms. Faulkner's sex discrimination suit against the state-supported all-male institution, Ms. Faulkner has been admitted provisionally, allowed to take daytime classes but not to live on campus or to join the corps of cadets. The cadets are reported to be unhappy; one cadet told the *New York Times:* "The majority of people are just going to give her the cold shoulder. She's not wanted here."

January 23 / The Clinton Administration regards helping the world's women to control their fertility as key to promoting worldwide stability and family economic well-being, according to an article by Steven Greenhouse in today's *New York Times.* The Administration's policy for helping developing countries emphasizes not only family planning but also education for women. Mr. Greenhouse notes that the Clinton policy represents a "sharp departure" from the policies of Presidents Reagan and Bush.

January 24 / The *Washington Post* reports that researchers may have accidentally found the key to developing a male contraceptive pill when they noticed the effect of nifedipine, a drug widely prescribed to control blood pressure, on the ability of a spermatozoon to fertilize an egg. Nifedipine seems to interfere with the biochemical arrangements that normally help sperm penetrate the outer coating of an egg. The research findings were published in this month's issue of the *Journal of NIH Research.*

January 24 / In a unanimous decision the U.S. Supreme Court rules that abortion clinics can use the federal antiracketeering law to sue anti-abortion protesters who conspire to shut the clinics down. Groups convicted of breaking that law—the Racketeering-Influenced and Corrupt Organizations Act, or RICO—can be liable for triple damages. The decision reinstates a case *(National Organization for Women* v. *Scheidler)* that NOW filed in 1986 against Operation Rescue and other anti-abortion groups and individuals. NOW charges them with a nationwide conspiracy to put abortion clinics out of business through a campaign of violence and intimidation. To win its case, NOW must prove that the anti-abortion activities were part of a "pattern of racketeering activity."

January 25 / A federal district judge in South Carolina lifts his four-day-old order barring lawyers for the plaintiffs in a suit filed on behalf of drug-addicted pregnant women from talking to the press about the suit. The New

York–based Center for Reproductive Law and Policy has filed suit against the Medical University of South Carolina, charging that the university tested prenatal care patients for drug use without their knowledge and gave law enforcement authorities information about the tests, even though the women involved had not waived their right to confidentiality.

January 25 / The U.S. Court of Appeals for the Second Circuit rules that a victim of sexual harassment on the job can sue her employer even if she suffered no economic harm from the harassment. Stating that an employee's legal right to a workplace free of harassment and the employer's responsibility to provide such a workplace are the same whether or not she submits to unwelcome sexual advances, the court holds that "the focus should be on the prohibited conduct, not the victim's reaction." The ruling reinstates in lower court a suit *(Karibian v. Columbia University)* brought by a woman who charges that her supervisor forced her to have sexual relations with him in exchange for raises and promotions. The lower court judge had dismissed the suit because she had not proved that the harassment resulted in economic loss.

January 25 / Four girls are among the top 10 winners of this year's prestigious Westinghouse Science Talent scholarship awards, Westinghouse announced today. The four are: Jennifer Yu-Fe Lin of Flushing, New York (second place); Flora Tartakovsky of Queens, New York (sixth place); Jennifer Melissa Kalish of Baltimore, Maryland (eighth place); and Margaret Chalmers Bothner of Falmouth, Massachusetts (ninth place).

January 25 / In his televised State of the Union address to Congress, President Clinton focuses most of his attention on the deficiencies of America's health care system and urges Congress to act on his plan to overhaul it. Following the President's speech, Senate Minority Leader Robert Dole (R-KS) gives the official Republican response. He says there is no health care crisis in the country.

January 26 / The Women's Research and Education Institute releases a report, *Women's Health Insurance Costs and Experiences,* showing that women of childbearing age use more health care services than men and spend more out of pocket on health care than men spend. Because of these costs, the majority of women of color, poor women, and women without health insurance fail to get preventive services.

January 27 / The Associated Press reports that the Northwest Georgia Girl Scout Council plans to teach girls between the ages of five and 17 how to protect themselves from the virus that causes AIDS. The council, made up of 40,000 Scouts, will reportedly use a two-year $50,000 grant from Levi Strauss & Company to train staff members and volunteers in how to educate the girls. The project was sparked by concern about the increase in HIV infections among women in Georgia.

January 28 / Hillary Rodham Clinton goes to bat in Nevada for the Administration's health care reform proposals. Speaking to a group of doctors in Las Vegas, Mrs. Clinton says the claim that there is no health care crisis is "unfair and in many ways cruel."

January 30 / Cammy Myler becomes the first U.S. woman ever to win a World Cup luge competition.

January 31 / After meeting with President Clinton to discuss his health care reform proposals, the chairman and vice chairman of the National Governors' Association (NGA) report that the President is "willing to be flexible on mandatory alliances and global budgets." The health care policy statement adopted today by the NGA calls for employers to make core insurance coverage available "to those employees who wish to purchase it" but does not call for requiring employers to pay for any part of the insurance.

January 31 / Betty Heitman, who cochaired the Republican National Committee during the Reagan years and served under President Bush as director of his Committee on Executive Exchange, dies at age 64 at her home in Baton Rouge, Louisiana. Ms. Heitman, a conservative, is credited with prodding Presidents Reagan and Bush to appoint more women to high-level federal posts.

February 1 / In an advisory issued today the American College of Obstetricians and Gynecologists says that when it comes to exercising, women with uncomplicated pregnancies can let their own stamina and abilities be their guide. The group's new guidelines represent a considerable change from its earlier ones, which urged restricting the intensity of exercise during pregnancy. However, the main author of the advisory told Jane Brody of the *New York Times,* "In my opinion, there is really no point in exercising strenuously, since a pregnant woman can maintain cardiovascular fitness through mild to moderate exercise."

February 1 / The U.S. State Department releases its 1993 report on human rights around the world. In a summary of the report furnished to the press, the department says, "[W]e have paid special attention in 1993 to the problem of rampant discrimination against women. Physical abuse is the most obvious example. . . . In addition, the political, civil, and legal rights of women are often denied. . . . All too often, women and girls find that their access to education, employment, health care, and even food is limited because of their gender."

February 3 / Sexual harassment of female students is pretty much the norm at the U.S. military academies, an analyst for the General Accounting Office (GAO) tells a Senate subcommittee. According to Mark Gebicke's testimony for the GAO, "although relatively few cases of sexual harassment were formally reported, responses to [the GAO] survey indicated that nearly all academy women reported experiencing at least one form of sexual harassment during the academic year 1991."

February 3 / National Women in Sports Day is celebrated across the country. In Washington, D.C., Tipper Gore presents golfer Patty Sheehan with the 1994 Flo Hyman award for her dignity, spirit, and commitment to excellence outside her sport. Ms. Sheehan is among the female athletes lobbying legislators for stricter enforcement of Title IX, as well as for more funds for research into women's diseases.

February 3 / The U.S. Department of Health and Human Services (DHHS) says that it has begun an investigation of the prenatal care program at the Medical University of South Carolina (*see* January 25, 1994). The program tests some pregnant women for drugs without their knowledge and threatens those whose tests are positive with jail if they do not agree to undergo treatment. The hospital could be violating federal civil rights laws if its staff singles out black women for drug testing.

February 6 / The deadlocked jury in the recent Menendez trial split strictly on gender lines, according to an article by Mary Tabor in today's *New York Times*. The six men voted to convict the Menendez brothers of murder; the six women voted to convict for manslaughter, a lesser charge. Can the split be attributed purely to gender differences? Experienced trial lawyers queried by Ms. Tabor disagree on whether female jurors' reactions predictably differ from those of male jurors.

February 8 / The director of the Congressional Budget Office (CBO) delivers an evaluation of the Administration's health care plan that is widely regarded as furnishing powerful ammunition to those who oppose the plan. The CBO's Robert Reischauer says his office has concluded that the plan will cost $133 billion more than the Administration has estimated and that its funding should be included in the federal budget.

February 10 / A federal appeals court upholds a North Dakota law requiring women seeking an abortion to wait 24 hours before having the procedure, rejecting the argument that the requirement presents an undue burden to women in North Dakota, which has only one clinic (in Fargo) that performs abortions. The decision, by two of the three judges on a panel of the U.S. Court of Appeals for the Eighth Circuit, says in effect that the state regulation is not to blame for the fact that a North Dakota woman may have to make several long-distance trips to get an abortion.

February 11 / Parents' Fair Share, a pilot program to help absent parents find work so that they can provide financial support for their children, has shown real promise. An evaluation released today by the Manpower Demonstration Research Corporation (MDRC) found that two-thirds of the 4,000 delinquent parents required to join the program actively participated in job search workshops and remedial education classes. Fathers accounted for nearly all of the 4,000 program participants, who were ordered into the program by courts.

February 11 / The Navy drops the last charges in connection with the Tailhook scandal (*see* October 15, 1993).

February 11 / A spokesman for the General Accounting Office tells a congressional subcommittee that states are having difficulty enforcing standards for child care centers, even, in some cases, standards set by state law. According to the GAO's Joseph F. Delfico, "the number of children in care is outstripping states' capacity to protect them while in that care. . . . As demand for child care continues climbing . . . states will be further challenged to ensure the health and safety of children in care."

February 12 / Elizabeth Fox-Genovese testifies for the defense (Virginia Military Institute), telling the court that she approves of VMI's plan to set up a separate, less rigorous program for women at Mary Baldwin College rather than integrate them into the VMI program (*see* November 15, 1993). According to Dr. Fox-Genovese, who was the founding director of the women's studies program at Emory University, "young women, by the time they reach college, for whatever reason have less confidence in themselves. . . . We really don't need to beat uppityness and aggression . . . out of young women."

February 14 / Most women—especially those who are actually at high risk—think they are not at risk of contracting sexually transmitted diseases (STDs), most women say they know little or nothing about STDs other than AIDS, and few women realize that STDs are more harmful to women than to men. These are the survey findings released today by the Campaign for Women's Health and the American Medical Women's Association. Women's health advocates call on the government to educate people about STDs as it does about AIDS.

February 15 / The U.S. Air Force introduces its first female combat pilot, First Lieutenant Jeannie Flynn. Lieutenant Flynn, who has completed nine months of training on the F-15E Eagle fighter-bomber, will join her operational unit after a course in pilot survival training. The Air Force is the third of the U.S. military services to assign female pilots to combat aircraft: The Army assigned its first (Second Lieutenant Charlene Wagner, assigned to a Cobra attack helicopter) last June and now has six women qualified to fly combat helicopters; the Navy's first female combat pilot, Lieutenant Shannon Workman, flies off a carrier in the Atlantic.

February 15 / Two groups file an administrative challenge with the U.S. Department of Education in which they allege that using a standardized test as the primary criterion in awarding National Merit Scholarships violates Title IX because it discriminates against girls. Sixty percent of Merit Scholarship winners are male. The American Civil Liberties Union and the National Center for Fair and Open Testing assert that the Preliminary Scholastic Assessment Test (PSAT), which is the main criterion used in awarding Merit Scholarships and on which girls typically do less well than boys, is not a good predictor of how girls will do in college. On average girls get higher grades than boys in most subjects in both high school and college.

February 16 / Dana Priest writes in today's *Washington Post* that senior citizens "have not turned out to be the cheerleaders for the [Administration's health care reform plan] that the White House had hoped for and desperately needs." A survey conducted in January by the American Association of Retired Persons (AARP) found that although a majority of seniors polled think major health care reform is needed, more than half of elderly Americans either opposed the Clinton plan or were unsure about whether they should support it. "A one-word summation would be 'confusion,' " said an AARP spokesman. "The TV ads have scared a lot of older people. . . ."

February 16 / The *Washington Post* reports that the Army top brass have approved a plan that will—for the first time—allow female soldiers to guard the Tomb of the Unknowns at Arlington National Cemetery. The traditional height requirements for soldiers in this assignment will not, however, be changed; all who serve must be between 5′10″ and 6′4″.

February 16 / College authorities are worried by signs that heavy drinking is increasing among female students, according to an article by William Celis III in today's *New York Times*. Mr. Celis reports that although the proportion of college women who say they drink has remained steady (34 percent, compared with 51 percent of college men), studies on some campuses have shown a sharp increase in the percentage of women who have five or more drinks at one sitting and in incidents of violent behavior and public drunkenness on the part of female students.

February 17 / Lori Alvord, believed to be the first Navajo woman to become a surgeon, is the subject of an article by Elizabeth Cohen in today's *New York Times*. Dr. Alvord, who got her undergraduate degree at Dartmouth and her medical education at Stanford, is general staff surgeon at the Gallup (New Mexico) Indian Medical Center.

February 17 / The State of New Jersey settles a six-year-old employment discrimination lawsuit by agreeing to pay seven million dollars to blacks and women who were denied jobs as law enforcement officers because they did less well than white males on certain tests administered by the state. The state will also give job placement priority to about 450 blacks and women who were previously rejected. The U.S. Justice Department brought the suit in 1988, charging that the state's written test, on which blacks tended to do less well than whites, and its physical test, on which women tended to do less well than men, were not related to job performance.

February 21 / "Women's religious orders [in America] appear to be dying out," according to an article by Larry B. Stammer in today's *Los Angeles Times*. That newspaper's recent nationwide survey of a representative sample found that more than one-third of Roman Catholic nuns in the United States and Puerto Rico are over age 70 and only three percent are age 40 or younger. Most of the youngest nuns are in their forties.

February 23 / American speed skater Bonnie Blair wins the women's 1,000-meter speed skating race at the Winter Olympics in Lillehammer, Norway. This—her second win at these Olympic games—brings to five the number of gold medals Ms. Blair has won over three Olympic competitions and makes her the most successful American Winter Olympian ever.

February 24 / A panel of the Institute of Medicine, which has been studying the status of women in health research at the request of the federal government, releases a report recommending that pregnant women be allowed to participate in medical research if they wish, as long as they are fully informed of the risks. Federal regulations currently bar research on pregnant women.

February 27 / The 1994 Winter Olympics wind up. Of the 13 medals won by U.S. athletes, women took nine—four of the six golds (including the two won by Bonnie Blair), three of the five silvers, and both of the two bronzes.

February 28 / Reversing its leadership's earlier support for key elements in the Administration's health care reform proposals, the board of the U.S. Chamber of Commerce votes to oppose requiring employers to pay any part of their employees' health insurance coverage and "to suspend its policy" that universal coverage should be the goal of any health reform proposal.

February 28 / Whether black, Hispanic, or white, women are more likely than their male counterparts to attend college, but the disparity is widest (eight percentage points in 1992) among African Americans, in part because black males' enrollment has been dropping. These findings, reported in today's *Washington Post,* are from a study of college enrollment trends prepared by the American Council on Education.

March 1 / The influence of lobby groups in the health care reform debate is the subject of an article by Michael Weisskopf in today's *Washington Post*. Mr. Weisskopf reports that lobbying by the National Federation of Independent Businesses was key to getting the American Medical Association (AMA) to drop its earlier endorsement for requiring employers to pay for at least part of their employees' health insurance coverage. Four years ago the AMA endorsed the so-called employer mandates, central to the Clinton reform plan. The article also notes that after being lobbied by Fortune 500 company chairmen who employ large numbers of uninsured workers, the Business Roundtable endorsed Representative James Cooper's bill and added fuel to business opposition to President Clinton's plan.

March 2 / Chief Justice William Rehnquist rejects Senator Bob Packwood's (R-OR) plea to withhold his private diaries from the Senate Ethics Committee. The committee is investigating evidence that Senator Packwood may have engaged in sexual and official misconduct (*see* December 17, 1993).

March 3 / Lisa Henson, reported to be the youngest head of a Hollywood studio (she's 33), takes over as president of Columbia Pictures. Ms. Henson attributes her success partly to Lucy Fisher, Warner Brothers' executive vice president for worldwide theatrical production, for whom Ms. Henson worked for several years.

March 3 / A government study released today estimates that at least six percent of pregnant women are battered by their spouses or partners. The study, conducted by researchers at the Centers for Disease Control and Prevention (CDC), is based on a sampling of about 13,000 women in four states. The figures show that although violence against women occurs in all social groups, it is most common among the young, the least educated, those in crowded living conditions, the unmarried, and those who do not seek prenatal care.

March 4 / Republican members of Congress hold a retreat on health care but have already acknowledged that it will not provide a consensus because GOP lawmakers are deeply split over fundamental principles as well as details of reform.

March 6 / The Navy announces that more than 60 women will soon join the crew of the aircraft carrier *Eisenhower,* with plans eventually to have a total of 500 female officers and enlisted personnel assigned to that ship. This is the Navy's first-ever permanent assignment of women to a combat ship, but it will not be the last this year: The Navy says it expects that women will be serving on eight combat ships by the end of 1994. Navy women have served on support vessels since 1978.

March 8 / The *Wall Street Journal* reports that women considerably outnumber men among black professionals employed in the corporate sector, and the disparity has been increasing. The *Journal*'s analysis of Equal Employment Opportunity Commission data found a female-to-male ratio of 1.8 to 1.0 among black professionals in companies that reported to the EEOC in 1992, compared with 1.2 to 1.0 in 1982. White female professionals have also been gaining on their male counterparts but are still outnumbered: The female-to-male ratio among white professionals in 1992 was 0.94 to one, up from 0.62 to one 10 years earlier.

March 8 / Sexual harassment and discrimination against women are pervasive in federal law enforcement agencies, and the government does little or nothing to help the victims. In fact, according to five women testifying today before a subcommittee of the House Post Office and Civil Service Committee, in their experience the government protects the harassers at the expense of the victims. Three of the women are employed by the Drug Enforcement Administration, one is with the Bureau of Alcohol, Tobacco, and Firearms, and one is former FBI Agent Suzanne Doucette (*see* October 11, 1993).

March 9 / Bill Koch, who successfully defended the America's Cup in 1992 with his yacht *America³*, announces that his entry in next year's America's Cup race will be crewed entirely by women. At a news conference in New York, Mr. Koch introduces eight of the nine women who will form the nucleus of a 22-woman team. Sixteen members of the team will sail the Koch yacht in January 1995, when it must compete with two other American yachts for the right to defend the cup against a foreign challenger.

March 9 / Four servicewomen tell the House Armed Services Committee that despite stronger antiharassment rules and other reforms adopted by the military, sexual harassment is still a problem in the U.S. armed services. They say that servicewomen who bring complaints of harassment to their superiors often find that they, not their harassers, face punishment, ostracism as "troublemakers," or reassignment to less desirable posts. The committee also heard the recommendations of several advocates for military women, among them Patricia Gormley, a retired Navy captain who is director of WREI's Women in the Military Project.

March 10 / Commenting on the testimony at yesterday's Armed Services Committee hearing, Secretary of the Navy John Dalton says he was shocked to hear that superiors retaliated against servicewomen who brought complaints about sexual harassment. What "made his blood boil," Dalton says, was the shoddy response by the very system the Navy has set up to handle complaints.

March 11 / Two female FBI agents file a sex discrimination suit against the bureau. Heather Power-Anderson and Boni Carr Alduenda charge that their boss sexually harassed them and that supervisors retaliated against them for making formal complaints about the harassment. The FBI is overwhelmingly male; women account for 11 percent of its agents.

March 14 / The National Council of Negro Women's plan to establish a National Center for African American Women comes closer to reality with a gift from Camille and Bill Cosby, a landmark building to house the center. Dorothy Height, president of the council, says the Cosbys have given "significant momentum" to the council's $30 million campaign for a center.

March 14 / Senator Bob Packwood (R-OR) announces that he will turn over his diaries to the Senate Ethics Committee, which is investigating charges against him of sexual and official misconduct (*see* March 2, 1994).

March 14 / A Massachusetts state law against hate-motivated violence is brought to bear for the first time in a case involving violence against women. The Suffolk Superior Court orders a man who battered not only his wife but several other women with whom he has recently had relationships to stay away from these women and to refrain from assaulting any woman. If he disobeys the court's order, he faces up to 10 years in prison.

March 14 / The principal researcher in a major breast cancer study that turned out to include some falsified data reports that a reanalysis without the false data produces the same conclusion: Survival rates for most women with breast cancer are the same whether they have a lumpectomy followed by radiation treatments or a mastectomy.

March 16 / The first round of the women's National Collegiate Athletic Association (NCAA) basketball tournament begins, with 64 women's teams taking to the boards today. This is the first time that there are as many teams in the first round of the women's tournament as there are in the men's.

March 17 / U.S. Surgeon General Joycelyn Elders attacks cigarette advertising and delivers a stern warning about the dangers of smoking for teenagers as she releases the latest Surgeon General's report on smoking and health, "Preventing Tobacco Use among Young People."

March 17 / Montefiore Medical Center has agreed to pay Heidi Weissmann $900,000 to settle a sex discrimination suit she brought seven years ago against Montefiore and the Albert Einstein College of Medicine, with which it is affiliated. Ms. Weissmann, who was a researcher in nuclear medicine and associate professor of radiology at these New York institutions, charged that they failed to promote her because she was a woman. Both institutions deny the charges. The settlement was announced today.

March 17 / Lawyers representing thousands of women with silicon breast implants announce that they have reached a four-billion-plus-dollar settlement with implant manufacturers, although Dow Corning says it is still negotiating. If the manufacturers' corporate boards approve the settlement, it will reportedly be the largest product liability agreement in U.S. history.

March 17 / Americans who were age 25 to 30 last year (1992–93) were 10 pounds heavier on average than their counterparts seven years previously, according to a federally sponsored study by Cora E. Lewis of the University of Alabama in Birmingham. Her findings, released today, were based on a 5,000-plus study population that was equally divided among blacks and whites and women and men. Only among black women did the increase in weight average less than 10 pounds. The gain among white women averaged 10.1 pounds. Dr. Lewis speculates that a decline in physical activity is probably responsible.

March 19 / High school students with college ambitions take the Scholastic Aptitude Test (SAT), which has been substantially revised in response to charges that the traditional test was, among other things, biased against women and minorities.

March 20 / Pennsylvania's "new" abortion law, which was enacted six years ago but has been in abeyance because of court challenges (*see* January 14, 1994), goes into effect. Under the law, women seeking an abortion must hear a physician's lecture about the risks of and alternatives to having an abortion and then wait 24 hours before having the procedure. The law also requires parental consent (with a judicial bypass provision) if the woman seeking an abortion is under age 18. This is the law that the U.S. Supreme Court ruled on in *Planned Parenthood of Southeastern Pennsylvania* v. *Casey* (June 1992). In that decision the Court upheld a woman's right to have an abortion but permitted the state to impose restrictions unless they cause an "undue burden" to women.

March 21 / According to today's *Washington Post,* the Freedom of Choice Act, a bill that would prohibit most state restrictions on abortion, is dead, at least for now. Pro-choice advocates say they must give priority to ensuring that abortion and other pregnancy-related services are included in the health reform package.

March 23 / An American immigration judge lifts a deportation order against Lydia Oluloro, a Nigerian citizen. She and her two little girls, who are American citizens, can stay together here in the United States. The judge accepted Ms. Oluloro's argument that to deport her to Nigeria would mean extreme hardship for her daughters: If they stayed behind, they would lose their mother; if they went with her, they would almost certainly be subjected to genital mutilation.

March 24 / The Associated Press reports that the FBI has moved to dismiss John Carpenter, a supervisor named in the sexual harassment lawsuit filed by agents Boni Carr Alduenda and Heather Powell-Anderson (*see* March 11, 1994). Mr. Carpenter was reportedly asked to vacate his office after FBI officials determined that there were grounds for his dismissal.

March 28 / The Census Bureau, releasing statistics on health insurance coverage in the years 1990–92, reports that one in four Americans was without insurance for at least part of that period. Lack of health insurance was most common among children (29 percent lacked coverage) and young adults (47 to 48 percent lacked coverage).

March 28 / The *New York Times* reports that a study released by Citizen Action showed that campaign contributions to congressional candidates by health and health insurance industries in 1993 totaled $11.3 million, up 22 percent from the comparable period of the last election cycle two years earlier. Contributions from doctors and other health care professionals totaled $2.6 million, up 39 percent from the earlier election cycle; contributions from drug companies and manufacturers of medical equipment totaled $1.5 million, up 21 percent. Top contributors were the political action committees (PACs) of the American Dental Association, the American Medical Association, the National Association of Life Underwriters, and the American Hospital Association.

March 29 / In today's *Wall Street Journal,* staff writer Rochelle Sharpe writes that a *Journal* analysis of 1992 data filed with the Equal Employment Opportunity Commission showed women holding less than one-third of the management jobs in the nation's companies overall and only one-quarter of the management jobs in 200 of the biggest companies. The study, based on data from more than 38,000 companies that report to the EEOC, also found that the percentages vary greatly by industry, with finance, insurance, and real estate having the highest proportion of female officials and managers (41.4 percent) and mining the lowest (9.8 percent).

March 29 / Two prominent Democratic women, Lynn Cutler and Ann F. Lewis, are leading an informal group in a campaign to defend Hillary Rodham Clinton against attacks in connection with the Whitewater affair, according to an article by Gwen Ifill in today's *New York Times*. Ms. Ifill writes that the group is "purposefully steering clear of direct Administration influence." With $50,000 raised from individuals across the country, the group placed a full-page ad in today's *Times*.

April 1 / A federal district court jury renders a landmark verdict finding that Margaret Jensvold, a research psychiatrist at the National Institute of Mental Health (NIMH), was the victim of illegal sex bias. Dr. Jensvold maintained that she was denied mentoring opportunities available to male scientists and, as a result, was placed at a disadvantage professionally. By defining the denial of mentoring opportunities as a form of sex bias under Title VII, the decision in this case sets a legal precedent that could have far-reaching implications for female scientists and other professionals in male-dominated fields.

April 5 / Planned Parenthood launches a national "equal health care for women" campaign with a full-page advertisement in today's *New York Times*. The ad features endorsements by 19 female members of Congress—16 representatives and three senators—who believe that health care reform must ensure a full range of reproductive services for women.

April 6 / Settling a sex and age discrimination suit brought by the Equal Employment Opportunity Commission, USAir agrees to drop weight limits as a condition of employment for flight attendants. "Performance on the job, not weight, should determine whether a flight attendant is capable," according to Carol Austin of USAir's flight attendants' union.

April 19 / In a six to three decision the U.S. Supreme Court rules that it is a violation of the equal protection clause of the Fourteenth Amendment for lawyers to exclude people from serving on a jury because of their sex. Justice Harry Blackmun's opinion for the majority stresses the harm caused by sex stereotyping: "It denigrates the dignity of the excluded juror, and, for a woman, reinvokes a history of exclusion from political participation." Interestingly, the case, *J.E.B.* v. *Alabama,* arose from the selection of an all-female jury in a routine paternity suit.

April 20 / A federal district court judge approves the settlement in a class-action sex discrimination suit against Lucky Stores, a chain of supermarkets on the West Coast. According to news reports, some 14,000 women—present and former employees in 188 stores in the chain's Northern California division—who were stuck in low-paying, dead-end jobs in the chain will share $60 million. The settlement also reportedly includes $20 million for new training and personnel programs, nearly $14 million in legal fees, and a $13 million penalty for noncompliance.

April 21 / The *Washington Post* reports that some white male Foreign Service officers are complaining of reverse discrimination. Women and minorities counter that the male-dominated character of the service remains unchanged. Using statistics furnished by Greta Hawkins Holmes, director general of the Foreign Service, the *Post*'s John Goshko writes that promotion rates averaged over the seven-year period 1987–93 were slightly higher for women and minorities than for white men. Nevertheless, as of 1993, 84 percent of senior Foreign Service officers—the group from which ambassadors and policymakers are chosen—are white males.

April 25 / Roper Starch Worldwide concludes a nationwide telephone survey asking teens about their sexual attitudes and sexual behavior. Among the survey findings: The majority of sexually active high school students of both sexes say they agree that "sex is a pleasurable experience," but boys are far more likely than girls to say they think so (81 percent versus 59 percent); the girls are also more likely than the boys to say they should have waited until they were older before having sex (62 percent versus 48 percent). The survey was commissioned by "Rolonda," a syndicated television talk show, in association with the Sexuality Information and Education Council of the United States.

April 28 / Today is the second annual Take Our Daughters to Work Day. Some people are complaining that to single out daughters discriminates against boys.

April 29 / Infant mortality rates dropped for both blacks and whites between 1980 and 1991, according to findings released today by the Centers for Disease Control and Prevention. However, partly because death rates declined more steeply among white babies than among black babies, the disparity between them was wider than ever (7.3 infant deaths for whites versus 17.6 infant deaths for blacks per 1,000 live births).

April 29 / Judge Jackson L. Kiser, of the U.S. District Court for the Western District, approves a plan by Virginia Military Institute to finance a special "leadership school" for women at another institution rather than opening VMI itself to women. The Virginia Women's Institute for Leadership will be at Mary Baldwin College, a women's college about 30 miles from VMI (*see* February 12, 1994).

May 3 / Admiral Jeremy M. Boorda, Chief of Naval Operations, tells reporters that he will try to move faster in opening assignments on all types of Navy ships to women but that meeting that goal will take time. He also says that he wants to recruit more women into the Navy, with the object of increasing the female proportion of enlisted personnel beyond its present 15 percent.

May 4 / New York City's fire department promotes Rochelle Jones to the rank of lieutenant. The daughter of a fireman (and now married to a fellow firefighter), Lieutenant Jones is the first woman ever to enter the top ranks of the city's fire department.

May 5 / The House of Representatives approves the House-Senate compromise version of a bill that would make blocking access to abortion clinics a federal crime. The Freedom of Access to Clinic Entrances Act provides criminal penalties for using force or threat of force to injure, intimidate, or block anyone trying to enter an abortion clinic. The full Senate must approve the compromise before it can go to President Clinton for signature.

May 5 / A study presented today at the annual meeting of the Population Association of America confirms that wives are contributing much more substantially to American families' income than was the case three decades ago. The proportion of marriages in which wives between the ages of 18 and 44 contributed between 30 and 70 percent of family income more than doubled between 1963 and 1992, from 26 percent to 56 percent among black couples and from 20 percent to 47 percent among white couples. Sociologists Aimee Dechter of the University of Wisconsin and Pamela Smock of the University of Michigan did the analysis using government survey data.

May 6 / A jury in Houston, Texas, finds that anti-abortion groups conspired to prevent women from entering abortion clinics in the Houston area while the 1992 Republican National Convention was being held in the city. The plaintiff in the case—Planned Parenthood of Houston and Southeast Texas—is awarded more than $200,000 (the cost of increasing security at the clinics) in actual damages; the jury will decide next week on punitive damages.

May 8 / The Colorado Silver Bullets, the first all-female professional baseball team to compete against a professional men's team, loses its first game by 19–0, but team members say they are not disheartened. The Silver Bullets face a 50-game schedule this year.

May 12 / The Senate votes 69 to 30 to approve the Freedom of Access to Clinic Entrances Act, which the House approved last week (*see* May 5, 1994). The measure now goes to the President, who has said he will sign it into law.

May 12 / The number of women—most of them mothers—who coach children's after-school sports has doubled to more than 20,000 in the last four years, reports Carin Rubenstein in today's *New York Times*. Female coaches are most likely to coach such newly popular sports as soccer; few, if any, coach Little League baseball.

May 12 / Many insurance companies make a practice of denying health and disability insurance coverage to battered women, according to the NOW Legal Defense and Education Fund and the Pennsylvania Coalition against Domestic Violence. Calling the practice discriminatory, the groups are asking Congress for legislation to prohibit it.

May 12 / Secretary of the Navy John H. Dalton writes to Lieutenant Darlene Simmons apologizing for the Navy's handling of her sexual harassment complaints: "[N]o-one in our Navy or Marine Corps should be treated as you were." Secretary Dalton has cleared her record and offered to extend her active duty in the Navy for two years. Lieutenant Simmons was one of the four servicewomen who testified about their experiences before the House Armed Services Committee earlier this year (*see* March 9, 1994), when she told the members, "I am regarded as a troublemaker with no future in the Navy."

May 14 / The Women's Research and Education Institute releases two reports, *Assessing and Improving Women's Health* and *The Health Status of Women of Color,* which argue that health reform, to be effective for women, must provide universal access to health care, as well as culturally sensitive preventive services for all women.

May 16 / Lawyers for Shannon Faulkner and the Citadel begin arguments in federal district court over Ms. Faulkner's right to attend the Citadel (*see*

January 20, 1994). Pending the outcome of her suit, she has been attending classes at the institution since January but has not been admitted to the corps of cadets.

May 16 / Judge Constance Baker Motley, of the U.S. District Court in Manhattan, rules that Vassar College discriminated against Cynthia J. Fisher when it denied her tenure. Dr. Fisher, an assistant professor of biology who was 53 when she filed the suit, charged that the college paid her less than similarly qualified men and that it denied her tenure partly because before coming to Vassar, she had chosen to teach part time when her children were young. Judge Motley finds the college guilty of sex, age, and salary discrimination against Dr. Fisher. In her written opinion the judge cites "the persistent fixation of the Biology Department's senior faculty on a married woman's pre-Vassar family choices, [a fixation that] reflects . . . a stereotype and bias that a woman with an active and on-going family life cannot be a productive scientist and therefore is not one, despite evidence to the contrary." Judge Motley also notes that no married woman had ever been granted tenure in Vassar's hard sciences in the 30 years before Dr. Fisher's tenure review.

May 16 / Roussel-Uclaf, the French manufacturer of RU-486, the so-called abortion pill, announces that it will give its patent rights to the drug to the Population Council, an American nonprofit organization that conducts contraceptive research. The council, which has applied to the Food and Drug Administration for approval of the drug, plans to find an American manufacturer for it and to conduct clinical trials. The hope is that RU-486 will be available to U.S. women in two years.

May 17 / Older fathers as well as older mothers are more likely than their younger counterparts to conceive children with congenital birth defects, according to a growing body of evidence discussed in an article by Natalie Angier in today's *New York Times*. Certain types of dwarfism are among the defects that can arise from small errors in the repeated replication of sperm cells over time. Unlike a woman's eggs, all of which are fully formed before she is born, sperm are first created when a man reaches puberty and are continuously manufactured thereafter.

May 18 / A lawyer for two female FBI agents who have sued the agency on sexual harassment charges (*see* March 24, 1994) says that the agency has agreed to a settlement that will include monetary compensation as well as a guarantee that the women will not be subject to retaliation or transfer.

May 18 / A group of female senators meet privately with the civilian secretaries of the Army, Navy, and Air Force and the military heads of the Army, Navy, Air Force, and Marine Corps to discuss what the services are doing to address equality for military women and to improve the handling of sexual harassment cases. The leaders also discussed their concern about growing family violence in military families. According to press reports, the "highly unusual" meeting was suggested by Senator Sam Nunn, chairman of the Senate Armed Services Committee, who also attended.

May 22 / Donna Shalala, Secretary of Health and Human Services, says that if RU-486 should be approved by the Food and Drug Administration (*see* May 16, 1994), it would not offer American women a cheap or easy way to get an abortion because at least three visits to a doctor would be required: to receive the first pill, to receive the second pill (two days after the first), and to be checked later for infection.

May 25 / Jockey Julie Krone rides at Belmont racetrack, the first time she has competed since she was severely injured after a fall at Saratoga nine months ago. Ms. Krone has won 2,000 races and $50 million in purses and is the only woman to have won a Triple Crown race (the Belmont Stakes in 1993).

May 26 / President Clinton signs the Freedom of Access to Clinic Entrances Act into law (*see* May 12, 1994).

June 1 / Judge Thomas Zilly of the U.S. District Court in Seattle orders the Army to reinstate Colonel Margarethe Cammermeyer in Washington State's national Guard. Colonel Cammermeyer was forced out of the Guard in 1992, when asked about her sexual preference during a security clearance interview, she acknowledged that she is a lesbian (*see The American Woman 1994–95*). Judge Zilly holds that the military policy on homosexuals that was in effect in 1992 was "grounded solely in prejudice" and violated the Constitution's equal protection clause. Under the policy now in effect, Colonel Cammermeyer would not be asked about her sexual preference, and if asked, she would not have to divulge it.

June 2 / The Women's Campaign School, sponsored by Yale University's Women's Studies Program, begins its first program. The four-day course, which is nonpartisan, will focus on building potential candidates' campaign skills, not on issues.

June 3 / Wide differences in the standards courts use in rulings on what constitutes rape are the subject of an article by Tamar Lewin in today's *New York Times*. Ms. Lewin contrasts two recent decisions: a May 27 ruling by the Pennsylvania Supreme Court that a man who did not use physical force when he had sexual intercourse with a woman who said no throughout the encounter could not be convicted of rape under Pennsylvania law, which requires "forcible compulsion," and a May 23 ruling by the California Supreme Court upholding the rape conviction of a man who was unarmed and whose victim submitted without a struggle.

June 7 / Vicki Van Meter, age 12, lands her single-engine Cessna at Glasgow, Scotland's airport, setting a record as the youngest female ever to pilot a plane across the Atlantic. Her previous record (subsequently topped by a nine-year-old) was as the youngest female to pilot a plane across the continental United States (*see* September 23, 1993). Ms. Van Meter was accompanied by an instructor on both flights because she is not old enough to fly solo legally.

June 7 / A study released today provides more evidence that drinking is a growing problem among college women (*see* February 16, 1994). The study, conducted by Columbia University's Center on Addiction and Substance Abuse, found that 35 percent of college women polled in 1993 said they drank to get drunk. The comparable proportion in 1977 was 10 percent. The study does not say how often college women indulged in this type of drinking, known as binge drinking.

June 8 / The National Institutes of Health Consensus Panel on Optimal Calcium Intake recommends higher levels of calcium intake than existing recommended daily allowances, particularly for adolescent girls and post-menopausal women, to reach and maintain peak bone mass and to minimize bone loss and the risk of osteoporosis in later adult years.

June 8 / The *Washington Post* reports that the Marine Corps, citing insufficient evidence, has dropped the last pending military case arising from the investigation of the Tailhook scandal (*see* February 11, 1994). Of the total of 140 cases referred to the Navy and Marine Corps by Pentagon investigators, not one went to trial.

June 9 / A survey of sex bias in the federal court system in Washington, D.C., found that female lawyers rarely encounter overt sex bias in federal courtrooms in that city. This is in marked contrast to the findings of similar surveys of a number of state court systems and one federal circuit. However, like their counterparts elsewhere, many female lawyers practicing in Washington's federal courts report bias and sexual harassment in pretrial work, such as depositions and conferences. And nearly 17 percent reported unwanted sexual advances from clients. These findings are presented in a draft report submitted today to the Judicial Council of the District of Columbia Circuit.

June 10 / Asserting that Judge C. Weston Houck may have already made up his mind to force the Citadel to admit women, that institution's lawyers ask that a mistrial be declared in the Shannon Faulkner suit (*see* May 16, 1994).

June 13 / Reacting to the Pennsylvania Supreme Court decision on May 27 (*see* June 3, 1994), the Pennsylvania Senate unanimously approves legislation to strike "forcible compulsion" from the statutory definition of what constitutes rape and to add "without consent of the other person."

June 13 / Beverly Sills becomes chair of the board of New York's Lincoln Center. Ms. Sills, who served as general director of the New York City Opera for five years after retiring from the opera stage, is the first woman ever to head Lincoln Center.

June 13 / Heidi Hartmann, the founder and director of the Institute for Women's Policy Research (IWPR) in Washington, D.C., is awarded a 1994 MacArthur Foundation fellowship—the MacArthur "genius award"—for her work in economics and public policy. Dr. Hartmann is one of seven women among the 20 recipients of this year's fellowships.

June 13 / Air Force Sergeant Zenaida Martinez, who has charged that she has been the target of reprisals from officials at her base since she testified about sexual harassment before the House Armed Services Committee (*see* March 9, 1994), meets with Air Force Secretary Sheila Widnall. Secretary Widnall promises that there will be no more reprisals and agrees to Sergeant Martinez's request that she be trained in a new career as an equal opportunity officer.

June 15 / Carol DiBattiste is named head of the Executive Office for U.S. Attorneys in the Justice Department. She is the first woman to hold that position. A former prosecutor in the Air Force (from which she retired as a major), Ms. DiBattiste has most recently been principal deputy general counsel for the Navy.

June 16 / The *Washington Post* reports that the Justice Department is appealing Judge Thomas Zilly's order to reinstate Colonel Margarethe Cammermeyer in the National Guard (*see* June 1, 1994).

June 16 / Dismissing the Citadel's motion for a mistrial as "totally frivolous," Judge C. Weston Houck hears final arguments in the Faulkner suit (*see* June 10, 1994). He says he will issue a ruling in July.

June 16 / A federal judge in Virginia rules that the Freedom of Access to Clinic Entrances Act is constitutional. The ruling, by Judge Leonie M. Brinkema of the U.S. District Court for the Eastern District, is the first to be handed down since the act was signed into law last month (*see* May 26, 1994). More rulings can be expected because anti-abortion groups have already brought suit in several states charging that the law violates protesters' First Amendment rights.

June 23 / A ruling by the Massachusetts Supreme Court forces the YWCA rape counseling center in Springfield to turn over counseling files to the attorney for the defendant in a rape trial. YWCA national officials say they intend to fight for federal and state laws to protect the confidentiality of rape counseling files. In the meanwhile, rape counseling clients will be warned that their records may not be confidential.

June 24 / Winn Newman, a labor lawyer revered for his pioneering efforts to end wage discrimination against female workers, dies at age 70. His achievements included successfully litigating several landmark pay equity suits on behalf of female public employees.

June 28 / Lawyers for both the Citadel and Shannon Faulkner present Judge C. Weston Houck with plans for admitting Ms. Faulkner to its all-male corps of cadets, should the judge rule next month that she must be admitted (*see* June 16, 1994). One of the Citadel's requirements would be that Ms. Faulkner's head be shaved, as is traditional for first-year cadets, who are known as knobs.

June 30 / With the release of advertisements prepared for TV, radio, and the print media, the Family Violence Prevention Fund launches a national media campaign intended to educate the public about domestic violence and the ways in which it can be prevented. The campaign's slogan is "There's no excuse for domestic violence."

June 30 / Ruling in *Madsen* v. *Women's Health Center,* the U.S. Supreme Court holds six to three that judges can bar demonstrators from coming within 36 feet of abortion clinics without violating the demonstrators' First Amendment rights. The High Court also upholds a lower court order that prohibited protesters from chanting, shouting, using bullhorns, and making other loud noises within earshot of the patients at the clinic during surgical and recovery hours. Anti-abortion protesters in Florida brought the appeal to the High Court after the Florida Supreme Court upheld the order.

July 1 / Barbara Landis Chase takes over as head of Phillips Academy (Andover, Massachusetts), a 217-year-old preparatory school that first admitted female students 21 years ago. Ms. Landis is the first woman in the school's history to hold that position, formerly headmaster, now head of school.

July 1 / Participation in sports and fitness activities dropped among both women and men between 1986 and 1990, but the drop was considerably steeper (13 percent) among women than among men (eight percent). The female-male disparity was even greater among people under age 35; their activities dropped 16 percent among women versus nine percent among men. These data are in "Healthy People 2000 Review 1992," a report released this month by the National Center for Health Statistics.

July 4 / In today's *New York Times,* Jane Gross writes that the O. J. Simpson case has heightened the public's awareness that domestic violence is a serious problem that can have fatal outcomes. Ms. Gross reports that calls to domestic violence hot lines have increased enormously and that more men are said to be seeking help in avoiding abusive behavior.

July 7 / Protesting Roussel-Uclaf's decision to allow RU-486 into the United States (*see* May 22, 1994), opponents of abortion announce that they will boycott 76 medicines made by Copley Pharmaceuticals and Hoechst-Roussel Pharmaceuticals, Roussel-Uclaf's American affiliates. The protesters want Roussel-Uclaf to rescind its agreement to turn over the American rights to RU-486 to the nonprofit Population Council.

July 8 / "Murder in Families," a Justice Department study released today, found that cases of one family member killing another accounted for 16 percent of all murders that went to court in 1988. Of these family murders, 40 percent involved one spouse killing the other. Husbands were the killers in 59 percent of spousal murders. However, 55 percent of the parents who murdered their offspring were women.

July 13 / Cathy E. Minehan is named president of the Federal Reserve Bank of Boston, becoming the second woman ever to head one of the 12 regional banks of the Federal Reserve and the only woman currently heading one. The first was Karen Horn, who was president of the Federal Reserve Bank of Cleveland from 1982 to 1987.

July 14 / Three Democratic senators blast the Democratic National Committee for the new advertisements it is running to shore up support for the Clinton health care reform plan. Senators Bob Kerrey (D-NE), Richard Bryan (D-NV), and Herb Kohl (D-WI) say the ads are not constructive because they are too partisan. According to Senator Kohl, "we should be trying to build a coalition behind a bipartisan health care bill."

July 14 / The Democratic leadership in the House of Representatives agrees to make the health care reform plan approved by the Ways and Means Committee the basis for crafting the leadership's reform bill. Under the Ways and Means Committee bill, employers would be required to provide health insurance for their employees and Americans not covered through employment would get coverage through an expanded Medicare program. Demonstrating the lack of consensus among Democrats, moderate and conservative Democratic lawmakers are pushing alternative, less ambitious plans.

July 14 / The public learns that a woman who holds a senior-level position in the clandestine operations directorate (the spy side) of the Central Intelligence Agency is suing the agency for sex discrimination. The suit filed by "Jane Doe Thompson" remains sealed—and her identity concealed—on the ground of national security, but court papers made public today allege many instances of discrimination and harassment. Among Thompson's allegations: that after she reported to her CIA superiors that a male subordinate was beating his wife, the subordinate was promoted rather than disciplined; that he—as well as other male subordinates whose misconduct she had reported—retaliated by filing untrue complaints against her; and that she was denied a promotion after a man who was to have become her subordinate said he would not work for a woman.

July 15 / Dana Priest writes in the *Washington Post* that although this Congress has only three more months in which to approve a health care reform bill proposal, "there are still no sure majorities in Congress for even the most basic elements, like whether to guarantee insurance for everybody."

This article also notes that the Health Care Leadership Council, a collection of the largest for-profit hospital, insurance, medical equipment, and pharmaceutical companies, has a $6 million annual budget aimed at influencing health reform legislation. "The money's there if we need it," says a for-profit hospital lobbyist and council member. The Health Care Reform Project, a pro–health reform coalition that endorses reform but not President Clinton's bill, has $1.5 million for pro-reform ads.

July 15 / Maria A. Chavez, serving aboard the USS *Mount Baker,* becomes a gunner's mate third class. She is the first woman ever to hold that position in the U.S. Navy.

July 15 / Tamar Lewin writes in today's *New York Times* about two lawsuits that have been brought by students since the U.S. Supreme Court ruled in *Franklin* v. *Gwinnett County Public Schools* (February 26, 1992). In that decision the Court held that students who are victims of sexual harassment and other forms of sex discrimination under Title IX can sue for monetary damages. The plaintiffs in both cases discussed by Ms. Lewin are girls—a seventh grader in Sonoma County, California, and a sixth grader in Delaware County, New York—who allege that school officials permitted egregious sexual harassment against them to continue despite their repeated complaints.

July 16 / The problems faced by Congress in devising a health care reform bill that both provides universal coverage and controls costs are the subject of a news analysis by Steven Pearlstein in today's *Washington Post.* He writes that the compromises that may be necessary to ensure political support from key constituencies with competing interests—such as large and small businesses—could undermine key cost control elements.

July 16 / In Pennsylvania, President Clinton makes a pitch for universal health care coverage with a direct appeal to America's middle class. President Clinton tells his audience, "the politicians have [coverage]. The wealthy have it. The poor have it. If you go to jail you've got it. Only the middle class can lose it."

July 17 / The National Governors' Association outlines its strong objections to certain components of several of the chief health care reform bills before Congress and declines to support any particular bill. In a speech to the group Senate Majority Leader George Mitchell (D–ME) says the question he is confronting is "how do we pay for benefits" without requiring employers to pay for a substantial part of the employees' coverage, but the NGA again declines to get behind such a requirement (*see* January 31, 1994).

July 19 / The National Association of Women Business Owners

(NAWBO) releases a new study concluding that women who own businesses typically have a management style different from that of their male counterparts. For example, according to NAWBO, female entrepreneurs are more likely than men to seek outside advice before making decisions, and the women "often describe their businesses as a family, [but] men business owners almost never do."

July 19 / Senate Minority Leader Robert Dole (R-KS) and President Clinton address the NGA on the subject of health care reform. Senator Dole says that President Clinton is pushing too hard for too much too quickly and tells the governors that the Administration's proposals for universal coverage and employer mandates are dead in the Senate.

President Clinton says that he would accept a health care reform plan that provided coverage to 95 percent of Americans. Since the President has previously made universal coverage his bottom line, his remarks today are interpreted as a sign that he is willing to be flexible even on this point if it will help get a reform bill through Congress with bipartisan support.

July 20 / In today's *Washington Post,* Walter Pincus reports that nearly one-third of the female case officers in the CIA's heavily male clandestine service have joined in allegations that the service has discriminated against women in promotions, country assignments, and spying tasks. Lawyers for the more than 100 women who have signed on to the complaint were reportedly ready to file a class action suit against the CIA last year but have held off because the agency agreed to enter into negotiations to settle the matter without going to court. The CIA says it has "been aware over the years that the statistics for women and minorities were not what they should be." Mr. Pincus writes that the "Jane Doe Thompson" suit could cause procedural complications (*see* July 14, 1994).

July 21 / House Majority Leader Richard Gephardt (D-MO) meets with the Congressional Caucus for Women's Issues to discuss caucus members' concerns about ensuring coverage for abortion and other women's health services in the health care reform legislation being developed by the Democratic leadership. The women lawmakers say that to win their support, the bill must include coverage for abortions.

July 21 / Democratic congressional leaders meet with the President and Hillary Rodham Clinton to say that they plan to draft a new health care reform bill that would phase in universal coverage more slowly than the White House recommends and would have a "less bureaucratic approach."

July 22 / Judge C. Weston Houck rules that the Citadel must admit Shannon Faulkner to its corps of cadets. (Still to be decided are such practical issues as whether Ms. Faulkner will live in the barracks, whether her uniform will include a skirt, and whether like male cadets, she will be required to shave her head.) Today's decision does not, however, apply to women applicants in general; the judge leaves open the possibility that the Citadel could establish a parallel program for women at another institution.

July 24 / Appearing on "Meet the Press," Vice President Al Gore and House Minority Leader Richard Gephardt (D-MO) indicate that both the Administration and the House Democratic leadership are ready to accept health care reform legislation with long phase-in periods for such key elements as employer mandates.

July 25 / A Michigan judge orders Jennifer Ireland to surrender custody of her three-year-old daughter to the child's father, Steve Smith. Judge Raymond Cashen of Macomb County Circuit Court says Mr. Smith ought to have custody of the child because Ms. Ireland puts the girl in daycare—"in essence [to be] raised and supervised by strangers"—while she attends the University of Michigan. In the father's custody, says the judge, the child will be "raised and supervised by blood relatives" because Mr. Smith will have his mother look after the little girl while he works.

July 26 / Anorexia nervosa and bulimia prove fatal to 22-year-old Christy Henrich, regarded as one of America's top gymnasts. Ms. Henrich's eating disorders are said to have begun when a gymnastics judge told her that unless she lost weight, she wouldn't make the 1988 Olympic team. In response to what appears to be a growing problem among young competitive female athletes, USA Gymnastics has reportedly stepped up its efforts to inform coaches and athletes about eating disorders.

July 28 / Secretary of Defense William Perry announces that the military will open more than 80,000 additional positions to women, effective October 1, 1994. As a result, 92 percent of the career fields and over 80 percent of the jobs in the armed services overall will be open to women. In approving the changes, Secretary Perry says, "I am confident that these policy changes will further enhance the already high state of readiness of our armed forces while at the same time expanding the opportunities for women in the military."

July 28 / WOMEN DOMINATE TOP JOBS AT JUSTICE is the headline of a front-page story by Pierre Thomas in today's *Washington Post*. Women hold the two top jobs—Attorney General (Janet Reno) and Deputy Attorney General (Jamie Gorelick)—and when the confirmation process is complete, women will fill seven of the 11 assistant attorney general positions. (However as Ms. Gorelick has pointed out, the balance of the sexes in senior jobs is more even when the male heads of the FBI and the Drug Enforcement Administration are taken into account.) Overall nearly one-third of Justice Department lawyers are female.

July 29 / A man with a shotgun opens fire outside an abortion clinic in Pensacola, Florida, killing a doctor and his security escort and wounding the escort's wife. The killer, arrested near the scene, is reported to be Paul Hill of the radical anti-abortion group Defensive Action.

July 30 / Many of the 11 women who, just 20 years ago, were the first to be ordained as priests in the Episcopal Church return to Philadelphia for a commemorative weekend. Their ordination there on July 29, 1974, was in defiance of church authorities, but the Episcopal priesthood was subsequently opened to women; indeed, three women are currently bishops in the Episcopal Church.

July 31 / A meeting of the Promise Keepers in Boulder, Colorado, draws 52,000 men to hear the organization's central message: that God has ordained that men must lead families and women must follow.

August 1 / The manufacturer of a new type of breast implant announces that the Food and Drug Administration will allow 50 American women to test the product, which is made of a fat derived from soybean oil. According to LipoMatrix, the manufacturer, the implant should be safer than silicone gel and saline implants and—unlike those types—can be seen through by mammography.

August 1 / In the wake of the July 29 killings in Pensacola, Florida, the Justice Department has sent U.S. marshals to guard a dozen abortion clinics across the country. Attorney General Janet Reno says the department is "trying to take all prudent steps using all federal tools" to prevent further violence and provide better security for doctors, clinic employees, and patients. Under the Freedom of Access to Clinic Entrances Act (*see* May 26, 1994), it is a federal crime to use force or threat of force to injure, intimidate, or block anyone trying to enter an abortion clinic.

August 7 / Senator Phil Gramm (R-TX), speaking on "Face the Nation," says, "I intend to use every power I have as just one member of the Senate to try to stop the Clinton [health care reform] bill."

August 9 / The Michigan Court of Appeals grants a delay in Judge Raymond Cashen's custody transfer order in the Ireland-Smith case (*see* July 25, 1994). The delay is approved pending a decision on Ms. Ireland's appeal, for which no hearing date has been set.

August 10 / In today's *Washington Post,* Michael Weisskopf reports that a coalition of leading business groups—including some that have previously supported broad principles of reform—has formed to lobby against the health care reform bills drafted by the Democratic leaders in the House and Senate. Although the disparate business groups making common cause against the bills object to them for widely different reasons, Mr. Weisskopf reports that businesses, both large and small, are increasingly of the view that the bills under consideration are "worse than the current system with all its flaws."

August 10 / In a historic double first the American Bar Association (ABA) elects women to fill its two top posts in 1995. Roberta Cooper Ramo will be the ABA's president, and Martha W. Barnett will chair its House of Delegates.

August 11 / A study of heterosexual couples in which one partner was HIV-positive showed that conscientious use of a condom can prevent HIV infection. Among the couples who consistently used condoms (about half of the total), none of the uninfected partners contracted HIV. By contrast, among the other couples, about 10 percent of the initially uninfected partners developed HIV. The study, published in today's *New England Journal of Medicine,* tracked 256 couples over four years.

August 15 / The University of Maryland names Deborah A. Yow its new athletic director. She is the first woman to head an athletic department in the Atlantic Coast Conference, regarded as one of the "powerhouse" athletic conferences in the country. Ms. Yow is the fourth woman to be appointed athletic director at an NCAA Division 1-A institution.

August 16 / The Commonwealth of Virginia is getting ready to implement a new child support enforcement tool: suspending the professional licenses of physicians, lawyers, and other professionals who fail to keep up with their child support payments. According to today's *Washington Post,* these parents will soon be notified that if they don't pay up, they will lose their licenses to practice their professions in Virginia.

August 16 / The Massachusetts Commission against Discrimination rules that the Commodore Club, composed of several hundred men who head local boat clubs in the state, must admit JoAnn Seidman, the female commodore of a yacht club in Cambridge. Ms. Seidman was turned down for membership because of her sex. The commission says Massachusetts's antibias laws apply to the Commodore Club because it is located on land leased from the state.

August 17 / The Federal Communications Commission (FCC) revises its rules with the intention of improving women's and minorities' chances to acquire wireless communications licenses.

August 18 / The National Museum of Women in the Arts announces that it will expand into the building next door, which has been bought with a million-dollar gift in honor of Elisabeth A. Kasser. The museum, located in a landmark building in downtown Washington, D.C., is the first and only museum devoted solely to "celebrating the achievements of women in the visual and performing arts." The Kasser wing is scheduled to open in 1997, the museum's 10th anniversary year.

August 24 / The president of the College Board, which administers the Scholastic Assessment Test, announces that the gender gap in SAT scores—

both verbal and math—has continued to narrow. Black women's scores have shown the most improvement over the past eight years.

August 25 / The Senate approves the Omnibus Crime Control and Safe Streets Act, clearing it for the President's signature. Two weeks ago the bill was thought dead when the House refused to consider it. Subsequently, however, the House changed its mind. The bill, familiarly known as the anticrime bill, incorporates the Violence against Women Act (VAWA), which includes many important initiatives designed to make homes and streets safer for women.

August 25 / The Senate Ethics Committee grants Senator Orrin Hatch (R-UT) permission to set up a legal defense fund for his aide Sharon Prost. Ms. Prost plans to appeal Judge Harriett Taylor's decision awarding custody of her two children to their father, Ms. Prost's ex-husband, Kenneth Greene. Senate rules bar senators or Senate staffers from setting up such funds in cases where "the legal expenses are for purely personal matters, to include . . . divorces. . . ." The committee justifies a fund in this case because "the judicial decision appears to implicate service in the Senate as a significant factor in that decision." Ms. Prost is minority counsel to the Senate Judiciary Committee. The judge's written opinion described her as "more devoted to and absorbed by her work and her career than anything else in her life, including her health, her children, and her family." By contrast, according to the judge, Mr. Greene puts his children first.

August 26 / A California jury awards $50,000 in compensatory damages to Rena Weeks, the plaintiff in a sexual harassment case against Baker & McKenzie, the world's largest law firm. Ms. Weeks, who was subjected to crude and repeated harassment by Martin R. Greenstein, a highly successful partner in the firm, where she was employed as a secretary, charged that Baker & McKenzie not only knew of his harassing behavior toward her but also knew that other female employees had made similar complaints, yet the firm did nothing to discipline Mr. Greenstein.

August 29 / The Michigan Supreme Court rules that the private counseling records of the plaintiff in a rape case can be used as evidence in court if the trial judge determines that the records are essential to a fair trial for the defendant.

August 30 / The Census Bureau reports that half of America's children live in situations other than a "traditional nuclear family," defined as a unit in which both parents are present, all the children in the household are the biological offspring of those parents, and no other persons are present. The data in the *Diverse Living Arrangements of Children: Summer 1991,* released today, come from the bureau's Survey of Income and Program Participation (SIPP).

August 31 / The *Washington Post* marks the first anniversary month of the Family and Medical Leave Act with an editorial observing that despite the "dire predictions" by some employers that the act would create a severe burden for them, the law seems to have created few problems and few complaints. Noting that many workers are not covered by the act, the *Post* opines, "[T]he first year's experience is encouraging and should prompt lawmakers to consider an expansion in coverage."

September 1 / The jury that last week awarded Rena Weeks $50,000 in compensatory damages (*see* August 26, 1994) today awards her a total of $7.1 million in punitive damages. Most ($6.9 million) of that sum, almost twice the amount Ms. Weeks sought, is to be paid by Baker & McKenzie; the remaining amount would come from Martin Greenstein. The jury's action reportedly is regarded as a wake-up call to employers, especially to law firms, that an employer has a responsibility to respond promptly and vigorously to complaints of harassment even when the victim is a low-level employee and the harasser a powerful professional.

September 1 / U.S. District Court Judge Sam Pointer gives final approval to a $4.24 billion settlement in the class action liability suit against the makers of silicon breast implants. More than 90,500 women have reportedly agreed to the terms of the settlement, which would provide American women with payments ranging from $105,000 to $1.4 million, depending on their age and the severity of their symptoms. (Nearly $97 million of the total is to be apportioned among foreign claimants.)

September 2 / A male air traffic controller files a sexual harassment lawsuit against his employer, the Federal Aviation Administration (FAA). Douglas P. Hartman charges that he was insulted and demeaned by being subjected to an all-female "gauntlet" that was part of an antiharassment workshop sponsored by the FAA.

September 6 / Details of the complaints of "Jane Doe Thompson" against the CIA emerge as her employment discrimination lawsuit is declassified (*see* July 14, 1994). She alleges that her 23-year career was ruined after a CIA report wrongfully portrayed her "as a drunk and sexual provocateur" and claims that the agency would never have even pursued such charges against a male CIA officer "because drinking and sexual prowess are not considered derogatory behavior for a man at the agency."

September 7 / Joanne E. Misko, who was among the FBI's first female special agents, files a sex bias suit against the bureau. She charges that she was repeatedly passed over for promotion to supervisory positions, losing out to men less qualified than she was. Ms. Misko has recently resigned from the FBI and gone to work for a bank, where she is said to think her opportunities for advancement will be better.

September 7 / A study comparing scores on the science section (Part I) of the medical licensing examination has found that non-Hispanic white men score better than men of color and women of every racial and ethnic group. The findings are described in today's issue of the *Journal of the American Medical Association*. The study did not include a comparison of scores on Parts II and III of the exam, which test clinical skills.

September 8 / An analysis released today by the National Women's Political Caucus (NWPC) concludes that success at the polls has nothing to do with sex. The study of more than 50,000 candidacies for Congress and the state legislatures found that "when male incumbents were compared to female incumbents, men running for open seats to women running for open seats, and male challengers to female challengers, women won as high a percentage of their races as men." According to the NWPC, the percentages of women in elected office are low because so few women run for office, not because female candidates are less likely to win.

September 8 / Two rival groups hope to launch cable television networks devoted to women's sports, according to today's *New York Times*.

September 8 / The U.S. Labor Department announces that it has reached a settlement in a 17-year-old employment bias case against the Honeywell Corporation. The case involved 6,000 female Honeywell employees who were discriminated against in promotions and job assignments between 1972 and 1977. The settlement includes $3.5 million in back wages and $3 million for future programs to promote diversity at Honeywell.

September 8 / The Women's Initiative of the American Association of Retired Persons releases "Going It Alone: A Closer Look at Grandparents Parenting Grandchildren," a report about people who care for their grandchildren in households where neither parent is present. Among AARP's findings: Forty-one percent of grandparent caregivers are either poor or near poor (i.e., have incomes below 150 percent of the poverty threshold) but often have difficulty in qualifying for foster care payments, AFDC, or other types of assistance.

September 9 / ABC News's "20/20" airs an interview with Barbara Bush, in the course of which she tells Barbara Walters that she believes in a woman's right to have an abortion. This is the first interview the former First Lady has given since her husband left the White House.

September 9 / In a speech to the National Baptist Convention, which is the largest black religious organization in the country, President Clinton says that the increase in out-of-wedlock births among blacks and whites is "a disaster. . . . Someone has to say again it is simply not right. You shouldn't have a baby before you're ready and you shouldn't have a baby when you're not married."

September 9 / Anna Quindlen, the only woman to have a regular column in the *New York Times,* says she is leaving the paper to pursue her career as a novelist. Ms. Quindlen is reported to have also turned down fast-track management assignments at the *Times* because she likes being able to spend a lot of time with her children.

September 12 / The State Department releases its first-ever report to the United Nations on human rights practices in the United States. Prepared for the UN Human Rights Commission, the report is composed mostly of federal and state statutes and case law, but its preface frankly acknowledges past and present problems. Among the present "areas of concern" identified in the preface are sex discrimination and attacks on abortion rights activists.

September 12 / Deborah Kent starts her new job as plant manager of the Ford Motor Company's vehicle assembly plant at Avon Lake, Ohio. The plant turns out more than 300,000 vans and minivans annually. Ms. Kent, a 17-year veteran of the automotive industry and the mother of two daughters, is the first woman to head one of Ford's vehicle assembly plants and the only African American female plant manager in the industry.

September 13 / President Clinton signs the anticrime bill into law (*see* August 25, 1994). Title IV of the new law (P.L. 103-322) is the Violence against Women Act, which includes dozens of provisions to improve the prevention and prosecution of sexual assaults and other violent crimes against women and children. VAWA also gives the victim of a gender-motivated hate crime the right to sue the perpetrator in federal court. Among several other provisions of P.L. 103-322 that have special relevance to women is one authorizing a demonstration project for persons convicted of nonviolent crimes to serve their sentences in a community facility with their children.

September 14 / The Census Bureau releases "Black Children in America—1993," which reports that the income gap between black and white families overall has widened in the past two decades. The gap has grown largely because the proportion of black families headed by women has grown. Among married-couple families the black-white income gap has narrowed.

September 14 / A group of research scientists announce that they have located the gene that appears to be responsible for about half of all cases of inherited breast cancer. (Inherited breast cancer accounts for only about five percent of all breast cancer cases.) Experts caution that while the discovery is important in advancing scientists' understanding of cancer, it is not a cure.

September 20 / Teenage mothers enrolled in Ohio's Learning, Earning, and Parenting program are more likely to stay in school and get their diplomas than their counterparts who are not in the program, according to a study conducted by the Manpower Demonstration Research Corporation and made public today. The Ohio program, known as LEAP, provides both monetary incentives and social services, such as daycare to teen mothers who attend school. The MDRC found LEAP's success was largely with mothers who had not already dropped out of school before entering the program.

September 20 / Controversy over the Sharon Prost child custody case (*see* August 25, 1994) is the subject of a front-page story by Susan Chira in today's *New York Times.* Ms. Chira writes: "To Ms. Prost and the feminist legal groups rallying around her, the judge's decision to remove the children [from Ms. Prost's custody] is chilling evidence of a judicial backlash against professional women. To her former husband [Kenneth Greene] . . . and his supporters, the decision is an overdue affirmation of fathers who have long been victims of bias in the courts themselves."

September 20 / The heads of the Central Intelligence Agency, Defense Intelligence Agency, National Security Agency, and Federal Bureau of Investigation testify before the House Intelligence Committee that they are working to eliminate sexual harassment and sex and race bias in their respective agencies. It is clear from their testimony, however, that these goals are far from being met.

September 22 / The National Institutes of Health selects 24 additional centers for its Women's Health Initiative, bringing the total to 40 centers to carry out this $628 million 15-year study of chronic diseases that affect women age 50 and older. The WHI goals are to recruit 63,000 women for clinical trials related to cancer, heart disease, and osteoporosis and another 100,000 women for an observational study of genetic, environmental, and lifestyle factors on health and disease.

September 22 / The House Judiciary Committee's Subcommittee on Crime hears testimony about enforcement of the Freedom of Access to Clinic Entrances Act. Staffers at abortion clinics say that they and their clients are still subjected to violence and harassment and complain of their frustration in trying to get federal authorities to enforce the law (*see* August 1, 1994).

September 26 / The effort to enact comprehensive health care reform is dead, at least in the 103d Congress. Senate Majority Leader George Mitchell (D-ME) makes the demise official when he announces that he cannot muster the 60 votes needed to end a filibuster that the Republicans in the Senate have said they will launch on any of the health care bills proposed by Democrats. Last month the House virtually gave up trying to pass its health care reform legislation.

September 28 / Breast cancer is twice as deadly for black women as for white women. Research published in today's issue of the *Journal of the American Medical Association* attributes 40 percent of the black women's higher death rate to the cancer's being more advanced when it is diagnosed. The study also found some evidence that cancerous tumors might be more aggressive in black women.

September 29 / "America's Children & the Information Superhighway," released today by the Children's Partnership of Santa Monica, California, reports a number of differences between boys and girls in their use of computers. For example, girls use home computers for schoolwork more than boys do, but "by the mid-teen years, when [school] computer courses are typically elective, girls [but not boys] begin to lose interest in computers at school, and the gender gap continues through college and graduate school."

September 30 / The Women's College Coalition and the Advertising Council announce the launching of a joint public service advertising campaign on the importance of women's education. The long-term goal is to create "a gender-equal education for girls and women, where females have every opportunity to achieve their full potential." The council has made an unprecedented 15-year commitment to the campaign and estimates the value of the donated media at $18 million annually.

October 4 / WREI presents its 1994 American Woman Award to syndicated columnist Ellen Goodman.

October 4 / The federal government has put the Medical University of South Carolina on probation for violating ethical research standards in its program for poor pregnant women (*see* February 3, 1994). The university could lose the more than $300 million it receives in federal funding if, after one year, its ethical standards still fail to pass muster. The Office of Civil Rights of the Department of Health and Human Services has already found that the program violated the women's civil rights.

October 5 / In the first case brought to trial under the federal Freedom of Access to Clinic Entrances Act, Paul Hill is convicted in federal court of killing two people and wounding another in an attempt to prevent legal abortions in a Pensacola, Florida, clinic (*see* July 29, 1994). Hill, who could get a life sentence under FACE, still faces trial for murder under Florida law.

October 5 / A House-Senate conference committee approves the final version of legislation revising the so-called nanny tax. Under the bill employers of household workers will not be required to pay Social Security taxes on a worker's pay unless it totals $1,000 or more annually. The bill also eases the paper work burden by allowing employers who must pay the tax to do so at the end of the year via their income tax returns. Current law requires household employers to file and pay Social Security taxes quarterly for any worker paid $50 or more in a quarter.

October 7 / The Senate confirms Ricki Tigert Helfer as chairman of the Federal Deposit Insurance Corporation (FDIC). Ms. Helfer is the first woman ever to head a federal banking agency.

October 7 / A new study of American sexual practices makes front-page news today. Called "the first comprehensive and scientifically accurate survey on sex in America," the study suggests that adult Americans are less sexually active and less sexually adventurous than many would have supposed. For example, fidelity in marriage appears to be the norm; 85 percent of wives and 75 percent of husbands said they have been faithful to their spouses. Among the troubling findings: Twenty-two percent of women said they have been forced by a man to do something sexual, and 17 percent of women (compared with 12 percent of men) said that as children they were touched sexually by an adolescent or adult. The study, conducted by a team of researchers based at the University of Chicago, is reportedly the first to question a random sample of adults about many aspects of sexuality.

October 10 / According to today's *New York Times,* a New York gynecologist has successfully performed more than 100 nonsurgical abortions using two prescription drugs that the Food and Drug Administration had approved for other uses. Richard Hausknecht uses methotrexate and misoprostal in a two-stage procedure. Reporter John Tierney writes that Dr. Hausknecht is a longtime abortion rights crusader who says his "goal is to show the medical community that there is a safe, simple, effective, legal technique of terminating pregnancies that is private and inexpensive." Several clinical trials of abortion involving the drugs that Dr. Hausknecht uses are under way.

October 13 / The National Women's Political Caucus reports that women were "slightly more successful than men" in winning congressional and gubernatorial primaries this year. The NWPC notes that a record number of women (111) are major-party candidates on November election ballots. Ten women (also a record) are running for governor; 9 (two less than in 1992) are running for the Senate.

October 13 / The Congressional Caucus for Women's Issues claims "record accomplishments for women in Congress." An analysis prepared by the bipartisan caucus for release today lists 66 measures of importance to women enacted by the 103d Congress, among them the Family and Medical Leave Act, the Freedom of Access to Clinic Entrances Act, the Violence against Women Act (enacted as part of the omnibus anticrime bill), the Defense Women's Health Act, and the Gender Equity in Education Act (enacted as part of the omnibus Elementary and Secondary Education Act).

According to caucus cochair Representative Patricia Schroeder (D-CO), "While the number of measures passed in this Congress is historic and impressive, the other story is the one behind the numbers: the cooperation between congresswomen, their persistence in working to bring legislation important to women to the House and Senate floors, and their political savvy in making this a record-setting Congress."

October 14 / The Women's Bureau of the Department of Labor releases the results of its survey "Working Women Count." The survey had two components: a popular questionnaire to which more than 250,000 women responded and a telephone survey with a scientifically selected, national, random sample. Asked what changes they would like to see in their workplaces, respondents in both surveys gave top priority to improving pay scales and health insurance for all. About half cited on-the-job training and giving employees more responsibility for how they do their jobs as important priorities. There was also consensus that workplace culture should support and respect families—and that it currently fails to do so.

October 17 / Judge Robert E. Cahill, a Maryland circuit court judge, sentences Kenneth Peacock to 18 months in prison for killing his wife with a hunting rifle several hours after finding her in bed with another man. In handing down the sentence (which includes 50 hours of community service), Judge Cahill says that he wishes he didn't have to send Mr. Peacock to prison at all. Says the judge: "I seriously wonder how many men married, five, four years would have the strength to walk away without inflicting some corporal punishment."

October 18 / At a panel on family violence sponsored by Women in Distress of Broward County (Florida), six men who are or have been members of the Miami Dolphins football team talk about their experiences with domestic violence. Dolphins cornerback Troy Vincent describes domestic violence as "the way of life in my [parents'] home" and says, "[I]t wasn't right." The slogan adopted by Women in Distress is "It's Not O.K."

October 19 / Researchers studying the effectiveness of a nonsurgical abortion procedure using methotrexate and misoprostal (*see* October 10, 1994) report their results and concerns in a "Preliminary Communication" in today's issue of the *Journal of the American Medical Association*. The researchers found the procedure comparable in efficiency and safety to RU-486, an abortifacient widely used in Europe but not yet approved for use in the United States. However, the researchers urged physicians not to use the procedure until more research is done.

October 22 / Four American Roman Catholic nuns who are concerned about the Pope's position on the ordination of women as priests demonstrate briefly in front of the papal apartments in the Vatican. The sisters chant,

"We will not be silenced," and display banners that read THEY ARE TALKING ABOUT US WITHOUT US and WOMEN WANT TO BE A PART, NOT APART. Earlier this year the Pope issued an encyclical in which he not only stated that ordination to the priesthood is reserved for men but also declared that the Catholic faithful should not even discuss the subject.

October 24 / The Justice Department announces that federal grand juries in California and Oregon have indicted Rochelle Shannon on 30 counts, charging her with arson and acid attacks at abortion clinics in Oregon, California, Nevada, and Idaho in 1992 and 1993. Ms. Shannon, an anti-abortion extremist, is in prison now for trying to murder a physician.

October 24 / A Florida circuit court judge rules that Paul Hill cannot use "justifiable homicide" as his defense against state charges that he murdered an abortion doctor and his escort. Mr. Hill could get the death penalty if he is convicted of murder by the Florida court; he has already been sentenced to life in prison under federal law (*see* October 5, 1994).

October 25 / Statistics on birthrates released today by the National Center for Health Statistics show that the rate among young teenagers (age 15 to 17) dropped slightly in 1992—the first decline for that age group since 1986. NCHS also found that the birthrate for women age 30 to 34 held steady for the second year in a row.

October 25 / Lieutenant Kara Hultgreen, one of the first two female Navy pilots to qualify for flying off the deck of an aircraft carrier, is killed when her F-14 fighter crashes into the sea as she approaches the carrier *Abraham Lincoln* for a landing.

October 25 / Proposed national standards for teaching history, released today, draw criticism from Lynne Cheney, who says they ignore the role of white male heroes in our history. Ms. Cheney, who headed the National Endowment for the Humanities under Presidents Reagan and Bush, says the curriculum guidelines (which would be voluntary) "present a very warped view of American history." Gary Nash, director of the history guidelines project, responds that the guidelines are intended to focus on broad themes, not individuals, and that in worrying about the omission of particular names, Ms. Cheney is "confusing a curriculum guidebook with a history textbook."

October 26 / Statistics released today by the Equal Employment Opportunity Commission show that job discrimination complaints to the commission doubled between 1990 and 1994. The backlog of complaints is the largest ever—more than 92,000 cases. Because EEOC staff has been cut even as the workload has been increasing, each EEOC investigator is now responsible for 116 cases, more than double the number per investigator in 1990.

October 27 / The Population Council says that clinical trials of RU-486, known as the abortion pill, have begun in the United States (*see* July 7, 1994). For reasons of privacy and safety, the group declines to give specifics about the clinics where the trials are going on, leaving the decision to do so up to individual clinics.

October 28 / The yacht *America³*, with an all-female crew (*see* March 9, 1994), takes second place in the first race of the International America's Cup Class World Championships. These are preliminaries to the actual America's Cup competition, which begins in January. The winning yacht, *One Australia,* is the only brand-new state-of-the-art yacht in today's six-boat race.

October 30 / The Justice Department reports that while violent crimes such as nonsexual assaults and robberies increased considerably in 1993, there were fewer rapes, attempted rapes, and other types of sexual assault. The information comes from the annual National Crime Victimization Survey conducted by the Bureau of Justice Statistics.

October 31 / Among recent college graduates who are black, women earn slightly more than men, according to today's *New York Times.* Researchers at the Economic Policy Institute and Queens College who conducted a study for the *Times* found a female/male wage differential of 1.01 among black recent graduates. Among their white counterparts the differential was 0.89.

October 31 / A federal jury, finding that the Hilton Hotel in Las Vegas failed to provide adequate security during the now-notorious 1991 Tailhook convention, orders the Hilton to pay former Navy Lieutenant Paula Coughlin $5 million in punitive damages in addition to $1.7 million in compensatory damages.

November 1 / Women who have sexual relations with HIV-infected men are at far greater risk of getting AIDS than are men who have relations with HIV-infected women. In fact, the risk for women is more than double that for men, according to findings reported in the November 1994 issue of *Epidemiology*.

November 1 / This month's issue of *Working Woman* reports on a Harris survey of top-level executive women that was conducted for the magazine earlier this year. The women polled were vice presidents or above at companies with $100 million or more in annual sales—mostly service companies. The executives gave their own companies higher marks as places for female executives to work than they gave large corporations in general. However, more than half identified a "male-dominated corporate culture" and "a glass ceiling" as obstacles to success for female executives at their companies. Over four-fifths thought mentoring programs and a top-level corporate policy to promote and train women would improve the corporate culture for women.

November 2 / After deliberating for only 20 minutes, a Florida jury composed of six women and six men convicts Paul Hill of two counts of first degree murder (*see* October 24, 1994).

November 3 / The contraceptive implant Norplant is much more effective than contraceptive pills in preventing inner-city teenagers from getting pregnant, according to a study of Baltimore teenagers described in today's *New England Journal of Medicine*. The study also found that the girls using Norplant are no less likely than the girls on "the pill" to use condoms.

November 4 / The U.S. Military Academy announces that it has benched three West Point football players who "groped" female cadets during a pregame pep rally last month. In addition to a 90-day restriction to grounds (which effectively prevents them from playing intercollegiate football), the offenders received 35 demerits and 80 hours of "walking punishment tours." Deputy Brigade Commander Stephanie Arnold, the highest-ranking woman in the corps of cadets, reportedly believes the punishment fits the crime.

November 7 / Today's teenagers are less physically active than the teenagers of a decade ago, and teenage girls are only half as likely as teenage boys to engage in physical activity. Overall only one-quarter of adolescent girls (compared with half their male peers) take part in vigorous exercise for at least 20 minutes at least three times a week. Moreover, the older they are, the less likely teenage girls are to do vigorous exercise. This pattern, particularly marked among black girls, is not found among teenage boys. These are among the findings of a new government study discussed today at an American Medical Association briefing.

November 7 / The Navy is investigating charges of sexual harassment at the Naval Training Center at San Diego, according to a statement released today by the center's commander, Captain John C. Ensch. Eight instructors at the training facility are alleged to have verbally or physically harassed enlisted women in their training classes. Captain Ensch asserts that the investigation began as soon as the allegations were brought to the attention of commanders back in September but has been slowed because many of the "possible victims and alleged harassers" are no longer at the San Diego center.

November 7 / In its third set of auctions of wireless radio licenses the Federal Communications Commission auctions 30 regional licenses for two-way paging systems. This time companies owned by women and minorities succeed in getting a piece of the action (*see* August 17, 1994). In an effort to encourage the participation of women- and minority-owned businesses, the FCC not only set aside some licenses for such businesses to

bid on but also provided generous financial incentives to help them afford
to bid.

November 8 / Americans go to the polls; the outcome will produce Republican majorities in both the Senate and the House. The election of eight-
term Representative Olympia Snowe (R-ME) to the Senate and the re-
election of the two incumbent female senators up this year—Dianne
Feinstein (D-CA) and Kay Bailey Hutchison (R-TX)—mean that when the
104th Congress convenes, there will be eight women in the Senate, an all-
time high. The number of women in the House will remain at 48, the high
established in the 103d Congress, although there will be 11 new faces (seven
Republicans and four Democrats) among them. In gubernatorial elections
Ann Richards of Texas loses her bid for a second term, and all of the six
other female gubernatorial candidates (four Democrats and two Republicans) lose as well. In other statewide races, however, the news for women
candidates is better, for 86 women win statewide offices.

November 10 / After analyzing more than 100 research papers claiming
that tax dollars spent on prenatal care save the taxpayers money in the long
run, two Seattle, Washington, physician-researchers conclude that the claims
are questionable because the studies on which they are based were seriously
flawed. However, the researchers—whose findings are published in today's
New England Journal of Medicine—stress that prenatal care is medically important and that all pregnant women should receive it.

November 10 / Election day exit polls published in today's *Washington
Post* revealed a yawning gender gap in the elections for the House of Representatives: Nationwide 54 percent of male voters voted for Republicans,
while 54 percent of female voters voted for Democrats. There was also a
considerable racial gap: Eighty-eight percent of black voters voted for Democrats; 58 percent of white voters, voted for Republicans. In several Senate races there were significant gender gaps among white voters. In California, for example, only 41 percent of white women, but 59 percent of
white men, voted for Michael Huffington, the Republican who challenged
incumbent Senator Dianne Feinstein.

November 10 / "Male Student-Athletes Reported for Sexual Assault: A
Survey of Campus Police Departments and Judicial Affairs Offices" is the
title of a paper presented today to the North American Society for Sports
Sociology. The authors—two professors and a graduate student, all at the
University of Massachusetts, all male—found that at 20 institutions with
highly rated NCAA Division I football and basketball teams, "athletes appear to be disproportionately involved in incidents of sexual assault on college campuses." The authors call for more research.

November 17 / Medical researchers studying the efficacy of hormone replacement therapy have found that a combination of estrogen and progestin is better than estrogen alone. The combination not only appears to offer post-menopausal women the same degree of protection against heart disease that is provided by estrogen alone but also offsets the risk of uterine cancer associated with estrogen alone. These findings are reported today at a meeting of the American Heart Association.

November 20 / To counter rumors and anonymous reports that Navy Lieutenant Kara Hultgreen was not properly qualified to land an F–14 on a carrier, Lieutenant Hultgreen's mother makes public her daughter's Navy flight records. The records, verified by the commander of fighter operations in the Pacific Fleet, show that Lieutenant Hultgreen had an "average to above-average" rating at the time she was killed during a carrier-landing attempt last month (*see* October 25, 1994).

November 21 / Beverly Harvard, a veteran officer with the Atlanta, Georgia, police department, is confirmed as Atlanta's new chief of police. She is the first black woman to head the police department of a major city.

November 25 / Judy Mann's column in today's *Washington Post* describes a study comparing the career paths of 46 women and 35 men who were the valedictorians of their high school classes in 1981 and who all went on to college. The researcher, Karen Arnold, began interviewing them when they were freshmen in college and has interviewed them periodically ever since. Among her major findings: While many of the women went on to get advanced degrees, overall they have achieved less professionally than the men, and they have made many more concessions to the competing demands of family than the men. Ms. Arnold's book *Valedictorians over Time* is due out in the fall of 1995.

November 28 / The Center for Reproductive Law and Policy files a citizens' petition urging the Food and Drug Administration to require the manufacturers of six oral contraceptives that can be used as "morning after" pills to include that information—and the dose to use—on the drugs' labels. The drugs are sold for emergency postcoital contraception in Europe, but the companies have not added that use to the labels of the drugs sold in this country. The petition, filed on behalf of the American Public Health Association, the American Medical Women's Association, and Planned Parenthood of New York, argues that the FDA's "failure to require manufacturers to provide [such] information . . . endangers women's health and increases the rates of unintended pregnancy and abortion."

December 1 / MORE MEN IN PRIME OF LIFE SPEND LESS TIME WORKING is the headline of an article by Sylvia Nasar in today's *New York Times*. Among her sources was a recent report prepared by Stephen J. Rose of the National Commission for Employment Policy. Citing the Rose study, Ms.

Nasar writes that the proportion of men age 22 to 58 who worked full time, year round, "year in, year out" (defined as in at least eight of ten years) dropped nine percentage points: from nearly 80 percent in the 1970s to 70 percent in the 1980s. This trend is evident largely among men with a high school diploma or less, reflecting the loss of decent jobs for unskilled and semiskilled men.

December 6 / The incoming Republican majority in the House of Representatives meets to make the House rules for the 104th Congress. Among its first actions is to vote to end funding for 28 legislative service organizations (LSOs), including the Congressional Black Caucus, the Environmental Study Group, and the Congressional Caucus for Women's Issues. Up to now LSOs have been permitted to have offices in the House office buildings and LSO staffers' salaries and other expenses have been paid for with dues from the office accounts of the members of Congress who belonged to them.

December 7 / ESPN announces that starting in 1996, ESPN and ESPN^2 will televise 23 games of the women's Division I basketball tournament, including the semifinals and finals, which are currently broadcast by CBS.

December 9 / Susan V. Berresford was selected to be the next president of the Ford Foundation, effective March 1996. Ms. Berresford became vice president for the foundation's U.S. programs in 1981 and has been vice president in charge of worldwide programming for the foundation since 1989. She will be the first woman to head the prestigious New York–based foundation.

December 9 / President Clinton asks for the resignation of the U.S. Surgeon General, Joycelyn Elders. Since she took the job, Dr. Elders's candor has caused many flaps. The most recent was triggered by a remark that was widely interpreted as an endorsement of teaching students about masturbation. She referred to the practice as "part of something that perhaps should be taught" in schools as a way of curbing the AIDS virus.

December 11 / Explaining to reporters why he fired U.S. Surgeon General Joycelyn Elders last Friday, President Clinton says that "at some point, the President is entitled to have people who . . . don't depart from the policy positions and personal convictions that a President has." Dr. Elders, interviewed today on "Meet the Press," says she believes "the President is doing what he needs to do" and that she still considers him a friend, but she doesn't regret her record of controversial statements: "I've tried to always speak what I knew to be a truth."

December 11 / The recipients of the 1994 Rhodes Scholarships are announced, and for the third year in a row the number of women among them breaks the record. Of this year's 32 winners, 18 are women. Rhodes Scholars are selected on the basis of academic achievement, integrity, leadership, and athletic ability.

December 12 / Many female students at Texas Woman's University (TWU)—the largest predominantly female university in the country—begin a sit-in protesting the TWU board's decision to allow male students in all the university's programs. Currently only three departments in this taxpayer-supported institution allow male students. The board voted to end the institution's mostly female status after a male student threatened a discrimination suit.

December 14 / The Navy announces that it has already punished six male instructors and plans to court-martial four more for sexually harassing enlisted women who were students at the Naval Training Center in San Diego (*see* November 7, 1994). The six received punishment ranging from reprimands and warnings to forfeiture of pay.

December 15 / Smith College announces that Ruth Simmons has been named its new president. Dr. Simmons is the first black person to be named president of one of the "Seven Sisters" colleges (Barnard, Bryn Mawr, Mount Holyoke, Radcliffe, Smith, Vassar, and Wellesley). Presently vice provost of Princeton University, Dr. Simmons will take the helm at Smith next July.

December 19 / In a report to Congress dated today, the General Accounting Office says that the Job Opportunities and Basic Skills (JOBS) program is not reaching most of the poor single mothers who have the greatest need for training and placement if they are to get off welfare and stay off it. For example, according to the GAO, only about one-fourth (24 percent) of all teenage mothers on AFDC were enrolled in the JOBS program.

December 20 / America's schools and parents have been doing a better job of educating children than they are usually given credit for, according to a new study released today by the Rand Corporation. The study found that between the mid-1970s and 1990, standardized test scores improved—slightly for white students and significantly for black and Hispanic students. The factor that helped students most was having better-educated parents. The Rand analysis also found that when considered alone, the increase in the number of working mothers and in the number of single mothers had no significant effect on students' performance.

December 20 / The percentage of abortion clinics experiencing violence and threats of violence from anti-abortion activists was only slightly higher in the first seven months of this year than in the comparable period of 1993 (52 percent versus 50 percent), according to a survey released today by the Feminist Majority. Death threats against doctors and clinic staff members increased; however, there were far fewer blockades of clinics, and clinics reported better cooperation and help from local law enforcement agencies.

December 22 / Researchers report in today's *Journal of the American Medical Association* that elderly women who smoke have poorer muscle strength, agility, and balance than their nonsmoking contemporaries. The findings are based on a study of 9,704 white women over age 65.

December 22 / About two million women quit smoking last year, according to a report released today by the Centers for Disease Control and Prevention. As a result, the percentage of women who smoke dropped from 25 percent in 1992 to 23 percent in 1993. Also released by CDC today are its most recent available statistics on abortion. The data show that the ratio of legal abortions to live births has continued to decline; in 1992 it was the lowest it had been since 1977.

December 22 / Today is Dee Dee Myers's last day as President Clinton's press secretary. She held the job for two years, having fought off an attempt earlier this year to replace her. The first woman and the youngest person to serve as a presidential press secretary, Ms. Myers was reportedly never part of Clinton's inner circle of advisers. She tells reporters, "I think that women, and particularly young women, have a little bit more trouble being taken seriously, being afforded the authority that you need to do this job."

December 24 / The Central Intelligence Agency and "Jane Doe Thompson" have agreed to settle the sex discrimination suit she brought against the agency (*see* September 6, 1994). According to today's *Washington Post,* the CIA will pay Ms. Thompson $410,000, most of which is to settle her claims for back pay, lost wages and benefits, and compensatory damages. The agency has also agreed to pay her legal costs. Ms. Thompson has retired from the CIA.

December 28 / Postmenopausal women who want to avoid falls and broken bones when they are old would do well to exercise regularly with weights, according to findings reported in today's *Journal of the American Medical Association.* Researchers found that postmenopausal women who trained strenuously and regularly with weights on exercise machines significantly strengthened their bones and muscles and improved their balance.

December 30 / Two women staffers are shot to death and several others are wounded by a man who opens fire with a rifle at two abortion clinics in Brookline, Massachusetts. The gunman flees the scene.

1995

January 4 / The 104th Congress convenes. It includes 55 women—47 in the House (17 Republicans, 30 Democrats); eight in the Senate (three

Republicans, five Democrats). Two women—both of them from Kansas—are chairs of permanent committees: Senator Nancy Landon Kassebaum (R) of the Senate Labor and Human Resources Committee (she is the first woman in a half century to chair a major Senate committee) and Representative Jan Meyers (R) of the House Committee on Small Business (the only permanent House committee currently chaired by a woman).

January 5 / John Salvi, who has been identified as the gunman who shot abortion clinic workers in Brookline, Massachusetts last week, is returned to Massachusetts, where he faces both federal and state charges (*see* December 30, 1994). Mr. Salvi was arrested in Norfolk, Virginia.

January 10 / The world's only manufacturer of contraceptive sponges announces that it will no longer make them. Whitehall-Robbins Healthcare says it would cost too much to bring the plant where the sponges have been made up to government safety standards.

January 13 / The all-female *America³* team wins the opening race of the first round of the trials that will determine which one of three American teams will defend the America's Cup in May (*see* March 9, 1994).

January 17 / By a vote of 390 to 0, the House clears the Congressional Accountability Act for the President's signature. The bill makes Congress subject to Title VII of the Civil Rights Act of 1964 and the Family and Medical Leave Act, as well as nine other federal employee protection laws that currently apply to the executive branch of government and to the private sector but not to Congress. (Congress has, however, previously adopted some measures intended to protect congressional employees from discrimination.)

January 18 / House Speaker Newt Gingrich's views on the roles of men and women in military combat are the subject of an item in today's *Washington Post*. Several weeks ago Representative Gingrich (R-GA) reportedly told the history class he teaches at a Georgia college that "females have biological problems staying in a ditch for thirty days because they get infections, and they don't have upper body strength." Men, on the other hand, "are basically little piglets; you drop them in a ditch, they roll around in it." But according to the Speaker, if being in combat means "being on an Aegis class cruiser managing the computer controls for twelve ships and their rockets, a female may be dramatically better than a male who gets very, very frustrated sitting in a chair all the time because males are biologically driven to go out and hunt giraffes."

After reading these quotations aloud on the House floor today, Representative Patricia Schroeder (D-CO), who serves on the House Armed Services Committee, says she is unaware that women get infections every 30 days. Moreover, she says, "I have been working in a male culture for a very long time and I haven't met the first one who wants to go out and hunt a giraffe."

January 20 / An electric guitar will be named after Bonnie Raitt, who will donate her royalties from sales of the Fender guitar to a program to encourage more girls to play. At a benefit today in California, Ms. Raitt reportedly raises $80,000 for the program, which will work through local charities to furnish guitar lessons and guitars to girls who could otherwise not afford them.

January 23 / Twenty-two years and one day after the Supreme Court's decision in *Roe* v. *Wade,* an estimated 45,000 anti-abortion advocates march in Washington to protest that decision and to rejoice in the strength of anti-abortion sentiment in the 104th Congress (abortion foes gained at least 39 House seats and 5 Senate seats in the last election). Speaking to the marchers, Representative Michael Forbes (R-NY) calls it "the most ardent pro-life Congress in memory."

January 26 / In a two to one ruling, a three-judge panel of the U.S. Court of Appeals for the Fourth Circuit approves the Virginia Military Institute's plan to establish a separate, state-subsidized program for women at Mary Baldwin College as an alternative to admitting women to VMI itself (*see* June 28, 1994). The Virginia Women's Institute for Leadership is scheduled to open in August at Mary Baldwin College. It is described as offering some military training, like drills and participation in the ROTC, but in an environment that is less "militaristic" than VMI.

January 26 / Ectopic pregnancies accounted for nearly one in every five (19.7 percent) of all pregnancies reported in 1992, according to figures released today by the federal Centers for Disease Control (CDC). The comparable proportion in 1970 was less than one in 20 (4.5 percent). CDC experts attribute the increas in the rise in the incidence of sexually transmitted diseases, such as chlamydia. Ectopic pregnancies, in which the fetus develops outside the uterus, are extremely dangerous.

January 29 / The Women's Voices for the Economy Campaign winds up a weekend meeting at which it endorsed goals expected to draw the support of women across partisan and socioeconomic lines. The goals: capital to start and expand businesses; job training, continuing education, and skill development; equitable pay and benefits for contingent workers; flexible schedules; and adequate care for children and the elderly. Women representing state and local groups across the country accounted for the majority of those who attended the meeting, which was organized by the Washington-based Center for Policy Alternatives.

January 30 / The same federal appellate judges who ruled a few days ago to let VMI remain all-male (*see* January 26, 1995) heard arguments in the matter of the Citadel, which has appealed Federal District Judge Weston Houck's ruling that Shannon Faulkner be admitted to the cadet corps of that all-male state-supported institution (*see* July 22, 1994). Pending the outcome of the appeal (not expected for several months), Ms. Faulkner is attending classes at the Citadel but is excluded from the military activities that are considered central to the institution's mission.

January 31 / Suzanne Doucette, a former FBI agent who brought a sexual harassment suit against the Bureau (*see* October 11, 1993), announces that she and the FBI have settled out of court. She will receive nearly $300,000. Ms. Doucette praises FBI Director Louis Freeh for "his personal efforts to resolve this case [and] his implementation of policies to insure . . . an [FBI] work environment that reflects the diversity of America."

January 31 / Several anti-abortion groups join in deploring the provisions of the Republican welfare overhaul legislation that would deny benefits to mothers under 18, disallow increased benefits for women who have additional children while on welfare, and disallow benefits for children whose paternity is not legally established. Anti-abortion advocates fear these provisions would result in more women having abortions.

February 2 / Today is National Girls and Women in Sports Day, and female athletes are lobbying Congress to urge that it maintain its commitment to Title IX, which bans discrimination on account of sex in all education programs that receive federal funds. Several weeks ago the American Football Coaches Association called on the new Congress to reconsider Title IX. The coaches complain that men's sports, especially football, are suffering because, they say, colleges are cutting funds for men's sports in order to beef up funds for women's sports.

February 3 / In her column today, entitled "A Goal for All: Fewer Abortions," Judy Mann reports on a recent seminar where pro-choice and anti-abortion advocates found common ground on the need to reduce unplanned pregnancies. Ms. Mann describes the seminar, jointly sponsored by the Kaiser Family Foundation and the American Enterprise Institute, as "one of those rare episodes in which evidence and ideas, rather than rhetoric, inform the debate."

February 3 / Secretary of the Treasury Robert Rubin reportedly approves a Special Olympics commemorative silver dollar bearing Eunice Shriver's image. Ms. Shriver founded the Special Olympics. She will be the first living woman (and only the third woman) to appear on an American coin.

February 5 / Two scholars who have studied the committee assignments of women and men on corporate boards describe their findings in today's *New York Times*. Diana Bilimoria and Sandy Kristin Piderit examined the membership of the six major committees on the boards of the 133 Fortune

300 companies that had at least one female director. They found that even after such factors as differences between women and men in experience had been taken, being male was "a significant advantage" for appointment to the key executive, compensation, and finance committees. Being female was an advantage for appointment to the public affairs committee. Neither sex had an advantage with respect to the audit and nominating committees.

February 5 / The *New York Times* reports that the number of law school applicants was down slightly last year (1993–94), compared with the year before. Male applicants dropped by 2.8 percent; female applicants by only 0.1 percent. The data are from the Law Schools Admission Council.

February 6 / NBC television airs "Serving in Silence," a made-for-television movie about Colonel Margarethe Cammermeyer. It is the true story of Colonel Cammermeyer, a career Army officer with an exemplary record who was discharged from the Washington State National Guard after she told a security clearance investigator that she was a lesbian (*see* June 16, 1994). Barbra Streisand was the driving force behind the making of the film, in which Glenn Close plays Colonel Cammermeyer.

February 6 / John H. Dalton, Secretary of the Navy, signs the Navy's new policy on pregnancy. Based on the philosophy that pregnancy is a natural event that can occur in the lives of Navy and Marine Corps women and is not a presumption of medical incapacity, the policy begins by stating that pregnancy and parenthood are compatible with a naval career. This is the first time a secretary of a military service has issued a detailed policy with respect to pregnancy.

February 6 / When it comes to meeting children's intellectual and emotional developmental needs, most daycare centers are no better than mediocre, and many are downright poor, according to a study made public today. "Cost, Quality, and Child Outcomes in Child Care Centers" is particularly critical of the quality of care for infants and toddlers. The study was conducted by child psychologists and economists at four universities, each in a different section of the country.

February 7 / According to today's *Washington Post,* a nationwide poll of high school students found that girls who participate in high school sports are regarded as "cool" and "feminine" by most of their peers—boys as well as girls. And although less than half (47 percent) of high school girls said they themselves participated in sports, the overwhelming majority agreed that sports participation develops a sense of achievement, increases self-confidence, promotes healthy habits, and improves self-image. The poll was conducted by the Women Athlete's Voice of Encouragement program, sponsored by Ocean Spray.

February 7 / Representative Nita Lowey (D-NY) and other members of the House Pro-Choice Task Force hold a news conference to support the nomination of Henry W. Foster, Jr., President Clinton's choice to succeed Joycelyn Elders as U.S. Surgeon General (*see* December 11, 1994). Anti-abortion lawmakers have objected to the nomination because Dr. Foster, who is an obstetrician, has performed abortions.

February 8 / A major study of the connection between a woman's weight in middle age and her risk of heart attack finds that the risk increases if she has gained more than 10 pounds over her weight at age 18. The researchers urge that the federal weight guidelines for women age 35 and over be revised downward by 15 percent. The study is described in today's issue of the *Journal of the American Medical Association*.

February 10 / Research showing that men typically do better than women in law school is the subject of an article by Laura Lansnerus in today's *New York Times*. A study of law students at the University of Pennsylvania, recently published in that institution's law review, found that men are three times as likely as women to be in the top 10th of their class after the first year of law school, and although the gap narrows later, it never closes. Ms. Lansnerus writes that a larger study of 6,000 students at law schools across the country yielded similar results. First-year grades are reportedly crucial in the "distribution of [such] goodies" as membership on the law review, summer jobs, and judicial clerkships.

February 13 / The nomination of Air Force Brigadier General Marcelite Jordan Harris for promotion to major general is received by the Senate Armed Services Committee. If the Senate approves the promotion, as seems likely, General Harris will hold the highest rank so far achieved by any African American woman in any U.S. military service. General Harris is director of maintenance for the Air Force.

February 14 / The Accreditation Council for Graduate Medical Education votes to require that medical residents planning to be obstetricians or gynecologists be taught abortion skills unless they have moral or religious objections to abortion. Hospitals that have such objections can arrange to have their ob-gyn residents get abortion training at another institution. The requirement is supported by the American Board of Obstetrics and Gynecology, the American College of Obstetricians and Gynecologists, and the American Medical Association.

February 15 / The *America³* team wins the first race of round three in the America's Cup trials (*see* January 13, 1995). This is only the third win for the all-women's team, which has lost eight races so far.

February 15 / The political and practical challenges facing the Congressional Caucus for Women's Issues in the 104th Congress are the subjects of an article by Kevin Merida in today's *Washington Post*. He writes that the caucus's new cochairs, Representatives Connie Morella (R–MD) and Nita Lowey (D–NY), "hope the caucus can be a model of how to rise above the [partisan] fray" in the more contentious and partisan atmosphere of the present Congress. Like other legislative service organizations, the caucus has been stripped of the staff and budget (see December 6, 1994) that helped it successfully to develop and track key legislative initiatives on behalf of women, as well as to provide information. The bipartisan group has established a separate nonprofit arm, Women's Policy Inc., to assist with these tasks.

February 16 / There are dramatic differences between the sexes in how their brains handle certain language functions, according to researchers at Yale University whose findings are published in today's issue of *Nature*. Using magnetic resonance imaging, Dr. Sally Shaywitz and Dr. Bennett Shaywitz scanned the brains of 19 women and 19 men while they performed various mental tasks. When given the same word-rhyming task to do, most of the men used only one area in the left side of the brain; the women, on the other hand, used areas on both sides of the brain.

February 20 / Chevron Corporation agrees to pay $3.2 million to settle a sexual harassment suit brought by four women who worked for the Chevron Information Technology Company. The plaintiffs charged not only that they and other women who worked for the company were subjected to many and repeated instances of sexual harassment but also that after they and other women submitted a letter asking the company to address the problem, they were made the targets of retaliation by management.

February 21 / President Clinton names Laura D'Andrea Tyson head of the National Economic Council, a Cabinet-level position not previously held by a woman. Ms. Tyson currently chairs the Council of Economic Advisers.

February 22 / The federal government issues a proposal that physicians counsel all pregnant women about AIDS and urge them to be tested for the HIV virus that causes AIDS. A pregnant woman who is HIV-positive can take a drug—zidovudine—that reduces by two-thirds the chance that her unborn child will be infected by the virus.

February 22 / College-educated black women with full-time jobs now typically earn as much as their white counterparts earn. The birthrate among unwed black teenagers has not, as is commonly believed, been increasing but rather has remained virtually the same for two decades. Three-fourths of black single mothers are employed. These are some of the findings contained in two reports on the U.S. black population released by the Census Bureau today.

February 27 / President Clinton signs an executive order giving the federal government a more active role in helping states track down federal employees and military personnel who fail to pay child support.

February 28 / Americans United for Life, an anti-abortion group based in Chicago, announces that it has filed a citizens' petition with the Food and Drug Administration asking that the FDA apply the strictest possible standards in reviewing the abortifacient RU–486. The leading signer of the petition is U.S. Representative Thomas Bliley (R–VA), who is also one of the Republican members of Congress calling on the FDA to ease regulatory burdens on businesses that seek quick approval for new products. The easing would include allowing foreign approval and foreign data to count in assessing the safety of a drug. RU–486 has been used safely in Europe for years.

February 28 / Evidence that women's physiology makes it unlikely that they can match men's records in such sports as running and speed swimming is the subject of an article by Rick Weiss in today's *Washington Post*. Mr. Weiss writes that although women athletes have made steady gains on men in recent years, experiments conducted by Kirk Cureton, a physiologist at the University of Georgia, have led the latter to conclude that differences between the sexes in cardiovascular capacity (men have more) and percentage of body fat (men have less) will always give men the edge.

February 28 / The full House Ways and Means Committee begins fine-tuning one of the centerpieces of the Republican Contract with America, a complete overhaul of the country's welfare system. As reported out of the Human Resources Subcommittee earlier this month, the bill would do away with entitlement to public assistance. It would replace the current federal-state AFDC matching arrangement, under which needy families are guaranteed assistance if they meet certain criteria, with cash payments to the states that the states would not be required to match. It would set a two-year limit on public assistance, after which adult recipients would be required to work. It would make the children of unwed teenage mothers ineligible for assistance and deny additional payments for children conceived by women already on welfare.

March 1 / Marking Women's History Month with a speech to military and civilian officials at the Pentagon, Hillary Rodham Clinton tells the gathering she is honored to learn that she is the first First Lady to have had the opportunity to speak at the Pentagon.

March 2 / "The Beardstown Ladies" and their best-selling *Common Sense Investment Guide* are the subjects of an article by Hubert Herring in today's *New York Times*. The "Ladies" are 15 Illinois women who in 1983 formed an investment club into which each puts $25 a month. The club has achieved an average annual return of 23.4 percent on its investments.

March 2 / The space shuttle *Endeavor* lifts off with Navy Lieutenant Commander Wendy Lawrence aboard. She is the first female navy aviator to go into space and the first woman astronaut to have graduated from the U.S. Naval Academy. Lieutenant Commander Lawrence's father is Vice Admiral William Lawrence (ret.), a member of the advisory committee to WREI's project on women in the military.

March 3 / As the Big East women's basketball tournament gets under way, the spectacularly successful University of Connecticut women's basketball team is the subject of an article by Frank Litsky in today's *New York Times*. With a record of 26–0, the women Huskies enter the tournament as the only unbeaten major college team in the country—female or male.

March 5 / Candace Gingrich discusses her concerns about House Speaker Newt Gingrich's views on homosexuals and homosexuality. Ms. Gingrich, who is a lesbian, is the Speaker's half sister. She is in Washington at a conference sponsored by the Human Rights Campaign Fund, the country's largest gay and lesbian rights political organization.

March 5 / House Republicans say they want to cut billions of dollars in federal spending for the Food Stamp program by establishing strict new work requirements for Food Stamp recipients.

March 6 / The *Navy Times* reports that women accounted for 18 percent of new recruits to the nation's military services overall in the first quarter of the current fiscal year. The quarter marked the beginning of the Navy's gender-neutral recruiting policy, and the female percentage among Navy recruits was about 22.2, up from about 12.6 in the equivalent period a year ago.

March 7 / Speaking today in Copenhagen, Denmark, at the UN World Conference for Social Development, Hillary Rodham Clinton says that poverty will not end until the lives of women are improved and tells her audience that the United States has created a program to help keep girls in school in Africa, Asia, and Latin America. The official announcement of the program is scheduled for tomorrow, International Women's Day.

March 9 / Senator Paul Wellstone (D-MN) introduces a bill that would prohibit insurance companies from charging higher premiums or denying health insurance coverage or benefits to an individual purely because she was a domestic violence victim (*see* May 12, 1994).

March 9 / Senator Joseph Lieberman (D-CT) calls preference policies based on race and sex "patently unfair." He was responding to questions from reporters about affirmative action. Senator Lieberman, the new chairman of the Democratic Leadership Council, stresses that he is speaking as an individual "but I think reflecting the view of the DLC."

March 9 / A federal district court judge rules that the amount of Paula

Coughlin's award for $6.7 million in damages from the Las Vegas Hilton must be reduced by $1.5 million because she received the latter amount in a separate settlement with the Tailhook Association (*see* October 31, 1994).

March 14 / Representative Enid Waldholtz (R-UT) is expecting a baby in September, according to today's *New York Times*. Representative Waldholtz, a freshman, is believed to be the first Republican member—and the second member ever—to be pregnant while in Congress. The first was former Representative Yvonne Braithwaite Burke, a California Democrat who had a baby in 1973, a year after she was first elected to the House.

March 14 / Hillary Rodham Clinton addresses the "Women and the United Nations" conference at UN headquarters in New York. She tells the participants that "we should commend the United Nations for inviting serious discussion of the unique obstacles confronting women in every country, rich or poor." The conference is dedicated to the memory of Eleanor Roosevelt.

March 15 / The U.S. Court of Appeals for the District of Columbia orders the Federal Communications Commission (FCC) not to proceed with its next planned auction of wireless communications licenses until a legal challenge to the auction rules is resolved. At issue are the financial preferences for female- and minority-owned bidders (*see* August 17, 1994).

March 15 / Picabo Street wins the World's Cup in downhill skiing, the first time a U.S. woman has ever captured that title.

March 15 / The bipartisan Glass Ceiling Commission releases its report, the results of a three-year study of how women and minorities are faring in gaining the upper levels of corporate America. The report's conclusion: The glass ceiling remains virtually intact, although most corporate CEOs think that it no longer exists. The commission's research identified three levels of "artificial barriers" to the advancement of women and minorities: societal barriers that may be outside the control of business, internal structural barriers that are in the direct control of business, and governmental barriers, such as lack of vigorous monitoring and enforcement of employment laws.

March 15 / Senate Majority Leader Robert Dole (R-KS), speaking on the Senate floor, says he will introduce legislation this year to end federal affirmative action programs for women and minorities.

March 16 / In written responses prepared for a Senate Armed Services subcommittee hearing today, the chiefs of personnel for the various services and the top Pentagon civilian in charge of military personnel say that military readiness has not been hurt by opening new specialties to women.

March 16 / "Many women are very concerned about freedom of speech and freedom of association" at the upcoming UN International Women's

Conference in Beijing, says Representative Nancy Pelosi (D–CA), adding that "accreditation [to the conference] should not be a politicized process." The UN has denied credentials to a number of groups, in some cases reportedly because of pressure from the Vatican or the Chinese government. Representative Pelosi is chair of the international task force of the Congressional Caucus for Women's Issues.

March 18 / As of today the *America³* team is no longer entirely female. A male helmsman has joined the crew, which has a new boat, *Mighty Mary.* Going into the semifinals, the *America³* team is behind its competitors, *Young America* and *Stars and Stripes,* by two points and one point respectively.

March 18 / The Associated Press reports that a panel of the National Association of Insurance Commissioners is drafting model legislation that would bar insurance companies from refusing coverage to abused women (*see* May 12, 1994, and March 9, 1995).

March 19 / "The drumbeat for getting rid of [federal affirmative action requirements] doesn't seem to be coming from America's major corporations" but rather from some smaller businesses, particularly those owned by white men, according to an article by Jonathan Glater and Martha Hamilton in today's *Washington Post.*

March 21 / Saying that domestic violence is the number one health risk for women age 15 to 44 and that 700,000 rapes are committed every year, President Clinton names the head of the new Violence against Women office at the Justice Department. She is Bonnie Campbell, whose credentials include serving as Iowa's attorney general.

March 22 / Officials on the carrier *Eisenhower* are reported to be angry about a Navy announcement that 14 women crew members were sent home from the ship because of pregnancy, allowing the public to infer that the women became pregnant aboard ship, as is not the case. According to Rear Admiral Daniel J. Murphy, commander of the *Eisenhower* battle group, the announcement detracted from the group's historic accomplishment as the first carrier to put to sea with women as part of its permanent crew.

March 22 / In a unanimous decision the U.S. Supreme Court holds in *Anderson* v. *Edwards* that states may count all needy children living in a single household as one family for purposes of setting the amount of welfare payments for the household. The practical effect of the Court's decision will be lower payments for poor families in which some of the children are not the offspring of the householder.

March 25 / By a vote of 234 to 199, the House of Representatives approves a bill that would vastly change the "welfare" system in this country. The bill would replace more than 40 federal programs to assist poor people with five block grants to the states and give the states greater discretion in deciding who should get public assistance and under what circumstances. Among the bill's provisions: AFDC would no longer be an entitlement, and states would set their own eligibility criteria and benefit levels, although they could not use federal funds to provide cash assistance to unmarried women under age 18 or to children born to mothers already on welfare. Adult recipients would be expected to work after two years, and no family could receive cash assistance for more than five years. Legal aliens would be ineligible for most forms of assistance, including AFDC, Medicaid, and Food Stamps. The vote is largely along party lines; two women are among the five Republicans opposing the bill.

March 26 / Karen De Witt reports in today's *New York Times* that the Clinton Administration has "unfurled a strategy" to publicize the President's accomplishments on behalf of working women and to contrast his policies with those of the Republican Congress. Ms. De Witt writes that Alexis Herman, White House director of public liaison, Karen Nussbaum, director of the Women's Bureau, and Nancy-Ann Min, an associate director of the Office of Management and Budget, met with a dozen women journalists earlier this week to assert, among other things, that the Republican approach to balancing the budget would hurt such programs as the Women, Infants, and Children nutrition program, the school lunch program, and the rape crisis telephone line.

March 27 / Controversy over the reliability of statistics on rape and other acts of violence against women is the subject of an article by John Schwartz in today's *Washington Post*. David Murray, research director of the Statistical Assessment Service, has charged that in his remarks last week about the new Violence against Women office, the President used "fake numbers" that vastly overestimate the problem (*see* March 21, 1995). Experts consulted by Mr. Schwartz told him that some of the statistics the President cited last week may be questionable but that the statistics cited by Mr. Murray on rape—which he estimated at 150,000 annually—understate the problem. The latest estimate from the Bureau of Justice Statistics is 300,000.

March 30 / President Clinton nominates Shirley A. Jackson to chair the Nuclear Regulatory Commission, which regulates the civilian nuclear industry. If she is confirmed by the Senate, Dr. Jackson will be both the first African American and the first woman ever to head the commission. She is currently a physics professor at Rutgers University.

March 31 / Hillary Rodham Clinton speaks in Ahmadabad, India, with some members of the Self-Employed Women's Association, a group of 143,000 vegetable vendors, embroidery workers, and other poor women workers who have organized to push for improvements in their lot. Ms. Clinton is on a 12-day tour of South Asia, a trip focused on promoting better health, education, and opportunities for girls and women throughout the world.

March 31 / A law professor at Rutgers University who studied affirmative action court cases for the Labor Department has concluded that affirmative action has caused very few claims of reverse discrimination by whites, according to news reports today. Alfred W. Blumrosen reportedly says his findings poke holes in the theory that affirmative action programs unfairly benefit minorities at the expense of white workers. His report, characterized by the Labor Department as a draft, was prepared for the department's Office of Federal Contract Compliance Programs.

AMERICAN WOMEN TODAY: A STATISTICAL PORTRAIT

SECTION I:
DEMOGRAPHICS[1]

This section profiles the U.S. population and looks at some of the demographic trends that shape—and are shaped by—the lives of individual women and their families. The continued increase in the proportion of American families that are headed by women is reflected in the substantial percentage of children who live with only one of their parents, usually their mothers. Also striking is the number of elderly women who live alone.

- The majority of Americans are female. Only in the age groups under 30 do males outnumber females (see Figure 1-1).
- After dropping steeply for decades, fertility rates edged up slightly between 1980 and 1990 (see Figure 1-4).
- Age at first marriage has continued to rise for both women and men. The typical first-time bride in 1993 was nearly four years older than her counterpart in 1970 (see Figure 1-6).
- Women and men living together but not married to each other accounted for three and one-half million American households in 1993. Another one and one-half million households were same-sex partnerships (see Table 1-4).
- Families headed by women have accounted for a growing proportion of American families over the last two and one-half decades. The proportion headed by men, although it remained very small, grew slightly. Still, married couples continued to predominate except among black families,

[1]The editors are deeply indebted to Monique DeJong for identifying and gathering the necessary materials as well as for preparing tables and figures for this and the other statistical sections of *The American Woman 1996–97*.

where single-parent families have constituted an increasing majority throughout the 1990s (see Table 1-3).

- The divorce rate—the number of divorces in a given year per 1,000 persons in the population—has declined slightly in recent years (see Figure 1-7). Even so, the ratio of currently divorced Americans to currently married Americans is at an all-time high (see Table 1-5).
- In 1993 one in five white children and nearly three in five black children lived with a single parent, usually the mother (see Table 1-6).
- Between 1970 and 1993 there was a large increase in the percentage of women age 75 and over who lived alone: from 37 percent to 52 percent (see Figure 1-9). After age 85 only one in 10 women lived with a spouse and almost six out of every 10 lived alone (see Table 1-7).
- The population of the United States is expected to become dramatically more diverse. By the middle of the next century the non-Hispanic white population is expected to decline until it represents only one of every two people in the United States—instead of the three of every four it represents now (see Figure 1-3).

Table 1-1 · POPULATION OF THE UNITED STATES BY RACE AND SEX, 1990

The 1990 Census counted more females than males in every racial group except "other."

Race and Sex	Population
Whites	
Females	102,210,190
Males	97,475,880
Blacks	
Females	15,815,909
Males	14,170,151
American Indians, Eskimos, and Aleuts	
Females	992,048
Males	967,186
Asians and Pacific Islanders	
Females	3,715,624
Males	3,558,038
Others[1]	
Females	4,736,684
Males	5,068,163

[1]"Others" are persons who did not classify themselves as one of the identified races.

Source: Bureau of the Census, *1990 Census of Population: General Population Characteristics, United States*, 1992, Table 16.

Figure 1-1· POPULATION OF THE UNITED STATES BY AGE AND SEX, 1995[1]

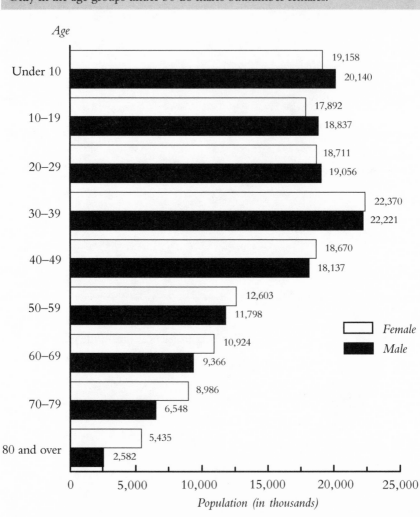

Only in the age groups under 30 do males outnumber females.

Age

Under 10	Female: 19,158	Male: 20,140
10–19	17,892	18,837
20–29	18,711	19,056
30–39	22,370	22,221
40–49	18,670	18,137
50–59	12,603	11,798
60–69	10,924	9,366
70–79	8,986	6,548
80 and over	5,435	2,582

☐ Female
■ Male

Population (in thousands)

[1]Projection of the resident population.

Source: Bureau of the Census, *Population Projections of the United States by Age, Sex, Race, and Hispanic Origin 1993–2050,* 1993, Table 2.

Figure 1-2 · POPULATION OF THE UNITED STATES BY SEX, RACE, AND HISPANIC ORIGIN, 1995[1] (percent distribution)

The proportion of non-Hispanic blacks is slightly larger among females than among males; the proportion of Hispanics is slightly larger among males than among females. In other respects, the distributions of the two sexes are nearly identical.

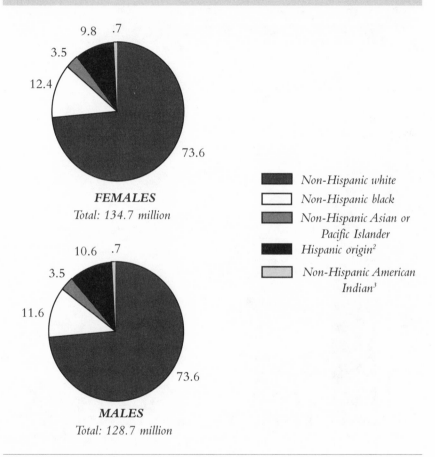

FEMALES
Total: 134.7 million

MALES
Total: 128.7 million

Legend:
- Non-Hispanic white
- Non-Hispanic black
- Non-Hispanic Asian or Pacific Islander
- Hispanic origin[2]
- Non-Hispanic American Indian[3]

[1]Projection of the resident population.
[2]Persons of Hispanic origin may be of any race.
[3]Includes non-Hispanic American Indians, Eskimos, and Aleuts.

Source: Bureau of the Census, *Population Projections of the United States by Age, Sex, Race, and Hispanic Origin 1993–2050,* 1993, Table 2.

Figure 1-3 · PROJECTED COMPOSITION OF THE POPULATION BY
RACE AND HISPANIC ORIGIN, 1995, 2000, 2020, AND 2050

The population of the United States is projected to become more diverse. By the
turn of the century the population is projected to comprise less than 72 percent
non-Hispanic whites with about 13 percent blacks, 11 percent persons of Hispanic
origin, four percent Asians and Pacific Islanders, and one percent American
Indians, Eskimos, and Aleuts. By 2050 the non-Hispanic white population
is expected to decline until it represents only one of every two people in the
United States.

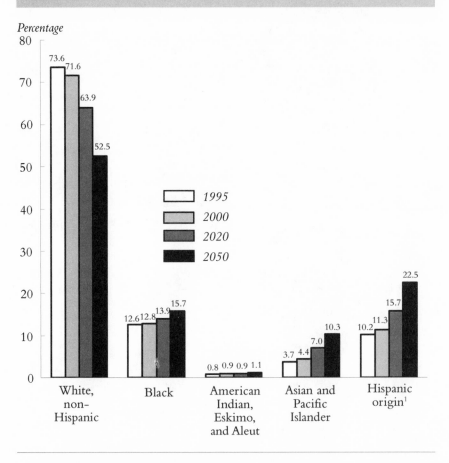

[1]Persons of Hispanic origin may be of any race.

Source: Bureau of the Census, *Population Projections of the United States by Age, Sex, Race,
and Hispanic Origin: 1993–2050,* 1993, Table J (middle series projections).

Figure 1-4 · U.S. FERTILITY RATES BY RACE OF CHILD, 1960–1990[1]

After dropping steeply for decades, fertility rates edged up slightly between 1980 and 1990.

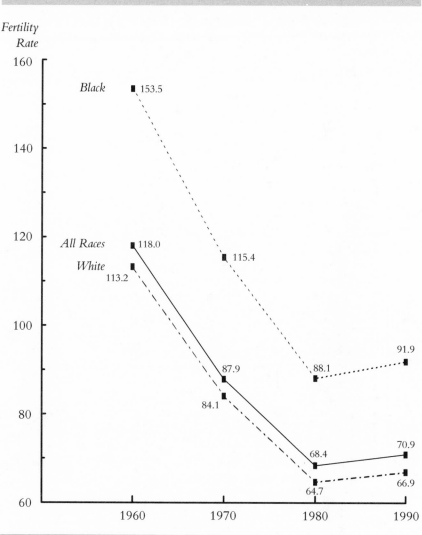

Fertility Rate

[1]Fertility rates are the number of live births per 1,000 women age 15 to 44.

Source: National Center for Health Statistics, *Health, United States, 1993,* 1994, Table 4.

Table 1-2 · MARITAL STATUS BY SEX, RACE, AND HISPANIC ORIGIN, MARCH 1993[1] (percent distribution)

A larger proportion of men than of women are either currently married and living with their spouses or have never married. This is because the formerly married account for a larger proportion of the women than of the men; in 1993, more than one-fifth of women overall were either widowed or currently divorced, compared with about 10 percent of men.

Marital Status	All Races		White		Black		Hispanic Origin[2]	
	Women	Men	Women	Men	Women	Men	Women	Men
Married, spouse present	55.6	60.4	58.8	63.2	31.8	40.2	54.2	53.4
Married, spouse absent	3.7	2.9	2.8	2.5	9.4	5.9	6.9	6.3
Widowed	11.5	2.8	11.6	2.6	12.0	4.4	7.0	1.7
Divorced	10.1	7.6	10.0	7.5	12.0	8.7	8.6	6.1
Never married	19.1	26.3	16.8	24.3	34.9	40.8	23.3	32.5
Total percentage[3]	100.0	100.0	100.0	100.0	100.0	100.0	100.0	100.0
Total number (in thousands)	97,442	89,693	82,111	76,618	11,695	9,622	7,493	7,420

[1]Persons age 18 and over.
[2]Persons of Hispanic origin may be of any race.
[3]Percentages may not add to 100 because of rounding.

Source: Bureau of the Census, *Marital Status and Living Arrangements: March 1993*, 1994, Table 1.

Figure 1-5 · CURRENTLY MARRIED AND NEVER MARRIED ADULTS BY SEX, RACE, AND HISPANIC ORIGIN, MARCH 1993 (in percentages)

For whites and persons of Hispanic origin, the percentage of currently married adults with a spouse present is significantly greater than the proportion that have never married. For both black men and women, the percentage of never married adults is slightly higher.

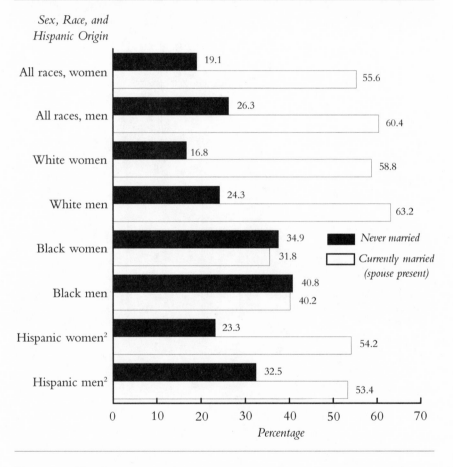

[1]Persons age 18 and over.
[2]Persons of Hispanic origin may be of any race.

Source: Bureau of the Census, *Marital Status and Living Arrangements: March 1993,* 1994, Table 1.

Figure 1-6 · MEDIAN AGE AT FIRST MARRIAGE BY SEX, 1970–1993

Age at first marriage has continued to rise for both women and men. The typical first-time bride in 1993 was almost four years older than her counterpart in 1970.

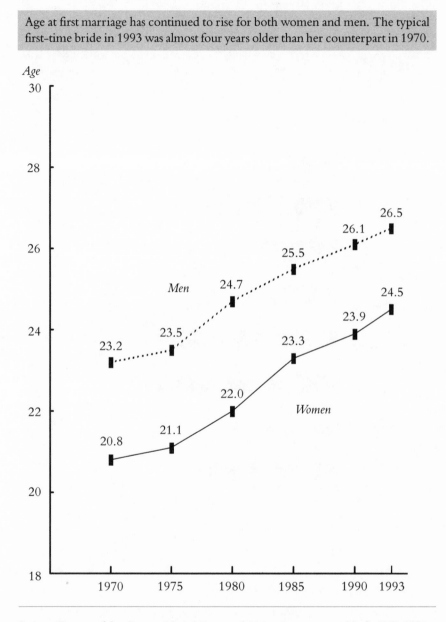

Source: Bureau of the Census, *Marital Status and Living Arrangements: March 1993,* 1994, Table B.

Table 1-3 · FAMILIES BY FAMILY TYPE, RACE, AND HISPANIC ORIGIN, 1970, 1980, 1990, AND 1993 (percent distribution)

Families headed by women have accounted for a growing proportion of American families over the last two decades. The proportion headed by men, although it remained very small, grew slightly—from 2.4 percent in 1970 to 4.3 percent in 1993. Still, although married couples account for a smaller proportion of families than they used to, they predominate except among black families.

Family Type	1970	1980	1990	1993
ALL RACES				
Married couple	85.7	81.7	78.6	77.6
Wife in paid labor force	33.6	41.0	45.7	47.0
Wife not in paid labor force	52.0	40.7	32.9	30.6
Male-headed, no spouse present	2.4	3.2	4.4	4.3
Female-headed, no spouse present	11.4	15.1	17.0	18.1
Total percentage[1]	100.0	100.0	100.0	100.0
Total number (in thousands)	52,227	60,309	66,322	68,506
WHITE				
Married couple	88.3	85.1	82.8	82.0
Wife in paid labor force	33.6	42.0	47.5	49.3
Wife not in paid labor force	54.7	43.1	35.2	32.7
Male-headed, no spouse present	2.3	3.0	4.0	4.0
Female-headed, no spouse present	9.4	11.9	13.2	14.0
Total percentage[1]	100.0	100.0	100.0	100.0
Total number (in thousands)	46,535	52,710	56,803	57,881
BLACK				
Married couple	65.6	53.7	47.8	46.5
Wife in paid labor force	35.5	32.0	31.4	30.2
Wife not in paid labor force	30.2	21.7	16.3	16.2
Male-headed, no spouse present	3.8	4.6	6.3	5.6
Female-headed, no spouse present	30.6	41.7	45.9	47.9
Total percentage[1]	100.0	100.0	100.0	100.0
Total number (in thousands)	4,928	6,317	7,471	7,993

(continued)

Table 1-3 (continued)

Family Type	1970	1980	1990	1993
HISPANIC ORIGIN[2]				
Married couple	—	73.1	69.3	67.9
Wife in paid labor force	—	33.8	35.2	35.7
Wife not in paid labor force	—	39.4	34.2	32.2
Male-headed, no spouse present	—	5.1	6.9	6.9
Female-headed, no spouse present	—	21.8	23.8	25.2
Total percentage[1]	—	100.0	100.0	100.0
Total number (in thousands)	—	3,235	4,981	5,946
ASIAN AND PACIFIC ISLANDER				
Married couple	—	—	80.0	82.1
Wife in paid labor force	—	—	—	—
Wife not in paid labor force	—	—	—	—
Male-headed, no spouse present	—	—	—	—
Female-headed, no spouse present	—	—	12.6	13.4
Total percentage[1]	—	—	—	—
Total number (in thousands)	—	—	1,536	1,737

[1]Percentages may not add to 100 because of rounding.

[2]Persons of Hispanic origin may be of any race.

Source: Bureau of the Census, unpublished data from the Current Population Survey, March 1971, 1981, 1991, and 1994.

Table 1-4 · HOUSEHOLDS WITH UNRELATED PARTNERS BY SEX OF
PARTNERS AND PRESENCE OF CHILDREN, 1993[1] (numbers in
thousands)

In 1993 more than five million households were composed of two adults living
together as partners. Over one-third of the households where the partners were
of different sexes contained children, as did about one-sixth of those with two
female partners. Children were rarely present in households where both partners
were male.

Household Type	Number of Households	With Children	
		Number	Percentage
Partners of opposite sex	3,510	1,236	35.2
Female householder, male partner	1,455	516	35.5
Male householder, female partner	2,055	720	35.0
Partners of same sex	1,509	132	8.7
Both partners female	713	119	16.7
Both partners male	796	13	1.6
Total	5,019	1,368	27.3

[1]Partners over age 18; children under age 15.

Source: Bureau of the Census, *Marital Status and Living Arrangements: March 1993,* 1994,
Table 8.

Figure 1-7 · THE DIVORCE RATE, 1970, 1980, 1990, AND 1994[1]

The divorce rate—the number of divorces in a given year per 1,000 persons in the population—has declined slightly in recent years.

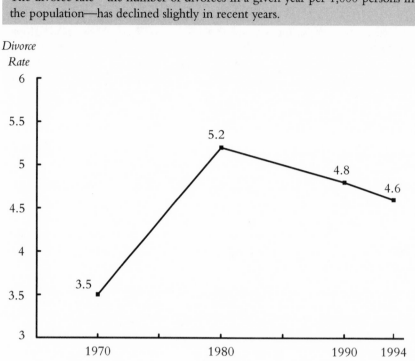

[1]The rate for 1994 is for the 12 months ending with September 1994.

Source: Bureau of the Census, *Statistical Abstract of the United States 1990,* 1990, Table 126, and *1992,* 1992, Table 134; and National Center for Health Statistics, *Monthly Vital Statistics Report,* March 1, 1995.

Table 1-5 · DIVORCE RATIOS BY SEX, RACE, AND HISPANIC ORIGIN, 1970, 1980, 1990, AND 1993[1]

Even though the divorce rate has declined recently (as shown in Figure 1-6), the divorce ratio has been rising because the number of currently divorced persons has continued to increase faster than the number of currently married persons. A relatively low proportion of currently married persons (as in the case of blacks— see Figure 1-4) helps produce a relatively higher divorce ratio.

Race and Hispanic Origin	1970		1980		1990		1993	
	Women	*Men*	*Women*	*Men*	*Women*	*Men*	*Women*	*Men*
All races	60	35	120	79	166	118	182	125
White	56	32	110	74	153	112	170	119
Black	104	62	258	149	358	208	378	216
Hispanic origin[2]	81	40	132	64	155	103	157	114

[1]The divorce ratio is the number of divorced persons per 1,000 married persons with spouse present.
[2]Persons of Hispanic origin may be of any race.

Source: Bureau of the Census, *Marital Status and Living Arrangements: March 1990,* 1991, Table C, and *Marital Status and Living Arrangements: March 1993,* 1994, Table 1.

Table 1-6 · CHILDREN'S LIVING ARRANGEMENTS BY RACE AND
HISPANIC ORIGIN, 1970, 1980, AND 1993[1] (percent distribution)

In 1993 one in five white children (21 percent) and nearly three in five black
children (57 percent) lived with a single parent, usually the mother. The proportion
was nearly one in three for Hispanic children (32 percent). Although the
percentages of children living in single-father families increased between 1970
and 1993, they remained very small.

Living Arrangements	1970	1980	1993
ALL RACES			
Living with two parents	85.2	76.7	70.5
Living with mother only	10.8	18.0	23.3
Living with father only	1.1	1.7	3.4
Other[2]	2.9	3.7	2.8
Total percentage[3]	100.0	100.0	100.0
Total number (in thousands)	69,162	63,427	66,893
WHITE			
Living with two parents	89.5	82.7	77.2
Living with mother only	7.8	13.5	17.4
Living with father only	0.9	1.6	3.5
Other[2]	1.8	2.2	1.9
Total percentage[3]	100.0	100.0	100.0
Total number (in thousands)	58,790	52,242	53,075
BLACK			
Living with two parents	58.5	42.2	35.0
Living with mother only	29.5	43.9	54.0
Living with father only	2.3	1.9	3.0
Other[2]	9.7	12.0	7.4
Total percentage[3]	100.0	100.0	100.0
Total number (in thousands)	9,422	9,375	10,660

(continued)

Table 1-6 (continued)

	1970	1980	1993
HISPANIC ORIGIN[4]			
Living with two parents	77.7	75.4	64.5
Living with mother only	—	19.6	28.0
Living with father only	—	1.5	3.8
Other[2]	—	3.5	3.6
Total percentage[3]	—	100.0	100.0
Total number (in thousands)	4,006	5,459	7,776

[1]Children under age 18.

[2]Living with relatives other than parents or with nonrelatives.

[3]Percentages may not add to 100 because of rounding.

[4]Persons of Hispanic origin may be of any race.

Source: Bureau of the Census, *Marital Status and Living Arrangements: March 1993*, 1994, Table F.

Figure 1-8 · NUMBER OF MEN PER 100 WOMEN BY AGE, 1992

The proportion of men to women decreases dramatically for every age group over age 24. Above age 85 there are fewer than four men for every 10 women in the United States. This imbalance is a major contributing factor to the large number of women who live alone in the United States.

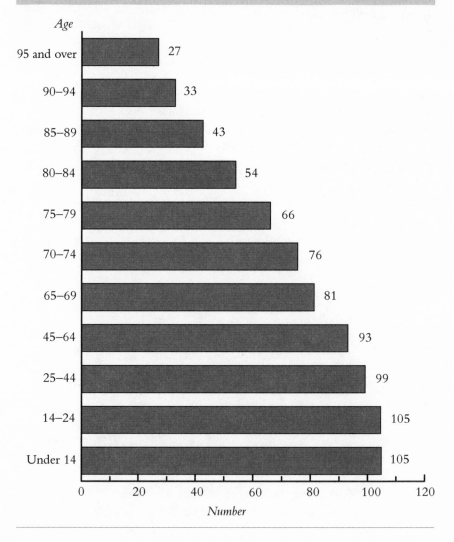

Source: Bureau of the Census, *Statistical Abstract of the United States, 1994*, 1994, Table 15.

Table 1-7 · LIVING ARRANGEMENTS OF WOMEN AGE 65 AND OVER BY AGE, RACE, AND HISPANIC ORIGIN, 1993[1] (percent distribution)

After age 85 only one in 10 women lived with a spouse, and almost six out of every 10 lived alone. For black women, the proportion of all older women living with a spouse was much lower, but they were less likely to live alone after age 75. Extended families are more prevalent for all minorities than for whites; white women are particularly vulnerable to the isolation that results from being widowed or divorced.

Age and Race	Living Alone	Living with Spouse	Living with Others
Age 65–74			
All races	32.0	52.3	15.7
White	32.1	54.4	13.4
Black	36.0	34.6	29.4
Hispanic origin[2]	22.1	46.1	31.8
Age 75–84			
All races	51.0	29.6	19.4
White	51.8	31.0	17.2
Black	47.9	16.0	36.1
Hispanic origin[2]	34.2	22.8	43.0
Age 85 and over			
All races	57.0	10.1	32.9
White	59.3	10.5	30.2
Black	31.4	5.8	62.8
Hispanic origin[2]	32.8	13.1	54.1

[1]Includes only the noninstitutional population.

[2]Persons of Hispanic origin may be of any race.

Source: Bureau of the Census, *Marital Status and Living Arrangements: March 1993*, 1994, Table 7.

Figure 1-9 · WOMEN AND MEN AGE 65 AND OLDER LIVING ALONE, 1970, 1980, AND 1993 (percent distribution)

This figure indicates the long-term consequences of women's longer life expectancy combined with their propensity to marry older men; a much higher percentage of women than men wind up living alone. Between 1970 and 1993 the percentage of older men living alone remained steady; however, there was a large increase in the percentage of women age 75 and over living alone, from 37 percent to 52 percent.

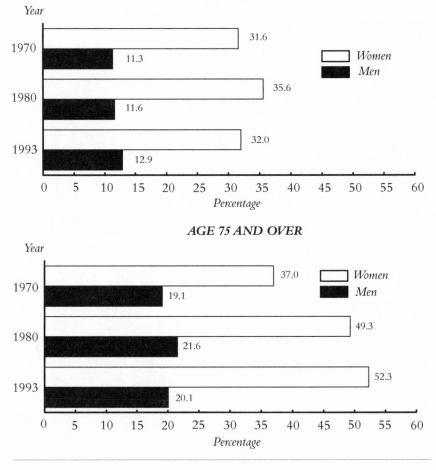

AGE 65 TO 74

Year

1970 Women 31.6 Men 11.3

1980 Women 35.6 Men 11.6

1993 Women 32.0 Men 12.9

Percentage: 0 5 10 15 20 25 30 35 40 45 50 55 60

☐ Women
■ Men

AGE 75 AND OVER

Year

1970 Women 37.0 Men 19.1

1980 Women 49.3 Men 21.6

1993 Women 52.3 Men 20.1

Percentage: 0 5 10 15 20 25 30 35 40 45 50 55 60

☐ Women
■ Men

Source: Bureau of the Census, *Marital Status and Living Arrangements: March 1993*, 1994, Table E.

SECTION 2:

EDUCATION

In the general population, the percentage of American women age 25 and over who have at least a high school education increased substantially between 1970 and 1993, particularly among black women. However, the trend with respect to college enrollment by blacks is not encouraging, and the lack of secondary education is a major problem among men and women of Hispanic origin.

At the postsecondary level women have made notable gains and have in some cases reversed the gender gap in higher education: Women now outnumber men among recipients of postsecondary degrees at every level except the doctoral level. In areas where women are still underrepresented, they continue to gain ground: Their share of college degrees in science and math has grown, and their presence among graduates of dental, medical, and law schools has continued to increase.

- As of 1993 almost two in five American women age 25 and older were high school graduates who had not gone on to college. Another 19.2 percent—nearly one in five—had finished at least four years of college (see Table 2-1).
- Although white women are still the most likely to have had 12 or more years of schooling, it was among black women that the proportion with at least 12 years of schooling increased most dramatically between 1970 and 1993 (see Figure 2-1).
- Lack of education is a particular problem among women and men of Hispanic origin. As of 1993 more than 30 percent of Hispanic women and men had no more than eight years of schooling (see Table 2-1).
- Between 1976 and 1992 non-Hispanic whites' predominance among col-

lege students declined a few percentage points as the Hispanic and Asian/Pacific Islander proportions of college enrollment increased. The trend with respect to black enrollment since 1976 is not encouraging (see Table 2-2).

- Of all female students in institutions of higher learning in 1991, more than one-third were at least 30 years old—more than double the proportion in 1970 (see Figure 2-2). Almost as many women went to colleges and universities part time as full time in 1991—a trend that is expected to continue through the end of the decade (see Figure 2-3).
- Between 1961/62 and 1991/92, women's share of biology and business degrees greatly increased. Although large gains have been made, women remain significantly underrepresented in the fields of computer and information sciences, engineering, and the physical sciences (see Table 2-3).
- Women outnumbered men among the recipients of postsecondary degrees in 1991/92 at every level except the doctoral level (see Figure 2-4).
- The presence of women in America's law, medical, and dental schools has increased significantly, as has the representation of minority women, between 1976/77 and 1991/92 (see Table 2-4).

Table 2-1 · EDUCATIONAL ATTAINMENT BY SEX, RACE, AND
HISPANIC ORIGIN, 1993[1]

As of 1993 slightly fewer than two in five (37.4 percent) of all American women age 25 and over were high school graduates who had not gone on to college. Another 19.2 percent—nearly one in five—had finished at least four years of college. A larger proportion of all men age 25 and older (24.8 percent) held a bachelor's degree or more. In recent years women have made real progress in reversing this gender gap in higher education; more women than men are currently enrolled in institutions of higher learning, as shown in Figure 2-3.

			Percent Distribution			
		—High School—			*—— College ——*	
	Number	*0–8*	*1–3*	*4*	*1–3*	*4 Years*
	(in thousands)	*Years*	*Years*	*Years*	*Years*	*or More*
All races						
Women	85,181	9.2	10.9	37.4	23.4	19.2
Men	77,644	9.4	10.1	33.2	22.6	24.8
White						
Women	72,222	8.7	10.0	38.0	23.6	19.7
Men	66,797	8.9	9.3	33.1	23.0	25.7
Black						
Women	9,833	11.4	17.6	35.8	23.0	12.4
Men	7,953	13.4	17.0	36.9	20.7	11.9
Hispanic origin[2]						
Women	6,097	31.6	15.2	27.6	17.1	8.5
Men	6,003	31.5	15.6	26.0	17.5	9.5

[1]Persons age 25 and over.

[2]Persons of Hispanic origin may be of any race.

Source: Bureau of the Census, *Educational Attainment in the United States: March 1993 and 1992*, 1994, Table 1.

Figure 2-1 · WHITE, BLACK, AND HISPANIC WOMEN AGE 25 AND OVER WITH 12 OR MORE YEARS OF EDUCATION, 1970, 1980, AND 1993[1] (percent distribution)

Although as of 1993 white women remained the most likely to have had 12 or more years of schooling, it was among black women that the proportion with at least 12 years of education increased most dramatically between 1970 and 1993. Among Hispanic women the proportion dropped significantly between 1980 and 1993.

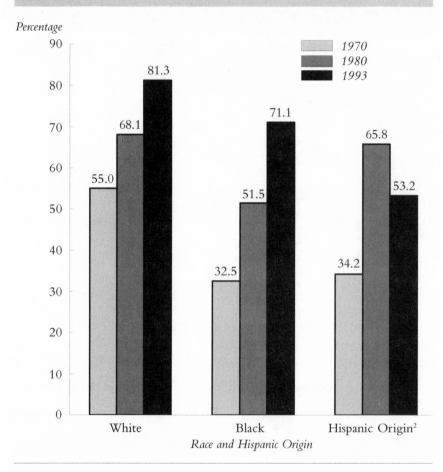

Percentage

[1]Prior to 1992 those with 12 years of schooling—whether or not they graduated.
[2]Persons of Hispanic origin may be of any race.

Source: Bureau of the Census, *Statistical Abstract of the United States 1994*, 1994, Table 233.

Table 2-2 · COLLEGE ENROLLMENT BY SEX, RACE, AND HISPANIC ORIGIN, 1976, 1984, AND 1992[1] (percent distribution)

Between 1976 and 1992 non–Hispanic whites continued to predominate heavily among college students of both sexes, although their proportion declined a few percentage points as the Hispanic and Asian/Pacific Islander proportions increased. This reflects not only higher educational attainment in these groups but also their increased numbers in the U.S. population.

	Women			Men		
	1976	*1984*	*1992*[2]	*1976*	*1984*	*1992*[2]
Non–Hispanic white	82.4	80.9	75.9	84.4	82.4	77.2
Non–Hispanic black	11.5	10.7	11.4	9.0	8.3	9.1
Hispanic origin[3]	3.6	4.7	7.2	4.0	4.8	7.3
Asian/Pacific Islander	1.7	2.9	4.5	1.9	3.7	5.6
Native American	0.8	0.8	0.9	0.7	0.7	0.9
Total percentage[4]	100.0	100.0	100.0	100.0	100.0	100.0
Total number (in thousands)	4,475	5,535	6,836	4,800	4,860	5,436

[1]Excludes nonresident alien students.

[2]Data for 1992 are preliminary.

[3]Persons of Hispanic origin may be of any race.

[4]Percentages may not add to 100 because of rounding.

Source: National Center for Education Statistics, *Digest of Education Statistics 1994*, 1994, Table 203.

Figure 2-2 · WOMEN ENROLLED IN COLLEGES AND UNIVERSITIES BY AGE, 1970, 1980, 1991, AND 1998[1] (percent distribution)

Of all women enrolled in institutions of higher learning in 1991, one-third were at least 30 years old—double the comparable proportion in 1970. The proportion over age 30 is projected to rise even higher (36.3 percent) by 1998.

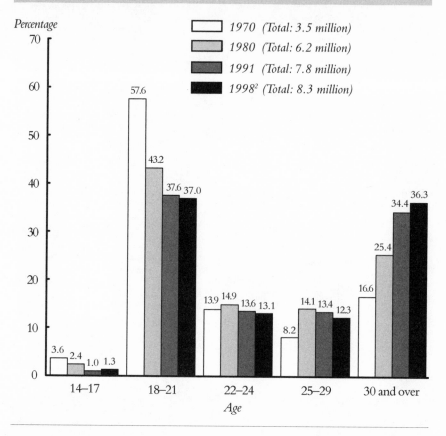

[1]Includes undergraduates, students in graduate programs, and students seeking first professional degrees (i.e., in law, medicine, etc.).
[2]Projected.

Source: National Center for Education Statistics, *Digest of Education Statistics 1994*, 1994, Table 171.

Figure 2-3 · STUDENTS ENROLLED IN COLLEGES AND UNIVERSITIES BY SEX AND FULL- OR PART-TIME STATUS, 1970, 1980, 1991, AND 1998[1]

In 1991 over four million women were enrolled as full-time students in institutions of higher learning, up from about 2.3 million in 1970. This was more than four times the increase in the number of men enrolled full time (only 425,000 over that period). The number of part-time students of both sexes increased, but much more dramatically for women—a trend which is projected to continue through 1998. In the 1990s women constitute the majority of both full-time and part-time students in institutions of higher learning.

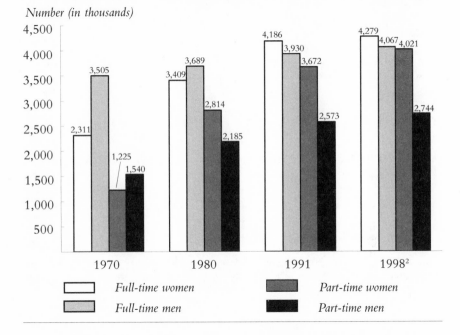

Number (in thousands)

Full-time women
Full-time men
Part-time women
Part-time men

[1]Fall enrollments. Includes undergraduates, students in graduate programs, and students seeking first professional degrees (i.e., in law, medicine, etc.).
[2]Projected.

Source: National Center for Education Statistics, *Digest of Education Statistics 1994,* 1994, Table 171.

Table 2-3 · WOMEN AWARDED UNDERGRADUATE DEGREES IN
SELECTED FIELDS, 1961/62–1991/92 (in percentages)

In the 30-year span between 1961/62 and 1991/92, women's share of all business
degrees awarded sextupled, and their share of biology degrees almost doubled.
Although large gains have been made, women today remain significantly
underrepresented in the fields of computer and information sciences, engineering,
and the physical sciences.

Field	Degrees Awarded to Women as a Percentage of All Degrees Awarded			
	1961/62	1971/72	1981/82	1991/92
Biological sciences	28.2	29.4	45.4	51.6
Business	7.8	9.5	39.4	47.2
Computer and information sciences	—	13.5	34.8	28.7
Education[1]	71.3	74.1	75.8	79.0
Engineering[1]	0.4	1.0	11.4	14.0
English[1]	62.3	64.6	65.8	66.3
Health professions	—	75.5	84.1	83.5
Mathematics[1]	27.2	38.9	42.8	46.6
Physical sciences[1]	12.5	14.9	25.7	32.6
Psychology[1]	40.8	46.2	66.9	73.2
Social sciences	—	36.2	44.6	45.5
Visual and performing arts	—	59.9	63.3	62.1

[1]Data are for 1959/60 rather than 1961/62.

Source: National Center for Education Statistics, *Digest of Education Statistics 1994*, 1994,
Tables 268, 270, 272, 273, 274, 276, 279, 280, 281, 283, 285, and 287.

Figure 2-4 · RECIPIENTS OF POSTSECONDARY DEGREES BY SEX, 1959/60–1991/92

In 1991/92 women outnumbered men among recipients of postsecondary degrees at every level except the doctoral level.

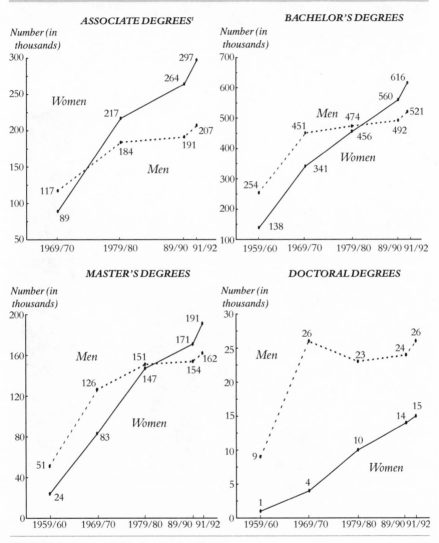

¹1959/60 data not available for associate degrees.

Source: National Center for Education Statistics, *Digest of Education Statistics 1990,* 1991, Table 156, and *Digest of Education Statistics 1994,* 1994, Table 234.

Figure 2-5 · FIRST PROFESSIONAL DEGREES AWARDED IN SELECTED
FIELDS BY SEX OF RECIPIENTS, 1991/92

Men predominated among those awarded their first professional degrees in dentistry, medicine, and law in 1991/92. However, as Table 2-4 shows, women have made a good deal of progress in these fields since 1976/77.

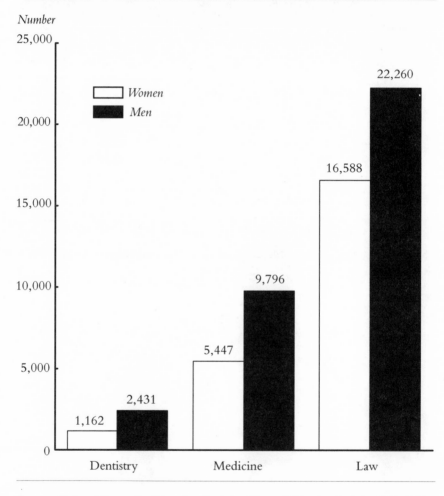

Source: National Center for Education Statistics, *Digest of Education Statistics 1994,* 1994, Table 264.

Table 2-4 · WOMEN AWARDED FIRST PROFESSIONAL DEGREES IN
SELECTED FIELDS BY RACE AND HISPANIC ORIGIN, 1976/77 AND
1991/92 (percent distribution)[1]

By 1991/92 the number of women who received dentistry degrees had nearly
tripled from 1976/77. The number of women receiving degrees in medicine
and law more than doubled over that same time. Minority representation was
highest among the recipients of dentistry degrees and lowest among law degree
recipients.

	Dentistry		*Medicine*		*Law*	
	1976/77	*1991/92*	*1976/77*	*1991/92*	*1976/77*	*1991/92*
Total number of degrees awarded to women	367	1,090	2,543	5,388	7,630	16,491
Non-Hispanic white	82.8	66.4	86.7	74.1	90.5	84.7
Non-Hispanic black	12.0	7.6	9.5	8.4	5.8	6.9
Hispanic origin[2]	1.6	6.4	1.7	4.2	1.6	4.2
Asian/Pacific Islander	3.0	19.4	1.9	12.6	1.7	3.7
Native American	0.5	0.2	0.2	0.6	0.4	0.5
Total percent	100.0	100.0	100.0	100.0	100.0	100.0
Degrees awarded to women as a percentage of all degrees	7.3	32.3	19.1	35.7	22.5	42.6

[1]Data exclude nonresident aliens.
[2]Persons of Hispanic origin may be of any race.

Source: U.S. Department of Health, Education, and Welfare, Office for Civil Rights, *Data
on Earned Degrees Conferred by Institutions of Higher Education by Race, Ethnicity and Sex,
Academic Year 1976–77* and National Center for Education Statistics, *Digest of Education
Statistics 1994*, 1994, Table 264.

Figure 2-6 · FACULTY WITH TENURE BY SEX AND TYPE OF INSTITU-
TION, 1980/81 AND 1992/93[1]

In 1992/93, as in 1980/81, the majority of men on the faculties of four-year
colleges and universities had tenure and the majority of their female counterparts
did not; in fact, the tenured proportions hardly changed for either sex between
1980/81 and 1992/93.

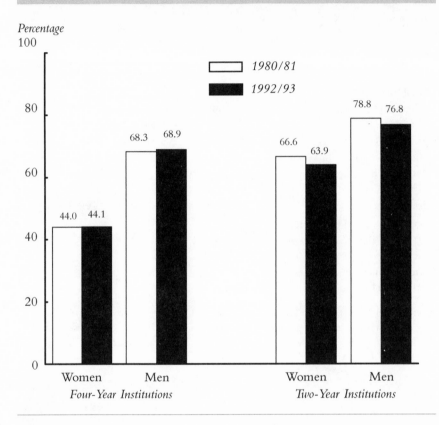

Percentage

[1]1992/93 is preliminary data.

Source: National Center for Education Statistics, *Digest of Education Statistics 1994*, 1994,
Table 230.

SECTION 3:
HEALTH

During this century life expectancy has increased dramatically for all Americans at birth: to almost 79 for a girl and 72 for a boy; this represents increases of more than 30 years for a girl and more than 25 years for a boy. Despite significant progress, the United States lags behind many other highly industrialized countries in life expectancy.

With the declines in death at birth, in childbirth, or from infectious diseases, most Americans now die in old age from cancer or heart disease. Breast cancer, lung cancer, cancer of other sites, heart disease, and AIDS remain significant causes of premature death for women. Inadequate access to preventive care and treatment remains a concern—especially for uninsured women, low-income women, and women of color.

- Life expectancy gaps—between women and men and among ethnic/racial groups—have widened. In 1991 life expectancy at birth was nearly seven years more for a girl than for a boy. For blacks this gender gap was more than nine years (see Table 3-1). For women life expectancy at birth is greater for Asian, American Indian, and Hispanic women than for black or white women (see Table 3-2).
- Although AIDS initially affected mostly men in the United States, it is now becoming a leading cause of death among young women. In 1994 black non-Hispanic and Hispanic women were overrepresented in the proportion of newly reported AIDS cases (see Table 3-11).
- Breast cancer and lung cancer are responsible for nearly half of all cancer deaths in women. Mortality rates for white women are higher than for black women for lung and ovarian cancer, but lower for breast, endometrial, and cervical cancer (see Table 3-8).

- Women with higher incomes and more education are more likely to obtain regular preventive care than their less well-off and well-educated counterparts. Less than half of women with family incomes under $20,000 a year or less than 12 years of education had a Pap smear or clinical breast exam in 1990 (see Table 3-9). Women of color are also less likely to obtain prenatal care; in 1991 only three out of five of all women of color received prenatal care in the first trimester (see Table 3-3).
- Although black and Native American infants had far higher infant death rates than white infants between 1985 and 1987, Hispanic infants had no higher rates than white infants—despite Hispanic mothers' lower rates of early prenatal care than white mothers' rates of prenatal care (see Table 3-3 and Table 3-4).
- Although most women age 18 to 64 worked in 1993, women were less likely than men to receive their private health insurance coverage through their own jobs (see Figure 3-7). In 1993 more women than men had coverage through a family member's job or through public insurance, such as Medicare and Medicaid (see Figure 3-7 and Figure 3-8).
- In 1993 more than a fifth of Americans with no health insurance coverage were children under age 18; another 13 percent were children over age 18 who lived with their families (see Table 3-12). In 1993 almost one in four young women age 18 to 24 had no coverage (see Figure 3-9), and more than half of all women age 18 to 64 without health insurance coverage were under age 35 (see Figure 3-10).

Table 3-1 · LIFE EXPECTANCY AT BIRTH AND AT AGE 65 BY RACE
AND SEX, 1900–2010 (in years)

Over time the life expectancy gap between women and men has widened. In
1991 life expectancy at birth was 78.9 for a girl and 72.0 for a boy. The gap was
even greater for blacks: 73.8 for a girl and 64.6 for a boy, more than a nine-year
difference. Although narrowing for all races, the gap remains in later years; on
average, in 1991 a woman who reached age 65 could expect to live 19.1 more
years and a man 15.3 more years.

		At Birth	*Life Expectancy*		*At Age 65*	
Race	*Both Sexes*	*Female*	*Male*	*Both Sexes*	*Female*	*Male*
All Races						
1900	47.3	48.3	46.3	11.9	12.2	11.5
1960	69.7	73.1	66.6	14.3	15.8	12.8
1970	70.8	74.7	67.1	15.2	17.0	13.1
1980	73.7	77.4	70.0	16.4	18.3	14.1
1991	75.5	78.9	72.0	17.4	19.1	15.3
2010[1]	77.9	81.3	74.5	19.0	20.8	17.2
Whites						
1900	47.6	48.7	46.6	—	12.2	11.5
1960	70.6	74.1	67.4	14.4	15.9	12.9
1970	71.7	75.6	68.0	15.2	17.1	13.1
1980	74.4	78.1	70.7	16.5	18.4	14.2
1991	76.3	79.6	72.9	17.5	19.2	15.4
2010[1]	78.8	82.0	75.6	19.1	20.8	17.4
Blacks						
1900[2]	33.0	33.5	32.5	—	11.4	10.4
1960	63.2	65.9	60.7	13.9	15.1	12.7
1970	64.1	68.3	60.0	14.2	15.7	12.5
1980	68.1	72.5	63.8	15.1	16.8	13.0
1991	69.3	73.8	64.6	15.5	17.2	13.4
2010[1]	71.3	76.0	66.5	16.9	18.9	14.9

[1]Projected.
[2]Number is for all "nonwhite" population.

Source: National Center for Health Statistics, *Health, United States, 1993,* May 1994,
Table 27, and Bureau of the Census, *Population Projections of the United States by Age, Sex,
Race, and Hispanic Origin: 1993–2050,* November 1993, Tables B-1 and B-2.

Table 3-2 · LIFE EXPECTANCY AT BIRTH BY SEX, RACE, AND HIS-
PANIC ORIGIN, 1995[1] (in years)

Among both whites and people of color, life expectancy from birth is greater for
women than for men. Among women in 1995, Asians and Pacific Islanders have
the longest life expectancy, followed by Hispanics, American Indians, Eskimos,
and Aleuts. White and black women have shorter life expectancies overall. The
life expectancy gender gap is greatest for blacks, American Indians, Eskimos, and
Aleuts.

Race and Hispanic Origin	Females	Males
White	80.3	73.7
Black	74.8	65.8
Hispanic origin[2]	83.0	75.2
Asian and Pacific Islander	86.2	80.2
American Indian, Eskimo, and Aleut	82.1	72.5
All races	79.7	72.8

[1]Projected.
[2]Persons of Hispanic origin may be of any race.

Source: Bureau of the Census, *Population Projections of the United States by Age, Sex, Race,
and Hispanic Origin: 1993–2050*, 1993, Table B-1.

Figure 3-1 · FEMALE LIFE EXPECTANCY AT BIRTH IN SELECTED
INDUSTRIALIZED COUNTRIES, 1990

Despite the significant increase in life expectancy for Americans during the
twentieth century, the United States is behind a number of highly industrialized
countries in this regard. Life expectancy is highest for females in Japan (82.5
years for those born in 1990).

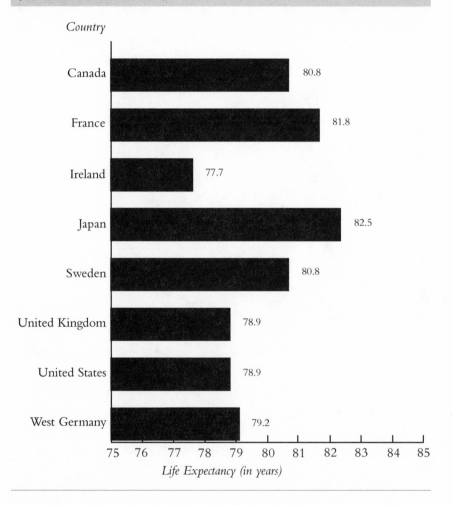

Country

Canada — 80.8
France — 81.8
Ireland — 77.7
Japan — 82.5
Sweden — 80.8
United Kingdom — 78.9
United States — 78.9
West Germany — 79.2

75 76 77 78 79 80 81 82 83 84 85

Life Expectancy (in years)

Source: National Center for Health Statistics, *Health, United States, 1993*, May 1994,
Table 26.

Table 3-3 · PRENATAL CARE FOR MOTHERS WITH LIVE BIRTHS BY RACE AND HISPANIC ORIGIN OF MOTHERS, 1991 (in percentages)

In 1991, although more than half of all women of color received prenatal care in the first trimester of pregnancy, a significant number did not. Over 87.7 percent of Japanese American women began prenatal care in the first trimester. At the other extreme, only 61.9 percent of black mothers, 59.9 percent of Native American, and 58.7 percent of Mexican American mothers received early care.

Race and Hispanic Origin	Percentage of Live Births for Which Mothers Received	
	Late or No Prenatal Care	Early Prenatal Care
Hispanic origin[1]		
Mexican American	12.2	58.7
Puerto Rican	9.1	65.0
Cuban American	2.4	85.4
Central and South American	9.5	63.4
Asian and Pacific Islander		
Chinese American	3.4	82.3
Japanese American	2.5	87.7
Filipino American	5.0	77.1
Native American	12.2	59.9
Black	10.7	61.9
White	4.7	79.5

[1]Persons of Hispanic origin may be of any race.

Source: National Center for Health Statistics, *Health, United States 1993*, May 1994, Table 9.

Table 3-4 · INFANT, NEONATAL, AND POSTNEONATAL MORTALITY
RATES BY MOTHERS' RACE AND HISPANIC ORIGIN, FOR BIRTH
COHORTS, 1985–1987 (number of deaths per 1,000 live births)

Most infant deaths between 1985 and 1987 were neonatal for all groups except
Native Americans. Blacks have by far the highest rate of total infant mortality at
18.2 infant deaths per 1,000 live births. The Asian and Pacific Islander American
groups had infant mortality rates lower than the infant mortality rates for whites.

Race and Hispanic Origin	Total Infant Deaths[1]	Neonatal Deaths[1]	Postneonatal Deaths[1]
TOTAL	10.1	6.6	3.6
RACE			
White	8.5	5.5	3.0
Black	18.2	12.0	6.2
Native American	13.3	6.1	7.2
Total Asian and Pacific Islander[2]	7.6	4.7	2.9
Chinese American	6.0	3.4	2.6
Japanese American	6.6	3.9	2.7
Filipino American	7.2	4.7	2.5
Other Asian and Pacific Islander	8.3	5.2	3.2
HISPANIC ORIGIN			
Total Hispanic origin[3]	8.5	5.5	3.0
Mexican American	8.1	5.2	2.9
Puerto Rican	10.9	7.3	3.6
Cuban American	7.7	5.5	2.2
Central and South American	7.8	5.2	2.6
Other and unknown	9.1	5.7	3.4
Non–Hispanic white[4]	8.4	5.4	3.0
Non–Hispanic black[4]	17.9	11.6	6.3

[1]Infant deaths are the sum of neonatal and postneonatal deaths; neonatal deaths occur
within the first 28 days of life; and postneonatal deaths occur after the 29th day but before
the 365th day of life.

[2]Includes native Hawaiians.

[3]Persons of Hispanic origin may be of any race.

[4]These data apply only to births in those states that specify Hispanic origin as well as race
on birth certificates. In the period from 1984 to 1986, 23 states and the District of
Columbia did so.

Source: National Center for Health Statistics, *Health, United States, 1993,* May 1994,
Table 18.

Figure 3-2 · LOW-BIRTHWEIGHT LIVE BIRTHS BY RACE, ETHNICITY, AND HISPANIC ORIGIN OF MOTHERS, 1991 (in percentages)

In 1991 the percentage of low-birthweight infants born to black mothers (13.6 percent) was more than twice that of any other racial or ethnic group for whom data were collected except Filipinos and Puerto Ricans. The percentage of low-birthweight infants of Puerto Rican mothers (9.4 percent) was about two-thirds higher than the percentage of low-birthweight babies born to Mexican American, Cuban, and Central or South American mothers.

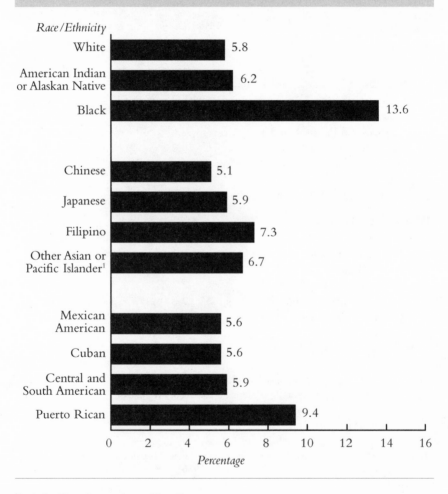

¹Includes Hawaiians and part Hawaiians.

Source: National Center for Health Statistics, *Health, United States, 1993*, 1994, Table 8.

Table 3-5 · CONTRACEPTIVE USERS AGE 15 TO 44 BY METHOD AND AGE, 1988

As women's reproductive goals change over the course of their reproductive lives, the types of contraception they choose also changes. Overall, sterilization (both female and male) was the most common form of birth control in 1988, followed by oral contraceptives ("the pill").

Age	Number (in thousands)	Contraceptive Methods (in percentages)					
		Female Sterilization	Male Sterilization	Pill	Intra-uterine Device	Dia-phragm	Condom
15–19	2,950	2	0	59	0	1	33
20–24	5,550	5	2	68	0	4	15
25–29	6,967	17	6	45	1	6	16
30–34	7,437	33	14	22	3	9	12
35–39	6,726	45	20	5	3	8	12
40–44	5,282	51	22	3	4	4	11
Total	34,912	28	12	31	2	6	15

Source: William D. Mosher, "Contraceptive Practice in the United States, 1982–1990," *Family Planning Perspectives*, 1990.

Table 3-6 · WOMEN EXPERIENCING CONTRACEPTIVE FAILURE
DURING THE FIRST 12 MONTHS OF USE BY MARITAL STATUS,
POVERTY STATUS, AND AGE, 1988[1] (in percentages)

The effectiveness of short-term contraceptive methods varied more by age, marital status, and poverty status than by method in 1988, suggesting that failure more often resulted from improper and irregular use than from a method's inherent limitations.

Marital Status, Poverty Status, and Age	Contraceptive Failure Using					
				Periodic		
	Pill	Condom	Diaphragm	Abstinence	Spermicide	Other
NEVER MARRIED						
Under 200% of poverty						
Under age 20	12.9	27.3	37.3	51.7	49.8	43.7
20–24	15.0	31.1	42.1	57.3	55.4	49.1
25–29	12.8	27.0	36.9	—[2]	49.4	43.5
30 and over	9.6	20.8	—[2]	—[2]	39.6	—[2]
At 200% of poverty and over						
Under age 20	5.9	13.2	—[2]	27.5	26.3	22.5
20–24	6.9	15.2	21.4	31.4	30.0	25.8
25–29	5.9	13.0	18.4	27.2	26.0	22.3
30 and over	4.4	9.8	14.0	—[2]	—[2]	—[2]
EVER MARRIED						
Under 200% of poverty						
Under age 20	26.8	51.3	—[2]	—[2]	—[2]	—[2]
20–24	14.0	29.3	39.8	54.7	52.8	46.6
25–29	8.8	19.0	26.6	38.3	36.7	31.8
30 and over	6.2	13.8	19.5	28.7	27.5	23.6
At 200% of poverty and over						
Under age 20	12.9	—[2]	—[2]	—[2]	—[2]	—[2]
20–24	6.4	14.2	20.1	29.5	28.2	24.2
25–29	4.0	8.9	12.8	19.2	18.3	15.5
30 and over	2.8	6.4	9.1	13.9	13.2	11.2

[1]Percentages are adjusted for underreporting of abortion.
[2]Indicates subgroups represented in the *National Survey of Family Growth* by fewer than five intervals of contraceptive use.

Source: Elise F. Jones and Jaqueline D. Forrest, "Contraceptive Failure Rates Based on the 1988 National Survey of Family Growth," *Family Planning Perspectives*, 1992.

Table 3-7 · ABORTIONS BY WEEK OF GESTATION, 1991 (in numbers and percent distribution)

In 1991, 89 percent of all abortions performed in the United States took place in the first trimester, with half taking place at eight weeks or less from the time the woman had her last menstrual period. Almost 99 percent of all abortions in this country are performed before 21 weeks.

Week of Gestation[1]	Number	Percentage
8 weeks	726,414	52.3
9–10 weeks	348,623	25.1
11–12 weeks	159,728	11.5
13–15 weeks	84,725	6.1
16–20 weeks	54,169	3.9
21 weeks or more	15,278	1.1
Total	1,388,937	100.0

[1]Week of gestation is calculated from last menstrual period.

Source: Centers for Disease Control and Prevention, *Abortion Surveillance: Preliminary Data—United States, 1992,* December 22, 1994, Table 1.

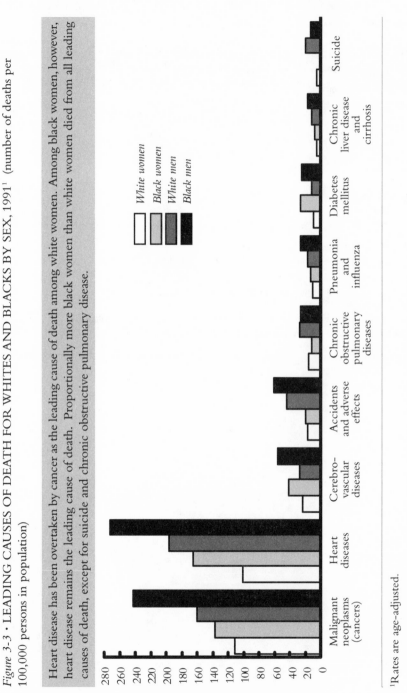

Figure 3-3 · LEADING CAUSES OF DEATH FOR WHITES AND BLACKS BY SEX, 1991[1] (number of deaths per 100,000 persons in population)

Heart disease has been overtaken by cancer as the leading cause of death among white women. Among black women, however, heart disease remains the leading cause of death. Proportionally more black women than white women died from all leading causes of death, except for suicide and chronic obstructive pulmonary disease.

White women
Black women
White men
Black men

Malignant neoplasms (cancers)

Heart diseases

Cerebro-vascular diseases

Accidents and adverse effects

Chronic obstructive pulmonary diseases

Pneumonia and influenza

Diabetes mellitus

Chronic liver disease and cirrhosis

Suicide

280
260
240
220
200
180
160
140
120
100
80
60
40
20
0

[1]Rates are age-adjusted.

Source: National Center for Health Statistics, *Health, United States, 1993*, May 1994, Table 28.

Figure 3-4 · MORTALITY RATES AMONG WHITE AND BLACK WOMEN
FROM LUNG AND BREAST CANCER, 1950–1991[1] (age–adjusted rates)

The death rate from lung cancer for American women continues to rise sharply.
Among both white and black women it has grown from a mortality rate of
approximately 10 in 1970 to 27 in 1991. Meanwhile, in the late 1970s the breast
cancer mortality rate for black women surpassed that of white women and has
continued to rise while that of white women has slightly dropped.

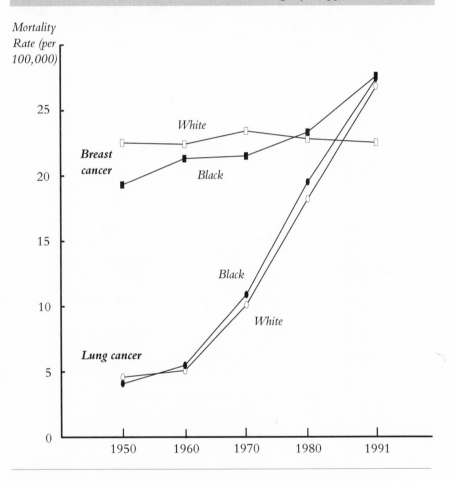

[1]A mortality rate is the number of deaths in a given year per 100,000 persons in the
population.

Source: National Center for Health Statistics, *Health, United States, 1993,* Tables 45 and
46.

Table 3-8 · INCIDENCE AND DEATH RATES FOR SELECTED CANCERS AMONG WOMEN BY CANCER SITE AND RACE, 1989 (per 100,000 women)[1]

Not only are breast cancer and lung cancer the most commonly occurring cancers in women, but together they are also responsible for nearly half of all cancer deaths in women. Mortality rates for white women are higher than for black women for lung and ovarian cancer, but lower for breast, endometrial, and cervical cancer. These differences by race may be related to the availability of preventive care and access to treatment.

	Incidence		*Deaths*		
Cancer Site	*White*	*Black*	*All Races*	*White*	*Black*
Breast	108.2	87.6	23.1	23.1	26.5
Lung and bronchus	40.1	45.2	24.9	25.3	25.0
Endometrium	21.9	16.7	2.6	2.4	4.5
Ovary	15.8	10.6	6.4	6.6	5.0
Cervix	8.2	12.8	2.7	2.3	6.2

[1]Rates are age-adjusted.

Source: National Center for Health Statistics (NCHS), *Health, United States, 1991 and Prevention Profile,* 1992 (incidence rates); NCHS, unpublished cancer statistics, January 1993 (mortality rates).

Figure 3-5 · BREAST CANCER: INCIDENCE AND MORTALITY RATES
FOR WHITE AND BLACK WOMEN, 1991[1]

Although the incidence of breast cancer is higher among white women than
among black women, the latter are more likely to die from this disease.

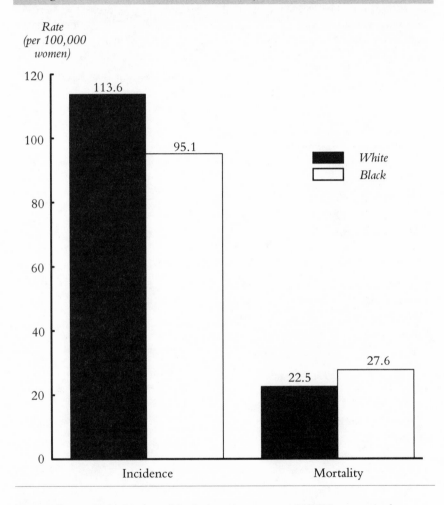

[1]A mortality rate is the number of deaths in a given year per 100,000 persons in the
population. An incidence rate is the number of new cases in a given year per 100,000
persons in the population.

Source: National Center for Health Statistics, *Health, United States, 1993*, May 1994,
Tables 46 and 67.

Table 3-9 · WOMEN WHO HAD SELECTED PREVENTIVE SERVICES IN THE PAST YEAR BY SELECTED CHARACTERISTICS,[1] 1990

In 1990 a greater percentage of women with high incomes and those with more education obtained regular preventive services than those with lower incomes or less education. Older women were less likely to receive regular preventive services than younger women. All women were much more likely to have had their blood pressure checked in the past year than to have had a Pap smear or breast exam.

| | *Percentage That Had* | | |
Characteristics	*Pap Smear*	*Clinical Breast Exam*	*Blood Pressure Check*
Total, age 18 and over	50.1	53.1	90.8
Family income			
Less than $10,000	41.0	45.5	89.5
$10,000–$19,999	44.0	47.0	89.2
$20,000–$34,999	50.1	53.0	90.4
$35,000–$49,999	55.2	58.3	91.0
$50,000 or more	58.9	61.4	92.6
Age			
18–29	63.9	62.2	92.1
30–44	55.2	55.6	89.9
45–64	43.6	49.1	90.0
65 and over	30.4	42.0	91.7
Race			
White	49.7	53.1	90.6
Black	54.3	55.3	92.6
Hispanic origin			
Hispanic[2]	49.1	50.4	88.3
Non-Hispanic	50.1	53.4	90.9
Education			
Less than 12 years	37.9	43.0	88.9
12 years	49.6	52.2	89.9
More than 12 years	57.2	59.7	92.7

[1]Data for mammograms in the past year are not available from the National Center for Health Statistics.

[2]Persons of Hispanic origin may be of any race.

Source: A. Piani and C. Schoenborn. "Health Promotion and Disease Prevention," National Center for Health Statistics, *Vital and Health Statistics*, 1993.

Table 3-10 · WOMEN WHO HAVE RECEIVED A BREAST EXAMINATION
AND MAMMOGRAM BY SELECTED CHARACTERISTICS, 1992 (in
percentages)

In 1992 only half of all women age 50 and over had received a breast exam and
mammogram in the preceding two years. For those living in low-income
households and those without a high school diploma the percentage was even
lower, with only a third of women age 50 and over receiving screening for breast
cancer in the preceding two years. Among younger women, age 40 and over,
only two-thirds had ever received this very important exam.

Characteristic	Percentage That Had Breast Exam and Mammogram
Ever received	
All races, 40 years and over	66
Hispanic, 40 years and over	66
Black, 40 years and over	62
Less than a high school education, 40 years and over	50
Low income, 40 years and over[1]	47
All races, 70 years and over	55
Received within preceding 2 years	
All races, 50 years and over	51
Hispanic, 50 years and over	47
Black, 50 years and over	48
Less than a high school education, 50 years and over	35
Low income, 50 years and over[1]	32
All races, 70 years and over	39

[1]Annual family income less than $10,000.

Source: National Center for Health Statistics, *Healthy People 2000 Review 1993,* 1994,
Table 16.

Figure 3-6 · AIDS CASES IN FEMALES AGE 13 AND OVER BY RACE AND HISPANIC ORIGIN, 1987–1994

Although the initial impact of AIDS in the United States was primarily on men, the disease is now becoming a leading cause of death among young women; the number of new cases among females has increased steadily. The peak in 1993 is in part due to an expansion of reporting definitions which included significant numbers of cases not captured in prior years. After 1994 the overall number of new AIDS cases in women is expected to return to an upward trend.

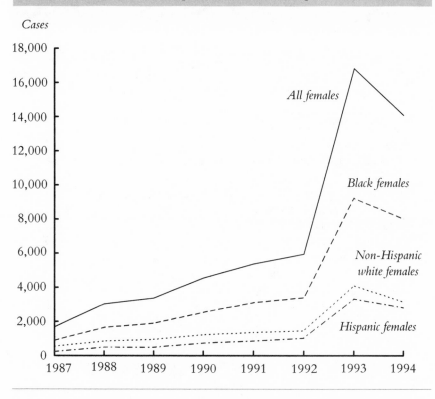

Source: National Center for Health Statistics, *Health, United States, 1993,* May 1994, Table 61; Centers for Disease Control and Prevention, *HIV/AIDS Surveillance Report,* 1993, Table 9, and 1994, Table 9.

Table 3-11 · DISTRIBUTION OF NEWLY REPORTED AIDS CASES AMONG WOMEN AGE 13 AND OVER BY RACE AND HISPANIC ORIGIN, 1994

In 1994 black non–Hispanic and Hispanic women were overrepresented in the proportion of newly reported AIDS cases when compared with their proportions in the total female population, while white, Native American, and Asian and Pacific Islander American women were underrepresented. Although black non–Hispanic women constituted only 11.7 percent of all women, they accounted for over one-half of all new AIDS cases among women.

Race and Hispanic Origin	Percent Distribution of AIDS Cases	Percent Distribution of All Women
Non-Hispanic white	24.2	75.7
Non-Hispanic black	54.5	11.7
Hispanic origin[1]	20.4	8.6
Asian and Pacific Islander	0.5	3.3
Native American	0.3	0.7
Total percentage[2]	100.0	100.0

[1]Persons of Hispanic origin may be of any race.

[2]Totals may not add to 100 because of rounding.

Source: Centers for Disease Control and Prevention, *HIV/AIDS Surveillance Report,* 1994, Table 9; Bureau of the Census, *Population Projections of the United States, by Age, Sex, Race, and Hispanic Origin: 1993–2050,* 1993, Table 2.

Figure 3-7 · PERSONS AGE 18 TO 64 WITH PRIVATE HEALTH
INSURANCE BY SEX AND SOURCE OF COVERAGE, 1993[1] (percent
distribution)

Only slightly more than half of all women with private health insurance in 1993
were covered through their own jobs, compared with nearly three-fourths of
privately insured men.

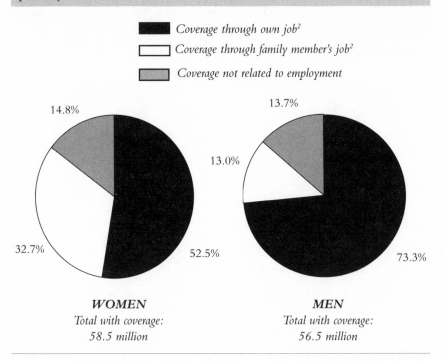

■ *Coverage through own job*[2]

□ *Coverage through family member's job*[2]

▨ *Coverage not related to employment*

14.8%

13.7%

13.0%

32.7%   52.5%

73.3%

WOMEN
Total with coverage:
58.5 million

MEN
Total with coverage:
56.5 million

[1]Persons with coverage for all or part of the year.
[2]Coverage related to current or past employment.

Source: Bureau of the Census, unpublished data from the Current Population Survey,
March 1994.

Figure 3-8· HEALTH INSURANCE COVERAGE BY SEX AND TYPE OF
INSURANCE, 1993[1] (in percentages)

A larger proportion of males than of females lacked health insurance of any kind
in 1993. A larger share of females than of males had public coverage through
Medicaid and Medicare. Seven out of 10 women and men had private insurance
coverage.

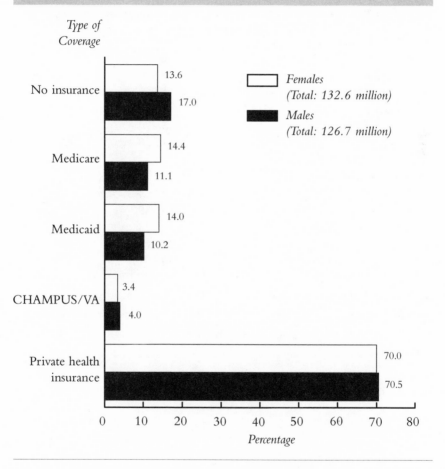

[1]Persons of all ages. The "insured" had coverage for all or part of 1993; the uninsured had
no coverage at any time during 1993. Percentages for each sex add up to more than 100
percent because some insured had coverage from more than one source.

Source: Bureau of the Census, unpublished data from the Current Population Survey,
March 1994.

Table 3-12 · PERSONS WITH NO HEALTH INSURANCE COVERAGE BY FAMILY RELATIONSHIP, 1993[1]

More than a fifth of Americans with no health insurance coverage are children under 18; another 13 percent are children *over* 18 who live with their families.

Relationship	Number (in thousands)	Percentage of Uninsured
Persons living in families		
Wives	5,478	13.8
Husbands	5,520	13.9
Female householders	1,962	5.0
Children under age 18	8,554	21.6
Children over age 18	5,274	13.3
Other[2]	4,228	10.7
Persons not living in families		
Unrelated females	2,964	7.5
Unrelated males	5,138	13.0
In unrelated subfamilies	473	1.2
Total	39,591	100.0

[1]Persons who had no health insurance coverage at any time during the year.

[2]Could include male householder with no spouse present, as well as other relatives.

Source: Bureau of the Census, unpublished data from the Current Population Survey, March 1994.

Figure 3-9· PERSONS WITH AND WITHOUT HEALTH INSURANCE COVERAGE BY SEX AND AGE, 1993

The majority of people of all ages are covered by some form of health insurance, but coverage varies by both sex and age. For example, in 1993, of the roughly 34 million females under 18 years of age, 4.7 million—almost 14 percent—had no coverage. Almost one in four young women age 18 to 24 had no coverage during these important reproductive years.

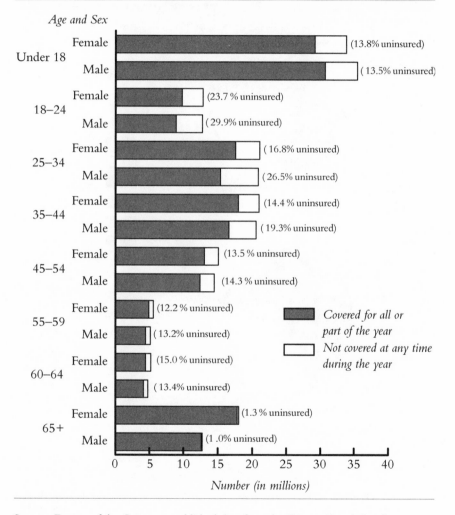

Source: Bureau of the Census, unpublished data from the Current Population Survey, March 1994.

Figure 3-10 · PERSONS AGE 18 TO 64 WITH NO HEALTH INSURANCE
COVERAGE BY SEX AND AGE, 1993[1] (percentage distribution)

In 1993, 56 percent (9.3 million) of all uninsured men between the ages of 18
and 64 were under age 35. The comparable proportion of women was smaller
(50 percent); however this group, which represented half of all uninsured women
(over 6.5 million), was in its prime reproductive years.

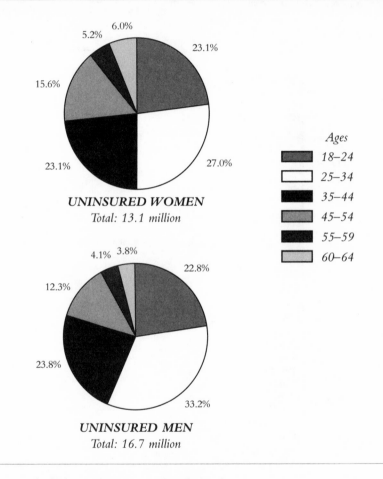

UNINSURED WOMEN
Total: 13.1 million

Ages
18–24
25–34
35–44
45–54
55–59
60–64

UNINSURED MEN
Total: 16.7 million

[1]Persons who had no coverage at any time during the year.

Source: Bureau of the Census, unpublished data from the Current Population Survey,
March 1994.

Figure 3-11· PERSONS AGE 16 TO 64 WITH NO HEALTH INSURANCE COVERAGE BY SEX AND WORK EXPERIENCE, 1993[1] (percent distribution)

Most people of working age who have no health insurance do work. In 1993 one-fourth of uninsured women and well over one-third of uninsured men worked full time, year round.

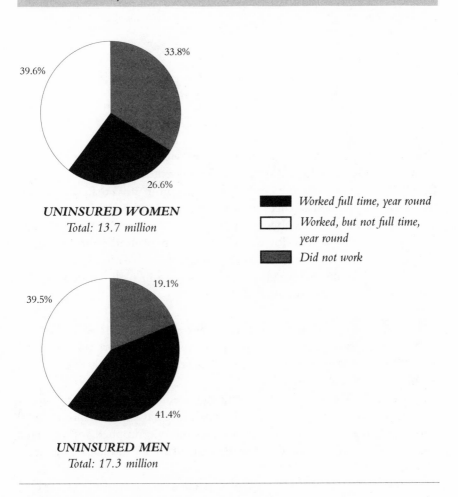

UNINSURED WOMEN
Total: 13.7 million

■ *Worked full time, year round*
□ *Worked, but not full time, year round*
▨ *Did not work*

UNINSURED MEN
Total: 17.3 million

[1]Persons with no coverage at any time during the year.

Source: Bureau of the Census, unpublished data from the Current Population Survey, March 1994.

SECTION 4:

ECONOMIC SECURITY[1]

The real median income of married couples with working wives increased between 1973 and 1993—although 1993 represented a decrease from 1988. Families of other types were typically less well off in 1993 than their counterparts in 1973. Median income of families headed by persons under age 45 and by single men declined steeply between 1988 and 1993. Although as a rule poverty rates are low for married couples, nearly one-quarter of Hispanic couples with children were poor in 1993. Nearly one in two female-headed families with children and one in four male-headed families with children lived in poverty in 1993.

- The net increase in family incomes between 1973 and 1993 was driven almost entirely by the gains for married couples with working wives, the only family type for which real income increased significantly over the period (see Figure 4-1).
- Between 1983 and 1993 real income increased for black married couples, remained about the same for black female-headed families, and declined for black male-headed families. Median income dropped for Hispanic families of every type except female-headed families and married couples with working wives (see Table 4-1).
- Families with a head of household over age 45 were typically doing better in 1993 than their counterparts in 1973, but those with a head of household under age 45 were not doing as well. The decline in the income of these families between 1988 and 1993 was striking (see Figure 4-2).

[1]Health insurance coverage is an important factor in determining American's economic security. Statistics on health insurance coverage can be found in Section 3 (Health) of this book.

- A family headed by a woman is much more likely to be poor than a married-couple family. Although the most dramatic drop in income from 1978 to 1993 was for male-headed families, they are still less likely to be poor than female-headed families (see Figure 4-3).
- A family with children is much more likely to be poor than its counterpart without children. When a family with children is headed by a women, the odds that it is in poverty approach one in two, versus one in four for a male-headed family (see Figure 4-4).
- In 1993, 23.7 percent of Hispanic couples with children were poor—a poverty rate far higher than those of their black and white counterparts (see Table 4-5).
- Poverty rates are higher at every age for women who live alone or with nonrelatives than for their male counterparts. The disparities are widest for the 18 to 24 age group and for those age 65 and over (see Table 4-4).
- Men age 65 and over received an average of $20,505 in 1993, about 80 percent more than the average of $11,383 for women in that age group. The women were less than half as likely as the men to be receiving a pension (see Table 4-6) and almost twice as likely to be living in poverty (see Table 4-3).
- The percentage of American households that owned their homes declined between 1983 and 1993 in every age group except those age 65 and over. The drops were most noticeable in the age groups under age 45 (see Figure 4-5). In 1993 female-headed families with children were less likely to own their own homes than any other family type (see Figure 4-6); they were more likely to rent than to own their own homes (see Figure 4-7).

Figure 4-1 · MEDIAN FAMILY INCOME BY FAMILY TYPE, 1973–1993 (in constant 1993 dollars)[1]

Married couples with two working partners were the only family type whose 1993 median income was above the 1973 level. However, between 1988 and 1993 income for these two-earner families also declined.

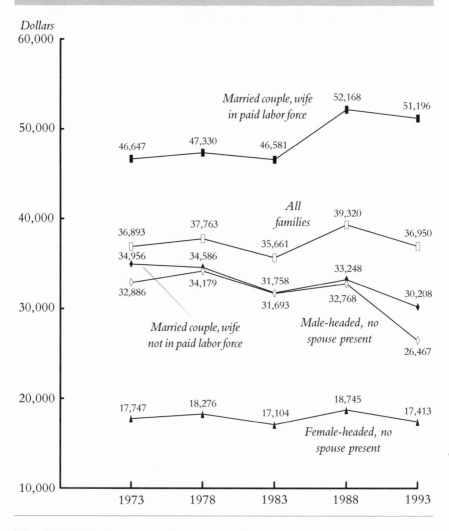

[1]The CPI-U-X1 inflator was used.

Source: Bureau of the Census, unpublished data from the Current Population Survey, March 1974, March 1979, March 1984, March 1989, and March 1994.

Table 4-1 · MEDIAN INCOME OF WHITE, BLACK, AND HISPANIC
FAMILIES BY FAMILY TYPE, 1983, 1988, AND 1993 (in constant 1993 dollars)[1]

> Real income increased through the late 1980s, only to decline again in the early
> 1990s. This was true for families of every type except black male-headed households,
> whose income steadily dropped over the decade, and Hispanic married families
> without working wives, whose median income remained level between 1983 and
> 1988 and fell by 1993.

| Race, Hispanic Origin, | Median Income | | |
and Family Type	1983	1988	1993
WHITE			
All family types	37,368	41,426	39,291
Married couple	40,174	44,999	43,659
Wife in paid labor force	47,251	52,746	51,621
Wife not in paid labor force	32,439	34,150	30,867
Female-headed, no spouse present	19,965	21,586	19,962
Male-headed, no spouse present	33,670	35,343	28,269
BLACK			
All family types	21,045	23,610	21,535
Married couple	31,686	37,114	35,181
Wife in paid labor force	38,285	44,839	44,805
Wife not in paid labor force	20,052	22,616	22,207
Female-headed, no spouse present	11,605	13,017	11,905
Male-headed, no spouse present	22,563	21,807	19,476
HISPANIC[2]			
All family types	24,600	26,590	23,649
Married couple	29,324	31,351	28,454
Wife in paid labor force	35,427	38,921	35,973
Wife not in paid labor force	23,356	23,351	20,721
Female-headed, no spouse present	11,312	13,054	12,047
Male-headed, no spouse present	26,161	26,795	21,643

[1]The CPI-U-X1 inflator was used.

[2]Persons of Hispanic origin may be of any race.

Source: Bureau of the Census, unpublished data from the Current Population Survey,
March 1984, March 1989, and March 1994.

Figure 4-2 · MEDIAN FAMILY INCOME BY AGE OF HOUSEHOLDER, 1973–1993 (in constant 1993 dollars)[1]

Families in all age groups over 45 were typically doing better in 1993 than their counterparts in 1973, but those under the age of 45 were not doing as well. In the five years between 1988 and 1993 median income for all groups except those age 45 to 54 declined.

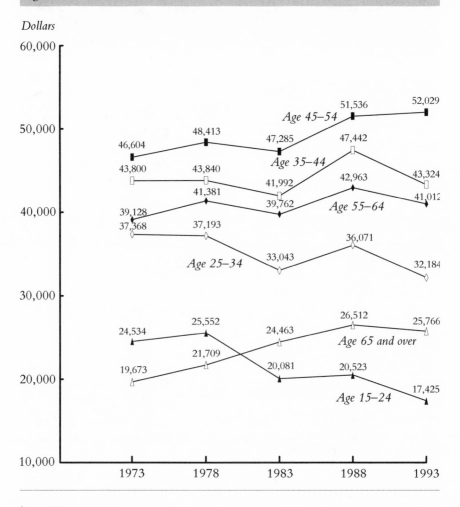

Dollars

[1]The CPI-U-X1 inflator was used.

Source: Bureau of the Census, unpublished data from the Current Population Survey, March 1974, March 1979, March 1984, March 1989, and March 1994.

Figure 4-3 · MEDIAN INCOME OF FAMILIES WITH CHILDREN BY FAMILY TYPE, 1978–1993 (in constant 1993 dollars)[1]

The typical married couple with children had a higher real income in 1993 than its counterpart in 1978. This was not true of single-parent families with children, whose purchasing power was lower at the end of the period than at the beginning. The most dramatic drop in income was for families headed by men.

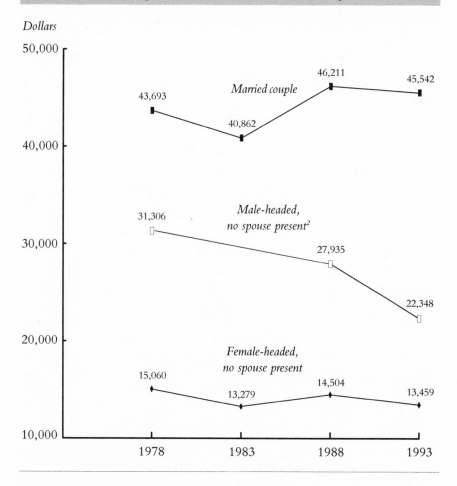

Dollars

¹The CPI-U-X1 inflator was used.
²1983 data were not available for male-headed families.

Source: Bureau of the Census, unpublished data from the Current Population Survey, March 1979, March 1984, March 1989, and March 1994.

Table 4-2 · SOURCES OF INCOME FOR WOMEN AGE 15 TO 64 BY RACE AND HISPANIC ORIGIN, 1992

A woman may have personal income from more than one source, but wages or salaries are by far the most common source of income for nonelderly women. In 1992, among nonelderly women of all races who had income, 76 percent had wage-and-salary income. The average amount was $16,978.

| Source of Income, Race, and Hispanic Origin | With Income From Source | | Mean Income From Source (in dollars) |
	Number (in thousands)	Percentage	
Total[1]			
All races	75,876	100.0	15,745
White	63,056	100.0	16,056
Black	9,593	100.0	13,529
Hispanic origin[2]	6,049	100.0	12,128
Wage and salary			
All races	57,643	76.0	16,978
White	48,310	76.6	17,140
Black	6,997	72.9	15,492
Hispanic origin[2]	4,458	73.7	13,578
Self-employment[3]			
All races	4,180	5.5	9,450
White	3,786	6.0	9,338
Black	217	2.3	7,139
Hispanic origin[2]	182	3.0	7,888
Unemployment compensation			
All races	3,525	4.6	2,460
White	2,885	4.6	2,440
Black	522	5.4	2,479
Hispanic origin[2]	368	6.1	2,179

[1]Totals comprise women who had income from any source in 1992. However, not every source of income is detailed in this table.

[2]Persons of Hispanic origin may be of any race.

[3]Excludes farm self-employment, from which 209,000 women had income in 1992.

Table 4-2 (continued)

Source of Income, Race, and Hispanic Origin	With Income From Source		Mean Income From Source (in dollars)
	Number (in thousands)	Percentage	
AFDC[4]			
All races	3,863	5.1	3,525
White	2,211	3.5	3,554
Black	1,482	15.4	3,371
Hispanic origin[2]	671	11.1	4,369
Interest			
All races	43,597	57.5	816
White	39,102	62.0	842
Black	2,731	28.5	348
Hispanic origin[2]	2,010	33.2	454
Child support			
All races	4,368	5.8	3,152
White	3,614	5.7	3,346
Black	638	6.7	1,982
Hispanic origin[2]	318	5.3	2,820

[4]Excludes women who had income from other forms of public assistance as well as from Aid to Families with Dependent Children (AFDC).

Source: Bureau of the Census, unpublished data from the Current Population Survey, March 1993.

Table 4-3 · POVERTY STATUS OF WOMEN AND MEN BY AGE, RACE, AND HISPANIC ORIGIN, 1993

Women are more likely than men to live in poverty at all ages past childhood. By the time a woman is 65 years old, she is almost twice as likely as her male counterpart to be living in poverty. Nearly one-third of all black women and 29 percent of Hispanic women live below the poverty level; about one in five men in these groups is also poor.

	Women		Men	
	Total		*Total*	
	Number	*Percentage*	*Number*	*Percentage*
Characteristic	*(in millions)*	*Poor*	*(in millions)*	*Poor*
Total, age 18 and over	98.8	14.9	91.2	9.7
Age				
18–24	12.8	23.3	12.7	14.8
25–44	42.0	14.9	41.4	9.5
45–64	25.9	10.3	24.4	8.3
65 and over	18.0	15.2	12.7	7.9
Race				
White	82.6	12.2	77.6	8.2
Black	12.0	31.7	9.8	19.9
Asian/Pacific Islander	2.9	15.3	2.5	12.8
Hispanic origin[1]				
Hispanic	8.5	29.3	8.6	20.6
Non-Hispanic	90.3	13.5	82.6	8.6

[1]Persons of Hispanic origin may be of any race.

Source: Bureau of the Census, unpublished data from the Current Population Survey, March 1994.

Table 4-4 · POVERTY RATES OF UNRELATED INDIVIDUALS BY SEX AND AGE, 1993[1]

Poverty rates are higher at every age for women who live alone or with nonrelatives than for their male counterparts. The disparities are widest for the 18 to 24 age group and for those 65 and over.

	Women		Men	
Age	Number (in thousands)	Percentage in Poverty	Number (in thousands)	Percentage in Poverty
Under 18	94	96.7	93	87.8
18–24	2,235	40.0	2,397	28.2
25–34	3,293	17.6	5,423	14.2
35–44	2,342	19.2	4,014	14.8
45–54	2,152	19.9	2,312	17.9
55–59	953	23.7	784	22.7
60–64	1,223	33.1	735	25.1
65 and over	7,608	26.7	2,380	16.0
Total	19,901	25.7	18,137	18.1

[1]Persons who live alone or with nonrelatives.

Source: Bureau of the Census, unpublished data from the Current Population Survey, March 1994.

Figure 4-4 · POVERTY RATES OF FAMILIES BY FAMILY TYPE AND PRESENCE OF CHILDREN, 1993[1]

When a family with children is headed by a woman, the odds that it is in poverty approach one in two; 46 percent of female-headed families with children were poor in 1993.

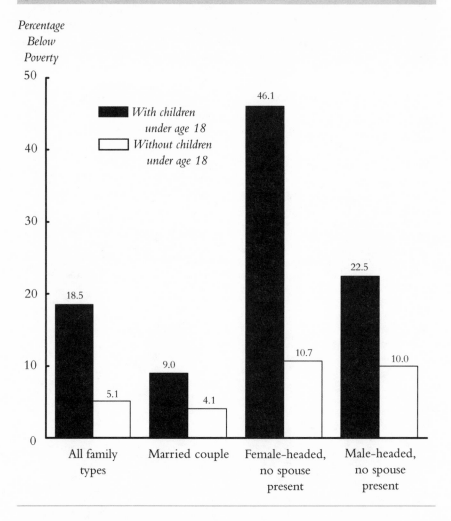

Percentage Below Poverty

[1]Related children under age 18.

Source: Bureau of the Census, *Income, Poverty, and Valuation of Noncash Benefits: 1993*, 1995, Table D-6; unpublished data from the Current Population Survey, March 1993.

Table 4-5 · POVERTY RATES OF WHITE, BLACK, AND HISPANIC FAMILIES
BY FAMILY TYPE AND PRESENCE OF CHILDREN, 1993[1]

Although married-couple families with children are more likely to be poor than couples without children, they are less likely to be poor than other types of families with children. However, it is notable that in 1993, 23.7 percent of Hispanic couples with children were poor—a poverty rate far higher than the poverty rates for black and white couples with children. Also striking is the disproportionately high rate of poverty for black male-headed families without children.

| | *Percentage in Poverty* | | | |
| | *All Family Types* | *Married-Couple Families* | *Families with* | |
Race and Hispanic Origin and Presence of Children			*Female Head*[2]	*Male Head*[2]
WHITE				
All families	9.4	5.8	29.2	13.9
Families with children	14.5	8.2	39.6	19.5
Families without children	4.3	3.6	9.1	7.7
BLACK				
All families	31.3	12.3	49.9	29.6
Families with children	39.3	13.9	57.7	31.6
Families without children	13.3	10.2	17.2	25.6
HISPANIC[3]				
All families	27.3	19.1	51.6	20.2
Families with children	34.3	23.7	60.5	27.6
Families without children	11.2	9.1	19.9	9.9

[1]Related children under age 18.
[2]With no spouse present.
[3]Persons of Hispanic origin may be of any race.

Source: Bureau of the Census, *Income, Poverty, and Valuation of Noncash Benefits: 1993*, 1995, Table D-6.

Table 4-6 · SOURCES OF INCOME FOR PERSONS AGE 65 AND OVER BY SEX, 1993

In 1993 average income for women age 65 and over was $11,383, slightly more than half of the average income of $20,505 for men. The most common sources of income for both sexes were Social Security (received by over 90 percent of both men and women) and interest.

Source of Income	Persons With Income From Source		Mean Income From Source (in dollars)
	Number (in thousands)	Percentage	
Total[1]			
Women	17,641	100.0	11,383
Men	12,463	100.0	20,505
Earnings			
Women	1,909	10.8	9,769
Men	2,552	20.5	20,219
Social Security			
Women	16,489	93.5	5,854
Men	11,425	91.7	7,757
Supplemental Security Income (SSI)			
Women	1,246	7.1	2,289
Men	447	3.6	2,234
Survivors' benefits			
Women	1,806	10.2	6,100
Men	303	2.4	8,756
Pensions			
Women	3,807	21.6	5,433
Men	6,132	49.2	10,041
Interest			
Women	11,437	64.8	2,759
Men	8,679	69.6	3,234
Dividends			
Women	2,917	16.5	3,272
Men	2,673	21.4	3,318
Rents and royalties			
Women	1,604	9.1	4,435
Men	1,413	11.3	4,321

[1]Totals comprise persons who had income from any source in 1993. However, not every source of income is detailed in this table.

Source: Bureau of the Census, unpublished data from the Current Population Survey, March 1994.

Table 4-7 · SOURCES OF INCOME FOR WHITE, BLACK, AND
HISPANIC WOMEN AGE 65 AND OVER, 1993

> Elderly white women have, on average, a higher total income than their black
> and Hispanic counterparts. However, elderly black women are slightly more
> likely than their white counterparts to have earnings, while black and Hispanic
> women who have pensions receive, on average, a larger dollar amount than their
> white counterparts.

Source of Income, Race, and Hispanic Origin	Persons With Income From Source		Mean Income From Source (in dollars)
	Number (in thousands)	Percentage	
Total[1]			
White	15,829	100.0	11,761
Black	1,483	100.0	7,851
Hispanic origin[2]	700	100.0	7,778
Earnings			
White	1,707	10.8	9,725
Black	169	11.4	9,613
Hispanic origin[2]	64	9.1	11,977
Social Security			
White	14,896	94.1	5,946
Black	1,339	90.3	4,963
Hispanic origin[2]	582	83.1	4,886
Supplemental Security Income (SSI)			
White	821	5.2	2,272
Black	358	24.1	2,081
Hispanic origin[2]	181	25.9	3,107
Survivors' benefits			
White	1,704	10.8	6,132
Black	92	6.2	5,523
Hispanic origin[2]	33	4.7	3,374
Pensions			
White	3,547	22.4	5,371
Black	209	14.1	5,960
Hispanic origin[2]	68	9.7	6,128

[1]Totals comprise women who had income from any source in 1993. However, not every
source of income is detailed in this table.

[2]Persons of Hispanic origin may be of any race.

(continued)

Table 4-7 (continued)

| Source of Income, Race, and Hispanic Origin | Persons With Income From Source | | Mean Income From Source (in dollars) |
	Number (in thousands)	Percentage	
Interest			
White	10,931	69.1	2,819
Black	349	23.5	1,432
Hispanic origin[2]	236	33.7	1,753
Dividends			
White	2,851	18.0	3,308
Black	28	1.9	1,279
Hispanic origin[2]	33	4.7	4,148
Rents and royalties			
White	1,520	9.6	4,493
Black	61	4.1	3,409
Hispanic origin[2]	38	5.4	2,301

Source: Bureau of the Census, unpublished data from the Current Population Survey, March 1994.

Figure 4-5 · HOMEOWNERSHIP BY AGE OF HOUSEHOLDER, 1983 AND 1993[1]

In 1993 householders in every age group under 65 were less likely to own their own homes than their counterparts in 1983. The differences are most noticeable for the groups under age 45.

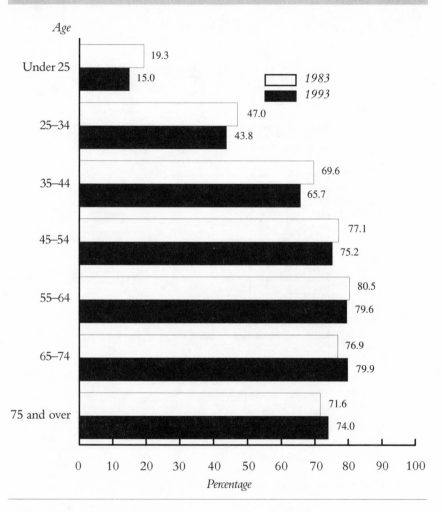

[1]March 1983 and March 1993.

Source: Bureau of the Census, *Household and Family Characteristics: March 1983*, 1984, Table 24, and *March 1993*, 1994, Table 16.

Figure 4-6 · HOMEOWNERSHIP BY FAMILY TYPE, PRESENCE OF CHIL-
DREN, RACE, AND HISPANIC ORIGIN, MARCH 1993[1] (in percentages)

Whether it is white, black, or Hispanic, a female-headed family with children is less
likely to own its home than any other type of family of the same race or ethnicity.
However, a white family of any given type is more likely to own its home than a
black or Hispanic family of the same type. As a rule, homeownership rates are lower
for families of any particular type if they have children.

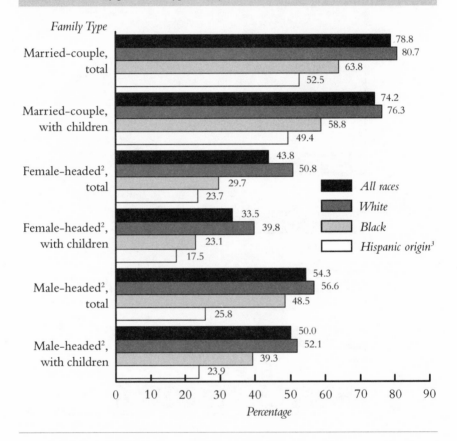

[1]Related children under age 18.
[2]With no spouse present.
[3]Persons of Hispanic origin may be of any race.

Source: Bureau of the Census, *Household and Family Characteristics: March 1993*, 1994,
Table 16.

Figure 4-7 · FEMALE-HEADED HOUSEHOLDS BY TYPE AND
PRESENCE OF CHILDREN, MARCH 1993[1] (percent distribution)

Women who head families with children account for a much higher percentage
of female householders who rent (38.3 percent) than of those who own (20.2
percent). Most of the women who own their own homes live alone; in 1993
they accounted for 57 percent of female homeowners.

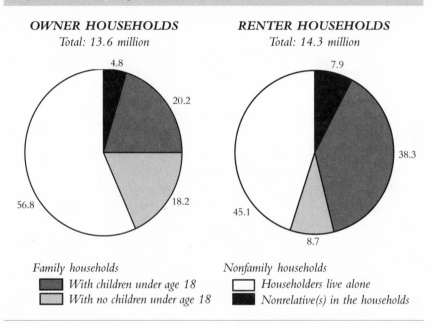

OWNER HOUSEHOLDS
Total: 13.6 million

4.8
20.2
18.2
56.8

RENTER HOUSEHOLDS
Total: 14.3 million

7.9
38.3
8.7
45.1

Family households
■ *With children under age 18*
▫ *With no children under age 18*

Nonfamily households
□ *Householders live alone*
■ *Nonrelative(s) in the households*

[1]Related children under age 18.

Source: Bureau of the Census, *Household and Family Characteristics: March 1993,* 1994,
Table 16.

SECTION 5:

WOMEN IN THE MILITARY

Women in the U.S. armed forces continue to make progress. The proportion of the services that is female has increased despite the ongoing military
drawdown, and black women still find the armed forces, particularly the
Army, an attractive career choice. New jobs and occupations have opened
to women: In late 1993 Congress repealed the last combat exclusion law
that prohibited Navy and Marine Corps women from being permanently
assigned to combat ships, and in early 1994 the Navy began assigning women
to the carrier USS *Eisenhower*. In July 1994 Secretary of Defense William
Perry approved proposals to open some 32,700 Army and 48,000 Marine
Corps positions to women.

On the other hand, women are still excluded from the premier ground
fighting units of infantry, armor (tanks), and field artillery. Although increased opportunities are available to military women in nontraditional career fields, they remain clustered in traditional occupations. Servicewomen
are well educated and have competed successfully for promotions in the junior and middle pay grades. At the senior ranks, however, the glass ceiling
is very apparent: Of the 968 generals and admirals, only 11 are women. In
addition, female veterans have a higher unemployment rate and substantially
lower median incomes than men.

- Since the beginning of the all-volunteer force in 1973 the percentage of
  enlisted women has increased eightfold, while the percentage of female
  officers has more than tripled (see Figure 5-1).
- The Air Force has the highest percentage of women, and the Army has
  the highest proportion of black women (see Table 5-1).
- Military women may enter almost all military occupations but still tend

to pursue careers in the traditional fields of administration and health care (see Figures 5-2 and 5-3).
- Military women consistently have higher educational levels than military men (see Table 5-2).
- Women in the armed forces are competitive for promotion in the lower and middle pay grades but are underrepresented in the senior ranks (see Table 5-3).
- Female veterans have a higher unemployment rate than male veterans, although it varies by race and ethnicity (see Table 5-4). White male veterans earned the highest median income by far, twice that of female veterans of all races and of Hispanic origin (see Figure 5-4).

Table 5-1 · U.S. ACTIVE DUTY SERVICEWOMEN BY BRANCH OF
SERVICE, RANK, RACE, AND HISPANIC ORIGIN, FISCAL YEAR 1994

In 1994 women in the military numbered 198,083, 12.1 percent of the total
armed forces. The Air Force had the highest percentage of women of any service,
the Marine Corps the lowest. The Army had by far the largest proportions of
black women; they accounted for nearly half of the Army's enlisted women and
one-fifth of its female officers in fiscal year 1994.

Service and Rank[1]	Number of Women	Women as a Percentage of Total Personnel	Percent Distribution of Women			
			White	Black	Hispanic	Other
Total armed forces						
Enlisted	165,745	12.0	—	—	—	—
Officers	32,338	12.8	—	—	—	—
Army						
Enlisted	58,395	12.9	41.8	48.1	4.3	5.8
Officers	10,889	12.8	71.4	20.0	2.9	5.7
Navy						
Enlisted	44,339	11.0	64.1	24.7	7.2	4.0
Officers	7,978	12.9	84.0	8.6	3.2	4.2
Marine Corps						
Enlisted	7,029	4.5	58.5	26.3	10.2	5.0
Officers	642	3.6	84.0	8.7	4.8	2.5
Air Force						
Enlisted	53,433	15.7	68.6	23.9	3.8	3.7
Officers	12,322	15.2	82.9	10.2	2.1	4.8
Coast Guard						
Enlisted	2,549	8.8	73.2	15.6	5.6	5.6
Officers	507	6.8	87.2	3.7	3.4	5.7

[1]Officers include warrant officers.

Source: U.S. Department of Defense, Defense Manpower Data Center, unpublished data,
September 30, 1994.

Figure 5-1 · DEPARTMENT OF DEFENSE ACTIVE DUTY WOMEN
PERSONNEL BY OFFICER/ENLISTED STATUS, 1972–1994[1]

Since 1972, the year before the beginning of the all volunteer force, the percentage
of enlisted women increased eight fold, while the percentage of women officers
more than tripled. Although the actual number of women in the armed services
decreased since 1990 as a result of the military drawdown, the percentages of
both officers and enlisted women continued to rise.

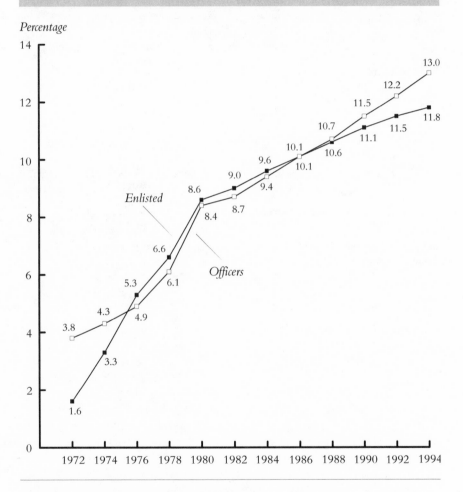

[1]Does not include the Coast Guard, which is a part of the Department of Transportation.

Source: Washington Headquarters Services, Directorate for Information Operations and
Reports, September 30, 1994.

Table 5-2 · EDUCATIONAL ATTAINMENT OF ACTIVE DUTY DEPART-
MENT OF DEFENSE PERSONNEL BY OFFICER/ENLISTED STATUS
AND SEX, FISCAL YEAR 1994[1] (cumulative percent distribution)

Women in the military, both enlisted and officers, consistently had higher levels
of education than their male counterparts.

Status and Level of Education	Women	Men
Officers		
Postgraduate work	40.3	38.9
Graduated from college	97.0	93.7
Completed some college	99.0	96.6
Graduated from high school	100.0	99.9
Enlisted		
Graduated from college/postgraduate work	4.7	3.2
Completed some college	30.6	23.2
Graduated from high school	98.8	95.9
Completed some high school	100.0	100.0

[1]Does not include the Coast Guard, which is a part of the Department of Transportation.

Source: U.S. Department of Defense, Defense Manpower Data Center, unpublished data,
September 30, 1994.

Table 5-3 · ACTIVE DUTY PERSONNEL BY PAY GRADE GROUPING, BRANCH OF SERVICE, AND SEX, FISCAL YEAR 1994 (in percentages)

The representation of women in the junior and middle pay grades was approximately the same as their proportion in each service. At the senior ranks women were substantially underrepresented, especially in the officer corps.

Status and Pay Grade	Army		Navy		Marine Corps		Air Force	
	Women	*Men*	*Women*	*Men*	*Women*	*Men*	*Women*	*Men*
Officers								
Percentage of service	12.8	87.2	12.9	87.1	3.6	96.4	15.2	84.8
Pay grade grouping								
Senior (06–010)	5.0	95.0	5.0	95.0	1.3	98.7	0.2	99.8
Mid-grade (04–05)	12.1	87.9	12.7	87.3	3.1	96.9	4.0	96.0
Junior (01–03, W1–W5)	13.7	86.3	13.8	86.2	3.9	96.1	8.4	91.6
Enlisted								
Percentage of service	12.9	87.1	11.0	89.0	4.5	95.5	15.7	84.3
Pay grade grouping								
Senior (E7–E9)	8.8	91.2	5.8	94.2	3.7	96.3	9.5	90.5
Mid-grade (E4–E6)	13.1	86.9	9.8	90.2	5.2	94.8	15.0	85.0
Junior (E1–E3)	14.7	85.3	15.6	84.4	4.0	96.0	21.1	78.9

Source: U.S. Department of Defense, Defense Manpower Data Center, unpublished data, September 30, 1994.

Figure 5-2 · POSITIONS AND OCCUPATIONS OPEN TO ACTIVE DUTY
WOMEN BY SERVICE, AS OF OCTOBER 1, 1994 (in percentages)

Although the proportion of occupations open to women was above 90 percent
in each of the services, the percentage of positions open to women in the Army
and Marine Corps was substantially lower because infantry, armor (tanks), and
field artillery remained closed to them.

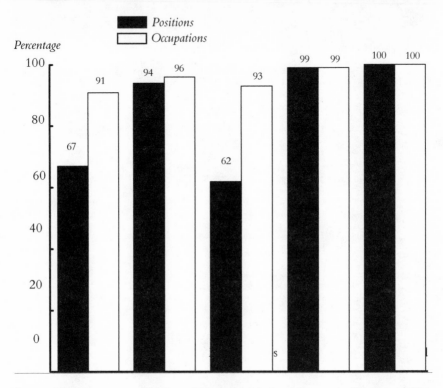

Source: U.S. Department of Defense, Office of the Assistant Secretary of Defense, Public
Affairs News Release no. 449-94, July 29, 1994.

Figure 5-3 · OCCUPATIONAL PROFILE OF ACTIVE DUTY WOMEN IN THE DEFENSE DEPARTMENT, FISCAL YEAR 1994[1] (percent distribution)

Although most occupations were open to women in the military, enlisted women remained concentrated in the support and administrative fields and female officers were overwhelmingly in the health care field.

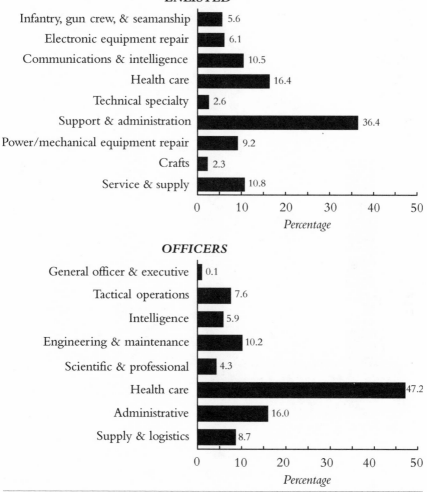

ENLISTED

Infantry, gun crew, & seamanship	5.6
Electronic equipment repair	6.1
Communications & intelligence	10.5
Health care	16.4
Technical specialty	2.6
Support & administration	36.4
Power/mechanical equipment repair	9.2
Crafts	2.3
Service & supply	10.8

Percentage

OFFICERS

General officer & executive	0.1
Tactical operations	7.6
Intelligence	5.9
Engineering & maintenance	10.2
Scientific & professional	4.3
Health care	47.2
Administrative	16.0
Supply & logistics	8.7

Percentage

[1]Does not include the Coast Guard, which is a part of the Department of Transportation.

Source: U.S. Department of Defense, Defense Manpower Data Center, unpublished data, September 30, 1994.

Table 5-4 · UNEMPLOYMENT OF VETERANS BY SEX, RACE, AND
HISPANIC ORIGIN[1], ANNUAL AVERAGE 1994 (in percentages)

Overall, female veterans had higher unemployment rates than male veterans, but
major differences existed when men and women veterans were compared by race
and Hispanic origin.

Race and Hispanic Origin[1]	Women	Men
White	6.0	4.5
Black	6.8	8.1
Hispanic	1.6	7.2
Total	6.3	4.9

[1]Persons of Hispanic origin may be of any race.

Source: Bureau of Labor Statistics, unpublished data from the Current Population Survey,
March 1994.

Figure 5-4 · MEDIAN INCOME OF VETERANS BY SEX, RACE, AND HISPANIC ORIGIN, 1990

The median income of male veterans was substantially higher than that of female veterans. White male veterans earned the highest median income by far, twice that of female veterans of all races and of Hispanic origin.

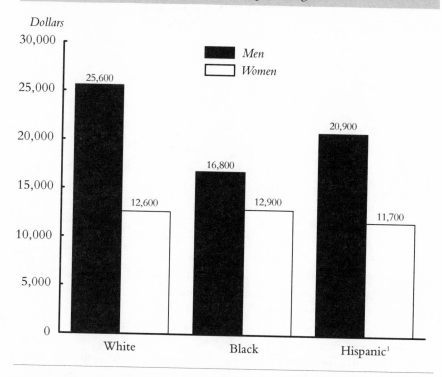

[1]Persons of Hispanic origin may be of any race.

Source: U.S. Department of Veterans Affairs, *Chief Minority Affairs Officer Report 1991–1993*, December 1993.

SECTION 6:

ELECTIONS AND OFFICIALS

In every national election beginning with 1980, not only have more women than men gone to the polls, but larger percentages of women than of men voted. Women's increased political participation has been reflected in a larger percentage of women among high-level federal appointments. After 24 months in office, 29 percent of President Clinton's appointments to positions requiring Senate confirmation were women, a considerably better record in this regard than previous administrations. With the confirmation of Ruth Bader Ginsburg to the U.S. Supreme Court in the summer of 1993, there are now two women serving on the Court.

Over the past several decades an increasing number of women in America have been elected to public office. However, considering that more than half the U.S. population is female, women remain significantly underrepresented in 1995 among both elected officials and high-level appointed officials.

- White, black, and Hispanic women were more likely than their male counterparts to vote in the 1992 national election. However, voter participation was lower among black women and men than among their white counterparts and very low among women and men of Hispanic origin (see Table 6-1).
- Voter participation has consistently been low in the age group just old enough to vote, but women age 18 and 19 have been consistently more likely to vote than their male peers (see Table 6-2).
- In the age groups over 55, turnout has tended to be relatively high for both sexes, but higher for men than for women. Nevertheless, voter participation has been generally increasing among older women (see Table 6-2).

- The election of 1992 increased the number and percentage of elected women in the U.S. Congress (see Table 6-3). The election of 1994 brought to eight the number of women in the U.S. Senate, where as recently as 1991 there were only two elected women.
- American women's increased participation in the political process is reflected in the growing presence of women in high-level federal appointed jobs. Twenty-nine percent of President Clinton's appointments to Senate-confirmed positions in the first 24 months of his Administration were women (see Table 6-5).

Table 6-1 · VOTER PARTICIPATION IN NATIONAL ELECTIONS BY SEX, RACE, AND HISPANIC ORIGIN, 1976–1992[1] (in percentages)

A greater proportion of white women and men turned out for the 1992 election than for any of the previous four national elections. However, for black and Hispanic voters of both sexes, the 1984 election was the recent high-water mark of voter participation.

Year	All Races		White		Black		Hispanic Origin[2]	
	Women	Men	Women	Men	Women	Men	Women	Men
1976	58.8	59.6	60.5	61.5	49.9	47.2	30.1	33.9
1980	59.4	59.1	60.9	60.9	52.8	47.5	30.4	29.2
1984	60.8	59.0	62.0	60.8	59.2	51.7	33.1	32.1
1988	58.3	56.4	59.8	58.3	54.2	48.2	30.1	27.4
1992	62.3	60.2	64.5	62.6	56.7	50.8	30.9	26.8

[1]Persons who reported having voted as a percentage of the population age 18 and over.
[2]Persons of Hispanic origin may be of any race.

Source: Bureau of the Census, *Voting and Registration in the Election of November 1976*, 1976, 1978, Table 2; *Voting and Registration in the Election of November 1980*, 1982, Table 2; *Voting and Registration in the Election of November 1984*, 1986, Table 2; *Voting and Registration in the Election of November 1988*, 1989, Table 2; and *Voting and Registration in the Election of November 1992*, 1993, Table 2.

Table 6-2 · VOTER PARTICIPATION IN NATIONAL ELECTIONS BY SEX AND AGE, 1976–1992[1] (in percentages)

Voter participation has consistently been low in the age group just old enough to vote, but women age 18 and 19 have been consistently more likely to vote than their male peers. In the age groups over 55, by contrast, turnout has tended to be relatively high for both sexes, but higher for men than for women. Nevertheless, the general trend has been one of increasing participation among the older female voters.

Age	1976		1980		1984		1988		1992	
	Women	*Men*	*Women*	*Men*	*Women*	*Men*	*Women*	*Men*	*Women*	*Men*
18–19	38.8	34.6	34.5	33.9	37.6	32.5	34.4	29.9	39.5	36.2
20–24	45.3	43.7	43.9	40.4	44.6	41.0	39.7	35.8	47.2	42.1
25–29	53.9	51.6	52.4	50.0	53.3	48.2	46.0	41.2	52.8	46.8
30–34	58.9	58.2	59.6	56.7	61.1	56.1	54.1	50.2	58.5	53.6
35–44	64.1	62.5	66.0	62.7	64.9	62.0	63.3	59.1	65.7	61.5
45–54	67.9	67.9	67.6	67.3	68.0	67.0	66.6	66.6	69.2	68.2
55–64	67.9	71.8	70.2	72.6	71.5	72.7	68.9	69.8	71.4	71.9
65–74	63.0	70.9	66.7	72.7	70.2	73.9	71.5	75.0	71.8	76.2
75 and over	50.1	62.9	52.9	65.7	57.2	68.3	57.5	70.2	60.8	71.4
Total	58.8	59.6	59.4	59.1	60.8	59.0	58.3	56.4	62.3	60.2

[1]Persons who reported having voted as a percentage of the population age 18 and over.

Source: Bureau of the Census, *Voting and Registration in the Election of November 1976*, 1978, Table 1; *Voting and Registration in the Election of November 1980*, 1982, Table 1; *Voting and Registration in the Election of November 1984*, 1986, Table 1; *Voting and Registration in the Election of November 1988*, 1989, Table 1; and *Voting and Registration in the Election of November 1992*, 1993, Table 1.

Table 6-3 · WOMEN IN ELECTIVE OFFICE, SELECTED YEARS, 1975–1995[1]

In 1995 the number and percentage of women serving in elective offices continued to rise. The elections of 1994 brought the number of women serving in the U.S. Senate to eight, the highest number ever. In the U.S. House of Representatives 48 women were elected, including 13 women of color. Although significant gains have been made over the past 20 years, the percentages of women holding office remain very low.

| Elected Officeholders | Percentage Women | | | | | Number of Women |
	1975	1981	1987	1991	1995	1995
Members of Congress	4	4	5	6	11	56[2]
Statewide elected officials[3]	10	11	14	18	26	84
State legislators	8	12	16	18	21	1,536
Mayors[4]	5	8	11	17	18	178

[1]As of January 1995.
[2]Includes 48 women in the House of Representatives (one of whom is the nonvoting delegate from the District of Columbia) and eight women in the Senate.
[3]Does not include officials in appointive state cabinet-level positions, officials elected to executive posts by state legislatures, members of the judicial branch, or elected members of university boards of trustees or boards of education.
[4]Mayors of cities with populations over 30,000.

Source: Center for the American Woman and Politics, *Women in the U.S. Senate 1922–1995*, 1995; *Women in the U.S. House of Representatives 1995*, 1995; *Statewide Elective Executive Women 1995*, 1995; *Women in State Legislatures 1995*, 1995; National Women's Political Caucus, *Fact Sheet on Women's Political Progress*, 1995.

Table 6-4 · WOMEN ON THE FEDERAL BENCH, 1995

Although improvements have been made, women continue to be vastly underrepresented on the federal bench. With the exception of the Supreme Court, women represent less than 20 percent of the judiciary on the federal level.

| | *Female Judges* | |
	Number	*As a Percentage of All Judges*
Supreme Court justices	2	22.2
Circuit court judges[1]	23	17.4
District court judges[2]	72	14.6
Bankruptcy court judges	50	15.7
U.S. magistrates (full time)	71	20.3

[1]Includes judges on the Temporary Emergency Court of Appeals.

[2]Includes Territorial Courts, Claims Court, Court of International Trade, Special Court– Regional Rail Reorganization Act of 1973, and Judicial Panel on Multidistrict Litigation.

Source: Administrative Office of the United States Courts, unpublished data, June 1995.

Table 6-5 · FEMALE PRESIDENTIAL APPOINTEES TO SENATE-CONFIRMED POSITIONS, 1977–JANUARY 1995[1]

After 24 months in office, 29 percent of President Clinton's appointments to Senate-confirmed positions were women—a notably higher percentage than in previous admininstrations.

President	*Total Number of Appointments*	*Number of Women Appointed*	*Percentage Women*
Jimmy Carter (1977–81)	919	124	13.5
Ronald Reagan (1981–89)	2,349	277	12.0
George Bush (1989–92)	1,079	215	19.9
Bill Clinton (1993–January 1995)	1,244	364	29.0

[1]Figures for the Clinton Administration reflect the first 24 months only and are not really comparable to data for earlier administrations. Included in the Clinton data are some positions not counted for earlier administrations and vice versa.

Source: National Women's Political Caucus, *Factsheet on Executive Appointments of Women,* February 1995.

WOMEN IN THE 104TH CONGRESS*

AFTER THE INROADS MADE BY WOMEN in the 1992 election, the results in 1994 were somewhat disappointing. Women did not significantly increase their ranks in the 104th Congress. However, neither did they lose ground. Five Democrats and three Republicans brought the Senate total to eight, up from seven in the 103d Congress. In the House the number of women remained constant at 48, after almost doubling in 1992.

Altogether women in the 104th Congress represent 23 states and the District of Columbia, down from 28 states in the 103d Congress. California has the largest number of female legislators; both California senators and eight of the state's representatives are women. Two women—Senator Nancy Kassebaum and Representative Jan Meyers—chair congressional committees.

Despite the changing political climate, women continue to make progress. However, it is important to remember that women still constitute only a little over 10 percent of Congress, even though they account for more than half of the U.S. population.

WREI is pleased to include, in this sixth edition of *The American Women,* brief biographies of 55 of the 56 women serving in the 104th Congress. The biographies are followed by a list of the members of the Congressional Caucus for Women's Issues, which is cochaired by Representatives Nita Lowey (D-NY) and Constance Morella (R-MD).

*Information on Representative Helen Chenoweth (Republican, 1st District, Idaho) was not available.

Senator Barbara Boxer *(Democrat, California)* is in her first term as a member of the U.S. Senate, following 10 years as a member of the House of Representatives.

Senator Boxer sits on the Banking, Housing, and Urban Affairs Committee, the Environment and Public Works Committee, and the Committee on the Budget. She also sits on the Joint Economic Committee.

During her tenure in the House, Representative Boxer led the fight for federal funding of abortions for women who are the victims of rape or incest. In the Senate she has championed the Violence against Women Act and legislation to make threatening or harassing behavior a federal crime.

Born in Brooklyn, New York, in 1940, Senator Boxer has a B.A. degree in economics from Brooklyn College. She is married and the mother of two adult children. Prior to coming to Congress, she was a six-year member of the Marin County Board of Supervisors.

Representative Corrine Brown *(Democrat, 3d District, Florida)* was first elected to Congress in 1992.

Representative Brown holds B.S. and M.A. degrees from Florida A&M University and an education specialist degree from the University of Florida. She has served as a member of the faculty at Florida Community College of Jacksonville as well as on the faculties of the University of Florida and Edward Waters College. Representative Brown was born in 1946 in Jacksonville, where she still resides.

Prior to her election to Congress, Representative Brown served for 10 years in the Florida House of Representatives, where she was the chair of the Prison Construction and Operations Subcommittee and vice chair of the Regulatory Subcommittee.

In Congress, Representative Brown serves on the Committee on Transportation and Infrastructure and the Committee on Veterans' Affairs. Her legislative priorities include education, aging, economic development, and women's issues.

Representative Eva Clayton *(Democrat, 1st District, North Carolina)* was first elected to the House in a combination general and special election in November 1992 to fill the seat left vacant by the death of her predecessor.

Representative Clayton was not only the first woman elected to Congress from North Carolina but also the first woman to be elected president of a Democratic freshman class. Representative Clayton sits on the Agriculture Committee and on the Small Business Committee, where she is the ranking Democrat on the Subcommittee on Procurement, Exports, and Business Opportunities. She has been an active advocate for rural health care, housing assistance, and job training.

Congresswoman Clayton was born in 1933 in Savannah, Georgia. Prior to her election to Congress she served as a member of the Warren County Board of Commissioners. She is married and has four children and two grandchildren.

Representative Barbara-Rose Collins *(Democrat, 15th District, Michigan)* is serving her third term in the House of Representatives. She sits on the Transportation and Infrastructure Committee and the Committee on Government Reform and Oversight. After the 1994 election she was able to retain her position on the latter committee as the ranking Democrat on the Subcommittee on Postal Service. Representative Collins also serves on the Subcommittee on the District of Columbia.

Congresswoman Collins was a member of the Detroit City Council from 1982 until her election to Congress. She also served for six years in the Michigan House of Representatives, where she chaired the Standing Committee on Urban Affairs. Born in 1939 in Detroit, Michigan, Representative Collins attended Wayne State University. She has two children and four grandchildren.

Representative Cardiss Collins *(Democrat, 7th District, Illinois),* the longest-serving African American woman in Congress, was first elected to the House of Representatives in June 1973 in a special election to fill the seat of her late husband.

Representative Collins sits on the Commerce Committee, where she is the ranking Democrat on the Subcommittee on Consumer Protection and Competitiveness. She is also a member of the Government Operations Committee and the ranking minority member of the Committee on Government Reform and Oversight. She has long been an advocate of universal health insurance as well as a champion for increased funding for breast cancer research and screening.

Congresswoman Collins was born in 1931 in St. Louis, Missouri, and earned her B.A. degree at Northwestern University.

Representative Barbara Cubin *(Republican, at Large, Wyoming)* is serving her first term in the House of Representatives.

She is a member of the Committee on Resources and the Committee on Science, Space, and Technology. Prior to coming to Congress, Representative Cubin served in both the Wyoming House and Senate. She is a graduate of Creighton University and is pursuing a master's degree in business administration. A fifth-generation Wyomingite, Representative Cubin is married and has two children.

Representative Patricia Danner *(Democrat, 6th District, Missouri)* was elected to Congress in 1992. She is a member of the Committee on Transportation and Infrastructure.

Before her election to Congress Representative Danner served for 10 years as a member of the Missouri Senate, where she chaired the Transportation Committee. During her tenure in the state senate she worked on legislation to enhance federally funded vocational technical programs by providing tuition waivers for displaced homemakers. She also authored Missouri's Extended Day Child Care Act, which provided funds for after-school child care services.

Representative Danner was born in 1934 in Louisville, Kentucky. She graduated with honors from Northeast Missouri State University, where she earned her B.A. degree. She is married and has four children.

Representative Rosa DeLauro *(Democrat, 3d District, Connecticut)* was first elected to Congress in 1990. She sits on the Committee on National Security. She also serves as the chief deputy whip.

Representative DeLauro was born in New Haven, Connecticut, in 1943, and has been in public service for much of her lifetime. She was the first woman to serve as executive assistant to the mayor of New Haven and was chief of staff to Connecticut Senator Christopher Dodd. Prior to her election she was the executive director of EMILY's List, a national organization committed to increasing the number of women in elected office.

Congresswoman DeLauro has made improving the delivery of health care a priority of her tenure in Congress, sponsoring legislation to increase funding for medical research into women's health.

Representative DeLauro received her B.A. degree from Marymount College and her M.A. degree in international politics from Columbia University. She is married and has three grown children.

Representative Jennifer Dunn *(Republican, 8th District, Washington)* was one of two women elected to Congress from Washington State in the November 1992 election. She serves on the Ways and Means Committee and the Oversight Committee. Her policy priorities include women's health issues as well as middle-class and small business tax relief.

Prior to her election to Congress, Representative Dunn was chairperson of the Washington State Republican party, a position to which she was reelected five times. Congresswoman Dunn was born in Seattle, Washington, in 1941 and holds a B.A. degree from Stanford University. She is the mother of two children.

Representative Anna Eshoo *(Democrat, 14th District, California)* was elected to her first term in Congress in 1992. She sits on the Committee on Commerce.

As a 10-year member of the San Mateo County Board of Supervisors, Representative Eshoo was responsible for securing funds for California's first freestanding nursing facility for AIDS patients. In Congress she has played an active role in women's health issues.

Congresswoman Eshoo was born in New Britain, Connecticut, in 1942. She holds her A.A. degree from Canada College in Redwood City, California, and is the mother of two children.

Senator Dianne Feinstein *(Democrat, California)* was first elected to the Senate in November 1992 to complete the unexpired term of California Governor Pete Wilson. She was reelected in 1994 to her first full six-year term.

Senator Feinstein served as mayor of San Francisco from 1978 to 1988. Prior to her election as mayor she was a member of the San Francisco Board of Supervisors.

Senator Feinstein sits on the Judiciary, Rules Administration, and Foreign Relations committees. She was instrumental in the 1994 passage of legislation banning military assault weapons.

A native of San Francisco, Senator Feinstein was born in 1933. She is married and has one child and three stepchildren.

Representative Tillie Fowler *(Republican, 4th District, Florida)* is serving her second term as a member of the House of Representatives, where she sits on the National Security Committee and the Transportation and Infrastructure Committee.

Prior to her election to Congress, Representative Fowler was a member of the Jacksonville City Council for seven years and was the council president for two years. She began her career of public service on the staff of former Representative Robert Stephens, Jr. (D-GA), and then served as general counsel in the White House Office of Consumer Affairs during the Nixon Administration.

Congresswoman Fowler was born in 1942 in Milledgeville, Georgia. She holds both a B.A. degree and a law degree from Emory University. She is married and has two daughters.

Representative Elizabeth Furse *(Democrat, 1st District, Oregon)* was elected in 1992 to her first term in Congress. She was born in Nairobi, Kenya, in 1936 and was raised in South Africa. She came to the United States as a young woman and became an American citizen in 1972.

In the House, Representative Furse sits on the Commerce Committee. She has placed emphasis on domestic violence prevention, winning enactment of legislation during 1994 to help local communities better coordinate their response to incidents of domestic violence.

A longtime community activist, Congresswoman Furse worked during the 1960s as a community organizer in Los Angeles and on behalf of Northwest Native Americans during the 1970s. In 1986 she founded the Oregon Peace Institute, the goal of which is to resolve conflict through nonviolence.

Representative Furse received her B.A. degree from Evergreen State College in Olympia, Washington. She is married and has two children.

Representative Jane Harman *(Democrat, 36th District, California)* is serving her second term in Congress, where she sits on the committees on National Security and on Science, Space, and Technology.

Representative Harman worked in Washington during the 1970s as legislative director to then Senator John Tunney (D–CA) and as chief counsel and staff director of the Senate Judiciary Subcommittee on Constitutional Rights. She also served in the Carter Administration as deputy secretary to the Cabinet and eventually as special counsel to the Department of Defense.

Born in New York City in 1945, Congresswoman Harman is a graduate of Smith College and Harvard University Law School. She is married and has four children.

Senator Kay Bailey Hutchison *(Republican, Texas)* was elected in June 1993 to fill the unexpired seat of then Secretary of the Treasury Lloyd Bentson (D-TX). She serves on the Armed Services Committee, the Small Business Committee, and the Committee on Commerce, Science, and Transportation. She also serves on the Select Committee on Intelligence. She has used her position on the Armed Services Committee to address the needs of military families.

Prior to her election to the Senate Senator Hutchinson was elected Texas state treasurer, making her the first Republican woman chosen for a statewide office. This former member of the Texas House was earlier appointed by President Ford to be vice chair of the National Transportation Safety Board.

Raised in La Marque, Texas, Senator Hutchinson is a graduate of the University of Texas at Austin and the University of Texas School of Law. She is married.

Representative Eddie Bernice Johnson *(Democrat, 30th District, Texas)* is serving her second term as a member of the House of Representatives, where she sits on the Transportation and Infrastructure Committee and the Committee on Science, Space, and Technology.

Before her election to Congress, Representative Johnson enjoyed a distinguished career as a business entrepreneur, professional nurse, health care administrator, and member of the Texas House of Representatives, where she was the first African American woman since 1935 to be elected to public office in Texas. She left the state legislature in 1977 to become the regional director of the Department of Health, Education, and Welfare during the Carter Administration. In 1986 she successfully sought a seat in the Texas Senate, which she held until her election to Congress. She is the only member of Congress who is licensed as a registered nurse.

Representative Johnson is a graduate of Texas Christian University and earned her M.P.A. degree from Southern Methodist University. She was born in 1935 in Waco, Texas, and is the mother of one child.

Representative Nancy Johnson *(Republican, 6th District, Connecticut)* was first elected to Congress in 1982. In 1988 she became the first Republican woman to be named to the Ways and Means Committee, and she chairs its Subcommittee on Oversight. She is the first woman to chair a Ways and Means subcommittee. She also chairs the Committee on Standards of Official Conduct.

Congresswoman Johnson has spent much of her congressional career advocating for women in the areas of health care, child care, welfare reform, and reproductive rights.

Representative Johnson was born in Chicago, Illinois, in 1935. She received her B.A. degree from Radcliffe and served as a civic leader and adjunct professor before embarking on her political career. Prior to her election to Congress she served three terms in the Connecticut Senate. She is married and has three children.

Representative Marcy Kaptur *(Democrat, 9th District, Ohio)* has been in Congress since 1983 and sits on the Appropriations Committee.

Representative Kaptur was born in 1946 in Toledo, Ohio, and earned her B.A. degree from the University of Wisconsin and her M.A. degree in urban planning from the University of Michigan. She practiced as an urban planner for 15 years before seeking office and was a doctoral candidate at the Massachusetts Institute of Technology in urban studies. She also served as an urban adviser during the Carter Administration and as the first deputy director of the National Cooperative Consumer Bank.

In the House Congresswoman Kaptur has long advocated on behalf of small businesses, particularly those with female entrepreneurs, as well as for tighter restrictions on trade and tougher lobbying restrictions on top-level federal officials.

Senator Nancy Landon Kassebaum *(Republican, Kansas)* was first elected to the Senate in 1978. She chairs the Labor and Human Resources Committee. She also sits on the Committee on Foreign Relations and on the Committee on Indian Affairs.

Born in Topeka, Kansas, in 1932, Senator Kassebaum earned her B.A. degree from the University of Kansas and her M.A. degree in diplomatic history from the University of Michigan. A former radio executive, she entered politics as a member of the Maize, Kansas, school board. She is the mother of four children.

From her position as chair of the Labor and Human Resources Committee, Senator Kassebaum has been able to play a leading role in welfare reform, education, and children's issues. She also has led the fight on funding for international family planning programs and abortion rights.

Representative Sue Kelly *(Republican, 19th District, New York)* is serving her first term in the House of Representatives, where she sits on the Transportation and Infrastructure, the Small Business, and the Banking and Financial Services committees. Her legislative priorities include greater opportunities for small business owners, an end to the capital gains tax, and a balanced budget.

Before coming to Congress, Representative Kelly worked as an educator, small business owner, patient advocate, rape crisis counselor, and community leader. She is a graduate of Denison University and has a master's degree in health advocacy from Sarah Lawrence College.

Congresswoman Kelly was born in 1936 in Lima, Ohio. She is married and has four children and one grandchild.

Representative Barbara Kennelly *(Democrat, 1st District, Connecticut)* has served in Congress since 1982. She is one of three women who sit on the Ways and Means Committee. She is also the vice chair of the Democratic Caucus.

Born in 1936 and raised in Hartford, Connecticut, Representative Kennelly earned her B.A. degree from Trinity College in Washington, D.C., and her M.A. degree from Trinity College in Hartford. She is married and has four children. Before her election to Congress she served as secretary of state in Connecticut and as a member of the Hartford Court of Common Council.

During her tenure in Congress, Representative Kennelly has championed welfare reform, tax policies that help families, and long-term care insurance. She served as a member of the U.S. Commission on Interstate Child Support and has long advocated improved child support enforcement.

Representative Blanche Lambert Lincoln *(Democrat, 1st District, Arkansas)* was elected to her first term in Congress in 1992. She is a member of the Commerce Committee.

Congresswoman Lambert Lincoln began her political career as an aide to former Representative Bill Alexander, whom she defeated in the 1992 primary. Before her election to Congress she spent several years doing legislative research at law and governmental lobbying firms.

Born in 1960 in Helena, Arkansas, Representative Lambert Lincoln is a graduate of Randolph-Macon Women's College and is married. Her legislative priorities include job creation and development, agricultural incentives, and rural development.

Representative Sheila Jackson Lee *(Democrat, 18th District, Texas)* is serving her first term in the House of Representatives, where she serves on the Judiciary Committee and the Committee on Science, Space, and Technology.

Before coming to Congress, Representative Lee was a member of the Houston City Council. Prior to that she served as an associate municipal court judge. She is a graduate of Yale University and holds a Juris Doctorate from the University of Virginia Law School.

Congresswoman Lee is married and has two children.

Representative Zoe Lofgren *(Democrat, 16th District, California)* was elected to the House in 1994. Before her election to Congress she served on the Santa Clara County Board of Supervisors.

Representative Lofgren is a graduate of Stanford University and received her law degree from the University of Santa Clara Law School. Following her graduation from college, she worked on the Watergate hearings with former Representative Don Edwards, who preceded her in Congress.

Congresswoman Lofgren sits on the Science, Space, and Technology Committee and the Judiciary Committee. Her legislative priorities include health care for children and the elderly.

She is married and has two children.

Representative Nita Lowey *(Democrat, 18th District, New York)* was first elected to the House of Representatives in 1988. She is a member of the Appropriations Committee, serving on the Labor, Health and Human Services, and Education Subcommittee and on the Subcommittee on Agriculture, Rural Development, Food and Drug Administration, and Related Agencies.

Congresswoman Lowey was elected to cochair the bipartisan Congressional Caucus on Women's Issues in the 104th Congress, and she serves as the chair of the Pro-Choice Task Force. She is also a member of the Presidential Glass Ceiling Commission.

Representative Lowey is an advocate of biomedical and breast cancer research, women's preventive health programs, aid to Israel, worker retraining initiatives, and educational reform. She supports tough anticrime legislation and has authored a welfare reform bill that will encourage work, job training, and personal responsibility.

Born in 1937 in Bronx, New York, Representative Lowey graduated from Mount Holyoke College. She is married and is the mother of three grown children.

Representative Carolyn Maloney *(Democrat, 14th District, New York)* was first elected to Congress in 1992. She is a member of the Banking and Financial Services Committee and the Committee on Government Reform and Oversight.

Representative Maloney brings to Congress a strong interest in women's and children's issues. During her 10 years on the New York City Council she offered a comprehensive legislative package to increase the availability and affordability of child care services. During her first term in Congress she advocated on behalf of children in the child welfare system.

Congresswoman Maloney is a native of Greensboro, North Carolina, where she was born in 1948. She is a graduate of Greensboro College. She is married and has two daughters.

Representative Karen McCarthy *(Democrat, 5th District, Missouri)* was elected to Congress in November 1994. She serves on the Science, Space, and Technology Committee and the Committee on Small Business.

Prior to her election to Congress, Representative McCarthy served as a member of the Missouri legislature, chairing the Ways and Means Committee. She received her B.A. from Kansas University, her master's degree in English from the University of Missouri at Kansas City, and her M.B.A. from the University of Kansas.

Representative Cynthia McKinney *(Democrat, 11th District, Georgia)*, serving her second term in Congress, is the first African American woman elected to the House of Representatives from Georgia. She sits on the Agriculture and the International Relations committees.

Born in 1955 in Atlanta, Georgia, Representative McKinney is a graduate of the University of Southern California. She is presently a Ph.D. candidate in international relations at Tufts University. Before her election to Congress she was a professor of political science at Agnes Scott College in Decatur, Georgia.

Congresswoman McKinney's legislative priorities during this Congress include rural development, reinventing government, and children's issues.

Representative Carrie Meek *(Democrat, 17th District, Florida)* was first elected in November 1992. She is a member of the Appropriations Committee.

Representative Meek came to Congress following a dozen years of service in the Florida legislature, where she served in both chambers. During her final term in the Florida Senate she chaired the Appropriations Subcommittee on Education.

Congresswoman Meek was born in 1926 in Tallahassee, Florida. She is a graduate of Florida A&M University and holds an M.A. degree from the University of Michigan. She has three children.

During her first term in Congress, Representative Meek championed legislation to provide retirement security to domestic workers, such as household workers, gardeners, and nannies. She also has worked to improve the access that low-income individuals have to such government services as housing and education.

Representative Jan Meyers *(Republican, 3d District, Kansas)* was first elected to Congress in 1984. As the chairwoman of the Small Business Committee she is the first woman to chair a House committee since 1976. She also serves on the International Relations Committee and the Economic and Educational Opportunities Committee.

Born in Lincoln, Nebraska, in 1928, Representative Meyers earned a B.A. degree in communications from the University of Nebraska. She served for five years on the Overland Park, Kansas, City Council and for 12 years in the Kansas Senate before her election to Congress. She is married and has two children.

In the House, Congresswoman Meyers has given her attention to older women's issues and to women's health care.

Senator Barbara Mikulski *(Democrat, Maryland)*, who was first elected to the Senate in 1986, is the first Democratic woman to hold a Senate seat not previously held by her husband, as well as the first Democratic woman to have served in both the House and the Senate.

Senator Mikulski came to Congress in 1976 as a member of the House of Representatives, where she distinguished herself as the first woman ever appointed to the Energy and Commerce Committee.

Senator Mikulski began her career in public service as a social worker in Baltimore, Maryland, and entered politics with her election to the Baltimore City Council. Born in Baltimore in 1936, she earned her B.A. degree from Mount Saint Agnes College in Baltimore and received her M.S.W. degree from the University of Maryland.

In the Senate, Senator Mikulski has been a leader on women's health issues, winning enactment of legislation requiring licensing of clinical laboratories to ensure proper analysis of Pap smears and access to mammograms for low-income women.

In 1994 Senator Mikulski was unanimously elected secretary of the Democratic Conference for the 104th Congress—the first woman to be elected to a leadership position in the Senate. She is the ranking member of the Appropriations Subcommittee on Veterans' Affairs, Housing and Urban Development, and Independent Agencies. She is also the ranking member of the Labor and Human Resources Subcommittee on Aging and serves on the Senate Ethics Committee.

Representative Patsy Mink *(Democrat, 2d District, Hawaii)* was first elected to Congress in 1964 and served until 1977. She returned to the House in 1990, when she was elected to complete the unexpired term of Daniel Akaka, who was appointed to the Senate.

In the House, Representative Mink sits on the Economic and Educational Opportunities Committee and the Budget Committee. She has been a leader on welfare issues, sponsoring legislation to provide education and other supportive services to help welfare recipients become self-sufficient. She also has been an advocate for women's health issues, introducing the Ovarian Cancer Research Act.

Congresswoman Mink was born in 1927 in Paia, Hawaii, and has been in public service for more than 35 years. After earning a B.A. degree from the University of Hawaii and a Doctor of Law from the University of Chicago, she went on to serve in Hawaii's house and later in the state senate. Between her congressional terms Representative Mink was appointed by President Carter to be Assistant Secretary of State for Oceans and International, Environmental, and Scientific Affairs. She also served on the Honolulu City Council and as chair of the council for two years. She is married and has one daughter.

Representative Susan Molinari *(Republican, 14th District, New York)* came to Congress in a special 1990 election to fill the seat left vacant by the election of her father, Guy V. Molinari, as mayor of Staten Island. She serves on the Committee on Transportation and Infrastructure, for which she chairs the Subcommittee on Railroad, and on the Budget Committee. She is also the vice chair of the Republican Conference.

Born on Staten Island, New York, in 1958, Representative Molinari earned both her B.A. and M.A. degrees from the State University of New York at Albany. In 1985 she became the youngest person ever elected to the New York City Council, where she served before entering the House of Representatives.

Representative Molinari is an advocate for women's rights, introducing and pushing through to passage the Glass Ceiling Initiative.

Representative Constance Morella *(Republican, 8th District, Maryland)* was first elected to the House in 1986. She sits on the Science, Space, and Technology Committee, and she chairs its Subcommittee on Technology. She was elected to cochair the Congressional Caucus on Women's Issues in the 104th Congress, and she is also a member of the Government Reform Committee.

Congresswoman Morella was born in Somerville, Massachusetts, in 1931. She received her A.B. degree from Boston University and her M.A. degree from the American University in Washington, D.C. She served for eight years in the Maryland General Assembly. Prior to entering politics, she was a professor of English at Montgomery College. She is married and has raised nine children.

Representative Morella has been a leader on women's issues, championing legislation to increase research and prevention of AIDS in women. She also has been a leader in the fight against domestic violence, winning enactment of several bills addressing this issue.

Senator Carol Moseley-Braun *(Democrat, Illinois),* who is serving her first term, is the first African American woman to be elected to the Senate. She sits on the Finance Committee, the Banking, Housing, and Urban Affairs Committee, and the Special Committee on Aging.

Senator Moseley-Braun was born in 1947 in Chicago. She is a graduate of the University of Illinois in Chicago and earned her law degree from the University of Chicago. Following law school, she worked as a prosecutor in the U.S. Attorney's office.

In 1978 she was elected to the Illinois legislature, where she earned a reputation as a leader in the field of education. In 1987 Senator Moseley-Braun was elected Cook County recorder of deeds. She is the mother of one child.

Senator Patty Murray *(Democrat, Washington)* was elected in 1992 to the Senate, where she sits on the Appropriations Committee and the Committee on Banking.

Prior to her election to Congress, Senator Murray served in the Washington Senate, where she championed legislation to provide family leave to parents of terminally ill children. Senator Murray earned attention during her U.S. Senate campaign when she ran as a "mom in tennis shoes." She is a strong advocate for families and children, supporting family and medical leave, abortion rights, and tax relief for the middle class.

Born in 1950, Senator Murray is a native of Seattle. She is married and has two children. She earned her B.A. degree from Washington State University.

Representative Sue Myrick *(Republican, 9th District, North Carolina)* was elected to her first term in November 1994. She served as mayor of Charlotte, North Carolina, for two terms before being elected to Congress.

A member of the Budget Committee, the Small Business Committee, and the Committee on Science, Space, and Technology, Representative Myrick has championed small business issues.

Congresswoman Myrick was born in 1941 in Tifflin, Ohio. She is a graduate of Heidelberg College. She is married and has five children and six grandchildren.

Delegate Eleanor Holmes Norton *(Democrat, District of Columbia Delegate)* was elected to Congress in 1990 as the nonvoting delegate from the District of Columbia. She is the first woman elected to represent the District in the House.

Congresswoman Norton serves on the Government Reform and Oversight Committee, and she is the ranking Democrat on its District of Columbia Subcommittee. She is also a member of the Transportation and Infrastructure Committee.

Born in the District of Columbia in 1937, Congresswoman Norton is a graduate of Antioch College. She holds both her M.A. and law degrees from Yale University. Prior to her election to Congress, she was a professor of law at Georgetown University. She was the chair of the Equal Employment Opportunity Commission under President Carter.

In the House, Congresswoman Norton has been a champion for civil rights issues and for the economic and political independence of the District of Columbia.

Representative Nancy Pelosi *(Democrat, 8th District, California)* was elected to Congress in 1987. She sits on the Appropriations Committee and the Committee on Standards of Official Conduct.

Born in 1940 in Baltimore, Maryland, Representative Pelosi earned her B.A. degree from Trinity College in Washington, D.C., and later served as the state chair of the California Democratic party. She and her husband have five children.

In the House, Congresswoman Pelosi has focused much of her attention on funding for AIDS research and prevention and on increasing prenatal care for low-income families. She also authored legislation, which was enacted, to preserve the existing supply of housing for low-income families and to establish programs to alleviate homelessness among individuals with AIDS.

Representative Deborah Pryce *(Republican, 15th District, Ohio)* was first elected to the House of Representatives in 1992. She sits on the Rules Committee.

Prior to her election to Congress, Representative Pryce served as a judge on the Franklin County Municipal Court. She is a graduate of Ohio State University and holds a law degree from Capital University in Columbus, Ohio. She was born in 1952 in Warren, Ohio, is married, and has two children.

Representative Pryce has a strong interest in family and child welfare issues.

Representative Lynn Rivers *(Democrat, 13th District, Michigan)* was elected to the House in 1994. She sits on the Budget Committee and the Science, Space, and Technology Committee.

Congresswoman Rivers began her public service career as a member of the Ann Arbor school board, where she served as president for three years. Prior to her election to Congress she served one term in the Michigan legislature.

Representative Rivers was born in 1956 in Au Gres, Michigan. She received her bachelor's degree in 1987 from the University of Michigan and was awarded a J.D. degree from Wayne State University Law School in 1992. She and her husband live in Ann Arbor with their two daughters.

Representative Ileana Ros-Lehtinen *(Republican, 18th District, Florida)*, first elected in a special election in 1989, was the first Hispanic woman elected to Congress. She is a member of the Committee on International Relations and the Government Reform and Oversight Committee.

Representative Ros-Lehtinen was a member of the Florida legislature for seven years, serving for three years in its House and four years in its Senate.

Congresswoman Ros-Lehtinen was born in Havana, Cuba, in 1952. She obtained her A.A. degree from Miami-Dade Community College and her B.A. and M.S. degrees from Florida International University. She is married and has two daughters.

Representative Marge Roukema *(Republican, 5th District, New Jersey)* was first elected to Congress in 1980. She sits on the Banking Committee, where she chairs the Subcommittee on Financial Institutions, and on the Committee on Economic and Educational Opportunities.

Congresswoman Roukema was born in 1929 in Newark, New Jersey. She holds a B.A. degree from Montclair State College in New Jersey. Prior to her election to Congress she was a secondary school teacher. She is married and has two children.

Representative Roukema has been active on a variety of women's issues, including family and medical leave, welfare reform, and child support enforcement.

Representative Lucille Roybal-Allard *(Democrat, 33d District, California),* elected in 1992, was the first Mexican American woman elected to the House of Representatives. She filled the seat vacated by the retirement of her father, Edward Roybal.

Congresswoman Roybal-Allard sits on the Budget Committee and on the Banking and Financial Services Committee. Before her election to Congress, she served in the California Assembly. At the state level she was active on women's issues, authoring and winning passage of legislation requiring the courts to take an individual's history of domestic violence into consideration during child custody hearings. In Congress she has played a major role in highlighting health issues relating to Latinas, enacting the Violence against Women Act, and protecting small business programs for women and minorities.

Representative Roybal-Allard was born in Los Angeles, California, in 1941. She received her B.A. degree from California State University at Los Angeles. She is married and has two children.

Representative Patricia Schroeder *(Democrat, 1st District, Colorado)* is the most senior woman in Congress, having served in the House of Representatives since 1972.

Representative Schroeder sits on the Judiciary Committee, and she serves as the ranking Democrat on its Subcommittee on Courts and Intellectual Property. She also is a member of the National Security Committee.

Congresswoman Schroeder was born in Portland, Oregon, in 1940. She earned her B.A. degree from the University of Minnesota and her J.D. from Harvard University. Before her election to Congress she practiced law. She is married and has two grown children.

In the House, Representative Schroeder has been a leader on women's issues, focusing on family issues, women's health, and civil and constitutional rights. She is the author of the Family and Medical Leave Act.

Representative Andrea Seastrand *(Republican, 22d District, California)* was elected to Congress in 1994. She sits on the Transportation and Infrastructure Committee and the Committee on Science, Space, and Technology.

Congresswoman Seastrand campaigned diligently for the 104th Congress's Contract with America, whose goals—such as tax cuts for working Americans, term limits, and tough crime legislation—she championed.

Representative Seastrand served in the California Assembly from 1990 until her election to Congress. A graduate of De Paul University, she was an elementary school teacher before entering politics. She has two adult children.

Representative Louise Slaughter *(Democrat, 28th District, New York)* was elected to the House of Representatives in 1986. She is a member of the Budget Committee and the Committee on Government Reform and Oversight.

Congresswoman Slaughter was born in Harlan County, Kentucky, in 1929, and received both her B.S. and M.S. degrees from the University of Kentucky. She entered the Monroe County legislature in New York in 1975 and went on to serve in the New York Assembly before she ran successfully for Congress. She is married and the mother of three grown children.

In the House, Representative Slaughter has fought for programs to provide educational opportunities to homeless children, to broaden the safeguards for victims of domestic violence, and to expand the funds available for women's health research.

Representative Linda Smith *(Republican, 3d District, Washington)* was elected to the House of Representatives in 1994, the first person in Washington State's history to qualify for the general election ballot as a write-in candidate.

Congresswoman Smith sits on the Committee on Resources and the Committee on Small Business; she was appointed chair of the latter's Subcommittee on Taxation and Finance.

Representative Smith began her public service career in the early 1980s and served in both houses of the Washington State Congress. She was born in La Junta, Colorado, in 1950 and operated a tax consulting business for 14 years.

Senator Olympia Snowe *(Republican, Maine)* is serving her first term as a U.S. senator. Before her election to the Senate she served eight terms in the House of Representatives.

She sits on the Commerce, Science, and Transportation Committee, the Budget Committee, and the Foreign Relations Committee.

Senator Snowe was born in Augusta, Maine, in 1947 and received her B.A. degree from the University of Maine. She began her political career in 1973, when she was first elected to the Maine House to fill the seat vacated by her late husband. She is married.

In the House, Senator Snowe focused her energies on ensuring that women were included in medical research by establishing an Office of Research on Women's Health at the National Institutes of Health. She also has been a leader on international family planning issues.

Representative Karen Thurman *(Democrat, 5th District, Florida)* was first elected to the House of Representatives in 1992. She sits on the Agriculture Committee and the Committee on Government Reform and Oversight, and she is the ranking Democrat on the latter's Subcommittee on National Security, International Affairs, and Criminal Justice.

Born in Rapid City, South Dakota, in 1951, Representative Thurman is a graduate of the University of Florida. She is married and has two children.

Prior to her election to Congress, Representative Thurman served on the Dunnellon, Florida, City Council and was the city's mayor from 1979 to 1981. She also served for 10 years in the Florida Senate, where she chaired the Agriculture Committee.

Congresswoman Thurman is a supporter of abortion rights and is working to broaden traditional women's issues to areas beyond health care and jobs.

Representative Nydia Velazquez *(Democrat, 12th District, New York),* who is serving her second term in Congress, is the first Puerto Rican woman elected to the House of Representatives.

Born in Puerto Rico in 1953, Representative Velazquez received her B.A. degree from the University of Puerto Rico and her M.A. degree in political science from New York University.

In the House, she sits on the Banking Committee and the Committee on Small Business. As a member of Congress she is continuing her work on women's and poverty issues.

Prior to her election to Congress, Representative Velazquez worked as a liaison between the Puerto Rican government and the Puerto Rican community in New York, where she organized efforts to increase AIDS education and to register voters. She also was the first Hispanic woman to be elected to the New York City Council, on which she served from 1984 to 1986.

Representative Barbara Vucanovich *(Republican, 2d District, Nevada)* is serving her sixth term in the House of Representatives. She is the first woman to be elected to federal office in Nevada.

Representative Vucanovich sits on the Appropriations Committee and chairs its Subcommittee on Military Construction. She also serves as the secretary of the Republican Conference. The issues of prevention and treatment of breast cancer are a top priority to Congresswoman Vucanovich.

Prior to her election to Congress, Representative Vucanovich was active in politics, managing several successful campaigns in Nevada. She served as district director for Senator Paul Laxalt from 1974 until she ran for Congress in 1982. Born at Camp Dix, New Jersey, in 1921, she is married and has five children, 15 grandchildren, and two great-grand-children.

Representative Enid Greene Waldholtz *(Republican, 2d District, Utah)* was elected to the House in 1994. Born in 1959, she is a graduate of the University of Utah. She earned her law degree from Brigham Young University.

Congresswoman Waldholtz sits on the Rules Committee; she is the first freshman Republican to have been appointed to the committee in 80 years. Prior to coming to Congress, she was corporate counsel to Novell, Inc., a software company. She also worked as a commercial litigator. She and her husband are expecting their first child in September 1995; this will make her the first sitting congresswoman since Yvonne Braithwaite Burke to have a child while serving in Congress.

Representative Maxine Waters *(Democrat, 35th District, California)* was elected to the House in 1990. She sits on the Banking Committee and the Committee on Veterans' Affairs.

Congresswoman Waters served for 15 years in the California Assembly, where she was the first woman in the state's history to be elected chair of the Democratic Caucus. She was born in St. Louis, Missouri, in 1938, and holds a B.A. degree from California State University at Los Angeles. She is married and has two children.

Representative Waters has been a leader on the issue of AIDS in the African American community. She also has been a vocal advocate of increased investment in programs and services in the nation's urban areas.

Representative Lynn Woolsey *(Democrat, 6th District, California)*, elected to the House of Representatives in 1992, is the first former welfare mother ever elected to Congress.

Congresswoman Woolsey is a member of the Committee on Economic and Educational Opportunities and the Budget Committee. She has been a leader on welfare reform and children's issues.

Before her election to Congress, Representative Woolsey was a member of the Petaluma, California, City Council, and she was the city's vice mayor. She was successful in her efforts to expand available low- and moderate-income housing and led the fight to build the first emergency family shelter for homeless families in Sonoma County.

Representative Woolsey was born in Seattle, Washington, in 1937 and has four children. She is a graduate of the University of San Francisco.

Congressional Caucus
for Women's Issues

Corrine Brown (D-FL)

Cynthia McKinney (D-GA)

Eva Clayton (D-NC)

Carolyn Maloney (D-NY)

Barbara-Rose Collins (D-MI)

Carrie Meek (D-FL)

Cardiss Collins (D-IL)

Jan Meyers (R-KS)

Pat Danner (D-MO)

Patsy Mink (D-HI)

Rosa DeLauro (D-CT)

Susan Molinari (R-NY)

Anna Eshoo (D-CA)

Constance Morella (R-MD)

Tillie Fowler (R-FL)

Eleanor Holmes Norton (Del-D-DC)

Jane Harman (D-CA)

Nancy Pelosi (D-CA)

Eddie Bernice Johnson (D-TX)

Deborah Pryce (R-OH)

Nancy Johnson (R-CT)

Lynn Rivers (D-MI)

Marcy Kaptur (D-OH)

Marge Roukema (R-NJ)

Sue Kelly (R-NY)

Lucille Roybal-Allard (D-CA)

Barbara Kennelly (D-CT)

Patricia Schroeder (D-CO)

Sheila Jackson Lee (D-TX)

Louise Slaughter (D-NY)

Blanche Lambert Lincoln (D-AR)

Karen Thruman (D-FL)

Zoe Lofgren (D-CA)

Nydia Velazquez (D-NY)

Nita Lowey (D-NY)

Maxine Waters (D-CA)

Karen McCarthy (D-MO)

Lynn Woolsey (D-CA)

References

AFFIRMATIVE ACTION: UNDERSTANDING THE PAST AND PRESENT

Bendick, Marc. "Research Evidence on Racial/Ethnic Discrimination and Affirmative Action in Employment." Testimony prepared for informational hearing on affirmative action before the Assembly Committee on the Judiciary, California Legislature, May 4, 1995.

Bureau of the Census. "The Earnings Ladder: Who's at the Bottom? Who's at the Top?" *Statistical Brief,* June 1994.

Bureau of Labor Statistics. *Employment and Earnings.* Washington, DC: U.S. Government Printing Office, January 1994.

Costello, Cynthia, and Anne J. Stone. *The American Woman 1994–1995: Where We Stand.* New York: W. W. Norton & Company, 1994.

"Draft Report on Reverse Discrimination Commissioned by Labor Department." *Daily Labor Report,* March 23, 1995.

Equal Employment Opportunity Commission (EEOC). "EEOC Chairman Announces Task Forces to Address Operational Issues; Releases FY 1994 Enforcement Results." News release, December 1, 1994.

Glass Ceiling Commission. *Good for Business: Making Full Use of the Nation's Human Capital.* Washington, DC: U.S. Government Printing Office, 1995.

Granovetter, Mark. *Getting a Job: A Study of Contacts and Careers.* Chicago: University of Chicago Press, 1995.

Institute for the Study of Social Change. *The Diversity Project Final Report.* University of California at Berkeley, 1991.

Institute for Women's Policy Research. "Restructuring Work: How Have Women and Minority Managers Fared?" *Research-in-Brief* (January 1995).

National Committee on Pay Equity. "Background on the Wage Gap." 1993.

Needleman, Ruth. "Raising Visibility, Reducing Marginality: A Labor Law Reform Agenda for Working Women of Color." Paper prepared for the U.S. Department of Labor, October 1993.

Swisher, Kara. "At the Checkout Counter, Winning Women's Rights." *Washington Post* (June 12, 1994).

Watson, Warren E., Kamalesh Kumar, and Larry K. Michaelson. "Cultural Diversity's Impact on Interaction Process and Performance: Comparing Homogeneous and Diverse Task Groups." *Academy of Management Journal* 38 (June 1993): 590–602.

Wilkins, Roger. "The Case for Affirmative Action: Racism Has Its Privileges." *Nation* (March 27, 1995): 409–415.

ONE   WOMEN IN THE WORKFORCE: AN OVERVIEW

Administration for Children and Families. *Characteristics and Financial Circumstances of AFDC Recipients, FY 1992*. Washington, DC: U.S. Government Printing Office, 1994.

Bureau of the Census. *Historical Statistics of the United States, Colonial Times to 1970*. Series D 29-84. Washington, DC: U.S. Government Printing Office, 1975.

———. *Marriage, Divorce and Remarriage in the 1990s*. Current Population Reports, Series P-23, No. 180. Washington, DC: U.S. Government Printing Office, October 1995.

Bureau of Labor Statistics. *Current Population Survey March 1971 Supplement*. Washington, DC: Bureau of the Census, 1971.

———. *Current Population Survey 1974 Annual Averages*. Washington, DC: Bureau of the Census, 1974.

———. *Current Population Survey March 1975 Supplement*. Washington, DC: Bureau of the Census, 1975.

———. *Current Population Survey 1948–1994 Annual Averages*. Washington, DC: Bureau of the Census, 1994b.

———. *Current Population Survey March 1994 Supplement*. Washington, DC: Bureau of the Census, 1994c.

———. *Employment and Earnings*. Washington, DC: U.S. Government Printing Office, January 1995.

———. *Employment, Hours, and Earnings, United States, 1909–94*, Volumes I and II. Bulletin 2445. Washington, DC: U.S. Government Printing Office, September 1994a.

———. *Handbook of Labor Statistics*. Bulletin 2340. Washington, DC: U.S. Government Printing Office, August 1989.

———. *Industry Wage Surveys: Help Supply Services October 1989*. Bulletin 2430. Washington, DC: U.S. Government Printing Office, September 1993.

———. *Labor Force Statistics Derived from the Current Population Survey, 1948–1987*. Bulletin 2307. Washington, DC: U.S. Government Printing Office, August 1988.

————. Occupational Employment Statistics. Unpublished three-digit SIC tabulations, 1993.

Cohany, Sharon R., Anne E. Polivka, and Jennifer M. Rothgeb. "Revisions in the Current Population Survey Effective January 1994." *Employment and Earnings.* Washington, DC: U.S. Government Printing Office (February 1994): 13–37.

Deming, William G. "Work at Home: Data from the CPS." *Monthly Labor Review* 117, No. 2 (February 1994): 14–20.

Devine, Theresa J. "Characteristics of Self-Employed Women in the United States." *Monthly Labor Review* 117, No. 3 (March 1994): 20–34.

Gardner, Jennifer. "Worker Displacement: A Decade of Change." *Monthly Labor Review* 118, No. 4 (April 1995): 45–57.

Goodman, William, Stephen Antczak, and Laura Freeman. "Women and Jobs in Recessions: 1969–92." *Monthly Labor Review* 116, No. 7 (July 1993): 26–35.

Haveman, Robert, Philip DeJong, and Barbara Wolfe. "Disability Transfers and the Work Decision of Older Men." *Quarterly Journal of Economics* 106, No. 3 (August 1991): 939–949.

Hayghe, Howard V. "Family Members in the Work Force." *Monthly Labor Review* 113, No. 3 (March 1990): 14–19.

Howe, Wayne J. "Labor Market Dynamics and Trends in Male and Female Unemployment Rates." *Monthly Labor Review* 113, No. 11 (November 1990): 3–12.

Ippolito, Richard A. "Towards Explaining Earlier Retirement after 1970." Unpublished manuscript, Pension Benefit Guarantee Corporation, March 1989.

National Center for Health Statistics. "Advance Report of Final Marriage Statistics, 1988." *Monthly Vital Statistics Report* 40, No. 4, 1991.

————. "Annual Summary of Births, Marriages, Divorces and Deaths: United States, 1993." *Monthly Vital Statistics Report* 42, No. 13, October 11, 1994.

Rydzewski, Leo G., William G. Deming, and Philip L. Rones. "Seasonal Employment Falls over the Past Three Decades." *Monthly Labor Review* 116, No. 7 (July 1993): 3–14.

Shank, Susan E. "Women and the Labor Market: The Link Grows Stronger." *Monthly Labor Review* 113, No. 3 (March 1988): 3–8.

Wetzel, James R. "American Families: 75 Years of Change." *Monthly Labor Review* 113, No. 3 (March 1990): 4–13.

TWO WORK AND FAMILY: THE EXPERIENCES OF MOTHERS AND FATHERS IN THE U.S. LABOR FORCE

Baruch, Grace K., and Rosalind C. Barnett. "Role Quality and Psychological Well-Being." In *Spouse, Parent, Worker: On Gender and Multiple Roles,* edited by Faye J. Crosby. New Haven, CT: Yale University Press, 1987: 63–73.

Crouter, Ann C. "Spillover from Family to Work: The Neglected Side of the Work-Family Interface." *Human Relations* 37 (1984): 425–442.

Families and Work Institute. *National Study of the Changing Workforce.* New York: Families and Work Institute, 1992.

Galinsky, Ellen, James T. Bond, and Dana Friedman. *National Study of the Changing Workforce.* New York: Families and Work Institute, 1993.

Greenberger, Ellen, and Wendy A. Goldberg. "Work, Parenting, and the Socialization of Children." *Developmental Psychology* 25 (1989): 22–35.

Greenberger, Ellen, and Robin O'Neil. "Spouse, Parent, Worker: Role Commitments and Role-Related Experiences in the Construction of Adults' Well-Being." *Developmental Psychology* 29 (1993): 181–197.

Hofferth, Sandra L., April Brayfield, Sharon Deitch, and Pamela Holcomb. *National Child Care Survey 1990.* Washington, DC: Urban Institute, 1991.

Hughes, Diane, and Ellen Galinsky. "Balancing Work and Family Life: Research and Corporate Application." In *Maternal Employment and Children's Development, Longitudinal Research,* edited by A. E. Gottfried. New York: Plenum, 1988.

———, and Ann Morris. "The Effects of Job Characteristics on Marital Quality: Specifying Linking Mechanisms." *Journal of Marriage and Family* 54 (1992): 31–42.

Piotrkowski, Chaya S. *Work and the Family System.* New York: Macmillan, 1979.

———, and Paul Crits-Cristoph. "Women's Jobs and Family Adjustment." In *Two Paychecks: Life in Dual-Earner Families,* edited by Joan Aldous. Beverly Hills, CA: Sage Publications, 1982.

Quinn, Robert P., and Graham L. Staines. *The 1977 Quality of Employment Survey: Descriptive Statistics with Comparison Data from the 1969–1970 and the 1973–1974 Surveys.* Ann Arbor, MI: Institute for Social Research, 1979.

Repetti, Rena L. "Effects of Daily Workload on Subsequent Behavior during Marital Interaction: The Roles of Social Withdrawal and Spouse Support." *Journal of Personality and Social Psychology* 57 (1989): 651–659.

Shinn, Marybeth, Blanca Ortiz-Torres, Anne Morris, Patricia Simko, and Nora W. Wong. "Child Care Patterns, Stress and Job Behaviors among Working Parents." Paper presented at the annual convention of the American Psychological Association, New York, August 1987.

THREE WOMEN AND THE UNEMPLOYMENT INSURANCE SYSTEM

Advisory Council on Unemployment Compensation (ACUC). *Report and Recommendations.* Washington, DC: ACUC, 1994.

———. *Unemployment Insurance in the United States: Benefits, Financing, and Coverage.* Washington, DC: ACUC, 1995.

Bureau of the Census. *Survey of Income and Program Participation 1990 Panel File.* Washington, DC: Bureau of the Census, 1990.

Bureau of Labor Statistics. *Handbook of Labor Statistics. Washington, DC: U.S. Government Printing Office, 1989.*

————. *Employment and Earnings.* Washington, DC: U.S. Government Printing Office, January 1990.

————. *Employment and Earnings.* Washington, DC: U.S. Government Printing Office, January 1992.

————. *Employment and Earnings.* Washington, DC: U.S. Government Printing Office, January 1993.

————. *Employment and Earnings.* Washington, DC: U.S. Government Printing Office, January 1994a.

————. *Employment and Wages: Annual Averages 1993.* Washington, DC: U.S. Government Printing Office, 1994b.

————. Unpublished Statistics. December 1994c.

Congressional Budget Office. *Family Incomes of Unemployment Insurance Recipients and the Implications for Extending Benefits.* Washington, DC: Congressional Budget Office, 1990.

Council of Economic Advisers. *Economic Report of the President.* Washington, DC: U.S. Government Printing Office, 1994.

U.S. Department of Labor. *Comparison of State Unemployment Insurance Laws.* Prepared by Employment and Training Administration, Unemployment Insurance Service, 1994a.

————. *UI Data Summary.* Prepared by Employment and Training Administration, Unemployment Insurance Service, Division of Actuarial Services, March 1994b.

————. *UI Financial Data Handbook.* Prepared by Employment and Training Administration, Unemployment Insurance Service, 1994c.

FOUR   STRUGGLING TO SURVIVE: WELFARE, WORK, AND LONE MOTHERS

Administration for Children and Families. *Characteristics and Financial Circumstances of AFDC Recipients, FY 1992.* Washington, DC: U.S. Government Printing Office, 1994.

Amott, Teresa. "Black Women and AFDC: Making Entitlement out of Necessity." In *Women, the State, and Welfare,* edited by Linda Gordon. Madison: University of Wisconsin Press, 1990.

Bane, Mary J., and David T. Ellwood. "The Dynamics of Dependence: The Routes to Self-Sufficiency." Paper prepared for the U.S. Department of Health and Human Services, June 1983.

Blank, Rebecca. "Outlook for the U.S. Labor Market and Prospects for Low-Wage Entry Jobs." In *The Work Alternative: Welfare Reform and the Realities of the Job*

Market, edited by Demetra S. Nightingale and Robert Haveman. Washington, DC: Urban Institute, 1995.

Brock, Thomas, David Butler, and David Long. *Unpaid Work Experience for Welfare Recipients: Findings and Lessons from MDRC Research.* New York: Manpower Demonstration Research Corporation, 1993.

Burtless, Gary. "The Employment Prospects of Welfare Recipients." In *The Work Alternative: Welfare Reform and the Realities of the Job Market,* edited by Demetra S. Nightingale and Robert Haveman. Washington, DC: Urban Institute, 1995.

Duncan, Greg J., Martha S. Hill, and Saul D. Hoffman. "Welfare Dependence within and across Generations." *Science* 239 (January 1988): 467–471.

Esping-Anderson, Gosta. *The Three Worlds of Welfare Capitalism.* Princeton, NJ: Princeton University Press, 1990.

Freeman, Richard, editor. *Working under Different Rules.* New York: Russell Sage Foundation, 1994.

Gordon, Linda, editor. *Women, the State, and Welfare.* Madison: University of Wisconsin Press, 1990.

Greenberg, Mark. "Rethinking the Problem: How State Data on AFDC Length of Stay and Work Matter for the Time-Limited Welfare Debate." Mimeo. Washington, DC: Center for Law and Social Policy, July 1993.

Gueron, Judith, and Edward Pauly. *From Welfare to Work.* New York: Russell Sage Foundation, 1991.

Jencks, Christopher, and Kathryn Edin. "The Real Welfare Problem." *The American Prospect* (Spring 1990): 31–50.

Maynard, Rebecca. "Subsidized Employment and Non-Labor Market Alternatives." In *The Work Alternative: Welfare Reform and the Realities of the Job Market,* edited by Demetra S. Nightingale and Robert Haveman. Washington, DC: Urban Institute, 1995.

McFate, Katherine, Roger Lawson, and William J. Wilson. *Poverty, Inequality and the Future of Social Policy: Western States in the New World Order.* New York: Russell Sage Foundation, 1995.

Nelson, Barbara. "The Origins of the Two-Channel Welfare State: Workmen's Compensation and Mother's Aid." In *Women, the State, and Welfare,* edited by Linda Gordon. Madison: University of Wisconsin Press, 1990.

Nightingale, Demetra S., and Lynn Burbridge. *The Status of Work-Welfare Programs in 1986: Implications for Welfare Reform.* Washington, DC: Urban Institute, 1987.

Nightingale, Demetra S., and Robert Haveman. *The Work Alternative: Welfare Reform and the Realities of the Job Market.* Washington, DC: Urban Institute, 1995.

Pavetti, LaDonna. "The Dynamics of Welfare and Work: Exploring the Process by which Young Women Work Their Way off Welfare." Harvard University dissertation, 1992.

Rein, Martin. *Dilemmas of Welfare Policy: Why Work Strategies Haven't Worked.* New York: Praeger, 1982.

Spalter-Roth, Roberta, Beverly Burr, Lois Shaw, and Heidi Hartmann. *Welfare that*

Works: The Working Lives of AFDC Recipients. Washington, DC: Institute for Women's Policy Research, December 1995.

Spalter-Roth, Roberta, Heidi Hartmann, and L. Andrews. *Combining Work and Welfare: An Alternative Anti-Poverty Strategy.* Washington, DC: Institute for Women's Policy Research, 1993.

U.S. Congress, House Committee on Ways and Means. *Overview of Entitlement Programs: 1993 Green Book.* Washington, DC: U.S. Government Printing Office, 1993.

———. *Overview of Entitlement Programs: 1994 Green Book.* Washington, DC: U.S. Government Printing Office, 1994.

FIVE   WOMEN'S EMPLOYMENT PATTERNS, PENSION COVERAGE, AND RETIREMENT PLANNING

AARP Public Policy Institute. *Today's Careers, Tomorrow's Pensions: A Pension Portability Analysis.* Washington, DC: American Association of Retired Persons, July 1988.

Beller, Daniel J., and David D. McCarthy. "Private Pension Benefits." In *Trends in Pensions 1992,* edited by John A. Turner and Daniel J. Beller. Washington, DC: U.S. Government Printing Office, 1992.

KPMG Peat Marwick. *Retirement Benefits in the 1990s: 1994 Survey Data.* Washington, DC: KPMG Peat Marwick, 1994.

Merrill Lynch. "Retirement Savings in America." Fifth Annual Merrill Lynch Retirement Planning Survey. Princeton, NJ: Merrill Lynch, 1993.

Patterson, Martha Priddy. *The Working Woman's Guide to Retirement Planning: Saving & Investing Now for a Secure Future.* Englewood Cliffs, NJ: Prentice Hall, 1993.

U.S. Department of Commerce. *Statistical Abstract of the United States, 1993.* Washington, DC: U.S. Government Printing Office, 1993.

U.S. Department of Labor. *Employee Benefits in Medium and Large Private Establishments, 1991.* Washington, DC: U.S. Government Printing Office, 1991.

U.S. Department of Labor, Social Security Administration, Small Business Administration, and Pension Benefit Guaranty Corporation. *Pension and Health Benefits of American Workers: New Findings from the April 1993 Current Population Survey.* Washington, DC: U.S. Government Printing Office, 1994.

Wang, Penelope. "Brokers Still Treat Men Better than Women." *Money Magazine* 23, No. 6 (June 1994): 75.

SIX   WOMEN AND PENSIONS: A POLICY AGENDA

Beller, Daniel J. *Source 5500 Series Reports Filed with the Internal Revenue Service.* Washington, DC: U.S. Department of Labor, 1990.

Bureau of Labor Statistics. *Job Tenure Statistics*. Washington, DC: U.S. Government Printing Office, 1992.

Lewin/ICF. *Exploring the Dynamics of Poverty among Elderly People Living Alone in Future Years*. A background report commissioned by the Commonwealth Fund Commission. Baltimore, MD: Lewin/ICF, April 16, 1987.

General Accounting Office. *Women's Pensions: Recent Legislation Generally Improved Federal Entitlement and Increased Benefits*. GAO/T-HRD-92-20. Washington, DC: U.S. Government Printing Office, 1992.

Grad, Susan. *Income of the Population 55 and Older, 1992*. Washington DC: Social Security Administration, May 1994.

Reno, Virginia P. "The Role of Pensions in Retirement Income." Paper presented at the National Academy on Aging, Washington, DC, 1992.

Ross, Jane L. "Women's Pensions. Recent Legislation Generally Improved Pension Entitlement and Increased Benefits." Statement of Jane L. Ross, Associate Director, Income Security. Testimony presented before the Subcommittee on Retirement Income and Employment, Select Committee on Aging, U.S. House of Representatives, March 26, 1992.

Zedlewski, Sheila. *The Urban Institute's Dynamic Simulation of Income Model*. Washington, DC: Urban Institute, January 1988.

A STATISTICAL PORTRAIT

SECTION 1: DEMOGRAPHICS

Bureau of the Census. Current Population Reports, Series P-20, No. 450. *Marital Status and Living Arrangements: March 1990*. Washington, DC: U.S. Government Printing Office, May 1991.

———. Current Population Reports, Series P-20, No. 478. *Marital Status and Living Arrangements: March 1993*. Washington, DC: U.S. Government Printing Office, May 1994.

———. Current Population Reports, Series P-25-1104. *Population Projections of the United States, by Age, Sex, Race, and Hispanic Origin, 1993 to 2050*. Washington, DC: U.S. Government Printing Office, November 1993.

———. Current Population Survey, March 1971. Unpublished data, Washington, DC.

———. Current Population Survey, March 1981. Unpublished data, Washington, DC.

———. Current Population Survey, March 1991. Unpublished data, Washington, DC.

———. Current Population Survey, March 1994. Unpublished data, Washington, DC.

———. *1990 Census of the Population: General Population Characteristics. United States 1990*. Washington, DC: U.S. Government Printing Office, 1992.

———. *Statistical Abstract of the United States 1990.* Washington, DC: U.S. Government Printing Office, 1990.

———. *Statistical Abstract of the United States 1992.* Washington, DC: U.S. Government Printing Office, 1992.

———. *Statistical Abstract of the United States 1994.* Washington, DC: U.S. Government Printing Office, 1994.

———. National Center for Health Statistics. "Births, Marriages, Divorces, and Deaths for September 1994." *Monthly Vital Statistics Report* 43, No. 9 (March 1, 1995).

———. *Health, United States 1993.* Hyattsville, MD: U.S. Department of Health and Human Services, 1994.

SECTION 2: EDUCATION

Bureau of the Census. Current Population Reports, Series P-20, No. 476. *Educational Attainment in the United States: March 1993 and 1992.* Washington, DC: U.S. Government Printing Office, May 1994.

———. *Statistical Abstract of the United States 1994.* Washington, DC: U.S. Government Printing Office, 1994.

National Center for Education Statistics. *Digest of Education Statistics 1990.* Washington, DC: U.S. Government Printing Office, October 1991.

———. *Digest of Education Statistics 1994.* Washington, DC: U.S. Government Printing Office, October 1994.

U.S. Department of Health, Education, and Welfare. Office for Civil Rights. *Data on Earned Degrees Conferred by Institutions of Higher Education by Race, Ethnicity and Sex, Academic Year 1976–1977.* Photocopy, n.d.

SECTION 3: HEALTH

Bureau of the Census. Current Population Reports, Series P-25-1104. *Population Projections of the United States, by Age, Sex, Race, and Hispanic Origin, 1993 to 2050.* Washington, DC: U.S. Government Printing Office, November 1993.

———. Current Population Survey, March 1994. Unpublished data, Washington, DC.

Centers for Disease Control and Prevention. *HIV/AIDS Surveillance Report 6,* No. 2 (1994).

———. *HIV/AIDS Surveillance Report 5,* No. 4 (1993).

———. *Abortion Surveillance: Preliminary Data—U.S., 1992.* December 22, 1994.

Jones, Elise F., and Jacqueline D. Forrest. "Contraceptive Failure Rates Based on the 1988 National Survey of Family Growth." *Family Planning Perspectives* 24 (1992): 12–19.

Mosher, William D. "Contraceptive Practice in the United States, 1982–1990." *Family Planning Perspectives* 22 (1990): 198–205.

National Center for Health Statistics. *Healthy People 2000, Review 1993*. Washington, DC: U.S. Government Printing Office, 1994.

―――. *Health, United States, 1991 and Prevention Profile*. Hyattsville, MD: U.S. Department of Health and Human Services, 1992.

―――. *Health, United States, 1993*. Hyattsville, MD: U.S. Department of Health and Human Services, 1994.

―――. Unpublished cancer statistics, January 1993.

Piani, A., and C. Schoenborn. "Health Promotion and Disease Prevention." National Center for Health Statistics. *Vital and Health Statistics* 10, No. 185 (1993).

Section 4: Economic Security

Bureau of the Census. Current Population Reports, Series P-60, No. 388. *Household and Family Characteristics: March 1983*. Washington, DC: U.S. Government Printing Office, May 1984.

―――. Current Population Reports, Series P-60, No. 477. *Household and Family Characteristics: March 1993*. Washington, DC: U.S. Government Printing Office, June 1994.

―――. Current Population Reports, Series P-60, No. 188. *Income, Poverty, and Valuation of Noncash Benefits: 1993*. Washington, DC: U.S. Government Printing Office, February 1995.

―――. Current Population Survey, March 1974. Unpublished data, Washington, DC.

―――. Current Population Survey, March 1979. Unpublished data, Washington, DC.

―――. Current Population Survey, March 1984. Unpublished data, Washington, DC.

―――. Current Population Survey, March 1989. Unpublished data, Washington, DC.

―――. Current Population Survey, March 1993. Unpublished data, Washington, DC.

―――. Current Population Survey, March 1994. Unpublished data, Washington, DC.

Section 5: Women in the Military

Bureau of Labor Statistics. Current Population Survey, March 1994. Unpublished data, Washington, DC.

U.S. Department of Defense. Defense Manpower Data Center. Unpublished data, September 30, 1994.

―――. Office of the Assistant Secretary of Defense, Public Affairs, News Release no. 449-94, July 29, 1994.

U.S. Department of Veterans' Affairs. *Chief Minority Affairs Officer Report 1991–1993*. Washington, DC: Office of Planning and Policy, December 1993.

Washington Headquarters Services. Directorate for Information Operations and Reports, September 30, 1994.

SECTION 6: ELECTIONS AND OFFICIALS

Administrative Office of the United States Courts. Unpublished data, June 1995.

Bureau of the Census. Current Population Reports, Series P-20, No. 322. *Voting and Registration in the Election of November 1976.* Washington, DC: U.S. Government Printing Office, 1978.

———. Current Population Reports, Series P-20, No. 370. *Voting and Registration in the Election of November 1980.* Washington, DC: U.S. Government Printing Office, 1982.

———. Current Population Reports, Series P-20, No. 405. *Voting and Registration in the Election of November 1984.* Washington, DC: U.S. Government Printing Office, 1986.

———. Current Population Reports, Series P-20, No. 440. *Voting and Registration in the Election of November 1988.* Washington, DC: U.S. Government Printing Office, 1989.

———. Current Population Reports, Series P-20, No. 466. *Voting and Registration in the Election of November 1992.* Washington, DC: U.S. Government Printing Office, 1993.

Center for the American Woman and Politics (CAWP). *Statewide Elective Executive Women 1995 Fact Sheet, 1995; Women in State Legislatures 1995 Fact Sheet,* 1995; *Women in the U.S. Senate, 1922–1995 Fact Sheet,* 1995; and *Women in the U.S. House of Representatives 1995 Fact Sheet,* 1995. Rutgers, NJ: CAWP.

National Women's Political Caucus (NWPC). *Factsheet on Women's Political Progress,* 1995; and *Factsheet on Executive Appointments of Women,* February 1995. Washington, DC: NWPC.

NOTES ON THE CONTRIBUTORS

Laurie J. Bassi is the executive director of the Advisory Council on Unemployment Compensation and an associate professor of public policy at Georgetown University. At Georgetown, Dr. Bassi teaches courses in microeconomics, labor economics, human resource policy, social insurance, and income maintenance. Her research efforts have focused on corporate decisionmaking on training workers and the organization of work, the effects of training and job creation on the economy, and the economics of children's well-being. Dr. Bassi has published extensively and has just completed a manuscript entitled "Getting America to Work." Dr. Bassi received her B.S. in mathematics and economics in 1976 from Illinois State University, her M.S. in 1978 from the Industrial and Labor Relations School at Cornell University, and her Ph.D. in economics in 1983 from Princeton University.

James T. Bond is the vice president of the Families and Work Institute, a nonprofit organization that conducts applied research and strategic planning related to work and family issues. In addition to providing technical advice on survey design and data analysis to all major research projects of the institute, Mr. Bond has substantive responsibilities for projects focused on matters of public policy and the needs of low-income workers. Mr. Bond received both his undergraduate and graduate degrees in anthropology at the University of North Carolina, Chapel Hill. Before joining the institute, Mr. Bond was deputy director of the National Center for Children in Poverty at Columbia University, the founding director of the National Council of Jewish Women's Center for the Child, and director of research at the High/Scope Educational Research Foundation.

Amy B. Chasanov is a policy analyst at the Advisory Council on Unemployment Compensation in Washington, D.C. She has been working in the area of federal employment and training policy for the past seven years. Ms. Chasanov received her M.A. and B.A. in regional science and B.S. in economics from the University of Pennsylvania. Ms. Chasanov plans to attend law school in the fall of 1995.

Betty Dooley, WREI's president, has been with the Women's Research and Education Institute since its beginning in 1977. An early Texas feminist, she was active in state politics before moving to Washington, D.C. In 1964 she was a candidate for the U.S. House of Representatives from the 16th Congressional District of Texas. She served for several years as director of the Health Security Action Council, an advocacy organization based in Washington, D.C., that worked for comprehensive national health insurance. Ms. Dooley is a charter member of the National Council for Research on Women, a member of the Women's Health Advisory Board at Duke University, and a member of the Secretary of Labor's Advisory Committee on Employment and Training for Veterans.

Jocelyn C. Frye is policy counsel for work and family programs at the Women's Legal Defense Fund, focusing primarily on employment, job training, health care, and education issues. Prior to holding this position, she worked as an associate at Crowell & Moring, a Washington, D.C., law firm, practicing in the areas of defense procurement and fraud and labor. She is a graduate of the University of Michigan (1985) and Harvard Law School (1988).

Ellen Galinsky is the cofounder and copresident of the Families and Work Institute. At the institute Ms. Galinsky directs a nationally representative longitudinal study of the U.S. workforce, EQUIP (the Early Education Quality Improvement Project), and heads studies of family leave, parent education, and family involvement in children's education. Ms. Galinsky received her B.A. from Vassar College and her M.S. from Bank Street College. Prior to undertaking her responsibilities at the institute, Ms. Galinsky was part of the faculty of the Bank Street College of Education, where she helped institute the field of work and family life and directed numerous studies of work and family life, stress, and productivity. Ms. Galinsky is the author of several books and has published extensively in academic journals and magazines.

Diane E. Herz is an economist in the Division of Labor Force Statistics of the Bureau of Labor Statistics. Over the past eight years she has conducted research and written about many work-related issues, including employment characteristics of older women, labor market problems of older workers, job displacement, poverty among workers, early retirement, and employer-provided training. Ms. Herz received her B.A. in economics from the University of Maryland.

Cindy Hounsell is a staff attorney and director of the Women's Pension Project at the Pensions Rights Center, Washington, D.C. She coordinates the Women's Pension Policy Consortium and its national education campaign, Pensions Not Posies. Ms. Hounsell was a 1989–90 fellow with the Women's Law and Public Policy Fellowship Program at the Georgetown University Law Center and a former officer of the Independent Union of Flight Attendants and Stewardesses for Women's Rights.

Dr. Katherine McFate is an associate director of research at the Joint Center for Political and Economic Studies, a research and policy institute dedicated to examining issues of concern to African Americans. Before coming to the Joint Center, she lectured at Yale University and was the director of the Mayor's Special Commission on Poverty in New Haven, Connecticut. Dr. McFate has been studying welfare policy and urban poverty issues at the Joint Center since 1987 and regularly testifies before Congress. She is the editor (with William Julius Wilson and Roger Lawson) of *Poverty, Inequality, and the Future of Social Policy: Western States in the New World Order,* a comparative work that examines the way various European and North American countries have dealt with disadvantaged young people, minorities, and lone-parent families.

Martha Priddy Patterson is the director of Employee Benefits Policy and Analysis for KPMG Peat Marwick's Compensation and Benefits Practice. She is an attorney with 17 years of experience as a benefits consultant. Ms. Patterson advises companies on compliance with laws and regulations in the areas of tax policy, pensions, ERISA, and employment. She received her law degree from the University of Texas Law School. Before her appointment Ms. Patterson was a congressional staffer to Representative Bob Eckhardt and worked with federal agencies representing clients and issues.

Anne J. Stone is a consultant at WREI. Formerly WREI's senior research associate, she authored and coauthored policy analyses on various subjects including the federal budget, employment issues for women, and women in the military. She has also worked on the five previous editions of *The American Woman* and was the coeditor of the fourth and fifth editions.

Barbara Wootton is an economist in the Division of Labor Force Statistics of the Bureau of Labor Statistics. She has conducted research and written about the following areas: occupational employment trends, industry staffing patterns, work organization, skill needs, and training. She has also worked on the development of occupational and career information systems. Ms. Wootton received her B.A. in economics and government from Cornell University and her M.S. in industrial relations from the University of Wisconsin in Madison.

About the Women's Research and Education Institute

Betty Dooley, *President*
Shanda Boyett, *Research Assistant*
Leigh Carter, *Development Associate*
Cynthia B. Costello, Ph.D., *Research Director*
Barbara Kivimae Krimgold, *Women's Health Project Director*
Shari E. Miles, *Education and Training Program Director*
Kathleen Stevenson-Pagano, *Office Manager*
Georgia C. Sadler, *Women in the Military Project Director*
Anne J. Stone, *Editorial Consultant*

THE WOMEN'S RESEARCH AND EDUCATION INSTITUTE (WREI) is a nonprofit (501[c] [3]) organization in Washington, D.C. Established in 1977, WREI provides information, research, and policy analysis to the members of Congress who support equity for women. Over the years WREI's reputation as a source of reliable data and clear thinking about the status of American women has traveled far beyond the nation's Capitol.

- WREI's resources are among the nation's best and include research and policy centers throughout the country where scholars are conducting cutting-edge research on a host of issues concerning women.
- WREI puts vital information on key issues affecting women into the hands of policymakers in the form of reports and fact sheets that are prepared by WREI staff or outside scholars.
- WREI urges researchers to consider the public policy implications of their work and fosters the exchange of ideas and expertise between researchers and policymakers.
- WREI promotes the informed scrutiny of policies regarding their effect on women and encourages the development of policy options that recognize the circumstances of today's women and their families.

- WREI identifies and trains new leaders through its Congressional Fellowships on Women and Public Policy. Established in 1980, this program enhances the research capacity of congressional offices, especially with respect to legislative implications for women, and has given scores of promising women hands-on experience in the federal legislative process.
- WREI is a national information source and clearinghouse. Reporters, researchers, public officials, government agencies, advocacy organizations, and others contact WREI for information relating to women.

BOARD OF DIRECTORS

INDEX

italicized page numbers indicate photographs

abortion, 220
   abortions by week of gestation, 291 *table*
   anti-abortion rallies, 235
   clinic access, 205, 206, 210, 216, 222
   court cases, 185, 192, 195, 202, 211
   health care reform and, 214
   health insurance and, 180
   Medicaid coverage, 183, 188, 189,
      191–92
   prescription drugs used for, 224, 225, 230
   protesters' rights, 211
   reduction initiatives, 236
   restrictions on, 178, 190, 202
   RU-486 abortion pill, 207, 208,
      211–12, 227, 240
   violence at clinics, 215–16, 223, 226,
      228, 232–33, 234
   welfare reform and, 236
abortion training, 238
absenteeism, 97
Accreditation Council for Graduate Medical Education, 238
Administration for Children and Families,
   134, 139
AFDC, *see* Aid to Families with Dependent
   Children
affirmative action, 31, 32, 33, 241, 242, 243
   achievements of, 39

   broad economic benefits of, 38–40
   defining characteristics, 34–36
   historical framework, 33–34
   need for, 36–39, 42–43
   public support for, 36
   reverse discrimination, 41, 204, 245
   scapegoating of, 36, 40–42
   Supreme Court rulings, 35–36
African-Americans, *see* race/ethnicity
age:
   AFDC and, 133
   contraceptive failure during the first 12
      months of use by marital status,
      poverty status, and age, 290 *table*
   contraceptive users age 15 to 44 by
      method and age, 289 *table*
   earnings and, 68–69, 69 *table*
   homeownership by age of householder,
      321 *figure*
   labor force participation by women and,
      48, 49 *table,* 50, 50 *figure*
   median age at first marriage by sex, 258
      figure
   median family income by age of house-
      holder, 310 *figure*
   number of men per 100 women by age,
      266 *figure*
   persons age 18 to 64 with no health

age (*continued*)
  insurance coverage by sex and age, 304 *figure*
  persons with and without health insurance coverage by sex and age, 303 *figure*
  population of the United States by age and sex, 252 *figure*
  poverty rates of unrelated individuals by sex and age, 315 *table*
  poverty status of women and men by age, race, and Hispanic origin, 314 *table*
  voter participation in national elections by sex and age, 337 *table*
  women enrolled in colleges and universities by age, 274 *figure*
  see also elderly persons
Agency for International Development (AID), 185–86
AIDS and HIV infection, 193, 196, 217, 227
  AIDS cases in females age 13 and over by race and Hispanic origin, 298 *figure*
  distribution of newly reported AIDS cases among women age 13 and over by race and Hispanic origin, 299 *table*
  pregnancy and, 239
Aid to Families with Dependent Children (AFDC), 53, 105, 127–28
  AFDC-UP, 129
  age and, 133
  changes in AFDC population, 132–34
  conditional assistance, 134–38
  "dependency" issue, 135–36, 144–45
  earnings supplementation, 139
  education and, 133
  emergency assistance, 138–39
  establishment of, 129
  federal role, 132
  housing programs and, 132
  income support in lieu of work, 140
  intergenerational use, 136
  labor market prospects of low-skilled women, 140–42
  lone mothers and, 133–34, 138–40

  Medicaid and, 132
  race/ethnicity and, 133, 134–35
  reform initiatives, 138, 142, 144–47
  right to benefits, 135
  state benefit levels, 129, 130–31 *table*
  two-parent families and, 129
  unemployment assistance, 139
  value of benefits, 132
  work requirements, 135, 136–38, 142–44
Air Force, U.S., 180, 196
  see also military service
Albert Einstein College of Medicine, 201
Alduenda, Boni Carr, 200
Alvord, Lori, 197
American Bar Association (ABA), 180, 217
American Cancer Society, 187
American College of Physicians, 187
American Dental Association, 203
American Federation of State, County, and Municipal Employees, 143
American Hospital Association, 203
American Medical Association (AMA), 187, 198–99, 203
Americans United for Life, 240
American Woman series, 19
America's Cup race, 200, 227, 234, 238, 243
Amott, Teresa, 134
Anderson v. *Edwards,* 243
Andrews, L., 138, 139
Angier, Natalie, 207
Antczak, Stephen, 72
Army, U.S., 197
  see also military service
Arnold, Karen, 230
Arnold, Stephanie, 228
Asian and Pacific Islander women, *see* race/ethnicity
Aspin, Les, 190
Atwood, J. Brian, 186
Austin, Carol, 204
auto industry, 221

Baker & McKenzie law firm, 218, 219
Bane, Mary J., 136
Barnett, Martha W., 217
Barnett, Rosalind C., 81*n*

Bartolo, Sally, 177–78
Baruch, Grace K., 81*n*
baseball, 206
basketball, 201, 231, 241
Bassi, Laurie J., 27, 104–26
Beardstown Ladies, 240
Beller, Daniel J., 149, 171
Bendick, Marc, 37, 38
Berresford, Susan V., 231
Bilimoria, Diana, 236
birth defects, 207
Blackmun, Harry, 204
blacks, *see* race/ethnicity
Blair, Bonnie, 198
Blank, Rebecca, 140, 141, 142
Bliley, Thomas, 240
Bloom, Marc, 187
Blount, Linda, 44*n*
blue-collar occupations, 25
Blumrosen, Alfred, 245
boards of directors, 236–37
Bond, James T., 25, 79–103
Boorda, Jeremy M., 205
Bothner, Margaret Chalmers, 193
Boxer, Barbara, 342, *342*
Boyett, Shanda, 177*n*
brain functioning, 239
breast cancer:
    breast-feeding and, 190
    gene responsible for, 221
    incidence and mortality rates for white
        and black women, 222–23, 295 *fig-
        ure*
    mammography and, 183, 187
    mortality rates among white and black
        women from lung and breast can-
        cer, 293 *figure*
    treatment for, 201
breast-feeding, 190
breast implants, 201, 216, 219
bridge building, 188
Brinkema, Leonie M., 210
Brock, Thomas, 143
Brody, Jane, 194
Brown, Corrine, 342, *342,* 367
Bryan, Richard, 212
Burbridge, Lynn, 137
Burke, Yvonne Braithwaite, 242

burnout, job-related, 96, 98 *table,* 99–100
Burtless, Gary, 141, 142
Bush, Barbara, 220
Business Roundtable, 199
Butler, David, 143

caesarean section laws, 188
Cahill, Robert E., 225
calcium intake, 209
Cammermeyer, Margarethe, 208, 210, 237
campaign financing, 203
Campbell, Bonnie, 243
cancer:
    incidence and death rates for selected
        cancers among women by cancer
        site and race, 294 *table*
    mortality rates among white and black
        women from lung and breast can-
        cer, 293 *figure*
    see also breast cancer
Carpenter, John, 202
Casey, Robert, 191–92
Cashen, Raymond, 215
Catholic Church, 225–26
Celis, William, III, 197
Census Bureau, U.S., 38, 45
Central Intelligence Agency (CIA), 212,
        214, 219, 222, 233
Chamber of Commerce, U.S., 198
Chasanov, Amy B., 27, 104–26
Chase, Barbara Landis, 211
Chavez, Maria A., 213
Cheney, Lynne, 226
Chevron Corporation, 239
child care, 25
    children's intellectual needs and, 237
    custody and, 215, 216, 222
    parents in labor force and, 94–95
    standards for child care centers, 196
    welfare reform and, 145–46
    workfare and, 144
children:
    fathers as caretakers, 181
    female-headed households by type and
        presence of children, 323 *figure*
    homeownership by family type, presence
        of children, race, and Hispanic ori-
        gin, 322 *figure*

children (*continued*)
  infant, neonatal, and postneonatal mor-
    tality rates by mothers' race and
    Hispanic origin, 287 *table*
  labor force participation by women and,
    49 *table*, 51–52
  living arrangements, 218
    by race and Hispanic origin, 264–65
    table
  low-birthweight live births by race, eth-
    nicity, and Hispanic origin, 288 *fig-
    ure*
  median income of families with children
    by family type, 311 *figure*
  poverty rates of families by family type
    and presence of children, 316 *figure*
  poverty rates of white, black, and His-
    panic families by family type and
    presence of children, 317 *table*
  sick children, care for, 95, 96 *figure*
  workfare and, 144
child support, 146, 189, 195–96, 217, 240
Chira, Susan, 222
Citadel, the, 185, 189, 190, 192, 206–7,
  209, 210, 211, 214–15, 236
civil rights movement, 46, 134
Clayton, Eva, 343, *343,* 367
Clinton, Bill, 29, 183, 185, 239, 243, 244
  abortion policy, 188, 206
  child support policy, 240
  Elders's resignation, 231
  family planning policy, 192
  health care reform, 183, 193, 194, 213, 214
  judicial appointments, 191
  welfare reform, 138
Clinton, Hillary Rodham, 183, 194, 203,
  214, 240, 241, 242, 244
Close, Glenn, 237
coaches, female, 206
Cohany, Sharon R., 74
Cohen, Elizabeth, 197
colleges and universities:
  admissions policies, 41
  athletics programs, 186, 217
  college enrollment by sex, race, and His-
    panic origin, 273 *table*
  discrimination against female faculty,
    207

drinking by students, 197, 209
enrollment trends, 198
faculty with tenure by sex and type of
  institution, 280 *figure*
professional degrees awarded in selected
  fields by sex of recipients, 278 *figure*
recipients of postsecondary degrees by
  sex, 277 *figure*
sexual harassment, 229
students enrolled in colleges and universities by sex and full- or part-time
  status, 275 *figure*
women awarded first professional degrees in selected fields by race and
  Hispanic origin, 279 *table*
women awarded undergraduate degrees
  in selected fields, 276 *table*
women enrolled in colleges and universities by age, 274 *figure*
women's colleges, 191
women's educational aims, 189–90
see also specific institutions
Collins, Barbara-Rose, 343, *343,* 367
Collins, Cardiss, 344, *344,* 367
Colorado Silver Bullets, 206
Colorado State University, 186
Columbia Pictures, 199
Columbia University, 193
Commerce, U.S. Department of, 151
Commodore Club, 217
communications licenses, 217, 228–29,
  242
Community Work Experience Programs
  (CWEP), 137, 138
computer use, 223
Congress, U.S., 129, 132, 138, 145
  convening of 104th Congress, 233–34
  female committee chairs, 234
  legislative service organizations (LSOs),
    231
  1994 congressional elections, 31, 229
  Office of Fair Employment Practices
    (OFEP), 180–81
  sexual harassment in, 181–82
  women in 104th Congress, 341–66
  women's legislation, 186–87, 224–25
Congressional Accountability Act, 234
Congressional Budget Office, 143, 195

Congressional Caucus for Women's Issues, 224, 238–39, 367

contingent work, *see* part-time/temporary work

contraception:
contraceptive failure during the first 12 months of use by marital status, poverty status, and age, 290 *table*
contraceptive users age 15 to 44 by method and age, 289 *table*
male contraceptive pill, 192
Norplant contraceptive, 184, 228
sponges, 234

Contract with America, 240

Cooper, James, 199

coping ability, 99, 100–101 *table,* 102

Cosby, Camille and Bill, 201

Costello, Cynthia, 23–32

Coughlin, Paula, 227, 241–42

Council of Economic Advisers, 113

Covenant Investment Management, 39

Crits-Christoph, Paul, 81*n*

cross-country runners, 187

Crouter, Ann C., 81*n*

Cubin, Barbara, 344, *344*

Cureton, Kirk, 240

Current Population Survey (CPS), 45

custody issues, 215, 216, 218, 222

Cutler, Lynn, 203

Dalton, Clare, 181

Dalton, John H., 183, 200, 206, 237

Danner, Patricia, 344–45, *344,* 367

death:
breast cancer: incidence and mortality rates for white and black women, 222–23, 295 *figure*
incidence and death rates for selected cancers among women by cancer site and race, 294 *table*
infant, neonatal, and postneonatal mortality rates, 205
by mother's race and Hispanic origin, 287 *table*
leading causes of death for whites and blacks by sex, 292 *figure*
mortality rates among white and black

women from lung and breast cancer, 293 *figure*

Dechter, Aimee, 205

Defense Intelligence Agency, 222

Defense Women's Health Research Center, 178, 186

Defensive Action, 216

defined benefit pension plans, 149–51

defined contribution pension plans, 150–51

DeJong, Philip, 47

DeLauro, Rosa, 345, *345,* 367

Delfico, Joseph F., 196

Deming, William G., 54, 62

Democratic Leadership Council (DLC), 241

Democratic National Committee, 212

demographics, 249–50
children's living arrangements by race and Hispanic origin, 264–65 *table*
currently married and never married adults by sex, race, and Hispanic origin, 257 *figure*
divorce rate, 262 *figure*
divorce ratios by sex, race, and Hispanic origin, 263 *table*
families by family type, race, and Hispanic origin, 259–60 *table*
fertility rates by race of child, 255 *figure*
household types, 261 *table*
living arrangements of women age 65 and over by age, race, and Hispanic origin, 267 *table*
marital status by sex, race, and Hispanic origin, 256 *table*
median age at first marriage by sex, 258 *figure*
number of men per 100 women by age, 266 *figure*
women and men age 65 and older living alone, 268 *figure*
see also population of United States

dependent care benefits, 89–90

Deutsch, Claudia, 184–85

Devine, Theresa J., 61

Dewar, Helen, 181

De Witt, Karen, 244

DiBattiste, Carol, 210

discouraged workers, 75

discretionary income, 178
discrimination in workplace, 204, 220
    affirmative action and, 36–39
    at CIA, 212, 214, 219, 222, 233
    at colleges and universities, 207
    court cases, 203
    at FBI, 219, 222
    hiring practices, 41
    increases in, 226
    in law enforcement, 197–98, 200
    in legal system, 209
    parents in labor force and, 91
    prevalence of, 36–38
    race/ethnicity and, 37–38
displacement of workers, 73–74, 143
divorce:
    divorce rate, 262 *figure*
    divorce ratios by sex, race, and Hispanic
        origin, 263 *table*
    pensions/retirement planning and, 168–69
Dole, Robert, 193, 214, 242
Dooley, Betty, 23–32
Doucette, Suzanne J., 182, 200, 236
Dow Corning Company, 201
Driscoll, Dawn-Marie, 189
drug testing, 192–93, 195, 223
Duncan, Greg J., 136, 180
Dunn, Jennifer, 345, *345*

Earned Income Tax Credit (EITC), 28,
    141*n*, 145
earnings, 26
    AFDC and, 139
    age and, 68–69, 69 *table*
    decline in men's earnings, 31
    education and, 38, 67, 68 *table,* 227
    lone mothers and, 86–87
    median family income by age of house-
        holder, 310 *figure*
    median family income by family type,
        308 *figure*
    median income of families with children
        by family type, 311 *figure*
    median income of veterans by sex, race,
        and Hispanic origin, 333 *figure*
    median income of white, black, and
        Hispanic families by family type,
        309 *table*

men compared with women, 30, 38, 63,
    63 *table,* 64–65 *table,* 66, 68 *table,*
    69 *table,* 70 *table,* 191
men's earning capacity, 29–30, 31
minimum-wage workers, 70–71
occupational patterns and, 64–65 *table,*
    66
parents in labor force and, 79–80,
    85–87, 86 *table*
part-time/temporary work and, 70
pensions/retirement planning and, 151,
    153–54, 153 *table,* 162
race/ethnicity and, 67, 68 *table,* 70 *table,*
    221
sources of income for persons age 65 and
    over by sex, 318 *table*
sources of income for white, black, and
    Hispanic women age 65 and over,
    319–20 *table*
sources of income for women age 15 to
    64 by race and Hispanic origin,
    312–13 *table*
unions and, 69, 70 *table*
eating disorders, 215
Economic Policy Institute, 30
economic security, 306–7
    female-headed households by type and
        presence of children, 323 *figure*
    homeownership by age of householder,
        321 *figure*
    homeownership by family type, presence
        of children, race, and Hispanic ori-
        gin, 322 *figure*
    see also earnings; poverty
ectopic pregnancies, 235
Edelman, Marian Wright, 182
Edin, Kathryn, 139
education, 29, 269–70
    AFDC and, 133
    bias against girls, 186
    earnings and, 38, 67, 68 *table,* 227
    educational attainment by sex, race, and
        Hispanic origin, 271 *table*
    educational attainment of active duty
        Department of Defense personnel
        by officer/enlisted status and sex,
        328 *table*
    gender-equal education, 223

labor force participation by women and,
53–54
quality of education in America, 232
welfare reform and, 146–47
white, black, and Hispanic women age
25 and over with 12 or more years
of education, 272 *figure*
see also colleges and universities
Education, U.S. Department of, 179
elderly persons:
as caregivers, 220
exercise by, 233
health care reform and, 197
living arrangements of women age 65
and over by age, race, and Hispanic
origin, 267 *table*
poverty and, 167–68
sources of income for persons age 65 and
over by sex, 318 *table*
sources of income for white, black, and
Hispanic women age 65 and over,
319–20 *table*
tobacco use, 233
women and men age 65 and older living
alone, 268 *figure*
Elders, Joycelyn, 201, 231
Eleanor Roosevelt Monument, 182
elections, 334–35
congressional elections of 1994, 31, 229
gender gap, 229
sex of candidates and, 220
voter participation in national elections
by sex, race, and Hispanic origin,
336 *table*
voter participation in national elections
by sex and age, 337 *table*
women's success in, 224
Ellwood, David T., 136
Employee Retirement Income Security
Act (ERISA), 160, 161
Ensch, John C., 228
entrepreneurs, 213–14
Episcopal Church, 216
Equal Employment Opportunity Commission (EEOC), 36, 41
Equal Pay Act, 162
Erector Set Contest, 188
Eshoo, Anna, 346, *346,* 367

Esping-Anderson, Gosta, 128
ESPN, 231
exercise:
by elderly persons, 233
by pregnant women, 194
by teenagers, 228

Fair Employment Council of Greater Washington (FEC), 37–38
families:
by family type, race, and Hispanic origin, 259–60 *table*
female-headed households by type and
presence of children, 323 *figure*
homeownership by family type, presence
of children, race, and Hispanic origin, 322 *figure*
household types, 261 *table*
labor force participation by women and,
48, 52–53, 53 *table*
median family income by age of householder, 310 *figure*
median family income by family type,
308 *figure*
median income of families with children
by family type, 311 *figure*
median income of white, black, and
Hispanic families by family type,
309 *table*
parents in labor force and, 92–95, 94
table, 96 *figure*
persons with no health insurance coverage by family relationship, 302 *table*
poverty and, 76, 77 *table*
poverty rates of families by family type
and presence of children, 316
figure
poverty rates of white, black, and Hispanic families by family type and
presence of children, 317 *table*
Family and Medical Leave Act of 1993
(FMLA), 80, 84–85, 180, 219
family planning, 192
see also contraception
Family Support Act of 1988, 129*n*, 137
fathers as caretakers, 181
fathers in labor force, *see* parents in labor
force

Faulkner, Shannon, 185, 189, 190, 192,
206–7, 209, 210, 211, 214–15, 236
Federal Bar Association, 182
Federal Bureau of Investigation (FBI):
discrimination against female employees,
219, 222
sexual harassment in, 182, 200, 202,
207, 236
Federal Communications Commission
(FCC), 217, 228–29, 242
Federal Deposit Insurance Corporation
(FDIC), 185, 224
Federal Reserve, 212
Federal Unemployment Tax Act (FUTA),
107, 110
Feinstein, Dianne, 229, 346, *346*
Female Employment Initiative, 35
feminist movement, 46
Ferraro, Geraldine, 183
fertility rates by race of child, 255 *figure*
firefighting, 205
Fisher, Cynthia J., 207
Fisher, Lucy, 199
flexible time benefits, 89, 90 *table*
Flynn, Jeannie, 196
Flynn, Joanne T., 184
Food Stamps, 132, 241
Forbes, Michael, 235
Ford Foundation, 231
Ford Motor Company, 221
Foreign Service, 204
Foster, Henry W., Jr., 238
401(k) programs, 161
Fowler, Tillie, 346–47, *346,* 367
Fox-Genovese, Elizabeth, 196
Franklin v. *Gwinnett County Public Schools,*
213
Freedom of Access to Clinic Entrances Act,
205, 206, 208, 210, 216, 222
Freedom of Choice Act, 202
Freeh, Louis, 236
Freeman, Laura, 72
Freeman, Richard, 140
Friedman, Dana, 81
fringe benefits for parents in labor force,
88–90, 88 *table,* 90 *table*
Frye, Jocelyn C., 31, 33–43
Furse, Elizabeth, 347, *347*

Galinsky, Ellen, 25, 79–103
Garcia, Marie Reynolds, 179
Gardner, Jennifer, 74
Gebicke, Mark, 194–95
gender issues, *see* men compared with
women
General Accounting Office, 168
Gephardt, Richard, 214, 215
Gingrich, Candace, 241
Gingrich, Newt, 234–35
Ginsburg, Ruth Bader, 180
Girl Scouts, 193
glass ceiling, 24, 186, 189, 242
Glass Ceiling Commission, 24, 38, 40, 41
Glater, Jonathan, 243
Goldberg, Carol R., 189
Goldberg, Wendy A., 81*n*
Goldman, Sachs & Co., 183–84
Goodman, Ellen, 223
Goodman, William, 72
Gore, Al, 215
Gore, Tipper, 195
Gorelick, Jamie, 215
Gormley, Patricia, 200
Goshko, John, 204
Grad, Susan, 167
Gramm, Phil, 216
Granovetter, Mark, 41
Greenberg, Mark, 138
Greenberger, Ellen, 81*n*
Greene, Kenneth, 218, 222
Greenhouse, Steven, 192
Greenstein, Martin R., 218, 219
Gross, Jane, 211
Gueron, Judith, 137
gymnastics, 215

Hagen, Katherine A., 179
Hamilton, Martha, 243
Harman, Jane, 347, *347,* 367
Harris, Marcelite Jordan, 238
Harris v. *Forklift Systems,* 184
"Harry and Louise" advertisements, 180
Hartman, Douglas P., 219
Hartmann, Heidi, 138, 139, 210
Harvard, Beverly, 230
Harvard University, 181
Hatch, Orrin, 218

Hausknecht, Richard, 224
Haveman, Robert, 47
Hayghe, Howard V., 52
health, 281–82
    abortions by week of gestation, 291 *table*
    AIDS cases in females age 13 and over
        by race and Hispanic origin, 298
        figure
    breast cancer: incidence and mortality
        rates for white and black women,
        222–23, 295 *figure*
    breast examinations and mammograms
        by selected characteristics, 297 *table*
    contraceptive failure during the first 12
        months of use by marital status,
        poverty status, and age, 290 *table*
    contraceptive users age 15 to 44 by
        method and age, 289 *table*
    distribution of newly reported AIDS
        cases among women age 13 and
        over by race and Hispanic origin,
        299 *table*
    incidence and death rates for selected
        cancers among women by cancer
        site and race, 294 *table*
    infant, neonatal, and postneonatal mor-
        tality rates by mothers' race and
        Hispanic origin, 287 *table*
    leading causes of death for whites and
        blacks by sex, 292 *figure*
    low-birthweight live births by race, eth-
        nicity, and Hispanic origin, 288 *fig-
        ure*
    mortality rates among white and black
        women from lung and breast can-
        cer, 293 *figure*
    prenatal care for mothers with live births
        by race and Hispanic origin of
        mothers, 286 *table*
    preventive services in the past year by
        selected characteristics, 296 *table*
    see also life expectancy
Health, Education, and Welfare, U.S. De-
    partment of, 135
Health Care Leadership Council, 213
health care reform, 193, 206, 215, 222
    abortion and, 214
    campaign financing and, 203

    Clinton's program, 183, 185, 194,
        214
    defeat of, 222
    elderly persons and, 197
    opposition to, 180, 195, 198–99,
        212–13, 216
    reproductive services and, 203–4
health insurance, 26
    abortion and, 180
    health insurance coverage by sex and
        type of insurance, 301 *figure*
    parents in labor force and, 80, 88–89, 88
        table
    part-time/temporary work and, 27
    persons age 16 to 64 with no health in-
        surance coverage by sex and work
        experience, 305 *figure*
    persons age 18 to 64 with no health in-
        surance coverage by sex and age,
        304 *figure*
    persons age 18 to 64 with private health
        insurance by sex and source of cov-
        erage, 300 *figure*
    persons with and without health insur-
        ance coverage by sex and age, 303
        figure
    persons with no health insurance cover-
        age by family relationship, 302 *table*
    uninsured persons, 202–3
Health Insurance Association of America
    (HIAA), 180
Height, Dorothy, 201
Heitman, Betty, 194
Helfer, Ricki Tigert, 185, 224
Henrich, Christy, 215
Henson, Lisa, 199
Herman, Alexis, 244
Herring, Hubert, 240
Herz, Diane E., 23, 30, 44–78
Hill, Martha S., 136
Hill, Paul, 216, 223, 226, 228
Hispanics:
    active duty servicewomen by branch of
        service, rank, race, and Hispanic
        origin, 326 *table*
    AIDS cases in females age 13 and over
        by race and Hispanic origin, 298
        figure

Hispanics (*continued*)

children's living arrangements by race and Hispanic origin, 264–65 *table*

college enrollment by sex, race, and Hispanic origin, 273 *table*

currently married and never married adults by sex, race, and Hispanic origin, 257 *figure*

distribution of newly reported AIDS cases among women age 13 and over by race and Hispanic origin, 299 *table*

divorce ratios by sex, race, and Hispanic origin, 263 *table*

earnings of, 67, 68 *table,* 70 *table,* 221

educational attainment by sex, race, and Hispanic origin, 271 *table*

families by family type, race, and Hispanic origin, 259–60 *table*

homeownership by family type, presence of children, race, and Hispanic origin, 322 *figure*

infant, neonatal, and postneonatal mortality rates by mothers' race and Hispanic origin, 287 *table*

labor force participation by women, 49 *table,* 50–51

life expectancy at birth by sex, race, and Hispanic origin, 284 *table*

living arrangements of women age 65 and over by age, race, and Hispanic origin, 267 *table*

low-birthweight live births by race, ethnicity, and Hispanic origin, 288 *figure*

marital status by sex, race, and Hispanic origin, 256 *table*

median income of veterans by sex, race, and Hispanic origin, 333 *figure*

median income of white, black, and Hispanic families by family type, 309 *table*

occupational patterns, 24, 58–60, 59 *table*

population of the United States by sex, race, and Hispanic origin, 253 *figure*

poverty rates, 76, 76 *table*

of white, black, and Hispanic families by family type and presence of children, 317 *table*

poverty status of women and men by age, race, and Hispanic origin, 314 *table*

prenatal care for mothers with live births by race and Hispanic origin of mothers, 286 *table*

projected composition of the population by race and Hispanic origin, 254 *figure*

sources of income for white, black, and Hispanic women age 65 and over, 319–20 *table*

sources of income for women age 15 to 64 by race and Hispanic origin, 312–13 *table*

unemployment among, 73, 73 *table,* 111, 113 *figure*

unemployment of veterans by sex, race, and Hispanic origin, 332 *table*

voter participation in national elections by sex, race, and Hispanic origin, 336 *table*

white, black, and Hispanic women age 25 and over with 12 or more years of education, 272 *figure*

women awarded first professional degrees in selected fields by race and Hispanic origin, 279 *table*

history teaching standards, 226

HIV infection, *see* AIDS and HIV infection

Hofferth, Sandra L., 81*n*

Hoffman, Saul D., 136

Holmes, Greta Hawkins, 204

home-based work, 61–63

homelessness, 188

homeownership:

by age of householder, 321 *figure*

by family type, presence of children, race, and Hispanic origin, 322 *figure*

homosexuality, *see* sexual orientation

Honeywell Corporation, 220

hormone replacement therapy, 229–30

Horn, Karen, 212

horse racing, 208

Houck, C. Weston, 209, 210, 211, 214–15

Hounsell, Cindy, 27, 166–73

household types, 261 *table*
housing programs, 132
Howard Hughes Medical Institute, 182
Howe, Wayne J., 72
Huffington, Michael, 229
Hughes, Diane, 81*n*
Hultgreen, Kara, 226, 230
human rights, 194, 221
Hutchison, Kay Bailey, 229, 348, *348*
Hyde Amendment, 178

Ifill, Gwen, 203
Ilg, Randy, 44*n*
immigration, 179, 202
income, *see* earnings
Individual Retirement Accounts (IRAs),
    161
industry employment patterns, 60–61, 60
    table
infant mortality rates, 205, 287 *table*
inflation, 156, 172
Institute for the Study of Social Change, 41
integrated defined benefit plans, 150
International Labor Organization, 179
International Planned Parenthood Federa-
    tion, 185–86
International Women's Conference,
    242–43
International Women's Day, 241
Interstate Conference of Employment Se-
    curity Agencies, 121*n*
investments, 240
    pensions/retirement planning and,
        154–55, 155 *table*
Ippolito, Richard A., 47
Ireland, Jennifer, 215, 216
Ireland, Patricia, 177

Jackson, Shirley A., 244
Jancsy, Marilyn, 177–78
J.E.B. v. *Alabama*, 204
Jencks, Christopher, 139
Jensvold, Margaret, 203
Job Opportunities and Basic Skills (JOBS)
    program, 137–38, 232
job sharing, 190
job training, 29
John Paul II, Pope, 225–26

Johnson, Eddie Bernice, 348, *348,* 367
Johnson, Nancy, 349, *349,* 367
Joint Center for Political and Economic
    Studies, 143
Jones, Rochelle, 205
judges, female, 180, 191, 339 *table*
jury service, 204
Justice Department, U.S., 215
    Violence against Women office, 243

Kalish, Jennifer Melissa, 193
Kaptur, Marcy, 349, *349,* 367
Karibian v. *Columbia University,* 193
Kassebaum, Nancy Landon, 188, 234, 350,
    350
Kasser, Elisabeth A., 217
Kelly, Sue, 350, *350,* 367
Kennelly, Barbara, 351, *351,* 367
Kent, Deborah, 221
Kerrey, Bob, 212
Kiser, Jackson L., 205
Koch, Bill, 200
Kohl, Herb, 212
KPMG, 163
Krone, Julie, 208
Kumar, Kamalesh, 39
Kunde, Diane, 190

Labor, U.S. Department of, 41, 107, 113,
    135, 145, 149, 154, 156
    Women's Bureau, 25
labor force participation by women, 44–45
    age and, 48, 49 *table,* 50, 50 *figure*
    children at home and, 49 *table,* 51–52
    conclusions regarding, 77–78
    education and, 53–54
    families and, 48, 52–53, 53 *table*
    historical trends, 46–47, 47 *figure*
    low-skilled women, prospects of,
        140–42
    marital status and, 49 *table,* 51, 55–56
    multiple jobholding, 55–56
    race/ethnicity and, 49 *table,* 50–51
    work schedules, 54–55, 55 *figure*
    see also occupational patterns
Labor Statistics, U.S. Bureau of, 38, 45,
    122, 171
Lambert Lincoln, Blanche, 351, *351,* 367

Lansnerus, Laura, 238
law enforcement, 197–98, 200, 230
Lawrence, Wendy, 241
Lawrence, William, 241
law schools, 237, 238
Lawson, Roger, 128, 147
Lazarus, Ellen M., 182
Learning, Earning, and Parenting (LEAP)
    program, 221–22
Lee, Sheila Jackson, 352, *352,* 367
LeFevre, Jennifer, 177*n*
Lewin, Tamar, 208, 213
Lewin/ICF, 172
Lewis, Ann F., 203
Lewis, Cora E., 201–2
Lieberman, Joseph, 241
life expectancy:
    at birth and at age 65 by race and sex,
        283 *table*
    at birth by sex, race, and Hispanic ori-
        gin, 284 *table*
    female life expectancy at birth in se-
        lected industrialized countries, 285
        figure
    pensions/retirement planning and,
        151–52
Lincoln Center, 209–10
LipoMatrix company, 216
Litsky, Frank, 241
Lloyd, Marilyn, 178
Lofgren, Zoe, 352, *352,* 367
lone mothers, 25, 178, 220, 226
    AFDC and, 133–34, 138–40
    earnings and, 86–87
    female-headed households by type and
        presence of children, 323 *figure*
Long, David, 143
Lowey, Nita, 238, 239, 352–53, *352,*
    367
Lucky Stores, 37, 204

Madsen v. *Women's Health Center,* 211
Maloney, Carolyn, 353, *353,* 367
mammograms:
    breast cancer and, 183, 187
    breast examinations and mammograms
        by selected characteristics, 297
        table

managerial and professional occupations,
    23–25, 56–57, 199–200, 203,
    227–28
Mann, Judy, 182, 230, 236
Manpower Demonstration Research Cor-
    poration (MDRC), 137
Marcus, Ruth, 191
"marginally attached" workers, 75
Marine Corps, U.S., 186, 188, 209
    see also military service
marital status:
    contraceptive failure during the first 12
        months of use by marital status,
        poverty status, and age, 290 *table*
    currently married and never married
        adults by sex, race, and Hispanic
        origin, 257 *figure*
    labor force participation by women and,
        49 *table,* 51, 55–56
    median age at first marriage by sex, 258
        figure
    military service and, 188
    pensions/retirement planning and,
        168–69
    by sex, race, and Hispanic origin, 256
        table
    see also divorce
marriage relationships, 101
Martinez, Zenaida, 210
Massachusetts welfare program,
    190–91
Matthews, Elizabeth, 177*n*
McCarthy, David D., 149
McCarthy, Karen, 353, *353,* 367
McFate, Katherine, 28, 127–47
McKinney, Cynthia, 354, *354,* 367
McNeese, Yvonne, 177*n*
Medicaid, 28
    abortion coverage, 183, 188, 189,
        191–92
    AFDC and, 132
medical licensing, 220
medical schools, 177
Medical University of South Carolina,
    192–93, 195, 223
Meek, Carrie, 354, *354,* 367
men compared with women:
    active duty personnel by pay grade

grouping, branch of service, and sex, 329 *table*

brain functioning, 239

college enrollment by sex, race, and Hispanic origin, 273 *table*

college faculty with tenure by sex and type of institution, 280 *figure*

currently married and never married adults by sex, race, and Hispanic origin, 257 *figure*

divorce ratios by sex, race, and Hispanic origin, 263 *table*

earnings, 30, 38, 63, 63 *table*, 64–65 *table*, 66, 68 *table*, 69 *table*, 70 *table*, 191

educational attainment by sex, race, and Hispanic origin, 271 *table*

educational attainment of active duty Department of Defense personnel by officer/enlisted status and sex, 328 *table*

health insurance coverage by sex and type of insurance, 301 *figure*

industry employment patterns, 60–61, 60 *table*

labor force participation, 47, 47 *figure*, 50 *figure*

leading causes of death for whites and blacks by sex, 292 *figure*

life expectancy at birth and at age 65 by race and sex, 283 *table*

life expectancy at birth by sex, race, and Hispanic origin, 284 *table*

marital status by sex, race, and Hispanic origin, 256 *table*

median age at first marriage by sex, 258 *figure*

median income of veterans by sex, race, and Hispanic origin, 333 *figure*

number of men per 100 women by age, 266 *figure*

occupational patterns, 57–58, 58 *table*

pensions/retirement planning, 149, 150 *table*, 152 *table*, 153 *table*

persons age 16 to 64 with no health insurance coverage by sex and work experience, 305 *figure*

persons age 18 to 64 with no health in-

surance coverage by sex and age, 304 *figure*

persons age 18 to 64 with private health insurance by sex and source of coverage, 300 *figure*

persons with and without health insurance coverage by sex and age, 303 *figure*

physiological differences, 240

population of the United States by age and sex, 252 *figure*

population of the United States by race and sex, 251 *table*

population of the United States by sex, race, and Hispanic origin, 253 *figure*

postsecondary degree recipients by sex, 277 *figure*

poverty, 76, 76 *table*

poverty rates of unrelated individuals by sex and age, 315 *table*

poverty status of women and men by age, race, and Hispanic origin, 314 *table*

professional degrees awarded in selected fields by sex of recipients, 278 *figure*

professionals employed in corporate sector, 199–200

self-employment, 61, 62 *table*

sick children, care for, 95, 96 *figure*

sources of income for persons age 65 and over by sex, 318 *table*

students enrolled in colleges and universities by sex and full- or part-time status, 275 *figure*

unemployment, 72, 72 *figure*, 73 *table*, 111, 112 *figure*, 113 *figure*, 114 *table*

Unemployment Insurance benefits, 116, 117 *table*, 118 *table*, 119–20, 120 *table*, 123 *table*

unemployment of veterans by sex, race, and Hispanic origin, 332 *table*

valedictorians' careers, 230

voter participation in national elections by sex, race, and Hispanic origin, 336 *table*

voter participation in national elections by sex and age, 337 *table*

see also parents in labor force

Menendez trial, 195
menstruation, 180
Merida, Kevin, 239
Merrill Lynch, 156
Meyers, Jan, 234, 355, *355,* 367
Michaelson, Larry K., 39
Michelman, Kate, 189
Mikulski, Barbara, 355–56, *355*
military service, 324–25
 active duty personnel by pay grade
  grouping, branch of service, and
  sex, 329 *table*
 active duty servicewomen by branch of
  service, rank, race, and Hispanic
  origin, 326 *table*
 active duty women personnel by offi-
  cer/enlisted status, 327 *figure*
 educational attainment of active duty
  Department of Defense personnel
  by officer/enlisted status and sex,
  328 *table*
 equality for military women, 207–8
 Gingrich's views on, 234–35
 Harris's promotion, 238
 laws on, 178, 186
 marital status and, 188
 median income of veterans by sex, race,
  and Hispanic origin, 333 *figure*
 occupational profile of active duty
  women in Defense Department,
  331 *figure*
 positions and occupations open to active
  duty women, 215
  by service, 330 *figure*
 pregnancy and, 237, 243
 readiness issue, 242
 recruits to military services, 241
 risk rule, 190
 sexual harassment and, 194–95, 200,
  206, 210, 228, 232
 sexual orientation and, 208, 210, 237
 unemployment of veterans by sex, race,
  and Hispanic origin, 332 *table*
 veterans' benefits, 178
 see also specific branches
Min, Nancy-Ann, 244
Minehan, Cathy E., 212
minimum wage, 145

minimum-wage workers, earnings of,
 70–71
Mink, Patsy, 356, *356,* 367
Misko, Joanne E., 219
Mitchell, George, 213, 222
Molinari, Susan, 356–57, *356,* 367
Montefiore Medical Center, 201
Montells, Jessica, 179
Morella, Constance, 239, 357, *357,* 367
Morris, Ann, 81*n*
Morrison, Toni, 182
Moseley-Braun, Carol, 357, *357*
mothers in labor force, *see* parents in labor
 force
motion picture industry, 199
Motley, Constance Baker, 207
Murphy, Daniel J., 243
Murray, David, 244
Murray, Patty, 358, *358*
Myers, Dee Dee, 233
Myler, Cammy, 194
Myrick, Sue, 358, *358*

nanny tax, 223–24
Nasar, Sylvia, 230–31
Nash, Gary, 226
National Abortion and Reproductive
  Rights Action League (NARAL),
  189
National Academy for Science, Space, and
  Technology, 185
National Association of Life Underwriters,
  203
National Association of Women Judges,
  182
National Black Women's Health Project, 178
National Cancer Institute (NCI), 187
National Center for African American
  Women, 200–201
National Committee on Pay Equity, 38
National Economic Council, 239
National Girls and Women in Sports Day,
  236
National Governors' Association (NGA),
  194, 213
National Guard, 183
National Institute of Mental Health
  (NIMH), 203

National Institutes of Health (NIH), 184
National Longitudinal Survey of Youth (NLSY), 141
National Mammography Day, 183
National Merit Scholarships, 197
National Museum of Women in the Arts, 217
National Organization for Women (NOW), 177, 192
National Organization for Women v. *Scheidler,* 192
National Security Agency, 222
National Study of the Changing Workforce, 79, 81
National Welfare Rights Organization (NWRO), 135
National Women in Sports Day, 195
National Women's Health Network, 187
Navy, U.S., 186, 199, 205, 206, 213, 228, 232, 237
  see also military service; Tailhook affair
Needleman, Ruth, 34
Nelson, Barbara, 134
Newman, Maria, 191
Newman, Winn, 210–11
Nifediprine, 192
Nightingale, Demetra S., 137
Nobel Prize, 182
nonprofit organizations, workfare and, 143–44
Norplant contraceptive, 184, 228
North Dakota abortion laws, 195
Norton, Eleanor Holmes, 358–59, *358,* 367
Nuclear Regulatory Commission, 244
Nunn, Sam, 208
nursing profession, 188
Nussbaum, Karen, 244

occupational patterns, 56
  blue-collar occupations, 25
  earnings and, 64–65 *table,* 66
  home-based work, 61–63
  industry employment patterns, 60–61, 60 *table*
  managerial and professional occupations, 23–25, 56–57, 199–200, 203, 227–28

  men compared with women, 57–58, 58 *table*
  occupational profile of active duty women in Defense Department, 331 *figure*
  parents in labor force, 82–83
  positions and occupations open to active duty women, 215
    by service, 330 *figure*
  race/ethnicity and, 24, 58–60, 59 *table*
  self-employment, 61, 62 *table*
O'Connor, Sandra Day, 184
Office of Education Research and Improvement (OERI), 179
officials, 334–35
  female presidential appointees to Senate-confirmed positions, 339 *table*
  women in 104th Congress, 341–66
  women in elective office, 338 *table*
  women on federal bench, 191, 339 *table*
Okoed, Sandra, 177*n*
Old Age and Survivor's Insurance (OASI) program, 105
older persons, *see* elderly persons
Oluloro, Lydia, 202
Olympics, 198
Omnibus Crime Control and Safe Streets Act, 218, 221
O'Neil, Robin, 81*n*
Operation Rescue, 192

Packwood, Bob, 188, 199, 201
Panel Study on Income Dynamics, 136
parental leave:
  access to, 89, 90 *table*
  eligibility for coverage, 80, 84–85
  Family and Medical Leave Act, 80, 84–85, 180, 219
Parents' Fair Share, 195–96
parents in labor force, 25, 79, 205
  absenteeism, 97
  advantages of two incomes, 31
  aspirations for job advancement, 92, 93 *figure*
  burnout, job-related, 96, 98 *table,* 99–100
  child care and, 94–95
  conclusions regarding, 102–3

parents in labor force (*continued*)
  conditions on the job, 91
  coping ability, 99, 100–101 *table,* 102
  data on, 79, 81
  dependent care benefits, 89–90
  differences and similarities in life conditions and life outcomes between employed mothers and fathers, 79–80
  discrimination against, 91
  earnings and, 79–80, 85–87, 86 *table*
  employed parents with nonemployed spouses, 87
  employer characteristics, 84–85
  family life, 92–95, 94 *table,* 96 *figure*
  favorable outcomes, conditions fostering, 99–102
  feelings about jobs, employers, and work, 91–92
  flexible time and leave benefits, 89, 90 *table*
  fringe benefits, 88–90, 88 *table,* 90 *table*
  health insurance and, 80, 88–89, 88 *table*
  hours worked, 84
  interruption in employment, 84
  job characteristics, 82–84
  marriage relationships and, 101
  occupational patterns, 82–83
  parental self-image and, 101–2
  part-time/temporary work, 79, 83–84, 83 *figure*
  pensions/retirement planning and, 88–89, 88 *table*
  personal and family characteristics, 82
  personal outcomes and work, 80, 95–97, 98 *table,* 99–102, 100–101 *table*
  reasons for taking job with current employer, 90–91
  satisfaction with personal and family life, 97
  sexual harassment and, 91
  sick children, care for, 95, 96 *figure*
  spillover, home-to-job, 97
  stress and, 99, 100 *table,* 102
  work-family outcomes, 96–97
  work life outcomes, 95–96, 98 *table*
  workplace culture and, 91

part-time/temporary work, 26–27, 61
  earnings and, 70
  health insurance and, 27
  involuntary part-time work, 74–75
  parents in labor force, 79, 83–84, 83 *figure*
  pensions/retirement planning and, 154, 172–73
  unions and, 27–28
  vulnerability of workers, 27
Patterson, Martha Priddy, 27, 148–65
Pauly, Edward, 137
Pavetti, LaDonna, 138, 140
pay and benefits, *see* earnings
Peacock, Kenneth, 225
Pearlstein, Steven, 213
Pelosi, Nancy, 179, 243, 359, *359,* 367
Pennsylvania abortion laws, 191–92, 202
Pensions Not Posies program, 164
pensions/retirement planning, 148–49, 166
  annual pension benefit earned by women, 149, 150 *table*
  backloading formulas, 171
  changing jobs and, 156
  defined benefit plans, 149–51
  defined contribution plans, 150–51
  divorce and, 168–69
  earnings and, 151, 153–54, 153 *table,* 162
  examples of women's typical career patterns, 157–61
  40(k) programs, 161
  future prospects, 164–65
  improving retirement security, strategies for, 162–63
  Individual Retirement Accounts (IRAs), 161
  inflation and, 156, 172
  integrated defined benefit plans, 150
  investments and, 154–55, 155 *table*
  laws governing employer-provided retirement benefits, 161–62
  life expectancy and, 151–52
  lump sum at retirement, 159, 162
  marital status and, 168–69
  men compared with women, 149, 150 *table,* 152 *table,* 153 *table*

parents in labor force and, 88–89, 88
  table
part-time/temporary work and, 154,
  172–73
pension integration, 170
personal savings and, 159, 165, 167, 172
policy proposals, 173
portability of benefits, 162, 172
preparation for retirement, 155–56,
  162–63
preretirement consumption of retirement benefits, 157, 161
proportion of women receiving pension
  benefits, 149, 151, 152 *table,*
  169–70
protecting retirement financial security,
  163–64
reductions in benefits, 156
Simplified Employee Pensions (SEPs),
  169
Social Security benefits, 159, 160, 167
tenure and, 154
"three-legged stool" example, 167
time out of workforce and, 154, 156
vesting rights, 154, 156, 158, 160, 171
work after "retirement," 160
Perry, William, 215
Phillips Academy, 211
Piderit, Sandy Kristin, 236
Pincus, Walter, 214
Piotrkowski, Chaya S., 81*n*
Planned Parenthood, 203
Planned Parenthood of Southeastern Pennsylva-
  nia v. *Casey,* 202
Pointer, Sam, 219
Polivka, Anne E., 74
Population Council, 207
population of United States:
  by age and sex, 252 *figure*
  projected composition of the population
    by race and Hispanic origin, 254
    figure
  by race, sex, and Hispanic origin, 253
    figure
  by race and sex, 251 *table*
posttraumatic stress disorder, 189
poverty, 180, 241
  contraceptive failure during the first 12

months of use by marital status,
  poverty status, and age, 290 *table*
elderly women and, 167–68
families and, 76, 77 *table*
men compared with women, 76, 76 *table*
poverty rates of families by family type
  and presence of children, 316 *figure*
poverty rates of unrelated individuals by
  sex and age, 315 *table*
poverty rates of white, black, and Hispanic families by family type and
  presence of children, 317 *table*
poverty status of women and men by age,
  race, and Hispanic origin, 314 *table*
race/ethnicity and, 76, 76 *table*
Unemployment Insurance and, 124–25,
  124 *table*
working women and, 75–76, 76 *table,*
  77 *table*
Power-Anderson, Heather, 200
pregnancy:
  AIDS and, 239
  drug testing and, 192–93, 195, 223
  ectopic pregnancies, 235
  exercise and, 194
  medical research and, 198
  military service and, 237, 243
  prenatal care, 229
    for mothers with live births by race
      and Hispanic origin of mothers, 286
      table
  Unemployment Insurance and, 121
  violence against pregnant women, 199
Preliminary Scholastic Assessment Test
  (PSAT), 197
presidential appointees, 339 *table*
prevention services, 296 *table*
Priest, Dana, 197, 212–13
professional occupations, *see* managerial and
  professional occupations
Profet, Margaret, 180
Promise Keepers, 216
Prost, Sharon, 218, 222
Pryce, Deborah, 359, *359,* 367

Quality of Employment Survey, 81
Quindlen, Anna, 221
Quinn, Robert P., 81

race/ethnicity:

active duty servicewomen by branch of service, rank, race, and Hispanic origin, 326 *table*

AFDC and, 133, 134–35

AIDS cases in females age 13 and over by race and Hispanic origin, 298 *figure*

breast cancer: incidence and mortality rates for white and black women, 222–23, 295 *figure*

children's living arrangements by race and Hispanic origin, 264–65 *table*

college enrollment by sex, race, and Hispanic origin, 273 *table*

currently married and never married adults by sex, race, and Hispanic origin, 257 *figure*

discrimination in workplace and, 37–38

distribution of newly reported AIDS cases among women age 13 and over by race and Hispanic origin, 299 *table*

divorce ratios by sex, race, and Hispanic origin, 263 *table*

earnings and, 67, 68 *table,* 70 *table,* 221

earnings of college graduates, 227

educational attainment by sex, race, and Hispanic origin, 271 *table*

families by family type, race, and Hispanic origin, 259–60 *table*

fertility rates by race of child, 255 *figure*

homeownership by family type, presence of children, race, and Hispanic origin, 322 *figure*

incidence and death rates for selected cancers among women by cancer site and race, 294 *table*

infant, neonatal, and postneonatal mortality rates by mothers' race and Hispanic origin, 287 *table*

labor force participation by women and, 49 *table,* 50–51

leading causes of death for whites and blacks by sex, 292 *figure*

life expectancy at birth and at age 65 by race and sex, 283 *table*

life expectancy at birth by sex, race, and Hispanic origin, 284 *table*

living arrangements of women age 65 and over by age, race, and Hispanic origin, 267 *table*

low-birthweight live births by race, ethnicity, and Hispanic origin, 288 *figure*

marital status by sex, race, and Hispanic origin, 256 *table*

median income of veterans by sex, race, and Hispanic origin, 333 *figure*

median income of white, black, and Hispanic families by family type, 309 *table*

mortality rates among white and black women from lung and breast cancer, 293 *figure*

occupational patterns and, 24, 58–60, 59 *table*

population of the United States by race and sex, 251 *table*

population of the United States by sex, race, and Hispanic origin, 253 *figure*

poverty and, 76, 76 *table*

poverty rates of white, black, and Hispanic families by family type and presence of children, 317 *table*

poverty status of women and men by age, race, and Hispanic origin, 314 *table*

prenatal care for mothers with live births by race and Hispanic origin of mothers, 286 *table*

professionals employed in corporate sector, 199–200

projected composition of the population by race and Hispanic origin, 254 *figure*

sources of income for white, black, and Hispanic women age 65 and over, 319–20 *table*

sources of income for women age 15 to 64 by race and Hispanic origin, 312–13 *table*

unemployment and, 73, 73 *table,* 111, 113 *figure,* 114 *table*

Unemployment Insurance benefits and,

116, 117 *table,* 118 *table,* 119–20, 120 *table,* 123 *table*

unemployment of veterans by sex, race, and Hispanic origin, 332 *table*

voter participation in national elections by sex, race, and Hispanic origin, 336 *table*

white, black, and Hispanic women age 25 and over with 12 or more years of education, 272 *figure*

women awarded first professional degrees in selected fields by race and Hispanic origin, 279 *table*

Racketeering-Influenced and Corrupt Organizations Act (RICO), 192

Raitt, Bonnie, 235

Ramo, Roberta Cooper, 217

rape, 208, 209, 244

rape counseling, 210, 218

Ravitch, Diane, 186

Reagan Administration, 135, 136

Rehnquist, William, 190, 199

Reich, Robert, 25, 29

Rein, Martin, 135

Reischauer, Robert, 195

religious orders, 198

Reno, Janet, 182, 215, 216

Reno, Virginia P., 169

Repetti, Rena L., 81*n*

Retirement Equity Act of 1984 (REA), 161, 168

retirement planning, *see* pensions/retirement planning

reverse discrimination, 41, 204, 245

Rhodes Scholarships, 187, 231–32

Rice, Bridget, 177*n*

Rice, Stephen, 187

Richards, Ann, 229

Rivers, Lynn, 360, *360,* 367

Roberts v. *Colorado State University,* 186

Rodin, Judith, 187–88

Rones, Philip L., 54

Roosevelt, Eleanor, 182, 242

Rose, Stephen J., 230

Ros-Lehtinen, Ileana, 360, *360*

Rothgeb, Jennifer M., 74

Roukema, Marge, 360–61, *360,* 367

Roybal-Allard, Lucille, 361, *361,* 367

Rubenstein, Carin, 206

Rubin, Robert, 236

RU-486 abortion pill, 207, 208, 211–12, 227, 240

Rydzewski, Leo G., 54

Sadler, Georgia, 177*n*

Safeway company, 37

Salvi, John, 234

Scholastic Aptitude Test (SAT), 202

Scholastic Assessment Test (SAT), 217–18

Schroeder, Patricia, 178, 187, 225, 234–35, 362, *362,* 367

Schwartz, John, 244

scientists, female, 191

Seastrand, Andrea, 361, *361*

Securities and Exchange Commission (SEC), 163

Seidman, JoAnn, 217

self-employment, 61, 62 *table*

sex, *see* men compared with women

sexual harassment:
    at colleges and universities, 229
    in Congress, 181–82
    court cases, 179, 181, 184, 193, 201, 213
    in FBI, 182, 200, 202, 207, 236
    male victims, 219
    in military, 194–95, 200, 206, 210, 228, 232
    monetary damages for, 213, 218, 219, 239
    parents in labor force and, 91
    Unemployment Insurance and, 125

sexually transmitted diseases (STDs), 196
    see also AIDS and HIV infection

sexual orientation, 241
    military service and, 208, 210, 237

sexual practices of Americans, 204, 224

Shalala, Donna, 208

Shank, Susan E., 50

Shannon, Rochelle, 226

Sharpe, Rochelle, 203

Shaywitz, Bennett, 239

Shaywitz, Sally, 239

Sheehan, Patty, 195

Shinn, Marybeth, 81*n*

Shriver, Eunice, 236

Sills, Beverly, 209–10

Simmons, Darlene, 206
Simmons, Ruth, 232
Simplified Employee Pensions (SEPs), 169
Simpson, O. J., 211
single mothers, *see* lone mothers
Slaughter, Louise, 362, *362, 367*
Smith, Linda, 363, *363*
Smith, Steve, 215
Smith College, 232
Smock, Pamela, 205
smoking, 201, 233
Snowe, Olympia, 229, 363, *363*
Social Security Act of 1935, 104, 105, 107, 127
Social Security benefits, 159, 160, 167
space flight, 241
Spalter-Roth, Roberta, 138, 139, 141
Special Olympics, 236
spillover, home-to-job, 97
sports participation, 211, 236, 237, 240
Staines, Graham L., 81
Stammer, Larry B., 198
Stapleton, Jean, 19–20
Steadman, Cheryl Campbell, 179
Stone, Anne J., 23–32, 177*n*
Street, Picabo, 242
Streisand, Barbra, 237
stress:
   parents in labor force and, 99, 100 *table,* 102
   working women and, 25
Supreme Court, U.S., 180
   abortion rulings, 185, 192, 202, 211
   affirmative action rulings, 35–36
   jury service rulings, 204
   sexual harassment rulings, 184, 213
   welfare rulings, 243
Surgeon General, U.S., 231, 238
Swisher, Kara, 37

Tabor, Mary, 195
Tailhook affair, 183, 196, 209, 227, 241–42
Take Our Daughters to Work Day, 205
Tartakovsky, Flora, 193
taxes, payroll, 110–11
Tax Reform Act of 1986, 150, 161–62
Taylor, Harriett, 218

teenagers:
   exercise habits, 228
   sexual attitudes and behavior, 204
temporary work, *see* part-time/temporary work
tests, standardized, 185, 196–97, 202, 217–18
Texas Rangers, 179
Texas Woman's University (TWU), 232
Thomas, Pierre, 215
"Thompson, Jane Doe," 212, 214, 219, 222, 233
Thurman, Karen, 364, *364, 367*
Tierney, John, 224
Tigert, Ricki, *see* Helfer, Ricki Tigert
tobacco use, 201, 233
Tomb of the Unknowns, guards for, 197
Trowell-Harris, Irene, 183
Turner, James P., 185
Tyson, Laura D'Andrea, 239

UI, *see* Unemployment Insurance system
unemployment, 71–73
   AFDC and, 139
   government estimates, 185
   reasons for, 73 *table,* 112–13, 114 *table*
   trends in, 72 *figure,* 111, 112 *figure,* 113 *figure*
   unemployment of veterans by sex, race, and Hispanic origin, 332 *table*
Unemployment Insurance (UI) system, 104–5
   benefit levels, 108–10, 109 *table*
   continuing conditions to maintain benefits, 122–25
   covered individuals, 107
   creation of, 105
   eligibility requirements, 105–6, 107–8, 118–26, 120 *table*
   federal-state partnership, 106, 107
   financing of benefits, 110–11
   goals of, 106
   initial conditions to qualify for benefits, 121–22
   monetary eligibility requirements, 105–6, 107–8, 118–20, 120 *table,* 125

nonmonetary eligibility requirements, 106, 107–8, 120–23, 125–26
obstacles to women's access, 105–6, 125
percentage of eligible unemployed receiving benefits, 123–4, 123 *table*
poverty and, 124–25, 124 *table*
pregnancy and, 121
racial and gender composition of UI recipients, 116, 117 *table,* 118 *table*
sexual harassment and, 125
trends in receipt of UI benefits, 113–15, 115 *figure*
types of programs, 106
unions:
    earnings and, 69, 70 *table*
    part-time/temporary work and, 27–28
    workfare and, 143
United Nations, 183, 242–43
University of Maryland, 217
University of Pennsylvania, 187–88
USAir, 204

valedictorians' careers, 230
Van Meter, Vicki, 181, 208–9
Vassar College, 207
Velazquez, Nydia, 364, *364,* 367
vesting rights, 154, 156, 158, 160, 171
veterans:
    median income of veterans by sex, race, and Hispanic origin, 333 *figure*
    unemployment of veterans by sex, race, and Hispanic origin, 332 *table*
veterans' benefits, 178
Vincent, Troy, 225
violence against women, 199, 201, 206, 209, 211, 212, 225, 227, 241, 243, 244
Violence against Women Act (VAWA), 218, 221
Virginia Military Institute (VMI), 181, 185, 196, 205, 235
Vladeck, Robert, 189
voter participation in national elections:
    by sex, race, and Hispanic origin, 336 *table*
    by sex and age, 337 *table*
Vucanovich, Barbara, 365, *365*

Wagner, Charlene, 196
Waldholtz, Enid Greene, 242, 365, *365*
Walters, Barbara, 220
Wang, Penelope, 155
Waters, Maxine, 366, *366,* 367
Watson, Dan, 44*n*
Watson, Warren E., 39
Weeks, Rena, 218, 219
weight-gain patterns, 201–2
Weiss, Rick, 240
Weisskopf, Michael, 198, 216
Weissmann, Heidi, 201
Weld, William, 190–91
welfare:
    American approach to, 128–29
    households and, 243
    right to benefits, 135
    state benefit levels, 129, 130–31 *table*
    work requirements, 28, 30
    see also Aid to Families with Dependent Children (AFDC)
welfare reform, 138, 142
    abortion and, 236
    child care and, 145–46
    education and, 146–47
    low-skilled women, prospects of, 140–42
    Republican program, 240, 241, 243–44
    self-sufficiency issue, 144–45
    state programs, 190–91
    workfare, 135, 136–38, 142–44
Wellstone, Paul, 241
Westinghouse Science Talent scholarship awards, 193
West Point, 228
Whitewater affair, 203
whites, *see* race/ethnicity
Whitman, Christine, 184
Widnall, Sheila E., 180, 210
Wilkins, Roger, 33, 40
Wilson, William J., 128, 147
Wolfe, Barbara, 47
Women's Campaign School, 208
Women's Health Improvement Act of 1993, 178
Women's Health Initiative, 184, 222
Women's History Month, 240
Women's Policy Inc., 239

Women's Research and Education Institute (WREI), 19, 182, 193, 206
Women's Rights National Historical Park, 179
Women's Voices for the Economy Campaign, 235
Wood, Kimba, 184
Woolsey, Lynn, 366, *366,* 367
Wootton, Barbara H., 23, 30, 44–78
workfare, 135, 136–38, 142–44
Work Incentive (WIN) program, 135
working women, 20, 23–24
  changes preferred by, 225
  concerns of, 31–32
  conclusions regarding, 77–78
  discouraged workers, 75
  displacement of workers, 73–74, 143
  entrepreneurs, 213–14
  glass ceiling, 24, 186, 189, 242
  job training, 29
  labor law and, 182
  "marginally attached" workers, 75
  men's resentment of, 31

poverty and, 75–76, 76 *table,* 77 *table*
as proportion of labor force, 45
stress and, 25
see also affirmative action; earnings; labor force participation by women; occupational patterns; parents in labor force; part-time/temporary work; unemployment
"Working Women Count!" (report), 25, 26, 225
Workman, Shannon, 196
workplace culture, 91
World War II, 46
Wyeth-Ayerst Laboratories, 184

yachting, 200, 227, 234, 238, 243
Yow, Deborah A., 217
YWCA, 210
Yu-Fe Lin, Jennifer, 193

Zedlewski, Sheila, 171
Zilly, Thomas, 208

ABOUT THE EDITORS

CYNTHIA COSTELLO is WREI's director of research and senior editor of *The American Woman* series. Before coming to WREI, Dr. Costello was director of employment policy at Families U.S.A. and director of the Committee on Women's Employment at the National Academy of Sciences. She is the author of a book on organizing among clerical workers entitled *We're Worth It! Women and Collective Action in the Insurance Workplace*. Dr. Costello received her B.A. in sociology from the University of California in 1978 and her Ph.D. in sociology from the University of Wisconsin in 1984. She lives in the Washington, D.C., area with her husband, Peter Caulkins, and their son, Michael.

BARBARA KIVIMAE KRIMGOLD is the director of WREI's women's health project and assistant research director/coeditor of *The American Woman* series. Before joining WREI, she served as codirector of Working Mothers, Inc., and as a health policy consultant to George Washington University's National Health Policy Forum. Ms. Krimgold's other prior positions include professional staff member of the U.S. Senate Special Committee on Aging and senior budget examiner at the Office of Management and Budget. Ms. Krimgold received her bachelor's degree from Harvard University. She lives in McLean, Virginia, with her husband, Fred, and two of her five daughters.